ENTANGLED ALLIANCES

Racialized Freedom and
Atlantic Diplomacy During
the American Revolution

Ronald Angelo Johnson

Cornell University Press
Ithaca and London

Copyright © 2025 by Cornell University

All rights reserved. Except for brief quotations in a review, this book, or parts thereof, must not be reproduced in any form without permission in writing from the publisher. For information, address Cornell University Press, Sage House, 512 East State Street, Ithaca, New York 14850. Visit our website at cornellpress.cornell.edu.
First published 2025 by Cornell University Press

Library of Congress Cataloging-in-Publication Data

Names: Johnson, Ronald Angelo, 1970– author
Title: Entangled alliances : racialized freedom and Atlantic diplomacy during the American Revolution / Ronald Angelo Johnson.
Description: Ithaca : Cornell University Press, 2025. | Series: The United States in the world | Includes bibliographical references and index.
Identifiers: LCCN 2025003334 (print) | LCCN 2025003335 (ebook) | ISBN 9781501783708 hardcover | ISBN 9781501783715 paperback | ISBN 9781501783722 epub | ISBN 9781501783739 pdf
Subjects: LCSH: Slavery—Political aspects—United States—History—18th century | Slavery—Political aspects—Haiti—History—18th century | Racism—Political aspects—United States—History—18th century | Racism—Political aspects—Haiti—History—18th century | United States—Foreign relations—Haiti | Haiti—Foreign relations—United States | United States—History—Revolution, 1775–1783—Influence | United States—Race relations—History—18th century | Haiti—Race relations—History—18th century | Haiti—History—18th century
Classification: LCC E183.8.H2 J653 2025 (print) | LCC E183.8.H2 (ebook) | DDC 326.097294/09033—dc23/eng/20250408
LC record available at https://lccn.loc.gov/2025003334
LC ebook record available at https://lccn.loc.gov/2025003335

For Soleil and RJ

Contents

Prologue: "An Insurrection of the Negroes," 1758   1

Introduction: Between Two Treaties in Paris, 1763   9

Part I. In the Shadow of the Treaty of Paris: 1763–1775

1. "Their Colour Is a Diabolic Die": 1763–1769   25
2. "Kill Them! Kill Them!": 1770   60
3. "A Natural Right to Be Free": 1773–1775   94

Part II. The Dawn of a New Treaty in Paris: 1776–1783

4. "No More Talk of Reconciliation": 1775–1776   125
5. "Articles of Entangling Alliance": 1776–1778   155
6. "Armed, Disciplined and Battle-Hardened": 1779–1783   186

Epilogue: "The School of Liberty," Beyond 1783   213

Acknowledgments	221
Notes	227
Index	269

ENTANGLED ALLIANCES

Prologue

"An Insurrection of the Negroes"

1758

On Friday, 20 January 1758, at five o'clock in the afternoon, a Black man in Saint-Domingue (later Haiti), named Makandal, became a martyr for freedom in the Atlantic world.[1] No one in British North America (later the United States) realized it at the time, largely because of their preoccupation with the Seven Years' War. Newspapers across Europe and the imperial colonies ran stories centered on the war's third year, including troop movements, skirmish casualties, and epic sea battles. The Caribbean Sea served as a major theater of maritime warfare. On the day of Makandal's martyrdom, newspaper subscribers in Portsmouth, a major Atlantic port city in New Hampshire, learned that the commanding British admiral in the Caribbean theater had blockaded Martinique and Guadeloupe. He ordered the taking of ships "to any of the French Islands, of what Nation soever."[2] That day's print edition offered details about other sea skirmishes between British and French men of war. Throughout 1758, as colonial Britons remained focused on North American battles at Louisburg and Ticonderoga, Africans in Saint-Domingue's Limbé Valley, forcibly taken away from their families thousands of miles to the east, came together to create diaspora communities that affirmed the humanity of Black individuality in the face of their demeaning treatment by the plantation owners who enslaved them and their children.

Colonial Americans were not altogether unaware of the efforts by Black people across the Caribbean and the Atlantic world to eke out various levels of freedom from enslavement by Europeans. In the week before Makandal's execution, New York readers learned of a revolt in Suriname, where enslaved Black people wanting freedom "had destroyed three Plantations, and were continuing their Depredations." The same edition of the *New-York Mercury* also reported that around the time of the Suriname insurrection, "a young Negro Man called Hannibal," born in Barbados, took a less violent action to secure his freedom. He escaped from his enslaver in New York. Another "Negro Man, named Ralph," escaped bondage from a ship in the city. Black people conjured multiple forms of resistance to the eighteenth-century Atlantic slave regime that Europeans employed to subjugate people of African descent. Members of the African diaspora who did not take chances and succeed at self-liberation remained perpetually vulnerable to neglect, abuse, depravations, and trafficking, as in the case of a Black woman "to be sold," described in the *Mercury* as "a likely Negro Wench, about 26 Years of Age, with a Child of 16 Months old."[3]

British New Yorkers learned of the Makandal "insurrection" in Saint-Domingue several months after his martyrdom. News of the colony's most historically significant event of the year arrived in North America amid thorough reports of Franco-British naval warfare in the Caribbean Sea. The newspaper writer failed to fit the more salient points of a decisive moment in the history of Black Atlantic community resistance into the thirty-two-word summary of the episode. The thrust of the article centered on a British captain's "Engagement with the 7 Sugar Ships off" the northern port city Cap-Français, in which a British squadron "took a Ship and a Schooner." Near the end of the lengthy piece, which listed skirmishes, booty, and combatants with impressive attention to detail, was a cryptic description of intentional poisonings in Saint-Domingue. French prisoners taken during an encounter in the waters off Cap-Français informed Captain Seymour's crew that the city "was very sickly."[4]

White inhabitants believed they were being poisoned by members of the colony's African diaspora in acts of rebellion meant to help them gain freedom from slavery. The prisoners related that "in three Months," right around the time of Makandal's execution, "not a Vessel had arrived there."[5] According to their information, reports of African people poisoning white inhabitants, the execution of an important Black figure, and the resulting legal and societal fallout affected northern Dominguan municipalities enough to disrupt regular shipping operations at Cap-Français, one of the Caribbean's most important port cities. News of the insurrection and the resulting interruption of dock operations did not escape the notice of newspaper editors in another major port city along the Eastern Seaboard of North America. Three newspapers in Boston reprinted the *Mercury* story the following week.[6]

Yet most British North Americans remained measurably ignorant of the Black resistance movement to their south and to its contemporary and historical significance. The newspaper writer reported the account of French prisoners of war who said that "there had been an Insurrection of the Negroes lately."[7] No further information or context followed the succinct phrasing. It is unclear whether those words indicate the full extent of the detainees' intelligence or reflect the writer's discretion. The article did not mention Makandal by name. His life and beliefs, however, were central to the reported activities. Though his birth story remains unknown, he lived in the African region located today in the Democratic Republic of the Congo. He was trafficked across the Atlantic and arrived on Dominguan shores around 1730. A French planter enslaved him on an indigo estate just miles west of Cap-Français.[8] After the slaveholder converted the plantation's production to sugar, Makandal suffered a severe injury to his hand. The disability prompted the enslaver to move him to properties in the Soufrière Mountains, several miles to the south, to tend and safeguard cattle.[9] There, Makandal reclaimed his freedom. Around 1748, he walked away from the enslaver's properties to live *en marronage* among other self-liberated Black people in the Limbé Valley.[10]

The desire for freedom among Black people in Saint-Domingue predated Enlightenment writers, and the will to resist slavery lived in their hearts years before the fateful British standoff at Lexington and Concord in 1775. African-inspired leaders organized collective action within Saint-Domingue's Black community decades before the Haitian Revolution. Makandal and his fellow oppressed Black people knew they deserved to be free. Many of them, like Makandal, had been born and lived in freedom on the African continent before being captured and transported to the cash crop plantations of the western Atlantic world. They recognized their value as human beings, and, as such, they knew they did not deserve to be inventoried and treated as chattel. They designed and executed ways to live with dignity amid the regimes of racialized bondage.

In the middle of the eighteenth century, European thinkers began publishing radical treatises regarding natural law and the rights of humanity. Makandal and others in Saint-Domingue did not wait for French Enlightenment writers to express the horrors of slavery and the calls for freedom beyond the monarchy. A decade before Voltaire published his most popular novel, *Candide*, in 1759, Makandal had escaped slavery. Even before that, formerly enslaved Black people whose names largely remain unknown to us had recovered their freedom through self-liberation and established the maroon communities in which Makandal found affirmation, solace, and safety. Voltaire exhibited to a predominantly white reading audience the horrors of slavery through provocative interactions with enslaved African peoples in the western Atlantic world.[11]

In one instance, the novel's title character encounters an African whom Voltaire uncreatively named only "le Négre," who explains their condition to the European traveler, who expresses shock at "the horrible state in which I see you." Candide, in disbelief, after looking at the Black man's mangled body, asks incredulously if it was the enslaver "who treated [him] like this?"[12] Voicing one of the writer's more famous critiques of the Atlantic slave system, the Black man explains simply, "This is the price for you to eat sugar in Europe."[13] Voltaire's illustrious commentary on the abuses that white enslavers meted out to African children, women, and men may have enlightened (and perhaps appalled) some white Atlantic readers.

Makandal, however, did not need to read Voltaire's pontifications on the pains that life on plantations inflicted on African people. He and thousands of African diasporans, like the author's unnamed Black man, le Négre, lived daily at the unfortunate end of white ferocity. After securing his freedom and establishing relationships with likeminded African peoples in Soufrière, near the place where he had grazed another man's livestock, Makandal created ways to enrich the spiritual and emotional lives of the enslaved people across northern Saint-Domingue. He shared their indignity of being trafficked and forced to live as the property of other humans. He leveraged and risked his self-accomplished freedom to uplift fellow, less fortunate members of the African diaspora. Makandal's choice to move secretly between his maroon community and the plantations of the Soufrière region represented "a critical act of personal resistance that allowed him to work over many years building associations."[14]

Makandal established close communities based on shared African beliefs. He trekked clandestinely across the Limbé Valley, westward to Port Margot, and eastward to Cap-Français to nourish enslaved Black people through spiritual and collective healing. In some ways, his travels resembled circuits made by contemporary itinerant Protestant preachers across British North America. He did not have to convert enslaved Africans to the realization that they were oppressed and abused. They understood their plight and accepted that they were in need of healing. He called upon his lived experiences in the Congo Basin to create and distribute spiritually powerful objects made from organic and inorganic materials. Along his circuit of plantations, he distributed fetishes, conducted ceremonies to imbue the objects with powers, and taught believers how to properly care for and employ them.[15] The fetishes, the community-building rituals, and Makandal's physical presence strengthened and empowered the lives of people who believed in a higher power beyond that of their enslavers and enforcers.

Voltaire informed his readers about the importance of fetishes to the spiritual well-being of enslaved members of the African diaspora. In the novel, le Négre shares his mother's parting advice, on the coast of Guinea, after he was sold into slavery. "My dear child," she said to him, "bless our Fetishes, adore them always." The African mother believed that in the western Atlantic world, thousands of miles from his family, their fetishes "[would] bring [him] happiness."[16] Long before *Candide* was published and white readers learned about these spiritual beliefs, Africans in Saint-Domingue leaned on their faith in material objects imbued with life-sustaining spiritual power to retain their humanity despite legal papers and societal rules that treated Black people as inanimate beings.

Makandal played an important role in rallying descendants of Africa to recall principles instilled within them by families, friends, and communities whom they would never see again. He became so integral to the lives of believers that his particular fetishes became known as *macandals*. He became a legendary figure, garnering reverence among enslaved African believers—*macandalists*.[17] As a spiritual leader, he took on a status of esteem similar to that of the contemporary British evangelist George Whitefield, who was highly respected among Protestant converts and believers in British North America.[18] Like Whitefield, Makandal was not alone in the quest to spread his lifestyle and beliefs. Since he led a network of organizers across the region, his story cannot be separated from the history of maroon communities across northern Saint-Domingue that played important roles in maintaining and fostering resistance among the region's enslaved populations into the nineteenth century.[19]

The maltreatment of Africans in the Atlantic world already had a long history by the mid-1700s. The French legal system and colonial society deployed the word *black* to indicate enslavement. In many cases, the terms *nègre* and *noir* (black) practically equaled *esclave* (slave) and were regularly used in place of the latter.[20] Voltaire's literary character le Négre provides an example. In the Caribbean and North America, Europeans committed to enslaving African peoples endowed the identity of *Black*—in comparison to *white*—with the inherent status of inferiority and inequality. In slave societies throughout the eighteenth century, authorities passed laws and developed social norms to legitimize the dehumanization of African-descended women, children, and men. Successive acts of racecraft, the ritual repetition of social behaviors that made for the continuity of a racial ideology, fostered white Atlantic inhabitants' harmful views of Blackness and their perceptions of Black people as undeserving of humane treatment.[21]

During his life in Saint-Domingue, Makandal exhibited and encouraged a version of Blackness that actively countered the racist views of slaveholders who conflated African heritage with slavery.[22] He and his disciples promulgated a belief that Blackness offered those in the diaspora an unbreakable connection with their African roots, loved ones, and ancestors. The multitude of macandals that resided in dwellings on plantations represented daily, tangible proof that being Black did not warrant the pitiless treatment that Africans endured. Makandal, presiding over spiritual ceremonies among enslaved people across the Limbé Valley, affirmed that African lineage deserved to be cherished and honored in the face of persistent, racialized trauma.

The *New-York Mercury* characterized the collective actions of the diaspora community as "an insurrection of the Negroes."[23] The paper offered those five words to describe for British American readers the extent of the longing for freedom and dignity that enslaved Black people harbored.[24] The *Mercury*'s cursory coverage did not recount that a year earlier, in December 1757, Dominguan authorities had arrested Makandal and a number of his followers. White constabulary officials subjected the macandalists to heinous torture that forced them to implicate neighbors and family members who enlisted in the alleged conspiracy to poison slaveholders. Authorities detained hundreds of Black women and men—and Makandal. Magistrates convicted Makandal and sentenced him to death. The Superior Council of Cap-Français affirmed the verdict ordering Makandal to first make a show of repentance on the steps of the city's Our Lady of the Assumption Cathedral and then be burned alive at the stake.[25] Three decades later, at the start of the Haitian Revolution, the Superior Council sentenced the rebel of color Vincent Ogé to a similar show of repentance on the steps of the same church before white officials carried out his death sentence near the spot of Makandal's execution.[26]

Of Makandal's influence on his followers, New York readers in 1758 only learned "that 500 of them [macandalists] were hanged and burnt."[27] The newspaper left out details of a martyrdom that would inspire resistance among Saint-Domingue's Black populations for decades. Dominguan officials burned Makandal alive publicly on 20 January in a sickening exhibition of cruel and unusual punishment. White slaveholders forced many of his followers and unaffiliated Black people to watch, listen, and smell, in utter horror, the obliteration of a human body.[28] After Makandal's body was charred, French officials scattered his ashes to the wind.[29] Forty-five years later, French authorities treated the corpse of famed Haitian Revolution leader Toussaint Louverture in a similarly disgraceful fashion that robbed Black followers of an opportunity to appropriately mourn his passing. Their secret burial of Louverture in an unmarked mass grave prevented future generations from making a pilgrimage to the interment site of another martyr for freedom.[30] Despite such indignity in death, the life and legacy of Makandal, like those of Louverture later, continued to inspire hope in the hearts of his followers across Saint-Domingue.[31]

In death, Makandal became a symbol of Blackness across the Atlantic world and menaced the hold of white supremacy over African bodies. Black people believed in Makandal and his capacity to offer healing in a brutal world of despair. White people believed in Makandal too. They believed him to be a Black rebel leader, providing enslaved Africans with hope that inspired them to resist the indignities of an inhumane slavocracy. The actions and writings of white officials leave little doubt that Europeans viewed Makandal and his followers as architects of an insurrection meant to dismantle structures of white supremacy in Saint-Domingue. For the guarantors of the French imperial slavocracy, the colony's dominant class who exploited slave labor, Makandal and his form of Blackness represented an existential threat to the seemingly inexhaustible streams of power and profits derived from the forced transshipment, enslavement, and labor of people from the African continent.

Whether Makandal was rightly or wrongly executed for poisoning white people as part of a rebellion, Dominguan administrators began enacting reactive laws within weeks of the inspirational figure's death.[32] In March the "Regulatory Order of the Superior Council of Cap-Français, concerning the poisonings by the slaves," acknowledged "the large number of" enslaved Africans who possessed Makandal-produced amulets. The law denounced apostles of Makandal's spirituality as "so-called soothsayers & sorcerers" and ordered holders of macandals "to hand them over to their masters, or to the parish priests."[33] A subsequent regulation suggests that the previous law had a negligible effect on Makandal's esteem among Black believers and did not persuade Black families to relinquish their macandals. Broader in scope, the April directive established "the slave police" to root out belief in Makandal spiritualism and to control the lived experiences of Black people.[34] The laws sought to prevent the emergence of another popular, respected Makandal-like figure within the Black community.

The judicial actions of 1758, however, could not dampen the empowered sense of Blackness that Makandal's presence and practices had inspired in the enslaved populations of the African diaspora. They failed to diminish the fears of white inhabitants vulnerable to the ravages of rebellious Black people.[35] Three decades passed before another individual—named Toussaint Louverture—garnered similar levels of fear and respect among Dominguans. During the intervening years, the Seven Years' War concluded with a treaty in Paris, people of African descent in British and French colonies fought for freedom and equality, and a second treaty in Paris affirmed the independence of the United States.

The pages that follow tell a story of people across the Atlantic world who pursued freedom in a variety of ways, for diverse reasons, and with varying levels of success. This interconnected story, however, remains incomplete without an acknowledgment of the agency of Black diasporans to achieve their own liberty.

Introduction

Between Two Treaties in Paris

1763

A month after French and British diplomats signed the treaty to end the Seven Years' War "at Paris the tenth day of February, 1763," the Théâtre du Palais-Royal on the rue Saint-Honoré staged a play by the French playwright Charles-Simon Favart. King Louis XV commissioned the play to commemorate the Treaty of Paris. The preceding global conflict had proved to be very costly, in terms of lives and funds, for France and Britain. Favart's comedy *L'Anglois a Bordeaux* (*The Englishman in Bordeaux*) about reconciliation between rival empires remains one of his most remembered works. In it, the playwright explicitly attempts to reveal a path toward peaceful coexistence between the two warring empires. Favart's writing casts the war as a result of people being "born slaves to national prejudices." The plot revolves around transnational love affairs, following a French navy captain, Darmant, capturing a British captain, Brumpton, during the late war. The famous French actress Anne Catherine Dangeville offered the last public stage performance of her career in the Favart production. In the role of the Marquise de Floricourt, Darmant's sister, Dangeville delivered some of the play's most poignant criticisms of bigotry. In speaking of the British Brumpton, she says, "I am determined to cure him of his innate prejudices ... for the honor of our nation."[1] Over the course of the piece, as Darmant falls in love with Brumpton's daughter, the two men overcome pride and prejudices to make peace with each other and their past. Brumpton in the end marries the Marquise de Floricourt.

Favart's comedy about a lasting transnational peace gained broad success in Paris, "where it . . . had a more extraordinary run than any other new piece." Within a year, the play was translated into English and enjoyed runs in London and Dublin. One skeptical British reviewer provided a lukewarm reception to the comedy, in part because it was not "very consonant to probability, that Brumpton's prejudices against the French nation should so suddenly vanish upon the conclusion of a peace." However, he acknowledged that the ambition of the play was "laudable, as it tend[ed] to the removal of national prejudices."[2] Many French and Britons alike wanted to believe in Favart's presentation of human goodness overcoming intolerance. In scene 12, the character Darmant confidently proclaims, "Peace must unite France and England, and we will soon enjoy its sweetness." But the postwar Atlantic world of the 1760s seemed poised to embody Brumpton's rejoinder: "Peace! Peace! What a pipe dream!"[3]

Even as news of the treaty made its way across the Atlantic world, imperial officials in Paris and London prepared to face each other in a future war they foresaw as inevitable. The British government began stirring consternation across the empire's North American colonies with a slew of legislative measures to increase fiscal revenue in a desperate need to repay the massive debt incurred in the Seven Years' War. In Saint-Domingue, France's richest sugar colony, government administrators armed and trained men in the colonial militia to repel a British invasion as white planters steadily increased the numbers of African people they enslaved to replenish financial coffers diminished during the war. The colonists there, Black and white, soon rebelled. The uneasy peace that followed the Treaty of Paris of 1763 sent waves of contentious geopolitical reverberations across the western Atlantic world over the next twenty years.

The pages that follow tell the story of the challenges and limits of diplomacy, of the costs and complications of peace, of multiple and conflicting views of freedom, and of the importance and implications of racist inequalities across the eighteenth-century Atlantic world. The end of the Seven Years' War, though followed by temporary peace, set the stage for protests and fights over the meaning and scope of freedom. From 1763 to 1783, inhabitants in British North America and French-controlled Saint-Domingue battled their respective metropoles and fought among themselves over colonial leadership and social hierarchy in those territories.

Entangled Alliances is a US history of the American Revolution, which includes contemporary acts of rebellion by colonists—Black and white, free and enslaved—in the French colony of Saint-Domingue. In the history of Atlantic revolutions, as North American colonial ideals reached the full pitch of revolt and independence, free inhabitants and enslaved populations initiated similar acts of dissent, resistance, and rebellion in the land that later became the independent nation-state of Haiti. The story hinges on diplomatic negotiations conducted in Paris and their outcomes for the United States and the Caribbean, overlapping sociopolitical narratives that are generally written as unrelated occurrences.

This book recounts the oft-unintended impact of diplomacy on the evolution of revolutions and the increasing importance of racialized sociopolitical demarcations in the western Atlantic world as various claims to freedom competed for supremacy. It fuses the search for freedom, liberty, and equality by coalitions of multiracial founders in the United States and Saint-Domingue into a coherent story of revolutionary agency in the late eighteenth century. Acts of rebellion in these different regions affected one another. Afro-Caribbean and French colonists in Port-au-Prince embraced violence as protest during the 1760s, before Afro-Americans and Britons spilled blood and tea in Boston. In the decades that followed, North American and Dominguan colonists, Black and white, abetted one another's progress toward revolution and independence.

For all the scholarship on the revolutionary Atlantic world, there remains an untold story about the impact of the Treaty of Paris of 1763 on life in the North American colonies and Saint-Domingue. It is my story to tell. The historical analysis is written through the lens of the Treaty of 1763, looking forward to the Treaty of 1783. The book does not argue that the tenets of the first treaty in Paris led directly to the war that was ended by the second Treaty of Paris. The evidence presented does, however, suggest that actions taken by imperial leaders and colonial authorities in the intervening two decades between the two documents created environments of political unrest and social volatility. Inhabitants in the western Atlantic colonies adopted new ideologies and implemented radical methods of protest against egregious policies intended to solve problems derived from the Seven Years' War that the first Treaty of Paris could not solve. The Treaty of 1763 entangled the Atlantic world in imperial burdens that gave colonial peoples of all races and classes shared reasons for revolt. Subsequently, the diplomatic measures pursued by colonial leaders during this time reverberated across vast regions of North America and the Caribbean, shaping seemingly unrelated events.

The Treaty of Paris of 1763 and the Treaty of Paris of 1783 represent two of the greatest achievements of eighteenth-century diplomatic history in the

Atlantic world. The impacts that these two negotiated documents had on the lives of free colonists, subjected peoples, and imperial leaders are innumerable. The negotiated treaties acted as instruments of peace. Both signaled the end, or a temporary cessation, of widespread warfare that claimed the lives of thousands. The first treaty in 1763 changed the European colonial landscape of North America and the Caribbean. The second treaty affirmed the independence of the first republic in the western Atlantic world.

To Atlantic inhabitants who lived through the 1750s, which were marked by devastations and disruptions, the first Paris treaty promised "the Comforts of Peace to succeed to the Misfortunes of a long and bloody War." Governments, citizens, and subjects in North America, the Caribbean, Europe, Africa, and South Asia toasted and celebrated such hopes. Yet, as this book elucidates, parchment cannot protect peace from the hostile intentions of powerful people. As the negotiated language crossed the oceans, promising solace to war-torn populations, officials in London and Paris, suspicious of one another, began preparing for their next deadly encounters.

The 1763 treaty understood the Seven Years' War to have "arisen between England and France." Therefore, though the kings in Spain and Portugal also were signatories to the pact, the following narrative confines its scope predominantly to the British and French metropoles and territories. Potent diplomatic language proved optimistic, as did Article I, which proposed, "There shall be a general Oblivion of every Thing that may have been done or committed before, or since, the Commencement of War, which is just ended." Yet this hopeful declaration, despite being agreed to by signing parties, could not erase the balance sheets weighed down by the millions of pounds sterling and livres the respective monarchs borrowed over nearly a decade to wage war against one another. The financiers of global bloodshed demanded repayment. The era of peace laid down by the treaty provided an environment for each government to plan how to balance its war-ravaged fiscal ledgers. Both looked to their western Atlantic colonies for the much-needed revenue. The British king resorted to new taxes on items like sugar and paper products that had become staples of colonial North American life. The French accelerated trafficking in African people to increase the commercial output of Caribbean plantations.

A diplomatic historical framework equips this study to survey the increased instances of political tension and social transformation fueled, in part, by monarchical decisions after the Treaty of 1763. Much of the anti-imperial discord that paved the path toward renewed warfare involving two European powers can be found in interpretations and reactions of government officials to Articles IV–XXI of the treaty. These passages dictate the ceding and acquisition of physical territories across the globe. Article VII, for example, redrew the imperial borders across North America "in order to re-establish Peace on solid and durable Foundations, and to remove for ever a Subject of Dispute with regard to the Limits of the British and French Territories on the Continent of America." The concessions reset the European balance of power across the Atlantic world in favor of Britain. In response, French officials prepared to regain ground against their adversary, in part through the expansion of obligatory military service by colonists in Saint-Domingue. The British army, meanwhile, responded with intimidating force to colonists' demands for greater autonomy in Boston and New York. Reactions to royal and parliamentary actions in the aftermath of the first Paris treaty pit colonial resistance against imperial intransigence.

The outbreak of hostilities between Britain and its former colonies rechristened as the United States of America precipitated the negotiation of a Treaty of Paris in 1778. That important Atlantic diplomatic milestone occurred fifteen years (almost to the day) after the first Paris treaty ended a war involving the British and five years before the second Paris treaty concluded a war with Britain as a combatant. The major signatories of the 1778 treaty were the United States and France. Shortly after the Declaration of Independence, John Adams led the effort in Philadelphia to establish and articulate a nascent US foreign policy. Benjamin Franklin, the United States' first minister in Paris, employed creative, agile, and, according to Adams, eccentric methods of diplomacy abroad. Adams's vision and Franklin's adaptability secured France's recognition of American sovereignty and much-needed French financial support and naval engagement in the US War of Independence. Thus, bilateral negotiations in Paris helped US leaders and citizens defend their claims to independence. But the Franco-American alliance required a greater number of enlistments across the Caribbean colonies to bolster the French expeditionary army. In Saint-Domingue, for instance, service in the allied army to support the American rebels inadvertently opened pathways to freedom for enslaved Black men and equality for free men of color. Diplomatic arrangements and alliances that were formed on one side of the Atlantic opened opportunities in another.

This book examines afresh the contentious deliberations among US policymakers throughout the summer of 1776 over the contours of the foreign policy venture that eventually resulted in the ratification of the 1778 treaty. A sober narrative emerges to reveal the strongly held, shortsighted, albeit well-meaning belief of John Adams that early American diplomacy could be disconnected from "Articles of entangling Alliance."[4] Adams was not alone among the founding generation in viewing concession to entanglements in US diplomacy as a threat to American sovereignty. Later, as presidents, George Washington and Thomas Jefferson issued similar cautions to future generations of US foreign policymakers to not "entangle our peace" with other nations and to maintain "entangling alliances with none."[5]

In contrast, reading the American Revolution as a cross-colonial, transracial story between the two peace treaties of Paris, 1763 and 1783, can help us to investigate a myriad of unexpected ways that rebellion and resistance in North America and Saint-Domingue were intertwined. To this end, the book's title, *Entangled Alliances*, strives to capture unexplored inherent links between the jacquerie efforts of African diasporans and of European inhabitants. Their aspirations for freedom, liberty, and equality were inextricably "entangled" with one another.[6] The entanglement of race and freedom, in fact, was present throughout the era of the American Revolution. In Boston, enslaved African Phillis Wheatley and white colonist James Warren both put thoughts to parchment criticizing the reactionary practices of King George. Abigail Adams raised questions to her husband, John, a Continental Congress delegate in Philadelphia, about expanding women's rights and addressing the hypocrisy of slavery in debates over US independence.[7] In Port-au-Prince, Marie Carenan, a plantation owner of color, used the courts to challenge the colony's racialized understanding of freedom. In the same city, as patriot militiamen engaged redcoats at Lexington, an enslaved Yoruba woman given the name Léonore employed escape tactics to achieve a precarious freedom.[8] Newspapers carried along Atlantic shipping lanes kept rebels and revolutionaries abreast of protest movements across the colonies.

Elite white colonists assembled in Philadelphia at Independence Hall and at Cap-Français's Hôtel de Ville to demand their rights to liberty from the intellectual foundations of natural law and Enlightenment treatises. Barred from the vaunted chambers of deliberation, enslaved Black people secured their freedom under the cover of night and subterfuge, abetted by their communities. Still, on more than one occasion, Black and white inhabitants of both colonies found themselves fighting side by side against imperial forces. From the religious ceremonies of Makandal in 1758 to the multilateral diplomatic negotiations in Paris twenty-five years later, the stories in this volume present entangled histories of race and revolution that sent shock waves across the Atlantic world and shifted the meanings of freedom. Intersections with African-descended populations were not outcomes intended by white colonial leaders in Saint-Domingue and the emerging United States. Entanglements, nevertheless, were unavoidable.

What is new and important in this book is a contextual methodology that illuminates and connects concurrent, interracial resistance to imperial rule in the two colonial territories separated by five hundred miles across the Atlantic Ocean.[9] This analytical approach situates the commencement, progression, and conclusion of the American Revolution within a wider historical lens to present a United States in the world perspective. This book seeks to situate itself as a transnational study of how, after the Treaty of Paris of 1763, economic engagements, diplomatic negotiations, and military assistance informed and, at times, assisted concurrent, uncoordinated protest ventures by colonists across North America and Saint-Domingue.

This book makes no claim to proposing an exhaustive statement on its subject. Indeed, it strives to encourage continued interest in further scholarship that readily connects the histories of peoples in the early United States and its Caribbean neighbors. The cross-colonial historical method reveals an insightful story beyond the horrors that Europeans inflicted on African-descended peoples through slavery. It demonstrates the significance of free and enslaved Afro-Caribbean life to early US foreign relations. It integrates innovative reinterpretations of scholarly literature of early US history with the inclusion of French-language Haitian scholarship.[10] The narrative also offers fresh perspectives on historical events and actors through research in North American and Dominguan primary sources to expand our understanding of Atlantic resistance ideals during the American Revolution.[11]

Eighteenth-century English- and French-language newspapers serve as an important source base for this study. The methodological use of early North American and Dominguan print media is informed by the scholarship of historians Jeffrey Pasley, Adolphe Cabon, Leara Rhodes, and Robert Taber.[12] The narrative utilizes an innovative analysis of transracial relations in its incorporation of reports and opinion pieces from newspapers in Port-au-Prince and Cap-Français in conversation with their North American counterparts in Boston, New York, Philadelphia, Charleston, and Savannah. Editors and correspondents in these port cities informed Atlantic readers about the escape tactics employed by Black seekers of freedom from slavery and about companion acts of colonial rebellion against imperial forces. For historical analysis, these journalists left a record of important events with no known connections. For example, the court proceedings in Saint-

Domingue contesting the freedom status of Black plantation owner Paul Carenan occurred as Massachusetts lawyer John Adams defended British soldiers in the trial of the Boston Massacre. When discussed together, cross-colonial news stories help us more clearly see the costs of personal freedom and the dynamism in the collective search for liberty.

Books on the early United States abound. Recent works on the American Revolution have expanded our historical understanding of the period through analyses of gender and race that extend perspectives of continental and Atlantic history. The publication of scholarly works on early Haiti has increased over the two decades since the nation's bicentennial anniversary. Yet the robust collection of scholarly volumes on the United States in the age of Atlantic revolutions lacks a synthetic volume that addresses the broader connections between diplomacy, resistance, and race during the American Revolution. This book seeks to fill the lacuna. Despite the similarities in their respective radical origin stories and the challenges of their early national periods, historians continue to study the United States and Haiti predominantly along two parallel, separated tracks. This book aims to highlight the point that freedom seeking and rebellion by the colonial inhabitants of North America and Saint-Domingue were, instead, intertwined experiences.

The book employs a transnational approach to the history of the early American republic that integrates the development of racialized policies and societal norms in the United States alongside those in neighboring Saint-Domingue. The lived experiences of revolutionary Americans were shaped constantly and significantly by the changing decisions, conditions, and conflicts in the Caribbean, in Africa, and in Europe. An Atlantic world history of the American Revolution helps to explain the inconsistencies in idealistic white colonial discussions of liberty, the need for creative diplomacy to aid US independence, and the struggles of Black people across the western Atlantic world to secure a share of freedom during an extraordinary moment created by writers and rebels in North America.

The book's focus on bilateral diplomacy facilitates an intercultural analysis of multilingual sources to present an insightful look into the reactions of inhabitants on slave plantations and in port cities to erudite negotiations in Philadelphia, London, and Paris. An examination of the development of early US foreign relations with connections to Saint-Domingue across the scope of twenty years is grounded in a reading of published French-language colonial government documents and archival materials from Aix-en-Provence in conversation with diplomatic and personal correspondence, congressional records, legal cases, poetry, and political treatises from US-based repositories and digital humanities collections.

A transnational view of cross-colonial, companion hopes for freedom and liberty during the American Revolution encourages a revised vantage point from which to evaluate the Treaty of 1763's effects on events before the first militiaman fell at Lexington in 1775. The methodological approach invites scholars to more readily associate the famous statement by John Adams about the American revolutionaries with the experiences of Caribbean and Latin American rebels throughout the Age of Revolutions: "The Revolution was effected before the War commenced. The Revolution was in the Minds and Hearts of the People."[13] The diplomatic, political, and military actions that led to the Treaty of 1783 later influenced and, in some ways, inspired Black people on Saint-Domingue's northern plains to launch the military campaign of the Haitian Revolution.

The cornerstone of historical narratives about the foundational period of US independence remains a story of white colonial elites and a republican exceptionalism centered in North America. *Entangled Alliances* tells a different story. It connects the ideals and actions of Afro-Caribbean inhabitants in Saint-Domingue and multiracial founders in the United States to examine the various ways that inhabitants of both colonies—and future nation-states—understood their shifting place in the Atlantic world. Together, scholarship on revolution and Black freedom seeking can enhance our vision of this complex time period and also illuminate the widening divide between Atlantic inhabitants as the identity and the implications of Blackness evolved and empowered individuals and communities.

In the period between the two treaties, race was constantly entangled in calls for freedom. Therefore, it is important to explain my use of racial terminology in the narrative that unfolds, especially since the understandings of Blackness shifted over the twenty years examined in this history of Atlantic revolutions. In addition, colonists in British North America and Saint-Domingue appropriated racial designations in different ways. I am indebted to the work of writers across scholarly disciplines who have informed my understanding of race and racial taxonomy during this period.[14] This narrative employs terminologies of race in a manner that seeks to provide clarity in telling the story of dynamic shifts in the race relations and racialized treatment of Atlantic inhabitants. It also embraces the complexities and limitations of categorizing people who lived two centuries before us, in social settings that we may be able to analyze and imagine but will never fully understand. There are more words, particularly in reference to people of African descent, that could have been used to describe the human subjects in the stories that follow. My selections do not reflect a desire to limit or ban words. As Leslie Harris suggests, "Black history needs more language, not less."[15] The terms I selected best identify the individuals and groups of inquiry in relation to their status within communities and their relationships with fellow Atlantic inhabitants during a period of tremendous social and political change.

The terms *Black* and *African* are used to identify people, individually and collectively, from Africa or of African descent. In this usage, *Black*, as described by Elise Mitchell, refers "to a racial category and an elastic cultural, ethnic, and, arguably, political identity that is not defined by nationality or geopolitical boundaries."[16] In this book, *Black* also identifies people, enslaved and free, born of two parents of African descent in British North America or Saint-Domingue. *People of color* or *gens de couleur* indicates a racialized category of mixed-parentage inhabitants in Saint-Domingue. Members of this group could be either free or enslaved. A number a people of color discussed in this book enslaved Black people. In Saint-Domingue, as enslaved Black people sought to escape slavery, free people of color protested for their group's equal treatment with white Dominguans. In North America, British society generally referred to people of color, free and enslaved, using the outmoded term *mulatto*, which this narrative avoids except when presented in a period quotation.

Black people and people of mixed parentage, collectively, in British North America are referred to as *Afro-Americans* to distinguish them from *Afro-Caribbeans*, who were Black people and people of mixed parentage, collectively, in Saint-Domingue and Caribbean colonies. The terminology is especially useful when people of African descent from the British colonies and Saint-Domingue were mustered on the same battlefield at Savannah, Georgia, facing each other from opposite sides of the redoubts. Occasionally, to avoid repetition of the more cumbersome phrasing *Black people and people of color*, the term *Black* is employed to indicate a collective of people embodying various levels of African heritage—free and enslaved, in North America and Saint-Domingue—in reference to or being referenced by white people, to distinguish the latter from people with African lineage. The terms *white*, *blanc*, and *European* indicate non-Black people from Europe or of European descent in British North America and Saint-Domingue. Within the racialized societal and political realities of the period, *white* is also employed to indicate membership within the dominant racial class of the western Atlantic world.

After the Treaty of 1763, European and white Creole colonists refused to permit Black people, particularly those kidnapped and trafficked from Africa, to coexist as equals in the western Atlantic world. They deployed racialized categories to distinguish Black people from themselves. White British colonists used *Africans* interchangeably with *Negroes* and *blacks* to refer to people—whether born in Africa or in the western Atlantic world—whom Europeans forced into the African diaspora.[17] In North America, white colonists used *"negroes, slaves,* and *[n-----s]"* interchangeably to identify descendants of Africa.[18]

In Saint-Domingue, French leaders and citizens used a multitude of monikers like *black, negro, mulatto, gens de couleur,* and *sang-mêlé* to indicate that an individual or group was not white. The government and elite planter class implemented a host of racialized regulations to privilege and protect whiteness. Their campaign eventually spawned 128 distinctive racial designations to categorize the race of Dominguan colonists between Black and white with outdated classifications, including *mulatto, quarteron, marabou,* and *sacatra*. Only one division—white—received full liberty and respectability. Nonwhite inhabitants along the intricate racial spectrum contrived dynamic, uneven lifestyles under the scrutiny of a dominant, increasingly racist political culture. Disregarding individual self-perceptions or group aspirations toward greater socioeconomic standing, authorities relied on 127 levels of the racial system to, essentially, indicate that the vast majority of the Dominguan population was *not* white. As writer C. L. R. James put it succinctly, any person of any percentage of racially mixed parentage was treated as some version of a person of color, as inferior and unworthy of equality with white inhabitants.[19]

Regardless of how much or how little African blood one possessed, regardless of how much land and wealth one acquired in Saint-Domingue, over the two decades' scope of this book, white colonists subjected all descendants of Africa to humiliating, discriminatory rules that prohibited them from holding public office or militia commissions, wearing elite clothing, or sitting next to white neighbors in public spaces.[20] The shared Black identity of nonwhite Dominguans, in a myriad of ways, shaped their lives, occupations, cultures, and beliefs. My examination of Dominguan regulations in the 1770s illustrates how authorities legally prohibited *gens de couleur* with white fathers from dressing or behaving in ways that gave the appearance of them being *"blanc."* According to scholar Marlene Daut, French attempts to group individuals of African or Euro-African descent into a Black collective used "arbitrary and inconsistent markers of race and class" fashioned from "terms that had been contrived first to subject all the slaves to all the planters and the free colored planters to the white colonists."[21] Proponents of white supremacy created vocabulary, laws, histories, and traditions that established and upheld the notion of Black inferiority.

Race also entangles the concepts of freedom and liberty in this book. Black people and white people of the western Atlantic world sought freedom. However, the different groups fought for different kinds of freedom from different foes. This book illustrates how the meaning of freedom was racialized. In this book, *freedom* predominantly refers to what Black people sought in their search for an end to their enslavement by white colonists. After the Treaty of Paris of 1763, European writers and orators of British North America and Saint-Domingue regularly used terms like *slavery* and *freedom* to describe their increasingly contentious relationships with their respective imperial governments. *Liberty* is used herein to describe the objective of their demands for greater political autonomy, distinctive from seeking liberation from chattel slavery.

The words *slavery* and *freedom* encapsulate Black people's struggle against being forcibly kidnapped, trafficked, and enslaved by other human beings. European and white Creole inhabitants employed the terms to describe their protests over political disputes like taxation to pay down war debts without parliamentary representation and the imposed quartering of imperial troops in the homes of nonconsenting colonists. My distinctive use of *freedom* and *liberty* is intended to highlight the unbridgeable gulf between the concurrent use and disparate appropriation of the powerful, radical concept of freedom.

Free people of color, particularly those in Saint-Domingue, campaigned for *equality* with white inhabitants. During the examined period, they did not generally seek freedom, meaning emancipation from slavery, for Black people. Members of this group, most with European fathers, were born free or gained freedom from slavery. They refused to accept anything less than equal political and social standing. Despite my efforts at clarification, the lived experiences of Black and white people and people of color explored in the narrative did not exist consistently within the aforementioned frameworks. For example, Crispus Attucks, a man of mixed parentage, escaped slavery in Massachusetts, lived for decades as a free Black man in the Bahamas, and eventually lost his life alongside white rebels in Boston as the first martyr of the American Revolution. His biography reflects the complexities of racial experiences in the Atlantic world.

The story that follows is one of revolution and race. *Entangled Alliances* begins and ends with a diplomatic treaty in Paris. It unfolds in two parts over six chapters. Each chapter is centered on important developments spanning twenty years that affected populations in North America and Saint-Domingue. Some of the events are directly connected, with clear lines of correlation. Others occur in the two regions around the same time, without clear association. These moments facilitate a historical analysis that reveals similar resistance to imperial edicts and demands for freedom by disparate peoples across the Atlantic world as the American Revolution evolved.

Part I includes chapters 1–3. It describes the actions of British and French governments after the first Paris treaty and their importance in sparking and stoking the fires of rebellion in their colonial territories. Royal officials levied encumbrances on colonists across the postwar period. These autocratic decisions led to protest movements in North America, an increased dependence on African slavery in Saint-Domingue, and greater demands for autonomy in both colonies. Part I follows resistance actions in the advent of the Declaration of Independence.

Chapter 1 presents a textured exposition on the impact of the French-language newspaper coverage of the Stamp Act protests and the aftermath of an armed Dominguan rebellion that reflected the bitter relations between colonists, in both British North America and Saint-Domingue, and their respective imperial governments. Chapter 2 explores the life of Crispus Attucks before the racialized depiction of his martyrdom at the Boston Massacre to illuminate the networks of Black people in North America and the Caribbean who braved perilous journeys on the sea or *en marronage* (within maroon communities) in search of freedom, as white Americans protested monarchical rule with increasing anger and frustration. The Boston Tea Party anchors the analysis in chapter 3, facilitating a discussion of the diverse ways that Black people embraced methods of self-liberation and self-advocacy. The chapter explores Black Atlantic efforts to expand personal and socioeconomic prerogatives, including freedom petitions, poetry, education in Europe, escape from the clutches of enslavers, and the establishment of Black-governed civic institutions, in the context of growing white colonial political discontent.

The second half of the book involves intercolonial and bilateral actions during the US War of Independence. Part II, comprising chapters 4–6, is bookended by two important US foreign policy documents: the Declaration of Independence and the Treaty of Paris of 1783. Beginning with the involvement of Black soldiers at the battles of Lexington and Concord, chapter 4 addresses the influence of the Dunmore Proclamation on the strategies of the Continental Army and the Dominguan newspaper's thorough coverage of the momentous Continental Congress debates that resulted in the Declaration of Independence. Chapter 5 engages the Declaration as the foundational US foreign policy statement to the world. Its narrative offers a fresh perspective on the professional cooperation between John Adams's conception of the Model Treaty and the diplomatic ingenuity of Benjamin Franklin in Paris. Their collective vision of diplomacy secured the critical Franco-American alliance, as the Black abolitionist movement steadily took root in the nascent United States. The final chapter presents an expanded description of the contributions of the Chasseurs Volontaires, a battalion of Afro-Caribbean soldiers from Saint-Domingue, at the Siege of Savannah. Their involvement in the battle alongside white American rebels was a direct result of bilateral diplomacy. The presence of foreign Black soldiers on US soil, with hope for their own freedom, served as a hallmark of intercolonial connections and Black contributions to the American Revolution.

An epilogue explores how the ideals of liberty championed by white Americans resonated and resulted in freedom movements across the western Atlantic world in the aftermath of the Treaty of Paris of 1783. The book's narrative arc situates future leaders of the Haitian Revolution, including André Rigaud, Toussaint Louverture, and Jean-Baptiste Belley, alongside their colonial contemporaries, US revolutionaries George Washington, John Adams, and Alexander Hamilton. *Entangled Alliances*, as a whole, focuses attention on diplomacy as a transformative tool to encourage nations toward cooperating to effect change across geographies and cultures. The revolutionary actions of the United States over a twenty-year period between two treaties in Paris set the stage for successive waves of political shifts and racial transformations across Europe, the Caribbean, and Latin America over the next half century. The successes of American revolutionaries and rebellious Dominguans seeking greater freedom after the Seven Years' War illustrate the ways in which the age of revolutions was, in part, a collective effort.

Part I

IN THE SHADOW OF THE TREATY OF PARIS

1763–1775

There shall be a general oblivion of every Thing that may have been done or committed before, or since, the commencement of the war which is just ended.

—Article I, *The Definitive Treaty of Peace and Friendship, between His Britannick Majesty, the Most Christian King, and the King of Spain, 1763*

Chapter 1

"Their Colour Is a Diabolic Die"

1763–1769

The Treaty of Paris ended the Seven Years' War in 1763. The bilateral agreement also laid the foundation for political unrest and rebellion across the western Atlantic world over the next two decades. Article IV of the treaty stripped Quebec from Louis XV of France and gave it to Britain's monarch, George III.[1] The loss of Quebec and other territories in North America made Saint-Domingue more valuable and precious to France. The colony occupying the western one-third of the island of Hispaniola had been formally under French control since the Treaty of Ryswick of 1697. Leaders in Versailles felt their leverage within the European balance of power structure slipping. They increasingly viewed Saint-Domingue and other colonies as a bulwark to maintain and reinvigorate French imperial holdings in the Western Hemisphere.

The Paris treaty had similar and disparate effects on the global outlook within the British Empire. The terms signed by British Foreign Minister John Russell offered a resounding victory to George III, as they enlarged British colonial holdings in the western Atlantic world. However, the success also meant more territory and people to defend from French and Spanish intrigues. To establish and maintain the navy and colonial militia necessary to secure its hegemony, Britain anticipated greater military expenditures. The price

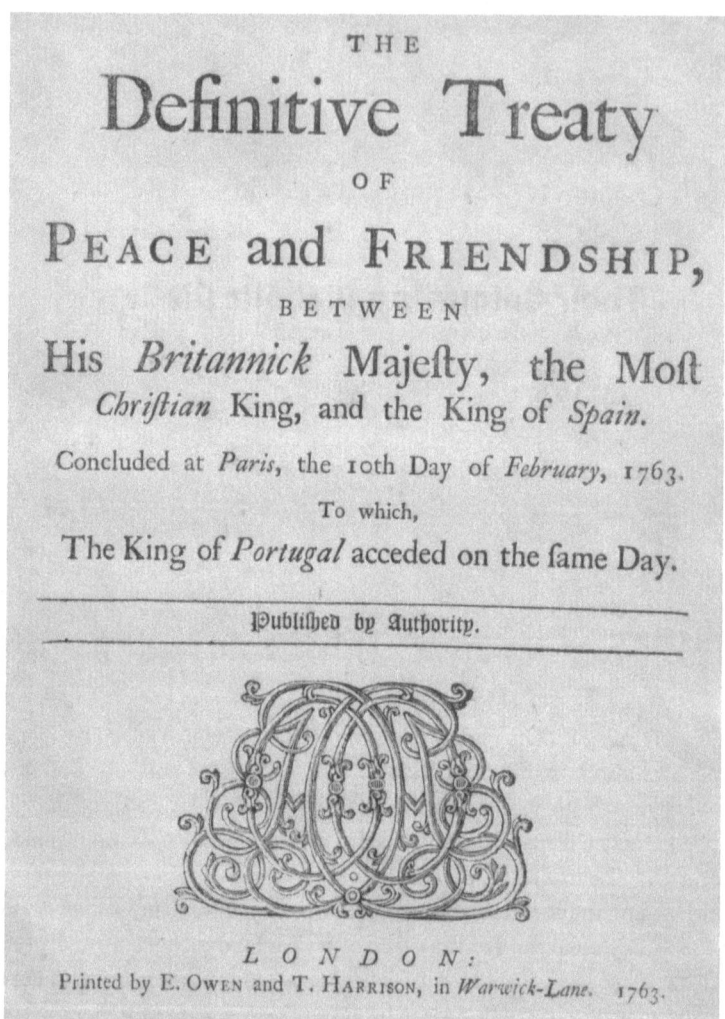

Figure 1.1. Title page of a published edition of the Treaty of Paris, 1763. Courtesy of the John Carter Brown Library.

George paid to ensure that the signature of his foreign minister held a place of honor on the Treaty of Paris above that of Louis's envoy had been exorbitant. Additionally, the military and diplomatic victories had put the British monarch some 130 million pounds sterling in debt. He and his Parliament looked to their colonies in North America to supply the extra funds needed to repay the war debts and to help shoulder the increased costs of expanding the empire.

Colonists in Saint-Domingue and British North America felt the pressures placed on them by their monarchs to fulfill grand imperial strategies devised on the other side of the Atlantic. The Seven Years' War changed the Creole inhabitants of Saint-Domingue as well. They had fought. Their friends and families had died. Dominguan residents had adjusted and risked their lives to bear and support military campaigns near and far. Western Atlantic colonists of both empires believed they had offered and sacrificed much during the war. Neither population was inclined to accept mildly the imperial dictates, which according to their reasoning infringed on their rights as subjects. Dominguan colonists and British Americans believed they had already given and paid enough for a war their side had won or lost. Though worlds apart in many ways, the revolutionary trajectories of colonists in British North America and French Saint-Domingue in the wake of the Seven Years' War illustrate shared desires for freedom and equality across national, imperial, and racial lines.

For a defeated France, threats, both foreign and domestic, seemed to be everywhere. And in this climate, Louis, shortly after signing the Treaty of Paris, authorized a plan to fortify French West Indian islands from British attack. After the war, in an effort to better balance its financial ledgers, the French government requested the colony of Saint-Domingue pay four million livres to relieve its white planter population of any service obligations to the militia.[2] Collecting and paying the special tax allowed planters more time to focus on crop yields and estate management while helping to replenish imperial coffers drained by the war. Though alleviating white colonists' responsibility for military service, the plan burdened free Black people and *gens de couleur*, or people of color, by making them almost solely responsible for colonial defense.

These changes in military policy became an important part of multiple lasting shifts in race relations in Saint-Domingue. Successive governors-general and regional administrators in the years following the 1763 treaty issued a number of racialized, discriminatory laws, which sought to redesignate the gens de couleur population into an intermediary caste between white inhabitants and the enslaved Black population. Many of them, in addition to being of African heritage, descended from elite European or Creole families. Members of this population had commanded influential positions within Dominguan society for decades. They owned and managed some of the colony's richest estates, particularly in areas along the southern coast. The evolving racist government rules regarding gens de couleur, in effect, defined their existence primarily as a racial category. Dominguan regulations asserted that their blood connections to the African diaspora rendered gens de couleur socially and legally inferior to white people.[3]

The enslaved African population, similar to most slave societies, greatly outnumbered white inhabitants. Relegating gens de couleur to the status of a "racially intermediary population" represented a strategic move to consolidate the powerful position of white colonists. The work of Marlene Daut, a leading scholar of Saint-Domingue's gens de couleur, suggests that white inhabitants followed racist colonial logic to reason that people of color would feel "beholden to the white colonists to whom they were putatively related" and "would be naturally opposed" to Black people. They believed gens de couleur would help white colonists to subdue and denigrate the Black population "in order to distance themselves from the slave status that being related to 'Africans' always had the ability to confer."[4]

Proponents of the new racialized military regime in Saint-Domingue looked to the Chasseurs Volontaires d'Amérique, the temporary military unit of free Black men, established in the final year of the Seven Years' War, as a model to fill gaps in the colony's defense. In that same year, Saint-Domingue produced a future military general of color with the birth in Jérémie of Thomas-Alexandre Dumas Davy de la Pailleterie, father of the famous French novelist Alexandre Dumas.[5] The Chasseurs detachment became popular among the gens de couleur. Within two months, some five hundred men of color joined the unit. According to one review of the Chasseurs, "There are few units who can shoot this well and as accurate; these [free people of color] are born with all the elements necessary to train a man for guerilla war."[6]

At the behest of French First Minister of State Étienne François de Choiseul, the colonial government speedily enacted a peacetime draft. Every male of color under forty years of age, some of whom possessed greater landholdings and financial assets than their white neighbors, was required to serve in the militia six months a year for ten years. Such a commitment would be professionally, financially, and personally ruinous. Social unrest and racial fear quickly began to erode support on both sides of the ocean for the Dominguan militia made up nearly exclusively of men of color since, numerically, there would not be enough white inhabitants to control the armed, trained ten thousand militiamen of color.

Across the colony, rumors spread of the *marrons*, or self-liberated Black people, like Makandal, who formed autonomous communities and conducted raids against the estates of the *grand blancs*, or white members of the colonial elite, planter class. The same reports claimed that members of the *petit blancs*—the population of poorer, laboring white colonists, many of them newly arrived from impoverished lives in France—had joined the raids. The possibility of a Black-white coalition against the planter class stoked racial fears. Within a year, the plan to alleviate white military service in Saint-Domingue was dead. Versailles instead decided to keep the multiracial militia to help control social unrest, much to the chagrin of the white colonists, some of whom had already paid their portion of the apparently nonrefundable fee to evade service.[7]

At Versailles, Choiseul remained alarmed by Britain's military dominance over his country. The Paris treaty signaled that empire's clear ascendance in the European balance of power. His suspicions of the British were not baseless. His government served as the diplomatic host for the final 1763 peace negotiations and, during the talks, had rebuffed any British moves to retain the French colonies Guadeloupe and Saint Lucia. Many in London disliked Articles VIII and XI, restoring those conquered territories to France, and wanted their victorious navy to expand Britain's Caribbean holdings. British writers continued to criticize the British negotiators in Paris and to voice dissatisfaction with the peace agreement over the next decade.[8]

Therefore, Choiseul made moves to support a future war and to deter the ever-present threat to France's colonial holdings in the Caribbean. In 1764, he dispatched Rear Admiral Charles Henri Hector d'Estaing, a wartime naval commander in the East Indies, as governor-general of Saint-Domingue. D'Estaing arrived with orders to reestablish the local militia. Without returning the submitted funds, he promptly rescinded the agreement exempting white planters from military service. The planter class viewed the actions of Choiseul and d'Estaing as duplicitous, and their support for imperial orders waned considerably. Consequently, the governor turned to other segments of the population to prepare the colony for defense. In a plan similar to that involving the Chasseurs d'Amérique, d'Estaing sought to increase the participation of people of color in the militia, despite racial fears, and make them the backbone of colonial defense. He reformed a mostly free constabulary of Black men into a light calvary troop called the Legion of Saint-Domingue. He required the enlistment of all boys and men of color ages sixteen to nineteen. Those who refused were imprisoned.

D'Estaing's military program also touched the lives of enslaved Black men. Across Saint-Domingue, wealthy free Black inhabitants and people of color enslaved other members of the African diaspora. Desperate for armed defense, the colonial government required these affluent Afro-Caribbean families to consign at least one of their enslaved males to service in the legion and offered freedom to any enslaved males who served in the calvary for three years. Given that the market value of a healthy enslaved male laborer was around two thousand livres, the constabulary requirement for enslaved servicemen and their subsequent freedom amounted to a tax on the affluent free Black population.

The Dominguan population of color viewed mandated service in d'Estaing's legion as an attack on their freedom and their ambition toward social mobility, which it was. Many refused to serve. They labeled compatriots of color who enlisted as *negres blancs*, an intraracial slur to indicate a Black person acting like, or submissively yielding to the demands of, white inhabitants. Yet d'Estaing jailed those who failed to report for duty, infuriating them even more. The detainees, free men of means, wrote to the Superior Council of Cap-Français, reminding the administrators of their loyal wartime service to the king.[9] They believed they had made enough military contributions.

D'Estaing planned to reestablish the militia for all men, though his racialized policies regarding service seemed at odds with that objective. White backlash against service meant the governor needed the support of servicemen of color. Their support, however, was undermined when d'Estaing ordered that there would be no Black officers in the new militia. He even proposed demoting officers of color who had served in the Seven Years' War to the ranks of noncommissioned officers. Resentment against the discriminatory policies swelled among men of mixed parentage. To secure their needed support, d'Estaing proposed designating anyone of one-eighth or less African ancestry as white. The ill-advised suggestion of an arbitrary change to the Dominguan color codes exhibited little appreciation for the complexity and the deep-rooted nature of the colony's racial designations, each accompanied by gradated legal and social protections.

In accordance with France's Code Noir of 1685, Saint-Domingue employed different versions of a racial scale that ranged from white European to Black African. Between the two poles existed various shades of color representing interracial relationships and different ancestral combinations across several generations. Racial scales worked to maintain a social and economic hierarchy grounded in white supremacy over Black Atlantic inhabitants. The racist priorities of the ruling class were complicated by the ever-increasing numbers of free (and freed) people of color. Many members of the population were of African-European ancestry, born to a mother of African descent and a father of European heritage.

During the Haitian Revolution, white French author Médéric Louis Élie Moreau de Saint-Méry published *Description Topographique, Physique, Civile, Politique et Historique de la Partie Française de l'Isle Saint-Domingue*

(1797–98). In this work, he drew up one of the most nuanced iterations of the racial scale in the history of the study of race. Moreau identified thirteen distinct categories of skin color among the populations of Saint-Domingue. His pseudoscientific promulgation of biological racism comprised a set of core racial combinations, which, when expanded and developed over seven hypothetical generations, resulted in a dizzying 128-point scale.[10] White Dominguans rebelled against d'Estaing's new racial color scheme and militia, and not necessarily because they cared about the concerns of the alienated servicemen of color whom Choiseul planned to use in Saint-Domingue to regain the geopolitical power ceded in the Paris treaty. White inhabitants coalesced against the governor's plan and, in a larger sense, against imperial rule, by voicing shared concepts of economic self-interest and a collective determination to bolster notions of racialized colonial rights and liberties.

Dominguans were not the only disgruntled colonists in the western Atlantic. American colonists pushed back concurrently against political machinations from Windsor. As insurgents in each region advanced assertions of liberty against imperial encroachments, they kept abreast of each other's progress and challenges. Print culture and transportation brought distant peoples into contact. Newspapers, carried by shipping vessels traversing the seas, served as the primary informational conduit between North America and the Caribbean on issues of growing cross-colonial tensions.

In the decade after the Paris treaty, ship captains and crews observed the different sets of sociopolitical changes in Atlantic port cities. They became eyewitnesses in written news articles consumed by readers from as far north as Portsmouth, New Hampshire, to Jacmel, on Saint-Domingue's southern coast. Their vessels carried stories of the French government levying new taxes on Caribbean subjects to fund new defensive fortifications across the region. A Rhode Island newspaper, for instance, reported the arrival of d'Estaing as governor-general. It followed his rapid plan of "strongly fortifying, with many additional new works" across the colony, including the cities Cap-Français, Port-de-Paix, l'Estère, and Port Saint-Louis.[11] As his measures took effect, disgruntled colonists responded by immigrating to British territories.

By the spring of 1765, the anger of white colonial planters ignited into "a most dangerous Insurrection at St. Domingo." According to a London-based writer, the Dominguan act of rebellion, if not tempered, could spark "a general Revolt in all the French Islands."[12] The analysis of the story, printed in the *New-York Gazette*, proved prescient. In 1766, in response to the considerable public backlash, Choiseul recalled d'Estaing and withdrew the former governor's militia plan. Meanwhile in British North America, angry colonists had brought about the repeal of the Stamp Act after engaging in protests also related to their rights as imperial subjects.

Aggrieved British colonists paid attention to, and likely found encouragement in, the collective acts of civil disobedience against French imperial plans in the Caribbean. In a similar fashion, colonists in Saint-Domingue closely monitored reactions to King George's authoritarian moves across North America. In 1764, the same year d'Estaing became governor-general, George III and his Parliament in London passed the Sugar Act as a means to service the empire's war debts. By one historian's estimate, the king's outstanding deficit, exacerbated by a postwar recession, topped 133 million pounds.[13] The Treaty of Paris had awarded the military victors a greater share of power in western Atlantic regions. It did not, however, alleviate the high costs of financing the war or the added expenses of controlling newly acquired territories. British American colonists at first accepted the tax rather benignly, a sign of war weariness rather than an implicit agreement to the idea of increased duties. That passive attitude changed in March 1765, when officials in London passed the Stamp Act.

The new direct tax required colonists to buy stamps from royal collectors and affix them to a wide variety of printed materials. Benjamin Franklin, residing at the time in London, suggested to officials during the Stamp Act debate that the colonies, at a minimum, deserved direct representation in Parliament. The reactions to the direct tax across British America were swift and unexpectedly hostile. One historian suggests, "The colonial reaction to the stamp tax was the most remarkable phenomenon of the lengthy pre-Revolutionary struggle."[14]

The Stamp Act became a popular news topic in Saint-Domingue, particularly in the French-language *Affiches Américaines*, printed in Port-au-Prince and Cap-Français. The operation of the state-sanctioned newspaper permitted Dominguan residents, free and enslaved, Black and white, to read or to listen to news about the revolutionary unrest in North America. Like its British American counterparts, *Affiches Américaines* compiled its international news section from a good mixture of rumor and reports, gathered from ship captains, sailors, Atlantic port merchants, and transatlantic personal and business correspondence. As Americans learned about the growing discontent with d'Estaing's effort to implement unpopular imperial reforms, Dominguan readers received reports about the opposition to George's encroachments on British American liberties.

Figure 1.2. Resistance to the Stamp Act in Boston in August 1765. Etching by Daniel Chodowiecki, 1783. Courtesy of the Library Company of Philadelphia.

The *Affiches'* coverage of the protests shaped Dominguan views about the American Revolution and their perspectives on what Atlantic colonial rebellions might achieve. On one occasion, it printed an inspiring story of how attacks by American rebels against tax collectors over the Stamp Act had forced the collectors to leave the colonies and discouraged others from taking up the posts.[15] Such reports may have encouraged Dominguan dissenters who later engaged in similar anti-imperial actions.

Though reactions to King George's moves toward greater control in North America were not initially as vehement as those of French subjects in Saint-Domingue, they were no less significant. The Stamp Act provided the colonists a sense of collective identity and a stake in shared grievances that even their hardships during the Seven Years' War did not create. For nine years, they had fought as members of different colonial militia with British regulars against French and Native American armies. Within three years after the Paris treaty, colonists from New Hampshire to Georgia banded together against British leadership in London. Similar to Dominguan inhabitants, colonists across Boston, New York, and Philadelphia made their voices heard through mob violence.[16]

Others employed ink and parchment as resistance. John Adams, a thirty-year-old lawyer in Braintree, Massachusetts, noted in his diary, "Our Presses have groaned, our Pulpits have thundered, our Legislatures have resolved, and Towns have voted."[17] Adams became a recognized revolutionary author by publishing his first major essay in the *Boston Gazette*. His argument in "A Dissertation on the Canon and the Feudal Law" that collective timidity, acquiescing to the king trampling on their rights, was equivalent to "consenting to slavery" captured the sentiments of many colonists.[18] He later observed, "The People, even to the lowest Ranks, have become more attentive to their Liberties . . . and more determined to defend them."[19]

In October 1765, delegates from the colonies took a defiant stance by assembling as the Stamp Act Congress in New York City to demand that there be no taxation of the colonists by a Parliament that did not permit them to seat a representative. Adams considered how London officials could react so unwisely to the congress's resolutions denouncing Parliament's actions. Astonished, he wrote, "What wretched Blunders do they make in attempting to regulate them. They know not the Character of Americans."[20] He and others hoped a spirit of defiance would spread across the Americas, embraced by white settlers in the Caribbean islands. Soon, British North Americans sought a coalition with British West Indians to leverage colonial complaints against London. In Antigua, white colonists formed an assembly and joined a petition against the Stamp Act. However, a broader coalition failed to form when other British subjects in Barbados and Jamaica declined to support western Atlantic colonists' opposition. One writer described Britons in Jamaica as "a low-lived spurious race" because there they used the required stamps and waited to see if the resistance of the Americans "in the cause of Liberty [would] get the act repealed." In Barbados, despite being "in Despair about the Affair," the white subjects blamed one another "in accepting the horrid Act, and thereby becoming Slaves."[21]

Adams's hopes for greater cross-colonial cooperation were disappointed. He confided to his diary a disdain toward white British subjects in Barbados and Jamaica for their lack of support for the Stamp Act resistance in North America. He described them vividly as "meeching, sordid, stupid Creatures, below Contempt, below Pity," and considered "their tame Surrender of the Rights of Britons" to be a "timid Resignation to slavery." To his private self, he suggested that the complacent white Caribbean colonists "deserve[d] to be made Slaves to their own Negroes," for "their Negroes seem[ed] to have more of the Spirit of Liberty, than they." Adams, interestingly, mused further that "we sometimes read of Insurrections" of enslaved rebellions that occurred periodically across the Caribbean.[22] Only several weeks before, a Boston newspaper had reported two separate attacks aboard slave ships, near Antigua and Barbados, in which Africans staged uprisings to overtake their captors. The crews "killed, wounded, and forced overboard" nearly a hundred Black freedom seekers in the failed escape attempts.[23] Out of apparent disgust with white British inaction in the Caribbean, Adams suggested hyperbolically, "I could wish that some of their Blacks had been appointed Distributors and Inspectors [etc.] over their Masters."[24]

During this period of American unrest, Benjamin Franklin served in London as a resident agent for the colony of Pennsylvania. Other colonies would later employ his services as transatlantic tensions increased. Operating as a kind of colonial diplomat, he was well placed to support a protest of the Stamp Act before it went into effect. Yet, despite growing angst back home about imperial legislative actions, Franklin initially hesitated to present colonial grievances to officials in the metropole. He did not consider the Sugar Act and the Stamp Act as exceptionally grievous. He believed that lawmakers themselves would come to see the legislations' risks for the English economy and repeal them. When Franklin met with Prime Minister George Grenville, he presented only rote protestations. He chose not to raise the contested principles of rights that troubled his constituents, reasoning that the issue would antagonize his interlocutors. Predictably, Franklin's effort proved unsuccessful in dissuading the British leader from implementing the controversial tax policies. Yet Franklin's self-assessment to a friend suggested, "I took every Step in my Power, to prevent the Passing of the Stamp Act."[25]

Franklin's objectives in London appeared entangled. He agreed with fellow colonists that Parliament's taxes without the subjects' consent violated the rights of Englishmen. He also held self-serving motives for trying to soft-pedal American complaints in the early stages of the Stamp Act controversy. He was beholden to George III as appointed deputy postmaster general back in Pennsylvania. To preserve his prospects, he encouraged colonists in Pennsylvania, in lieu of protesting, to comply with the Stamp Act and recommended a boycott of English goods as a preferable nonviolent form of protest. He asked his partner at the *Pennsylvania Gazette* to refrain from attacking the inflammatory tax in the paper.²⁶

After the passage of the Stamp Act, Franklin pivoted quickly when resentment and violence spread across colonial North America. News reached him of the destructive riots by crowds in Boston and the potential for mob unrest to spread to Philadelphia. Angry colonists questioned his loyalty to their cause and his efficacy after his failure to forestall Parliament's actions. His friends also scrutinized his weak efforts at opposing the legislation. In response, according to historian Sheila Skemp, "he swung into action." He began to post articles in London newspapers attacking the Stamp Act and defending the colonial outcry.²⁷ In late 1765, around the time disaffected colonial leaders back home convened the Stamp Act Congress, Franklin convinced a group of British merchants to endorse him as the authentic American voice in London. They succeeded, giving him a distinctive role in lobbying Parliament to repeal the tax law. Meeting regularly with British officials, he found that many parliamentary members possessed a surprisingly superficial understanding of American colonial affairs.

In February 1766, about a year after his failed meeting with Grenville, he addressed a committee of the whole in the House of Commons. He fielded about two hundred questions from lawmakers (some mean-spirited and belligerent) with his trademark patience, good judgment, and sweet reason, which would later make him one of America's most effective diplomats. One Commons member posed a question about the sentiment of the colonists toward the empire before the end of the Seven Years' War. Franklin responded that though some tension involving British leadership over the colonial militias had existed, the colonists had obeyed the laws of Parliament and the directives of the king. There had been little need for Britain to fortify garrisons or forts to keep the colonists in line.²⁸ Yet leaders at Windsor (and Versailles) took steps of militarization in the immediate postwar period, sowing seeds of discord among war-weary subjects in the western Atlantic world.

Franklin explained to Parliament that their actions had dimmed the loyalty of American colonists to the empire.²⁹ One member asked him about "a military force carry[ing] the stamp-act into execution." In response, he warned British leaders that if an expeditionary force was deployed against peaceful Americans, "they [would] not find a rebellion; they may indeed make one."³⁰ Newspapers in North America ran favorable accounts of Franklin's deft handling of the House. Within weeks of Franklin addressing parliamentary questions, pressures from home and abroad as well as the dismissal of members in the government cabinet caused the Parliament to repeal the Stamp Act. Though his exact role in influencing Parliament remains undetermined, after the repeal, he became the strongest voice in England for colonial interests. Franklin, despite missteps in his initial reaction to the Stamp Act, weathered the crisis to emerge as an American hero.[31] He officially began representing Georgia in 1768, New Jersey the year after, and Massachusetts in 1770. He continued as the official agent for his home colony Pennsylvania and an unofficial representative of all the colonies.

Franklin, like Adams, wielded the pen as his favorite weapon of revolt. He used his skills as a former newspaperman to draft vigorous rebuttals to any negative reporting in the London press regarding the colonists or their acts of defiance. He tried to counter every story, often anonymously, displaying a seemingly indefatigable stamina for agitation on behalf of his fellow colonists. He explained with care and coolness, a tone unlike that of Adams, why Americans took such a great offense to being taxed directly by the English Parliament. In one article, "On the Propriety of Taxing America," Franklin took up the most common arguments put forward by Parliament, then refuted each one in turn. He wrote articles, answered letters, and lobbied without ceasing for the American cause of greater latitude.

But Franklin still felt torn between various interest groups on both sides of the Atlantic. He believed that by achieving the American objectives, he was also helping Britain's cause to keep the colonies compliant in the long run.[32] He argued that the Stamp Act had weakened the attachment, once so firm, that Americans felt for Britain. Recalling the Plan of Union he proposed at the Albany Congress in 1754, popularized by the famous "Join, or Die" political cartoons, Franklin suggested that a united government of the thirteen colonies failed, in part, because the colonists identified as proud Englishmen.[33] The Stamp Act, however, had awakened colonists to the possibility of identifying as Americans as they assailed their unfortunate connections with Britain. The British, he suggested, were acting against their own interests by antagonizing the colonists.

While Britain was busy alienating Benjamin Franklin, France was trying to cultivate a closer relationship with him. In fact, French Foreign Minister Choiseul had tried to establish a diplomatic foothold in the British colonies via leaders such as Franklin, since positive relations with Americans were considered crucial for French survival where sheer power had failed to maintain their presence. The past war had embittered Anglo-French relations, and the Treaty of Paris of 1763 proved a bitter pill for the French Empire to swallow. With the loss of French Canada and Louisiana, Saint-Domingue became France's most prized colonial possession in the western Atlantic world. But the French had not given up on influencing North Americans. The terms of Article IV helped transform the North American continent into a virtual chess match for shifting the European balance of power. Even before the ink had dried on the parchment of peace, French officials sought ways to mitigate Britain's dominance in the Atlantic world and to secure their West Indian territories.[34] As British governors, judges, and military leaders loyal to George III enforced harsher policies from London to solidify firm imperial control across North America, French diplomats on behalf of Louis XV observed the American population and leadership, strategizing how to take advantage of the popular unrest over the more abrasive tax regime. The French, they reasoned, could support the disgruntled British colonists as a way to undermine Britain's power. However, some observers remained wary of giving British colonists too many grandiose ideas, which might inspire similar acts of rebellion in the Caribbean.

Foreign Minister Choiseul is not as well known among US history scholars as his more famous successors Charles Gravier de Vergennes and Charles-Maurice de Talleyrand-Périgord, both of whom served during the revolutionary and Federalist eras of the early American republic. He was, however, a strong political force within the Versailles government, and his presence shaped French foreign policy in the western Atlantic world across the 1760s. He assumed the position of chief diplomat in 1758, and the experience of shaping foreign policy in the midst of the global war influenced his decision-making throughout his tenure. Until the end of 1770, Choiseul also served as France's prime minister in every way except receiving the official title. Though Louis XV opposed having a chief minister, Choiseul held an outsize voice in directing government policies abroad and at home. Across those twelve years of service in high executive office, for only five of them did he not directly handle the diplomatic portfolio. Even then, he had his cousin César Gabriel de Choiseul fill the vacancy. At varied times during the decade, Choiseul served as the minister of war and the minister of the navy and the colonies.[35] Therefore, policy and life in colonial Saint-Domingue were never beyond his purview.

For Choiseul, the Seven Years' War did not end with the treaty. The period between 1763 and 1770 was marked by recurrent confrontations between France and Britain, over issues ranging from fishing rights in Newfoundland to the French purchase of the Mediterranean island of Corsica.[36] The bilateral conflicts held little threat of sparking all-out warfare, as neither nation's military was prepared to fight across the globe. Instead, the governments of Louis and George challenged each other in feints and countermoves to gauge the other's resolve.

Choiseul viewed his country as being in a constant state of rebuilding its international standing and of regaining its military and territorial losses. To move France toward those objectives, he dispatched officials across the Atlantic as the eyes and arms of French foreign policy. Between 1764 and 1768, as Parliament's tax policies caused steady estrangement between Britain and her colonists, the French sent secret agents to report on political developments in North America.[37] As early as 1764, Choiseul sent François de Sarrebourse de Pontleroy de Beaulieu to North America. Pontleroy was a navy lieutenant from the department of Rochefort, with strong skills in shipbuilding, piloting, and drawing. His mission was to gather intelligence regarding the port cities of the middle colonies. He could not write well; therefore, he passed his information to François-Marie Durand de Distroff, the French chargé in London. In letters to Choiseul, Durand shared Pontleroy's understanding that postwar legislation like the Stamp Act was causing a rift between the metropole and its American territories that could be exploited for France's benefit. He reported, "In all New England there were no citadels, from the people's fear of their being used to compel submission to Acts of Parliament infringing colonial privileges."[38]

The second agent Choiseul dispatched to North America, Johann Kalb, also known as Baron de Kalb, affirmed Pontleroy's analysis regarding the level of revolutionary fervor. Shortly after landing at Philadelphia in 1768, he learned of the lasting influence of the Stamp Act Congress, the Americans' rejection of Parliament's action as a free people with great unanimity, though the colonists from New Hampshire to Georgia were not connected in any formal way. To obtain a fuller view, Kalb left Philadelphia for New York, Boston, and Nova Scotia. After his tour, Kalb, unlike Pontleroy, concluded that despite hostile legislative disagreements, the colonists would remain firmly a part of the British Empire. He cautioned Choiseul that French actions leading to war would reunite the colonists with the Crown.[39]

Choiseul's envoys to North America agreed about threats regarding Saint-Domingue. Pontleroy reported that some American colonies wanted to conquer Saint-Domingue as an outlet for their products. This commercial strategy, he presumed, was a result of the close Dominguan-American trade beginning in the 1760s. Believing that the continental colonies would eventually declare independence from Britain, Pontleroy viewed them as a direct threat to Saint-Domingue and other French islands in the Caribbean. He assured Durand that the middle colonies, Pennsylvania, Maryland, and New York, were interested in taking control of Saint-Domingue. In relaying the reports to Choiseul, Durand seemed more interested in the potential threats to the French colony than in the colonists' complaints against their monarch. According to historian Josephine Pacheco, Durand used Pontleroy's findings to form the basis of a proposed plan for preemptively attacking the American colonies. His plan called for Pontleroy himself to lead swift attacks on New England, where defenses were weakest, while spreading alarm and fear along the Eastern Seaboard. The other colonies, occupied with rallying a defense, would be in no position to attack Saint-Domingue.

Though Durand's plan did not materialize, French interests in North American independence were sufficiently serious that as early as 1768 some officials considered a diplomatic alliance between France and the American colonies. The idea of a bilateral agreement hinged on the colonists' desire for national sovereignty. Kalb, for his part, was convinced that if Versailles engaged Britain in another war, the continental colonies, despite increasingly violent protests against imperial rule, would readily join their mother country in an effort to take Saint-Domingue and other territories of the French West Indies.[40] After the death of Louis XV in 1774, French fears of a British attack on Saint-Domingue remained so high that Louis XVI and Vergennes, who became the French minister of foreign affairs, consulted the reports from Pontleroy and Kalb on the subject.[41] Durand's successor in London, Louis-Marie-Florent de Lomont d'Haraucourt, duc du Châtelet, suggested that Choiseul should present the disgruntled British American colonists with a treaty of alliance and commerce that would offer greater gains than hostile intentions toward Saint-Domingue. In that way, the Americans could ensure their independence and establish their trade with France.[42] Though Châtelet's counsel was not followed in 1768, a decade later France ratified two such treaties with a nascent United States. One historian has suggested that France "secretly aided the colonies" throughout the 1760s and eventually signed the Franco-American alliance of 1778 "in order, among other things, to prevent an attack" from North America on Saint-Domingue and other French territories.

The political crisis precipitated by the Stamp Act provided France an opening to pursue its foreign policy agenda in North America, and it prompted the British colonists to think in collective terms and to consider shifting toward other players in the international arena. The postwar period of increasingly hostile rhetoric between George III and his subjects, therefore, became an important moment in the establishment of Franco-American diplomacy. The entanglements born at this early stage eventually would bind millions of people across the Atlantic world as diplomatic decisions made in one region reverberated in others.

Like imperial leaders, American colonists thought of foreign affairs in terms of the balance of power, which was fundamental to eighteenth-century European diplomacy across the Atlantic world. Inhabitants of North America, beyond simply following an inherited principle in international affairs, genuinely considered maintaining global equilibrium between major powers to be a progressive way of shaping foreign policy. According to historian James Hutson an extraordinary show of communal action resulting from shared anger over parliamentary actions was the development of a rudimentary American foreign service.[43] With a national government and official envoys over a decade away, the colonies' leaders utilized the foreign travel and international negotiating experience of colonial agents abroad to fashion the beginnings of a diplomatic corps. Prior to Kalb's departure for Philadelphia, Choiseul had instructed him to "seek to discover their plan of revolt, and the leaders who are expected to direct and control it."[44] The French foreign minister likely expected Kalb to prepare a list of names containing potential diplomats who would become his interlocutors on behalf of the continent. He had already identified Benjamin Franklin as a prospective target for an approach. In addition to sending agents to North America, Choiseul also deployed diplomats to London in an attempt to develop a friendship with Franklin.[45]

By the late 1760s, Franklin was probably the most recognizable American colonist around the Atlantic world. The Pennsylvania Assembly had sent him to London in 1757 as an agent. During his more than a decade of experience in living and working in the metropole, in the midst of war and as an advocate against the Stamp Act, Franklin had gained considerable notoriety. Choiseul tasked French chargé Durand to cultivate Franklin as a reliable source of information on conditions in North America regarding social unrest, attitudes toward the king, and military preparedness. The chargé did his best to convince the American agent to proffer the requested intelligence. He repeatedly called on Franklin, invited him to dinner, and, in general, treated him with the respect of a statesman. Once, when Franklin planned to visit Paris, Durand provided him with necessary letters of introduction to important Parisians. As the French diplomat perceived their relationship deepening, he took the bold step of asking Franklin for copies of his political writings to help him become better informed on affairs in British America. Franklin was too practiced a hand to give up his papers. Likely pressing a strategic advantage, he did share with Durand his view that the desire for more liberty and greater political rights among American colonists would only grow. There was no turning back. Durand's report of Franklin's conclusion would have pleased Choiseul, who would have understood it as encouragement to continue to help dividing North America from London. Franklin had grasped Durand's motives from their first encounters. He wrote to his son William that the French envoy pretended to have great respect for him and the British American cause. He, likewise, correctly understood "that intriguing nation [France] would like very well to meddle on occasion, and blow up the coals between Britain and her colonies." He maintained hope, however, that he and his disaffected countrymen "shall give them no opportunity" to entice them toward an irreparable rupture with the metropole.[46] Franklin, who disavowed a desire for French friendship prior to Lexington and Concord, became one of the most beloved US diplomats in France after American independence.

As the political crisis deepened on the continent, the colonists employed a new act of rebellion: the boycott. They refused to buy British goods as a way to avoid paying the despised taxes on those goods. Therefore, they turned to Saint-Domingue and other French Caribbean territories for certain essential items. Châtelet, in London, saw in American political protests a renewed opportunity for France to gain the friendship of the Americans. Though his plan for diplomatic alliance did not advance, this time he proposed that France relax the restrictions of the Exclusif trading system and extend commercial preference to the thirteen colonies to trade with Saint-Domingue. Choiseul wholly endorsed Châtelet's idea and presented it directly to the king and his council, who unanimously approved it. They all agreed the plan would injure Britain, Choiseul's enduring objective, and strengthen French diplomacy and commerce in the western Atlantic world.[47]

Emboldened by the support of the monarchy, Choiseul moved to construct stronger ties between Saint-Domingue and the American colonies. The Versailles government issued an ordinance making the northwestern port city of Môle-Saint-Nicolas one of two free ports in the French West Indies for the exchange of goods between the French and British colonies. The relatively freer policy within strict Exclusif and mercantilist regimes produced a brisk trade, with wood, tar, and livestock sailing southward and Dominguan molasses making its way to American ports. Across the decade, sugar and coffee departed from the Môle, Port-au-Prince, and Le Cap on ships to the continent. A mutual dependence and benefits from trade evolved between the two colonial peoples and endured into the early national periods of the United States and Haiti. According to historian Rayford Logan, Saint-Domingue and the American colonies "probably had as close and profitable relations with each other as with any other region except their respective mother countries."[48]

Choiseul left the government in 1770, after achieving closer and lasting commercial relations between Saint-Domingue and the British American colonies. He put much effort into intelligence gathering and diplomatic posturing to move the colonists closer to France. It remains difficult, however, to approximate the role of French diplomacy in the steadily increasing intensity behind continental resentment to monarchical rule, which led eventually to the US rupture with Britain. American colonists embraced greater access to Dominguan products, while many, including Benjamin Franklin, worked to keep France from exacerbating the colonial crisis. A Boston newspaper reprinted a story from London that exhibited a level of anxiety there about the plausibility of a Franco-American alliance. In an article laced with sarcasm and condescension, the writer asked, "Whether in the case North Americans should ever be such fools as to revolt against the English Government, and put themselves under that of France," would they continue "to enjoy their present civil and religious liberties?"[49] Many in England and France could not imagine the rebels existing as independent people, without the protection of a European empire. Before Lexington and Concord, neither could many American rebels.

The tightening entanglements between the French and American colonists as well as French Caribbean colonists were strengthened not only by diplomatic overtures but also by print culture. And in part because of its reliance on shipping as a means of communication across and around the ocean, print culture was not bound by race or class. John Adams, Benjamin Franklin, and other white male polemicists in the western Atlantic world added their views to an expanding print culture addressing questions of liberty and freedom across the 1760s. British North America had not yet developed a vibrant homegrown literary culture. Many of the names that would emerge as revolutionary intellectuals were virtually unknown as readers across the colonies encountered them in newspapers and pamphlets in the 1760s. As the scope of British colonial grievances broadened, writers of African descent, like their white counterparts, also published works that reflected the dynamic social and cultural contexts in which they were living. In doing so, they represented a diverse collective, engaging a variety of political, economic, historical, and spiritual concerns that influenced the full range of British life.[50]

Earlier, during the Seven Years' War, a Black writer exhibited the keen awareness that many Black Atlantic inhabitants had of imperial disputes and transatlantic conflicts. Briton Hammon endured an extraordinary thirteen-year adventure, crisscrossing the Atlantic world as European nations waged war against each other across the globe. Existing in various states of freedom, enslavement, and imprisonment, he journeyed from Boston to Cuba to Jamaica and England. Upon his return to Boston in 1760, Hammon wrote and published the story of his wartime expeditions.

Hammon was a man of African descent whose birthplace remains unknown. The complete, lengthy title of his book *Narrative of the Uncommon Sufferings and Surprizing Deliverance* includes the phrase "a negro man." Black writing, like much literature of the period, was produced by associative networks that included, among others, the author, publisher, and subscribers. Hammon's book identifies him as Black and English. Still, someone, likely the publisher, thought it important that the title also highlight that Hammon remained enslaved, a "servant to General Winslow." The book's opening paragraph, probably at the publisher's suggestion, emphasized that the Black man did not presume to write "as one in a higher Station."[51] Efforts to assuage readers potentially hostile toward Black voices by providing proof of African lineage and employing a language of obeisance were a common part of the eighteenth-century Black Atlantic literary tradition.[52]

Hammon left Boston in late 1747 as a sailor of some skill. He writes multiple times in the narrative "I ship'd myself," meaning he possessed the freedom to decide where he went and how to apportion his labor. He survived a shipwreck and months of captivity by American Indians in Florida. He spurned impressment in the service of the Spanish navy, refusing to sail against his countrymen. Resisting the Spanish cost him nearly five years' imprisonment "in a close Dungeon" in Havana before he escaped to London with the help of fellow English subjects.[53] Hammon singled out Captain Edward Gascoigne, "a true *Englishman*," for special note in substantiating his understanding of self-identification. When Spanish officials later boarded the *Beaver* and demanded the return of escapees, Gascoigne "refus'd them, and said he could not ... deliver up any *Englishmen* under English Colours."[54] An English captain's protection of him from the Spanish seemed to affirm his self-identification as English.

To aid his country in its global struggle against the French and the Spanish, Hammon enlisted in the Royal Navy. During the Seven Years' War, he served on several warships and participated in multiple naval battles. In 1759, he sustained injuries including being "disabled in the Arm" during a skirmish aboard the *Hercules*.[55] The following year, Hammon decided against hiring himself aboard "the ship bound to Guinea," an area of West Africa that served as a major embarkation point for enslaved Africans trafficked to the Americas.[56] Instead, he "return'd to [his] own Native Land" in North America. According to one literary scholar, Hammon had experienced an enduring cultural displacement that enabled him to consider himself English in London while identifying the region of New England as his "native land."[57] Despite being enslaved there, Hammon considered Boston more of a home to him than Africa. Authors of African descent in the British colonies shared their thoughts on different topics like abolition or life at sea using varied writing forms, from autobiography to philosophical poetry. Their use of multiple genres offered predominantly white readers multiple views of the broad diversity within Black lived experiences across the western Atlantic world.[58] As the rhetoric of liberty became pervasive among white colonists in the late eighteenth century, Black writers also expressed their experiences and their objectives in similar language. Using print culture, they too joined the chorus of colonists vying for "freedom," a development that bound their fates to those of white patriots who had mixed opinions about welcoming them into the revolutionary movement.

After Hammon, Phillis Wheatley, living in postwar British North America, used her writing skills to engage transatlantic discussions of imperial powers. As an enslaved Black writer, she was well versed in expressing the struggles of oppression and desire for freedom. Through her poetry, Wheatley joined John Adams and Benjamin Franklin in writing about the revolutionary developments across the continent. She contributed multiple poetic responses to the increasing conflict between Britain and its colonies during the twenty years between the two treaties in Paris, illustrating an extraordinary skill in employing interdisciplinary knowledge of classical mythology, theology, and philosophy to address the volatile political and social events of the day.[59]

Along with other writings around the Stamp Act, Wheatley penned "To the King's Most Excellent Majesty on His Repealing the American Stamp Act" in 1768. In verse, she lauds George III's repeal of the Stamp Act as "midst the remembrance of thy favors past" and suggests that "the meanest peasants most admire the last."[60] The poet's subtlety left unsaid that colonial protests like the Stamp Act Congress forced the king to rescind the odious law. The timing of the poem seems purposeful, given that it came two years after the revocation of the law. She wrote the poem after Parliament passed the Townshend Acts, named for the realm's Chancellor of the Exchequer Charles Townshend. Lawmakers, rejecting the arguments of Franklin and others, enacted the series of laws to establish the precedent that Parliament could levy taxes unilaterally on the colonies, over the objections of British subjects.

Figure 1.3. Phillis Wheatley. Engraving by Scipio Moorhead, 1773. Courtesy of the John Carter Brown Library.

The poem addressed to George III accompanied literary reactions by other white authors that year to the unpopular pieces of legislation. John Dickinson published twelve letters of protest in newspapers across the colonies under the heading "Letters from a Farmer in Pennsylvania."[61] Wheatley's engagement with British politics represented an attempt to urge the monarch toward less provocative measures against colonists already poised to rebel against despotic authority. She crafted it in the unthreatening form of a prayer, imploring, "Great God, direct, and guard him from on high, And from his head let ev'ry evil fly!" Wheatley, an enslaved Black teenager with no claim to the white revolutionaries' petitions for restored rights, gracefully ended the poem by encouraging George to act wisely and benevolently: "A monarch's smile can set his subjects free!"[62]

The work "To the King" was published five years later in a volume of her collected works titled *Poems on Various Subjects, Religious and Moral*. Wheatley's first book, published just months before the Boston Tea Party, represents the earliest known collection of poetry published by a person of African descent.[63] A decade after the Paris treaty, the British king had yet to reconcile taxation schemes to erase war debts with his subjects' demand for expanded political autonomy. The reach of Wheatley's writings indicates that Black authors "were significant, often central, actors in British and international networks" influential in developing an active print culture of protest.[64]

Phillis Wheatley was born in West Africa, likely present-day Senegal or the Gambia, around 1753. John and Susanna Wheatley of Boston enslaved the eight-year-old African girl in 1761 and named her Phillis, callously using the same name as the ship that had transported her in bondage to North America. At the age of fifteen, the writer exhibited remarkable skill and courage. The period of protest across North America that resulted in the Declaration of Independence was one in which women of any race or class rarely received an education beyond reading and writing. Poet-scholar June Jordan referred to the young Black female's capacity to learn English, Latin, history, and geography and her exhibition of literary talent under the challenging circumstances of enslavement as a "difficult miracle."[65] Wheatley's writings identify her as a Black woman who lived as a revolutionary New Englander. She signaled her African heritage, referring to herself as a "vent'rous *Afric*" in one poem and as "an Ethiop" in another.[66]

Wheatley's work also nudged white readers toward recognizing the entangled nature of their fight for liberty and the hopes Black people held for freedom. In the same year that she had admonished the king toward greater sagacity, she contemplated across a single eight-line stanza how white colonists of Massachusetts and British America forcibly brought Africans to North American shores and, simultaneously, resented their presence. "Some view our sable race with scornful eye," she observed.[67] White colonists seemed to believe God had marked Africans for enslavement and inequality in the color of their skin—one expression of their Blackness.

Wheatley's "On Being Brought from Africa to America" succinctly distilled the racialized and racist conditions under which Hammon, she, and so many other Black inhabitants of Massachusetts lived and suffered. The John and Abigail Adamses of North America, descendants of European immigrants, enjoyed lives and privileges that descendants of the African continent would never know. Wheatley, however, was not always understood. Some scholars have characterized this work as "the most reviled poem in African American literature." The first part of the poem, when not read carefully, can be construed as the poet accommodating slavery through her belief in Christianity.[68] However, in the third couplet, Wheatley challenges white readers to examine their personal positions on Blackness in the colonies. She reminds them that even when Black people achieve monumental tasks, for many white colonial inhabitants, "Their colour is a diabolic die."[69] She placed that six-word line between quotation marks to illustrate how ubiquitous that racist mindset had become. According to one scholar, "Thus, she locates in one line a complex of race, religion, history, and culture that captures the worldview of racism in her time."[70] The poem's last couplet forcefully states, "Remember, Christians, Negros, black as Cain, May be refin'd." Wheatley embraced Blackness in order to refute the racist mark-of-Cain thesis or any idea that Africans were beyond Christianity's salvation. The final four words suggest Black and white Christians share a measure of equality in God's sight and could together "join th' angelic train."[71]

Black writers in North America prior to the Haitian Revolution (1789–1804) gave little attention to the violence and inhumanity that generated the profitable Caribbean products that stimulated the British American economy. In the aftermath of the Seven Years' War, Hammon and Wheatley, two of the more famous Black Atlantic authors, identified with Blackness while not directly attacking the transatlantic system of human enslavement and the people who perpetuated it. According to biographer Vincent Carretta Wheatley used "subdued and indirect" references to present the inherently cruel nature of the Atlantic slave system. A reviewer highlighted the author's different approach to presenting Black Atlantic inhabitants, noting, "Negroes of Africa are generally treated as a dull, ignorant, and ignoble race of men, fit only to be slaves, and incapable of any considerable attainments in the liberal arts and sciences."[72] Her poetry placed the lives of Black people before the eyes of white readers and invited them to consider Christian and republican values in light of their plight.

In one of her first poems, the ode "Maecenas," Wheatley ensured that readers understood that "the happier *Terence* all the choir inspir'd" was "of *African* birth." She identified with Terence and "Afric's sable race." Carretta suggests that the move permitted her "to claim a place in the Western literary tradition, which had included Africans since its beginning."[73] Throughout her body of work, Wheatley claimed "the authority to converse with and chastise those individuals" holding social positions that generally permitted them to ignore someone of her race and gender.[74] Still, like Hammon, she was conscious in her writing not to risk her identification as a New Englander. Historian David Waldstreicher further argues that Wheatley employed the neoclassical language of contemporary US founding revolutionaries like Thomas Jefferson to offer readers "by stealth (or by simile) her African and female experience" and elucidated implicitly the ahistorical error in maintaining slavery in the new society.[75] Early Black writing attempted to provide readers tangible links between the arguments for freedom from slavery and those of other contemporary protest movements in the British

Atlantic world. Though the work of early writers of African descent remains absent in some historical scholarly literature, their critiques and insights made their way into eighteenth-century public discourse. Their collective intellectual endeavors, addressing racist and hostile readers, helped to shape British American life and, in the early United States, established a Black literary tradition of enlightenment and advocacy in the public sphere.[76]

In Saint-Domingue, people of African descent turned to more active means of rebellion than poetry to protest the king's actions that affected their lives in negative ways. D'Estaing's reorganization of the colonial militia and his insistence on the Legion of Saint-Domingue humiliated and angered men of color who saw the move as a way to restrict their rights and relegate their social standing primarily on the basis of race.[77] D'Estaing's successor, Louis-Armand-Constantin de Rohan, arrived in 1766. Over the next two years, he persisted with the racialized plans to put Dominguan soldiery more under Paris's control. His plan prompted fierce resistance from the colony's Afro-Caribbean and white populations.

In the face of opposition, Rohan asked Foreign Minister Choiseul to secure an arrêté, an order, from King Louis XV to authorize the reestablishment of the Dominguan militia.[78] Under such an order, colonists' refusal to serve in the reestablished militia would be tantamount to treason, defying the wishes of the king. In 1768, Choiseul obliged his appointee with the requested royal decree. Members of the Cap-Français Superior Council recorded the decree with little resistance. To Rohan's astonishment, however, colonial leaders in towns from Port-au-Prince to Les Cayes rebuked his heavy-handed tactics. They did not believe the governor was dealing with them in good faith. They refused to believe the king actually intended to reestablish the militia.[79] The members of the Les Cayes assembly signed a petition arguing that Saint-Domingue did not need military rule. Like their colonial neighbors in Boston, Dominguans interpreted imperial efforts to enlarge the military as a means to forcibly subjugate them to the king's will.[80]

Members of the Port-au-Prince Superior Council issued a statement expressing "the hope that [the king's] order would be revoked."[81] A few years earlier, Benjamin Franklin had explained to the Parliament in London that their actions were pushing loyal subjects toward rebellion. Similarly, Port-au-Prince councillors warned the governor-general that they could not accept the restoration of the colonial militia, even if it was authorized by the king. White inhabitants, many of them slaveholders, argued that compulsory "militia service was equivalent to slavery."[82] As they reaffirmed their loyalty

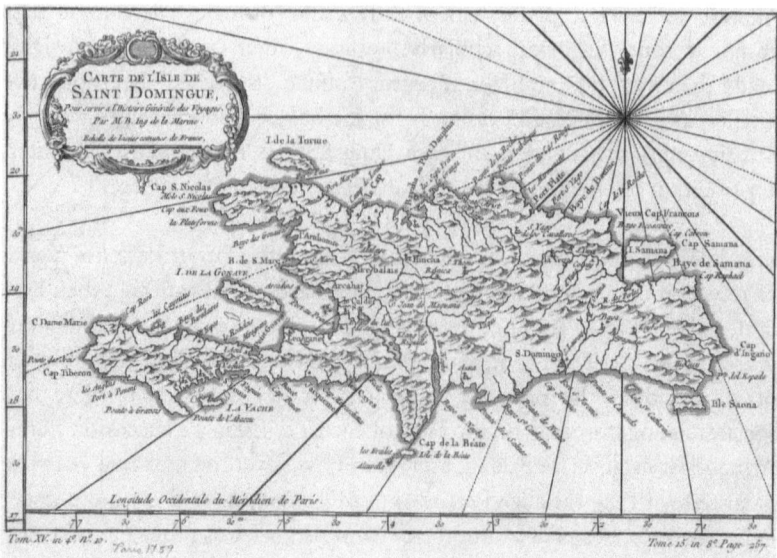

Figure 1.4. A map of the French colony Saint-Domingue, 1759. The map depicts the island of Hispaniola. Saint-Domingue occupies the western third of the island. Cap-Français, in the northwest, is listed as "le Cap." Port-au-Prince and Léogâne are on the central west coast of the colony. Les Cayes and Jacmel are in the south. Courtesy of the John Carter Brown Library.

to the throne, Dominguan colonists firmly pledged to "resist" the governor-general—and, if necessary, King Louis—in the reestablishment of the militia.[83] By year's end, armed revolt had erupted in Saint-Domingue.

Free Afro-Caribbeans also interpreted compulsory military service as an infringement on their freedom.[84] Their fellow white colonists used the term *slavery* as a metaphor to melodramatically express their grievances. The same word struck Afro-Caribbeans differently. Saint-Domingue was a society in which 90 percent of people with some percentage of African heritage lived and died enslaved by another human being. Therefore, the slightest hint of a threat of (re)enslavement posed an existential menace to the colony's free Afro-Caribbean population. After Rohan issued his plan, white opponents of the militia tried to persuade free Dominguans of color that the governor intended to throw them into chains of bondage.[85] In a much more real sense than their white counterparts could have ever imagined, free Afro-Caribbeans came to believe that the establishment of the militia planned to force them into slavery.[86]

Rohan attempted to quell what he characterized as "rumors that have been sown among the gens de couleur." One problem for the governor was that he made his rebuttals not to fearful Afro-Caribbeans but to audiences of white antimilitia groups, including the Port-au-Prince Superior Council. He worked diligently to characterize Louis XV as a protector of rights for all free colonists. In defense of that position, he argued that the king's 1768 law did not weaken any of the protections under law for "freedmen, mulattoes and free negroes and all other colored people." As Rohan put it, the law seemed to recognize the threats to freedom for the broad array of Saint-Domingue's Afro-Caribbean, or nonwhite, population. His characterization, however, was not completely accurate. The 1768 law sought to create a firmly racialized military structure in Saint-Domingue. In it, the king ordered that only white militiamen could replace other white militiamen in service or muster rolls.[87]

At Versailles, the authors of the royal decree seemed to understand that many people in Saint-Domingue were born of relationships between European men and women of African descent. They also appeared well aware that free people of varied percentages of African heritage self-identified as *blanc* or European. Under a previous law during d'Estaing's administration, a mixed-parentage person born of a gens de couleur and a blanc—resulting in a very light, not-white skin tone—"would be welcomed into the companies of whites." The authors of the 1768 militia decree rejected the principle of racial equality or the equal treatment of Afro-Caribbeans and white inhabitants. They sought to prevent integrated military units and to ensure that only white men served as officers. Therefore, they made the king's word an arbiter of racial status in the colony. Under the law, all free inhabitants of any percentage of African heritage, regardless of their self-identification, were characterized collectively "under the name gens de couleur"—meaning, pointedly, not white. Rohan insisted vigorously that the overriding purpose of the royal decree was to ensure the compliance by colonists of all races with the king's order to reestablish the militia in Saint-Domingue.[88]

Men of color, however, were not convinced by Rohan's remonstrances. They refused to overlook the obvious dishonoring of their long years of loyal service to the French military, and they resented the infringement on their rights and the rumored threats to their personhood. They considered his militia plan "infamous" since it stripped them of their status as military officers. The tensions and animosities expressed by Saint-Domingue's Afro-Caribbean population regarding the royal ordinance represented more than a dispute about military reorganization. Beyond affirming the position of King Louis XV's government, the military-necessity argument ignored the injustices targeting men of color for no apparent reason beyond racial prejudice. In late 1768, Rohan went to Croix-des-Bouquets, a parish city in the west of the colony, near Port-au-Prince, to enforce the ordinance reestablishing the militia. He planned to demote the parish's corps of Afro-Caribbean officers and commission white officers at the head of militia detachments of color.[89]

Race played a major role in the changes in military and social policies across Saint-Domingue. After the Paris treaty in 1763, French imperial and colonial leaders imposed legal, racialized restrictions on the colony's population of color. Not coincidentally, the changes in laws and racial norms occurred as the populations of free Afro-Caribbeans and, concurrently, the number of white transplants from France increased.[90] Across the decade, in addition to the dishonorable treatment Afro-Caribbean men endured as military members, they also suffered loss in their social status and injury to their personal dignity. The racist prohibitions had little or nothing to do with biology or genetics. The colony's white population, particularly the new arrivals, felt threatened socially and economically by the increase in the wealth and landholdings of their nonwhite counterparts.

As levels of white racism and Black discontent, in response, rose in the western and southern provinces of Saint-Domingue, free Afro-Caribbean men chose armed protest to express their outrage at the governor's attempts to relegate their status. The insurrection there began on Sunday, 11 December 1768. Men of color at Croix-des-Bouquets refused to muster under the demeaning orders for the restored militia. This act of defiance was quickly emulated in Cul-de-Sac and Mirebalais. The stated objective of those taking the defiant stance was to march on Port-au-Prince, remove Rohan from office by force, and replace him with an elected leader of their own choosing. Both the idea and action represented a direct challenge to colonial authority and the rule of King Louis XV.

Over the next couple of months, into the spring of 1769, the actions of Afro-Caribbean rebels in the west of the island inspired their fellow colonists of color in the south. There, the rebellion took hold when Jacques Delaunay, a prominent man of color, refused to muster with the militia as a noncommissioned officer. Delaunay had held an officer's commission and had served in the Seven Years' War, along with comrades of color like Guillaume Labadie and Jacques Boury. The local militia commander arrested Delaunay, and he emerged as a leader of the southern rebellion. His stance represented defiance against the government's social relegation and racial injustice. Some 150 men of color assembled to attempt to free him.[91] The French government later charged Delaunay with taking command of rebel forces and administering treasonous oaths of obedience and loyalty.[92] From

Torbeck to Tiburon, the insurrection spread rapidly, threatening to take hold of the region.[93] The rebels of the south supported the rebels in the west who maintained their pressure around Port-au-Prince.

What began as angst over militia realignments blossomed into an all-out defense of freedom for colonists. Men of African descent stood defiant upon the lives they had built in Saint-Domingue. They refused to relinquish the honor they had earned from their neighbors and colonial compatriots. This was a pivotal moment. There had been two previous revolts in Saint-Domingue to wrest authority from the metropole, in 1670 and 1722. Nineteenth-century Haitian historian Beauvais Lespinasse categorized the 1769 Revolt as the colony's third rebellion.[94] The distinctive element in the post-Paris treaty venture was that free Afro-Caribbean men formed the bulk of the rebel force, augmented by members of the petit blancs population.[95] The former wanted to be treated as subjects of the French Empire equal to affluent white colonists. Many gens de couleur were born free in Saint-Domingue to a mother of African descent and a European-descended father. They lived as free affluent colonial inhabitants. They made extended sojourns in France for a quality education and often possessed more land and wealth than many white locals or white immigrants to the island. People known as *les affranchis*, or freed people, in Saint-Domingue were individuals with different levels of African heritage who had endured some form of slavery. Through a variety of ways, they had achieved or received freedom. The Dominguan government did not afford gens de couleur or the affranchis the same national citizenship rights as white colonials. Still, members of these free Afro-Caribbean colonists had served in the king's military as officers and enlisted men during the Seven Years' War. The governmental reforms stripping them of their dignity earned as military officers challenged their allegiance to good order. Like white colonists in British North America, Saint-Domingue's free colonists of color refused to accept—without protest—the diminution of their rights at the hands of the monarch after the Paris treaty.

The 1769 Revolt amounted to a remarkable multiracial effort against the French king. Dominguan colonists, Black and white, divided themselves into two camps—rebels and Loyalists. Jean-Pierre Mallet, a white planter, became a leader in the southern resistance. Delaunay and Mallet led hundreds of rebels in roving campaigns across the region. They skirmished with local militia and abducted Black and white police and militia officers.[96] They burned the homes of Loyalists. They occupied captured plantations. Local administrators could not quell the rebellion because men of color had played such an important role in the constabulary. Militiamen and war veterans of color had helped to maintain law and order in the colony across the 1760s. Now they were disrupting it.

One future rebel, Julien Raimond, was a wealthy twenty-five-year-old indigo planter of color in 1769. He resided well to the east of sociopolitical turbulence. There is little evidence to suggest he participated with his fellow colonists in their rebellious activities against the king. But he later distinguished himself as one of most prolific revolutionary writers during the Haitian Revolution. From that vantage point, recalling his own experiences from two decades earlier, he suggested that "the jealousy of white people toward the people of color deployed itself with an unprecedented fury."[97] Racial envy led them to strip war veterans of color of their officer commissions. Raimond noted that the 1769 Revolt stemmed from actions and ideals beyond military ranks. Afro-Caribbeans had "watched the evolution of injustice [against them], as a succession of ordinances followed one after the other in tyranny, until they reached absurdity."[98] The terms imposed on France in the Treaty of Paris led Versailles officials to engineer measures to secure Saint-Domingue from external threats. Instead, King Louis and Governor Rohan destabilized the colony's internal security through racially injurious decrees.

March 1769 became a month of significant actions for the rebellion. Forces under Mallet's command took Les Cayes, the headquarters of the southern Loyalist militia commander. The city of Jérémie sided with the rebels after negotiating with their emissaries from the western province. Momentum appeared to swing toward the rebellion. But Rohan and Loyalist forces counterattacked with greater brutality. In Port-au-Prince, Rohan and 150 troops arrested members of the Superior Council and had them deported to France. His forces captured many of the western rebels as they tried to escape from the city. He ordered a general search of all city merchants suspected of arming, aiding, and abetting the insurgents. Rohan had initially planned to hang the white rebels and spare the partisans of color as a sign of the king's care for the latter group. However, he seemed to conclude that since the rebellion was multiracial, so should be the punishment for insurgency. He ordered Afro-Caribbean and white rebels to be hanged together in the grand marketplace of the city's center.[99]

After subduing Port-au-Prince, the militia forces focused on quelling rebellious embers in the south. They reestablished command in Les Cayes. There, too, the militia hanged Afro-Caribbean and white rebels together. The swift public executions helped to pacify the region. By the summer of 1769, a squadron of French navy ships landed in Dominguan ports, and troops from the metropole were deployed to restore the king's authority across the colony.[100] The French government ultimately sentenced Jacques Delaunay and three others to be hanged in Les Cayes's main marketplace. Presumably because of his status as a rebel leader, and very likely because he was a man of color, French officials singled out the body of Delaunay among those condemned to undergo additional indignities. After the execution, "the head was to be separated from the body," and the executioner was ordered to affix the severed head on a pike in the central marketplace of the southern port city of Côteaux.[101] Dominguan officials reserved special ignominy for convicted Afro-Caribbean rebels. A decade before, the body of condemned Black leader Makandal had been desecrated after his public execution. Twenty years after Delauney, colonial authorities publicly dismembered and dishonored the body of Vincent Ogé, a free man of color and one of the first martyrs of the Haitian Revolution. Jean-Pierre Mallet, the white 1769 Revolt leader, escaped to Jamaica.[102]

Colonists in British North America, protesting and preparing to rebel against the ordinances of their own king, followed closely the insurrectionist actions in Saint-Domingue. Newspapers along eastern port cities told the story of how fellow Atlantic colonists resorted to violence against unjust imperial mandates. Colonists in Boston read that "the inhabitants of Leogane and Goave had revolted and taken arms, and already musted 300 horsemen, and a great number on foot." The newspaper disclosed how the rebels threatened the property and the lives of Dominguan Loyalists.[103] In a matter of several years, American rebels would employ similar tactics to maintain cohesion within their insurrection. As legislatures across British America parried with King George over legal and political dominance, the successes and disasters of the 1769 rebels offered instruction and caution to their American counterparts.[104] They learned how the French military deployed "six frigates preparing to sail from Brest for St. Domingo, with additional civil and military power, to quell the malcontents of that island."[105] King Louis removed Rohan as governor-general of Saint-Domingue only months after the revolt. This news may have offered American rebels some glimmer of hope that protest proved effective.[106]

Protest also came with risks. White rebel lawmakers from New Hampshire to Georgia likely took particular interest in news about the French imperial show of force against members of the Port-au-Prince Superior Council.[107] Stories about the tragic end to the defiant council circulated widely. Americans read how "Rohan had himself seized, and sent the Sovereign Council home [as] prisoners . . . and then appointed a new Council."[108] They followed reports of "the eleven members" deported to France "guilty of sedition . . . and confined on their arrival at the Castle Trompette . . . [and] of the manner in which they were carried off by an armed force."[109] For some American readers, support for open rebellion may have faltered a bit as they learned the unpleasant fate of the deputies. According to a report, within a year of their arrest, "nine of the [eleven] principal ringleaders in the late disturbances at Cape Francois and St. Domingo, who had been sent home [as] prisoners, have since perished miserably in the Bastille."[110]

The writer of the story of the Dominguan prisoners reprinted in the *New-York Gazette* inserted an editorial remark at its end: *"Blessed Effects of arbitrary Power!"*[111] The remark exhibited a sense of injustice for the 1769 rebels who lost their lives without the semblance of due process. It illustrated a revolutionary understanding spreading across American colonies that would violently challenge their own king in a few years. It also indicates that American readers were aware of the horrors held within France's most famous prison, which became infamous after British writer Charles Dickens captured the despair of the then-four-hundred-year-old Bastille in his nineteenth-century novel *A Tale of Two Cities*. The book's opening section is titled "Recalled to Life." Through the character of Doctor Manette—"buried alive for eighteen years!" in the Bastille—it illustrates the unlikeliness of people surviving their imprisonment in the 1770s.[112] Dickens describes plainly what a sojourn in the French prison did to those fortunate to survive: "The task of recalling him from the vacancy into which he always sank when he had spoken, was like recalling some very weak person from a swoon, or endeavouring, in the hope of some disclosure, to stay the spirit of a fast-dying man." In one of the most memorable, heart-wrenching scenes in English literature, Doctor Manette, in Mr. Defarge's Parisian upper room, asks his former servant:

"Did you ask me for my name?"

"Assuredly I did."

"One Hundred and Five, North Tower."

"Is that all?"

"One Hundred and Five, North Tower."[113]

Three decades after the Port-au-Prince councillors' demise behind bars, the unforgiving despair, loneliness, and alienation of a French prison, as suffered by the fictious Manette, ended the real, heroic life of another revolutionary from Saint-Domingue: Toussaint Louverture, leader of the Haitian Revolution, who challenged French authority in the colony. In 1802, Emperor Napoleon I imprisoned Louverture with no trial at Fort de Joux prison in eastern France. Within months, a companion discovered the leader's lifeless body in his cell. The widely reported deaths of the 1769 Revolt councillors within the Bastille acted as warning signs for British American colonists in the western Atlantic world who contemplated revolution against their king.

The 1769 Revolt was a significant act of resistance. However, Black people had employed violence to achieve their objectives in the Atlantic world before the seventh decade of the eighteenth century. It joined the violent resistance of Black people in the Stono Rebellion, just south of Charleston, South Carolina, in 1739; the Makandal "insurrection" in Limbé, Saint-Domingue, in 1758; and Tacky's Revolt, across rural Jamaica in 1760. The 1769 Revolt was different. White colonials in this case joined Afro-Caribbeans in their action against authority. Also, previous revolts had been aimed at colonial, slaveholding white inhabitants. In closer relation to concurrent protests in British North America, the rebels in Saint-Domingue lashed out against the orders of the metropole and against changes to colonial life.

The lesson from Black engagement with Atlantic revolts is that the search for freedom, liberty, and equality was much more than the aspirations and actions of white people inspired by Enlightenment writers. People who had known freedom and had free family members in West Africa did not need European philosophies to tell them that white enslavers had unjustly stolen their lives and liberties. Free people of color in Saint-Domingue independently understood that France's laws and customs gave greater rights, privileges, and access to power to white French citizens who were less affluent and capable than they were, because the latter were white. Black writings in North America and violent protests by Afro-Caribbeans against the French Empire demonstrate the level of active resistance that brewed in the hearts of people of African descent across the western Atlantic world.

As a ship carried the 1769 Revolt leaders from Saint-Domingue to face condemnation in Paris, Edward Stevens began settling into his new surroundings in New York. The fifteen-year-old white native of Saint Croix was beginning his studies there at King's College (later Columbia University), the fifth-oldest institution of higher learning in the thirteen colonies. He wrote back home at least twice to his friend Alexander Hamilton. Both young men understood that the most effective means to the power and influence each hoped to attain meant leaving their island. While some colonists in British North America sought greater autonomy and rebels of color demanded equality in Saint-Domingue, other inhabitants across the western Atlantic world sought to reap the imperial benefits of education on the continent and in Europe. Stevens's family's financial situation allowed him to access education on the continent. Other children of affluent Caribbean colonists, Black and white, took advantage of opportunities to receive a quality education in the imperial cities of North America and Europe. British subjects routinely sent their children to famous schools in England, Scotland, Virginia, and Massachusetts. Nathan Hale, of Connecticut, attending Yale College, began his studies at the same time as Stevens. Parents from Saint-Domingue regularly sent their teenagers, including students of color, to France for higher learning. Vincent Ogé and André Rigaud, both adolescents of color, one from Dondon and the other from Les Cayes, were educated in Bordeaux. Ogé, Rigaud, and Stevens would return to establish adult professional lives on their home islands after educational sojourns abroad. Ogé and Hale died as revolutionary martyrs. Rigaud and Stevens served briefly as presidents of their respective islands.

Hamilton's reply to Stevens's missives made it clear that not every Caribbean child had access to off-island scholarly experience. Stevens and he, though best friends, did not come from the same economic class in Saint Croix. As an orphaned child, Hamilton possessed no guarantees of upward mobility afforded by education. He matched Stevens in ambition but was left behind to despise "the grov'ling and condition of a Clerk or the like, to which [his] Fortune &c. condemn[ed him]."[114] The young Hamilton understood the Atlantic class system but refused to accept a permanent place at the bottom of it. Hamilton's mother, Rachel Faucette, his sole guardian, died of yellow fever in 1768. He lamented having to settle as a clerk at Beekman and Cruger's shop in Christiansted "to build castles in the air" while preparing "the way for futurity."[115]

Five hundred miles to the northwest, an eleven-year-old slaved away, literally, in Dominguan sugarcane fields, before his enslaver sold him away to a free Black man named Dessalines. Jean-Jacques Duclos (later Dessalines), three years younger than Hamilton, was born enslaved in Grande-Rivière-du-Nord, Saint-Domingue. The child of two parents from western or central Africa, both of them bonded to a white enslaver on the Cormiers plantation, he resided at the lowest level of Moreau's 128-point racial category system.[116] Both Duclos and Hamilton—a Black Dominguan and a white Cruzan; one trafficked, one orphaned—made their way in the Atlantic world without the security of parental love and guidance. Duclos, who became Dessalines, remained enslaved. Toiling under the oppressive Caribbean sun, surrounded by other African-descended workers, Jean-Jacques Dessalines likely could not have imagined that, thirty-five years later, he would rule over that same ground and declare the colony of his birth as Haiti, the world's first independent Black republic. Hamilton, from the shop, with a view of the ships anchored along the wharf, dared to dream of grandeur beyond his island. To realize his ambitions, of which he pretended to be ashamed, Hamilton suggested to Stevens a solution: "I wish there was a War."[117] Rumors of war pervaded North America, the Caribbean, and Europe. One can appreciate the selfish musings of a poor teenage boy forced to watch his best friend excel at college while he remained stuck on the island, left to reconcile his hopes and dreams with the bleakness of his reality. Little could Hamilton have known the myriad of ways in which war over the next decade would change all their lives and irrevocably transform the world.

Chapter 2

"Kill Them! Kill Them!"

1770

Edward Stevens began his studies at King's College in New York in the same year revolutionary violence began to change the nature of life and politics in the North American colonies. He left his family in Christiansted, Saint Croix, to pursue an educational path toward becoming a physician. Saint Croix and other Caribbean islands consistently needed doctors for the free and enslaved populations, but his career path would first take him to the mainland colonies. He had discussed his academic and professional ambitions with his best friend in Christiansted, Alexander Hamilton. In a letter to Stevens from home, Hamilton referred to his fourteen-year-old companion as "Dr Edward." In 1767, two years before he set sail, King's College, under the leadership of President Myles Cooper (1763–75), established the second medical college in the western Atlantic world. Stevens relocated to British North America primarily as an academic necessity, not an act of political activism. There exists no evidence to suggest he gave much thought to the revolutionary rhetoric swirling about mainland British colonies. Hamilton acknowledged receipt of two letters from Stevens but made no response to news included in them about the stories that appeared regularly in Atlantic newspapers of rebellious indignation over parliamentary taxes and outrage over the imperial military occupation in Massachusetts. Stevens seemed to focus his letters on missing family and friends back home—a common first-year college sensation—and his academic experiences. Like a good friend, Hamilton reassured Stevens of "having soon the happiness of seeing" his parents and boyhood friend and encouraged Stevens by saying that he was "pleased to see [him] Give such Close Application to Study."[1]

New York during the volatile early 1770s did not exhibit the rebellious tendencies of other American cities. It possessed an influential Tory population and served as a stronghold of British imperial control. In 1770, the faculty of King's College, "housed in a stately three-story building with a cupola that commanded a superb view of the Hudson River," did not encourage or cultivate revolutionary fervor among the students. President Cooper, a vocal Loyalist who later left North America for Scotland, worked to maintain King's College as a fortress of British orthodoxy. He frowned on the increasing number of political protests that were happening nearby and segregated his students from "unwholesome" external forces across the city.[2] In the relatively sedate environment Cooper had established, Edward Stevens chose to focus on his studies, as indicated by Hamilton's letter, and not to participate directly in colonial revolutionary action.

Despite Cooper's best efforts, New York was still home to outspoken writers and newspaper publishers who spread the news about any brewing drama. One print journal reported that France, which had few serviceable ships of the line, or battleships, at the end of the Seven Years' War, had invested twenty-six million pounds sterling into naval power. Alluding to the threat posed by two former enemies of Britain, the writer noted that France and Spain, "ready to act in conjunction," had deployed twenty-five ships of the line, plus frigates, and over twenty thousand troops across the Caribbean.[3]

Another New York newspaper ran stories over several issues raising the specter of an imminent war with France less than a decade from the Treaty of Paris. One article warned, "The French court is preparing to break with us." As if building a sense of intrigue, another article informed readers that the French navy had "at [that] time 24 for ships of the line at Toulon, and 28 at Brest, none less than 50 guns, in fit order for sea on the shortest notice."[4]

Amid mounting fears of "our foreign dangers," an anonymous writer, probably based in London, published a volume offering "a proper sense of them and their causes." Seven years after its ratification, the author remained ardently critical of the first Paris treaty. After echoing a common sentiment that France had unjustly initiated the last war, they reminded readers of Britain's overwhelming defeat of the aggressor. Consequently, the essay faulted "improvident" British negotiators for ceding conquered territories. It blamed the peace deal for the French rearmament that prompted Britons' present fears. According to the author, "Giving up so great sources of commerce and naval power enabled [France] in so short time to renew the war."⁵

The essay also examined North American colonial discontent through the lens of "the malignant nature of the late peace." It considered the colonies a crucial part of the empire's economic and naval power. The author appeared empathetic to the cause of the colonists, reasoning that the "improvidence" that marred the treaty in 1763 continued to stymie government policymaking: "The consent of the people, in this kingdom and the colonies, hath been disregarded of late." To govern colonies in the western Atlantic world required "a patient hearing of the parties." The punitive Townshend Acts of the late 1760s, to the contrary, provoked mob violence. An imperial resolution to "the present dangers," both colonial and international, "the author presumes, [could] only be found in universal justice and equal social liberty."⁶ The author was not alone in doubting the government's willingness to adapt. Buried on the last page of a New York newspaper was a seemingly disjointed statement that, as events transpired, proved prescient: "It is rumoured that an entire new mode of government is to take place in the American part of the globe."⁷

Given the broad print coverage, Stevens and other King's College students were wary of rekindled hostilities and aware of the rebellious violence engulfing the city and North America. On 19 January 1770, townspeople clashed with British troops in the Battle of Golden Hill, along John Street between William Street and Pearl Street. There, soldiers attempted to take down a liberty pole and post a broadside with a pungent attack on the Sons of Liberty in New York. A crowd formed to stop them, and soldiers arrived with drawn bayonets. The ensuing clash between civilians and redcoats resulted in no gunfire and no deaths, but several injuries, including bayonet wounds, were reported on both sides of the skirmish. The melee occurred a half mile from King's College, and the students undoubtedly talked about it. A month later, the Sons of Liberty and sailors erected a liberty pole across from the campus commons.⁸

On the morning of Monday, 5 March 1770, Stevens may have read the *New-York Gazette* story about the white customs officer Ebenezer Richardson in Boston, who killed eleven-year-old Christopher Seider after "the Lads beat him [Richardson] off into his House, and broke his Windows, upon which he fired upon them."⁹ The "Lads" referred to in the story were the Boston Sons of Liberty, a riotous group that included famous revolutionaries like Samuel Adams. New Yorkers reading the Richardson story about white colonists fighting British Loyalists would have also read about Waverage, a "very black" man who, two days before the Seider killing, fled the home of his enslaver Joseph Cornwell. The newspaper featured the story of Waverage's escape to secure freedom at the top center of the front page. Just beneath the Richardson article was an article about an enslaver selling "a Negro man and a negro woman," both unnamed but listed as aged thirty-three and twenty-five years, respectively.[10]

In the era of revolution, across North American and Caribbean colonies, Black and white inhabitants debated, negotiated, and fought over the meaning of freedom and liberty. Along Atlantic sea lanes, multiracial crews forged a collective identity aboard maritime vessels. Formerly enslaved people of the African diaspora also formed bonds as they expanded notions of freedom within maroon communities. Many of their efforts transpired in the decade after the Treaty of Paris of 1763, which put pressure on a fragile peacetime still reeling from the previous war. During that period, British legislative reprisals and military occupation in Boston ignited a deadly riot. A post-treaty economic downturn in France prompted a broad migration to Saint-Domingue. Colonial administrators passed laws that disadvantaged the colony's *gens de couleur* population to accommodate the intolerant racial views of the new arrivals. As frustrations mounted between colonial rebels and imperial enforcers, the number of more direct actions, including violent encounters, increased. The peace terms of the Treaty of Paris were triggering new conflicts leading to war even if Atlantic inhabitants did not realize it at the time. From his college campus view of the Hudson River across a low, rambling meadow, Edward Stevens, on 5 March 1770, could not have known that by the evening's end, members of the British Twenty-Ninth Regiment of Foot would shoot to death five colonists in Boston.

When Crispus Attucks awoke on the morning of 5 March 1770, he did not imagine he would be dead before midnight. Attucks has generally entered the American historical narrative through his death at the Boston Massacre; however, his life warrants attention as well.[11] He exhibited much courage and faced many challenges when he became a fugitive freedom seeker. If, as Bernard Bailyn suggests, American revolutionary ideology was "a cluster of convictions focused on the effort to free the individual from the oppressive misuse of power," Crispus Attucks should also be known for achieving individual freedom fifteen years before white British colonists assembled at the Stamp Act Congress.[12]

Attucks was born around 1723. Similar to the rebels of color in Saint-Domingue's 1769 Revolt, he was born of mixed parentage. In Attucks's case, he was born to an African father and a Native American mother whose names biographers have yet to uncover. Unlike revolt leaders such as Jacques Delaunay, Attucks was not free at birth. A white British colonial subject, William Brown, enslaved the entire family on his plantation in Framingham, about twenty miles east of Boston. Attucks spent his first twenty-seven years in the Framingham area.

Though Black people did not need to be told their enslavement was inhumane and against God's will for humanity, white Christian enslavers and their allies in maintaining the systems of unjust servitude tried to convince Africa's children otherwise. Reverend Cotton Mather, one of the most influential New England Christian preachers and a slaveholder, proudly published *The Negro Christianized* with hopes to put a copy in the house of "every Family of New England, which has a Negro in it."[13] In the text, he instructed white enslavers, "Were your Servants well tinged with the Spirit of Christianity, it would render them exceeding Dutiful to their Masters, exceeding Patient under their Masters."[14]

To assist in convincing people of the African diaspora to accept their enslavement, he suggested that enslavers, instead of allowing their captives to read the Bible, "make them Learn by heart, certain Particular Verses of the Scriptures," including Ephesians 6:5, "Servants, Be Obedient unto them that are your Master—as the Servant of Christ, doing the will of God from the Heart." In the catechism for the enslaved, Mather instructed them not to "be Discontent with [their] Condition."[15] On one occasion, he encountered "a company of poor Negroes" who sought his assistance establishing a Christian society for members "of their miserable Nation that were servants among us." Mather prayed and preached at one of the meetings. In a most unabashedly paternalistic fashion, he gave "the following Orders" to "the miserable children of Adam, and of Noah," to "obtain some wise and good Man, of the English . . . and by their Presence and Council, do what they think fitting for us."[16]

Crispus Attucks was either unaware of or uninterested in the great preacher's instructions for Black salvation. Like so many before and after him, he was discontent with white people and racist laws perpetually subjugating him and his family to the status of property or taxable objects. On 30 September 1750, against the wishes of his white enslavers, he decided to search for freedom. He risked the emotional pains of forced relocation, loss of community, and a myriad of corporeal punishments if caught. He escaped captivity with a "Bearskin Coat, plain brown Fustian Jacket... new Buckskin Breeches, blue Yarn Stockings, and a check'd woollen Shirt." From that fateful moment, Attucks made for himself many decisions of which Brown's enslavement had robbed him and his parents. His new life represented not only the exercise of agency but also the most basic level of humans being treated as adults: choosing whether to stand or sit, eating what they wanted, dressing as they wanted, and living where they wanted. Had he not decided to control his own destiny as a freedom seeker, Attucks could have ended up like the nameless "Negro Woman" and "Negro Man" whose enslavers, on the same page that reported his escape, advertised those two "to be sold."[17]

The enslaver Brown placed announcements of Attucks's freedom trek in the newspaper on at least three occasions from 2 October to 20 November 1750. In them, he identified Attucks as "a Molatto fellow."[18] Between 1750 and 1775, newspapers across British North America used *Negro* and *Mulatto* roughly the same number of times to identify Black freedom seekers. In almost every advertisement—over 90 percent—editors used *Negro* or *Mulatto* to describe people of African descent. Both terms, according to historian Sharon Block, were "a manufactured invention" of Europeans and employed as a judgment of someone's personhood, connecting the subject of the term with the status of slavery. Notwithstanding multiracial heritage, Attucks and other people considered "mulatto" could not shed their primary identity, in the eyes of the arbiters of race across British America, "as an enslavable person of African descent."[19]

After his escape, Attucks no longer served Brown or increased the latter's wealth as property, a fact that made the enslaver eager to get him back. Brown used the *Boston Gazette* stories to alert "Masters of Vessels" in nearby harbors to Attucks's escape. He cautioned them "against concealing or carrying off" the man he had enslaved since birth. Despite the warning over several weeks, someone along the way assisted Attucks in the initial escape and his subsequent ventures to establish a self-governing life.[20] The need for Brown's alarm indicates that running away was not uncommon for enslaved Africans in Massachusetts.

At the close of the previous century, Mather had attempted to stem the tide of Black freedom seeking, or self-liberation, across the colony. He sought to use white Christianity to drive a wedge between oppressed members of the African diaspora. To assemble for religious meetings, Black Christians, at some level, had to pledge, "If any of them should *run away* from their Masters, wee will afford them no *Shelter*; but wee will do what in us *lies*, that they may bee discovered and punished: And if any of us, are found faulty in this Matter, they shall bee no longer *of us*."²¹ Mather was essentially demanding that free and enslaved Black people break the bonds of their diasporic spiritual communities, which mutually fed and sustained their spiritual and physical beings, to preserve white supremacy and the inhuman cruelty of slavery in colonial America.²² Social and religious rules such as those Mather implemented had limited effect, however, in convincing Blacks that it was sinful to escape slavery.

Mather was not alone in failing to stop African-descended people from seeking freedom. Marronage, the act of Black people creating Black-led communities, occurred and thrived across the western Atlantic world. These communities affirmed and supported acts of self-liberation, as they exercised differing levels of self-governance or autonomy beyond white control. The work of historian Sylviane A. Diouf defines maroons restrictively as people of African descent who "settled in the wilderness, lived there in secret, and were not under any form of direct control by outsiders." She notes that key differences existed between maroons and freedom seekers who lived in enclaves.²³ The research of geographer Celeste Winston affirms the difference, arguing, "Marronage must be understood not just as a fleeting practice of flight but also as a significant method of producing place."²⁴

People of African descent like Attucks did not only participate in marronage during the escape. They also constructed sites and networks to safeguard newly won freedom. Winston's examination of "maroon geographies" empowers scholars to understand the ways more fully that "self-emancipated Black people transformed their physical worlds to create zones of liberation." Members of the African diaspora across the Atlantic world chose and dared to live beyond enslavement "by mixing their labor with the external world to change the world and thereby themselves."²⁵

King's College student Edward Stevens had grown up in the slave society of the Danish West Indies. There, marronage was the most often used method of resistance to slavery. On Saint Thomas, people of the diaspora established freedom communities soon after planters developed a plantation culture. Slavery and Black freedom existed together from the beginning of unjust servitude. The island's primeval forest provided cover. The cliffs could not be scaled by catchers from the seaward side, and vegetation obstructed the landward approaches to maroon communities. The trees supplied wood for canoes to escape to nearby Spanish Puerto Rico, which lay within sight to the west. In 1706, the same year Mather published *The Negro Christianized*, the island's privy council ordered the destruction of all trees from which freedom seekers could make canoes. The clear-cutting policy spread to Saint

John and Saint Croix. The colonial government's tactic hurt the environment and robbed freedom seekers of refuge on the islands. Before the growth of cities like Christiansted and Frederiksted, the best chances for permanent escape from slavery on Saint Croix lay overseas. Historian Neville A. T. Hall describes the flight of fugitive freedom seekers across Caribbean islands as "maritime marronage." In 1748, for instance, forty-two maritime maroons seized a sloop in Saint Croix and sailed to freedom in the Spanish islands.[26]

Two years later and 1,800 miles to the north in another coastal colony, Attucks, at some point after leaving the Brown plantation, chose the sea as his vehicle to shape his own identity. He was not the only former enslaved person to do so. Throughout the eighteenth century, the ocean provided an effective cloak for Africans to shed their enslavement in exchange for the life of a sailor. Attucks obscured his identity within the complexities of the seaborne trade system to join the ranks of other sailors as "citizens of the world."[27] He chose the life of an Atlantic sailor, with experiences in the ports of the North American colonies and the Caribbean.[28] The seafaring profession allowed him a life in motion, riding the ocean waves and braving storms alongside his shipmates. Attucks's lived experiences as a free seaman of color resembled Ira Berlin's understanding of "Atlantic creoles" who created lives in the expanding commercial world that inextricably connected the destinies of Black men as sailors to enslaved people of African descent.[29]

It is unlikely that the harsh experience of being enslaved and having his family enslaved ever left Attucks. He, however, left behind that life. He lived under the name Michael Johnson and crafted a new identity as a free man of color. One can only speculate on the many untruths he had to tell and the many stories of birth, childhood, and family he had to concoct to secure and sustain his freedom. Unlike many people who were born, lived, and died under the oppressive inhumanity of white enslavers, Attucks, also known as Johnson, achieved the ability to depart the shores of British North America and make a new home for himself in a free Black community on the island of New Providence, Bahamas.[30] The British island colony, which had a Black population of 1,250 in the year Attucks escaped, attracted people from North America.

Attucks likely made his home in a community east of Nassau. There, sailors and fishermen maintained the village of New Guinea, "most of its inhabitants being free negroes and mulattoes." With Indian-African parentage, Attucks would have found camaraderie within the "complex social spectrum" of Bahamian society. Together, they forged a community that existed within the power structure of European authority and the dominant white Atlantic societal norms. The territory had a sizable population of "persons who were neither unequivocally black or white, and neither slave nor fully free." In the 1750s, lawmakers passed legislation "to ascertain who shall not be deem Mulattoes" in an attempt to address the complex racial question created by interracial sexual relations—predominantly between white males and Black females—that existed across the Atlantic world.[31]

In the early 1760s, as Bahamians of European descent crafted racial laws, Europeans negotiating the first Treaty of Paris haggled over the spoils of trafficking Black peoples on the high seas. London commentators condemned Article X of the treaty for ceding Gorée Island, site of the infamous "Door of No Return," to France. Article X, however, also guaranteed British access to important inland slave-trading posts along the Senegal River.[32] The imperial powers may not have agreed on many issues, but they did share a commitment to keeping Black populations under white authority. In the end, Bahamians were no more successful than any of the Caribbean or North American colonies in establishing an "almost-white" racial category that Europeans could accept as equal to themselves. The attempts to normalize people of African and European parents derived from a commitment to white supremacy. They "placed great stress on the social importance of aspiring to the white phenotype" as they devalued and degraded the genetics of Black women.[33]

Shortly after Attucks chose to live as a free man in the Bahamas, the island's population of color became the numerical majority. By 1767, Black Atlantic inhabitants, free and enslaved, constituted 64 percent of the New Providence population. Notwithstanding the island's "complex social milieu," lawmakers remained insistent that Black people would live differently than white inhabitants. Accordingly, they passed the "Act for governing Negroes, Mulattoes, and Indians," setting these groups as subordinate to white colonists. White leaders and residents considered the three nonwhite groups to be "a People of very bold daring Spirit . . . who live by Wrecking and Plunder" and regarded them as a collective socioeconomic and political threat to Bahamian society.[34]

Despite the restrictions, New Providence proved to be an accommodating home to sailors like Attucks and other transient residents involved in Atlantic commerce. Finding freedom on the seas, and working alongside their European counterparts, allowed Attucks and many sailors of African descent, like Olaudah Equiano, to cultivate an "African" identity that emphasized the racial and political realities of the Atlantic world.[35] Moving in and out of port cities that housed people hostile to their presence and trafficked openly in fellow members of the diaspora, Black sailors along with others created for themselves "a new diasporic identity" to protect and honor their heritage.[36]

Attucks lived and worked twenty years as a masterless inhabitant across the area Julius Scott called "Afro-America" and Paul Gilroy later described as "the Black Atlantic."[37] The spatial and racialized geography of both writers redirects historical attention toward ingenious ways that people of African descent, free and enslaved, created intercolonial communities, challenged the authority of local and imperial overlords, and forged a sharing of economic and cultural power within an Atlantic world framework centered on the political and economic power of Europeans.[38] The Treaty of Paris may have renegotiated territories involved in the slave trade, but Black inhabitants of the Atlantic world found communal and geographic gaps to transcend imperial boundaries.

Sailors like Attucks and other mobile migrants of color across colonial North America embraced an "African" identity though many Europeans considered the appellation degrading.[39] According to historian Leslie Alexander, a "Black transnational consciousness," rooted "in the horrors of the Trans-Atlantic trade in humans," developed across the western Atlantic world.[40] In this formulation, a Black Atlantic identity did not depend on skin complexion, location, social status, or wealth accumulation. Instead, peoples of various ethnic backgrounds, located across the Caribbean or North America, inhabited a racial identity through the common oppression of Atlantic slavery. White inhabitants refused to recognize efforts at self-identification by individuals with any percentage of African heritage. They generally viewed people of the African diaspora as a racially "Black" collective, arbitrarily employing terms like *negro, mulatto, affranchis,* and *gens de couleur* to perpetually link nonwhite inhabitants to the physical abuse, human indignities, and legal proscriptions associated with enslavement.[41]

Members of the African diaspora employed a myriad of ways to redefine Black humanity and freedom across an Atlantic world governed by enslavers and beneficiaries of the trafficking, sale, and involuntary labor of human beings. Novelist and scholar Stephen L. Carter developed the phrase "darker nation" to describe people of all levels of African ancestry, in an attempt to capture "a sense of solidarity and distinctiveness."[42] Members of the African diaspora did not consistently act in solidarity with the needs of different intraracial cohorts. Yet their collective nonwhite existence connected their lived experiences through injustices emanating from Europeans' commitment to slavery and white supremacy and set them apart as a distinct people within the Atlantic world.[43]

White Europeans were also migrating to create opportunities for themselves. Across the 1760s, middling and poorer white citizens who failed to secure satisfactory employment in France relocated to Saint-Domingue, perhaps thinking affluence would come more easily in the Caribbean. According to historian John Garrigus, "after 1763, about a thousand of them [poorer white people] arrived every year from France," and many of them found themselves at "the very bottom of the social hierarchy."[44] For the first time in their lives, these white subjects of the French Empire, funded in part by the enslavement of African people, were surrounded by Afro-Caribbean people who could read, who spoke more polished French, who dressed better, who were wealthier, and who owned more property than many white people.

These upstart French migrants had to adjust to many elements of Caribbean society, and oftentimes they did not fit in among white inhabitants on the island. Elite white members of Saint-Domingue considered the unwelcomed arrivals, called the *petits blancs*, to be responsible for the rise in urban crime, a "mob of vagabonds and adventurers hurling themselves upon these shores."[45] These lower-class white men, much less than becoming affluent in the New World, were forced to seek employment working alongside African descendants on plantations and in the cities. In a post–Seven Years' War Dominguan society that became increasingly racialized, in which white leaders passed legislation to regulate class and race, the position of the dream-seeking, aspiring white men eventually became demoralizing. They were easily convinced that their own status in society depended on keeping Afro-Caribbean men and women down.

Some people of African descent, however, refused to remain enslaved. Crispus Attucks escaped the bondage of white men by taking to the sea and adopting a new life within a Black community in the Caribbean. He lived there twenty years before sacrificing a life of Atlantic freedom in the cause of American liberty and independence.

Five hundred miles to the south of New Providence, Paul Carenan had lived as a free man of African and European descent for four decades. Carenan and Attucks, both of African descent with mixed parentage, established lives as consumers and beneficiaries of the Atlantic economy. The martyrdom of Attucks and the freedom trial of Carenan, pivotal moments in their lived experiences that occurred around the same time, did not directly inform or influence each other. Taken together, however, they illustrate the diverse threats across territorial boundaries that African-descended people frequently faced in the exercise of their freedom. Their stories reveal the methods employed to maintain white supremacy across the Atlantic world in the era of the American Revolution.

Beyond his residency and occupation, little is known of Attucks's personal life before his iconic death. Though Carenan's birth date remains elusive, more is known of him. By the year 1770, he had lived forty years, probably most of his life, as a free person. Carenan had no official papers of freedom. His enslaver, perhaps his father, manumitted him from slavery around 1730 using Article 55 of the Code Noir of 1685. The law permitted slaveholders to emancipate bonded persons. Few papers were required. Therefore, Carenan's enslaver completed or kept no official documents and did not register the manumission with the local notary. Historian Bernard Moitt describes people manumitted from slavery in this way across the French Caribbean as *libres de savane*, also known as *libres de fait*. Without documentation, they lived in a state of "quasi-freedom," a vulnerable position between slavery and freedom.[46]

Paul Carenan lived circumspectly over the course of his life, committing no acts to place him afoul of the law.[47] In 1757, a year into the war, Carenan married Marie-Jeanne Delaunay in "a union consecrated at the altar" of a Catholic church.[48] Marie-Jeanne came from an important family of color in Aquin that included her brothers, a master saddler named Julien and an indigo planter called Jacques.[49] Paul and Marie-Jeanne had six children and built a healthy, productive life together in southern Saint-Domingue. However, racist views regarding successes gained by free people of color brought changes to Dominguan laws and societal norms. Carenan became a target of white colonists who resented the achievements of enterprising Afro-Caribbeans.

In 1764, Carenan raised livestock on leased land. Three years later, he became a successful landowner, purchasing an indigo plantation in the Nippes region of southern Saint-Domingue. He paid Denis Carenan, a white resident and quite possibly his father, 130,000 livres for the land, which was worked by sixty enslaved Africans.[50] During the same period, the Cottineau plantation paid 52,700 livres to bond thirty-six Africans in the production of sugar in the northern region around Fort Dauphin.[51]

Around the same time as the 1769 Revolt, Denis Carenan filed a complaint with the attorney general in Petit-Goâve claiming that Paul Carenan was, in fact, an enslaved man posing as a free person of color. Since the complaint was made by a white male resident, the deputy attorney general arrested Paul Carenan and declared him to be a slave. Nineteenth-century Haitian writer Baron de Vastey suggested that Denis filed the initial complaint that cast suspicion on Carenan's freedom to take control of the Carenan plantation. It was a simple land grab. Connecting Carenan's case to the discriminatory racialization in which white inhabitants engaged across postwar Saint-Domingue, Vastey said, "One fact worth remarking upon, and which perfectly characterizes the way that justice was meted out in those days, is that this very same planter [who denounced Carenan] was the person who had sold the property [to him] in the first place."[52] Writing with utter disgust, the Haitian writer concluded that "this vile man," Denis Carenan, had defaulted on an agreement lasting forty years in "the despicable strategy" of defrauding his own son by declaring him a slave. Vastey characterized the racist white planter class more succinctly: "Kinship had no effect on those monsters!"[53]

Paul Carenan's case offers a solid example of the immediate impact of racially discriminatory laws and cultural outlooks in the 1770s. Nineteenth-century Haitian author Beauvais Lespinasse concluded that, during this period, white inhabitants would not allow Africans and their descendants to achieve the same level in Dominguan society as white people. In their eyes, no amount of white blood could overcome the stigmatization of Blackness.[54] On the word of a white inhabitant, the Petit-Goâve attorney general readily believed that a slaveholding planter, husband, and father of color had posed as a free man for four decades.

On Wednesday, 7 February 1770, a month before the martyrdom of Attucks and his fellow revolutionaries in Boston, in the spirit of the new racist atmosphere, the hands of white members of the Superior Council of Port-au-Prince deprived Paul Carenan of his freedom with the stroke of a pen. Mrs. Marie-Jeanne Carenan, "acting on her behalf and that of her children," appealed the decision of the Petit-Goâve attorney general regarding Paul Carenan's arrest and enslavement to the council. Members of the council, each of them prominent planters from the area, judged that Carenan was not free because he could not produce freedom papers signed by a notary or authorized by a court.[55]

Council members approached Carenan's case as if he were guilty of lying about being free until proven otherwise. In the records, they referred to him only by his first name, Paul. Enslaved people, in their view, did not merit surnames. They wrote that Carenan was "alleging to be a free person of color."[56] For the white planters, Carenan's freedom, and the freedom of thousands of Afro-Caribbeans, was a question of paperwork, merely a clerical or notarial transaction.

Council members knew Carenan was married to Marie-Jeanne. They knew Carenan was the father of six children. They saw his wife and children at the proceedings. Mrs. Carenan offered testimony attesting to his good character. The council members knew that Mr. Carenan owned a large plantation in Nippes and that the Carenan plantation shipped its indigo from Dominguan ports to Atlantic commercial hubs. Yet, for want of a piece of paper filed in a white notary's office, the members questioned Carenan's veracity. On the word of a lone white Dominguan man, they took it upon themselves to strip Carenan of the life that he and his wife had built together. With little reservation, "evoking the principal cause, and ruling thereon, the Court herewith declare[d] the mulatto Paul, known as Carenan, to be a slave, and to be confiscated to [their] use." The verdict, drafted with benign language, immediately transformed Paul Carenan from a man of influence, prestige, and wealth, beloved by Marie-Jeanne and their children, into an item of property, under the custody and control of the white council members, who planned to sell or use him for profit, like any other piece of inanimate property.[57]

The council took away Paul Carenan's plantation and gave it to Denis. If Vastey was correct, seizing the land was the intent of Denis's awful accusation. The white council members, despite meeting Carenan's family during the proceedings, gave little thought to the welfare and well-being of Mrs. Carenan and their children. Once they declared Paul to be enslaved, his marriage to Marie-Jeanne, according to civil and canonical laws, "was considered null and void, being the product of an error." The council rather callously ruled that since Mrs. Carenan and her children had brought the appeal that council members would "seek redress [from Carenan] as they [saw] fit for all costs incurred in the matter." Not only had the council taken from Mrs. Carenan her husband, her home, her land, and her livelihood; it also demanded that she pay the cost of Denis Carenan's court fees. In one decision, exhibiting legalized, racist malice, white authorities and a white resident destroyed the Carenan family. Paul's case was but one of countless instances of racial injustice inflicted on free Afro-Caribbeans, all along the colony's 127-point scale measuring African ancestry.[58]

As part of the French Empire, free Afro-Caribbean colonists like Carenan pursued opportunities to participate in the plantation labor system that made many Dominguan families rich. After military and diplomatic defeats that contracted France's territory and economy, French Caribbean colonies experienced a concurrent increase in their enslaved African and petit blanc populations. The preceding decades may have led people of color, particularly those closer to whiteness on the appointed racial scale than others, to believe that respectability would merit equality and acceptance by white inhabitants. They were wrong. There existed no security for the freedom of Black people anywhere in the Atlantic world. There was no talisman against the vengeance and scorn of white people's claim over Black freedom. Royal and colonial decision-making in response to the pressure placed on the French Empire after the Treaty of Paris of 1763 turned many pathways to Black social mobility into dead ends as competition for wealth and power fueled racial tensions.

Saint-Domingue's free people of color accumulated immense wealth, rose to the ranks of successful planters, and purchased properties that many white inhabitants could not afford. According to scholar C. L. R. James, plantations served as sanctuaries for planters of color: "Being so rich they imitated the style of the whites and sought to drown all traces of their origin."[59] Their success, through no fault of their own, may have garnered resentment from poorer white colonists intent on revenge. As Carenan's case illustrates, "the sacred rights of property, long possession, authentic titles, none of those things could prevent him, sooner or later, from being stripped of it by his covetous and powerful neighbour, and being himself persecuted and having his livestock attacked. Eventually, everything around him would fall prey to the predations of the [white] colonist."[60] No piece of paper could convince white colonists to view people of African descent, regardless of complexion, as political, economic, or social equals.

The persistent string of royal decrees and local restrictions during the 1760s and 1770s incrementally limited the freedom and blatantly insulted the dignity of free Afro-Caribbeans of every economic standing. Some of the colony's more successful planters possessed "some mixture of African blood—This description comprehends every shade complexion, from the slightest tinge of colour, to the original hue of the native African."[61] White French lawyer and author Jean-Philippe Garran de Coulon later wrote of the colony's commitment to white supremacy. He observed that though many planters of color secured lives of respectability, "as distinguished by their wealth, as for their talents and integrity," the white population religiously adhered to "the invidious distinction" between Afro-Caribbean and white. Garran-Coulon concluded that the white planters' racist regime of excluding planters of color "from their social circles, from their assemblies, from their municipal functions" helped to lay the foundation for the Haitian Revolution.[62]

Marie-Jeanne Carenan could not challenge the entire system that had destroyed the life that she and Paul Carenan had built, but she refused to idly sit by as white men destroyed her family. Across the Atlantic world, white men regularly bought, sold, and leased Black children, women, and men as commodities. In Port-au-Prince, on the day the council legally stripped her husband of his humanity, Mr. Belot, secretary to former governor Louis Rohan, advertised the sale of two Black teenagers without bothering to provide names for either.[63] In Savannah, Georgia, the white provost marshal Matthew Roche featured ten Black people for sale alongside "household furniture and shop goods." The advertisement included a woman named Sarah and her children Betty and Trimmer, along with another woman, Phillis, and her little boy Sam.[64]

As a wife and mother, Marie-Jeanne acted with utmost haste to save her husband and children from the cruel fate of enslavement. She had appealed the initial decision and lost. The tears she cried would not restore her husband's freedom. Therefore, she played the only legal card she had left to protect her family from the racialized injustice of the white members of the council. Marie-Jeanne appealed the unjust council decision to Governor-General Pierre Gédéon de Nolivos and Intendant Alexandre-Jacques de Bongars, the colonial government's two highest officials, to secure the freedom of her husband. Exhibiting grace, courage, and vulnerability, Mrs. Carenan explained the depth of her grief at the loss of her husband and asked the governor to grant clemency.

Because the council's decision effectively dissolved their marriage, she was free to form another marital union. But the unconquerable love Marie-Jeanne and Paul shared for each other and the fierce love of a mother for her children compelled her to plead before the colony's highest authority for "kindness toward her husband." Her familial petition was supplemented by an appeal to sentiment reminiscent of that of the beloved fictional maiden Héloïse, popularized across the 1760s in a French novel by renowned author Jean-Jacques Rousseau. In addressing the governor, one scholar suggests, Marie-Jeanne sought "relief from her troubles other than her tears."[65]

Marie-Jeanne's appeal, after much turmoil, was granted. The verdict was made plainly: "Please return her husband to her!" The governor and intendant witnessed an uninhibited expression of an Afro-Caribbean family's love for one another. It was recorded that the six children, likely metaphorically, "[threw] themselves at [the officials'] feet alongside their mother to plead for the freedom of their father." Governor-General Nolivos and Intendant Bongars made the order succinctly: "Give him his freedom." We do not know if Paul was present during these incredible outpourings of love. One can only imagine the force of Paul's gratitude and sadness had he seen his wife's public expressions of an unbreakable devotion and the dedication of his children to his return to their shared lives together. Despite facing seemingly insurmountable obstacles, Mrs. Carenan remained focused on the need to protect their livelihood. In addition to the restoration of Paul's free humanity, she also requested that the governor restore to them the property the council had given to Denis.[66]

Nolivos and Bongars viewed the Carenan appeal differently from that of the Superior Council of Port-au-Prince. They did not assume the appellants of color were inherently dishonest. They seemed to truly engage the arguments and emotions of Mrs. Carenan and her children. On Monday, 26 February 1770, one week before the Boston Massacre, the governor and intendant restored to Paul Carenan the status of a free person, "provisionally and until His Majesty [had] manifested his will to [them] in this regard."[67]

In the analysis of Lespinasse, the council's decision "was so iniquitous given the amount of time that Paul Carenan had been free . . . such an atrocious persecution," that Nolivos and Bongars had no choice but to overturn it.[68] Their reasoning for the decision is equally important. They admitted to being "touched" by the reasons, and likely by the expressions of love, presented by Marie-Jeanne. In discussing the provision of Article IX of the Code Noir of 1685, which prohibited slaveholders from manumitting their enslaved children, they chose to lean more toward "wishing, as much as [was] in [their] power, to reconcile the obedience that [they] owe[d] to the law with the reasons of humanity and religion."[69]

Nolivos and Bongars also restored the Carenan plantation to Paul and Marie-Jeanne, albeit provisionally, pending the king's statement on their decision; they were prevented from selling or significantly altering the property in the meantime. The order also forbade a despondent Denis from retaliating or doing "anything either to the person or to the property of the aforesaid Paul."[70] The reversal of the Carenan case must have given hope to colonists of color threatened by injustice. As Dominguan society became more racialized and white colonists sought to demean the personhood of their nonwhite neighbors, free Afro-Caribbeans continued to believe the colonial system of laws would protect their freedom and safeguard their status within the French imperial structure.

The Carenan family's freedom trial, the writings of Phillis Wheatley, and the actions of Crispus Attucks in Boston, when examined together, reveal the remarkable resilience of people in the African diaspora, who frequently faced a myriad of personal and collective struggles. Carenan, Wheatley, and Attucks did not know one another and never met, but their lives were entangled by the transatlantic crosscurrents of race and class. Each endured enslavement. Each ended their life as a free woman or man. Despite the misfortunes inflicted on them by societies constructed around white supremacy, they continued to believe in the power of resistance, sometimes in coordination with white inhabitants, to expand the reach of freedom in a moment of revolution across the Atlantic world.

Crispus Attucks was forty-six years old and had lived free for nineteen years when Jacques Delaunay defied racialized imperial French rule in Saint-Domingue during the 1769 Revolt. Delaunay and the rebels of color under his command became martyrs in the fight to secure their freedom and equality. They did not demand the abolition of slavery in Saint-Domingue. They died in the fight for citizenship rights and racial equality for free Black people and people of color. They sought to live free and enjoy the same political, economic, and social privileges as the colony's white inhabitants.

Atlantic revolts and revolutions were rarely completely successful or comprehensive actions, and theirs was no different. Each fight for freedom, however, set in motion the evolution of expanding rights and equity over long periods of time. The delegates at the Stamp Act Congress, for instance, did not address the racial, gender, or economic inequalities that were endemic to British North America. And the 1769 Revolt did not challenge the slave system in Saint-Domingue.

Likewise, Attucks and his fellow Black sailors did not dismantle the racist regimes of the Atlantic maritime community in short order. Building professional skills aboard transatlantic vessels and making extended calls in major port cities, they enjoyed economic privileges and the freedom of movement denied to the majority of the western Atlantic world's Black population. Ships employing sailors of color, though sailing under imperial flags and captained by white men, continuously cross-pollinated an emerging Atlantic world of new ecological, social, and racial relationships. Sailors like Attucks, therefore, "helped define and connect a new Black Atlantic world" that steadily became incrementally less unequal.[71] Similar to the actions of the Dominguan rebels of color, the movements of sailors of African descent, "their traditions of mobile resistance," as Julius Scott wrote, "assumed an even wider significance when political currents swirling about the Atlantic world brought an uncertainty to the shores of the American colonies."[72]

A year after the revolt in Saint-Domingue, a much smaller, more confined—albeit much more widely known—act of rebellious violence occurred in British North America. White rebels in Boston, on the evening of Monday,

5 March 1770, engaged in mob action against military oppressors. As a sailor who frequented Caribbean and North American ports, Attucks was aware of the revolutionary atmosphere gripping the Atlantic world. Attucks spent a lot of time on shore in port cities, picking up and sharing news. On various wharves and docks, he heard about and undoubtedly encountered men and women of color who, like him, had chosen to escape to freedom.

As plantation societies grew across the eighteenth century, port cities like Christiansted, Boston, Havana, Bridgetown, Cap-Français, and Philadelphia developed simultaneously as commercial hubs for slave labor products and attractive enclaves for fugitive freedom seekers, providing safety in sheltering communities and access to sea lanes that led toward liberation.[73] An important weekly newspaper in Saint-Domingue ran *Negres Marons*, a section that took up a full page in almost every edition to give details on the whereabouts and conditions of captured fugitive freedom seekers. Another half-page section in most editions, titled *Esclaves en Maronage*, reported stories of how two women from Congo fled to freedom while still in leg irons, how a Black fisherman branded with his enslaver's initials escaped "claiming to be free," how a man of color stole away with a gun, and how a woman of color, her face covered in spots (*taches de tortue*), continued to elude capture for over three months.[74]

In the 1770s, as revolutionary episodes changed Atlantic understandings of political and social liberty, Attucks and thousands of sailors of African descent who worked the North America–West Indies trade distributed news of freedom ventures and resistance to slavery across distant seaports.[75] Regional links of transmission carried news of interest to Black residents of the western Atlantic rim. Boston lawyer and later Continental Congress delegate John Adams marveled at the efficiency of Black communication networks. Though white elites controlled the production and distribution of books, newspapers, and most letters, he suggested, "The negroes have a wonderful art of communicating intelligence among themselves; it will run several hundreds of miles in a week or fortnight."[76]

Blackness served as a conduit between diasporic strangers across culturally diverse, multilingual communities of the Caribbean and North America. The movement of ships and sailors facilitated cross-colonial communication and allowed communities of color to follow developments in both regions. Diasporic cultural traditions and racially restricted literacy privileged channels of communications that depended on direct human contact for information, orally transmitted accounts, and shared public discourse of enslaved unrest and imperial conflicts.[77]

Attucks likely knew that men of color had led and participated in the 1769 Revolt. The news in early January along the port in New York detailed that some of the rebel leaders had landed in France, only to be "hurried to the Bastille, and never heard of since."[78] In February, a Savannah newspaper reported the French court continued to respond to colonial unrest, by deploying "six frigates preparing to sail from Brest for St. Domingo, with additional civil and military power, to quell the malcontents of that island."[79] Many of the Dominguan "malcontents" had a racial background similar to that of Attucks. Jacques Delaunay became a martyr in the fight for Afro-Caribbean equality. Attucks later joined Delaunay as a martyr of African descent during the age of Atlantic revolutions. And news from Port-au-Prince told of a white slaveholding native of Léogâne being installed as the new post-revolt governor-general of Saint-Domingue.[80]

On the day of his revolutionary martyrdom, Attucks was on shore leave in Boston, waiting for his ship to set sail for North Carolina.[81] Like Stevens in New York, Attucks was acquainted with the violent atmosphere of the rebellious colonies in general and Boston in particular. That morning's edition of the *Boston Gazette* informed readers, "The Particulars of several Rencountres between the Inhabitants and the Soldiery the Week past we are oblig'd to omit for Want of Room." Patrons of the taverns along the Boston shipyard, sailors, dockworkers, and locals would have been talking about the funeral of little Christopher Seider, which had taken place a week before. The *Gazette* featured a story of the funeral of Seider, "the unfortunate Boy who was barbarously murdered the 22d of February last." He had been shot during a protest against a local customs officer. Reports highlighted the sadness displayed across the city for the fallen rebel: "About Five Hundred School Boys preceded; and a very numerous Train of Citizens followed . . . at least Two Thousand of all ranks." Bostonians expressed much anger and hurt over Seider's passing. Because the newspaper connected the boy's death to the revolutionary movement, it was appropriate that "the little Corpse was let down under the Tree of Liberty," on which "the Sons of Liberty ordered a Board to be affix'd."[82] Tense revolutionary, anti-imperial sentiments and violence filled the streets of Boston.

Still, there was little about the evening of 5 March to indicate Crispus Attucks would not see the next morning. Much confusion about the nature and order of events reigned at the time of the Boston Massacre. Historians continue to offer varying versions and interpretations of the incident, reconceptualizing the actions by British soldiers and angry Bostonians.[83] The actions of Crispus Attucks are no less in dispute. Before the deadly episode began, Attucks was eating supper with other sailors at Thomas Symmonds's victualing house when British soldiers came in looking for part-time work.[84] When bells from Old South Church began to ring around nine o'clock, there was likely no dawning in Attucks's imagination that he was about to be thrust into a foundational moment of the American Revolution and the history of the new country his involvement would help to establish. British soldiers interpreted the bells as the beginning of an attack on their position on King Street. Most Bostonians, however, came running into the streets because they thought the bells signaled a fire alarm.[85] They were mistaken.

Within minutes of the bell ringing on 5 March 1770, Crispus Attucks was dead. After the gunfire rang out, Attucks became the first person in the American Revolution to be shot by the British military. Two balls penetrated his chest. A member of the crowd, John Hickling, went to Attucks where he was lying in the snow, saw him gasping, and held his head out of the gutter. Robert Goddard helped him get to a nearby house, where he died.[86] Some initially reported the fallen "Mollatto" man to be Michael Johnson but later identified him as Attucks.[87] After two decades of living, working, and traveling across the Atlantic world as a free man, he was killed in the struggle for American liberty and independence only forty miles from the Framingham plantation community in which the Browns had enslaved him for half his life. The reasons he chose to interrupt his evening and leave the tavern with twenty to thirty sailors to join the throng of Bostonians marching toward the Custom House on King Street remain a mystery. The showdown between townspeople and redcoats, many of whom had known one another well, had been building for years.[88] Insults, slights, fights, riots, and increasingly insulting engagements had elevated tension along the city's confined streets, alleyways, and public spaces.

Of all the North American port cities, the people of Boston mounted the fiercest resistance to a series of controversial taxes, more acutely since, in 1768, Parliament had stationed four regiments of soldiers in town.[89] The Treaty of Paris afforded the kingdom many economic and military advantages. It did not, however, erase "the debts [they] contracted." The British felt they needed to recoup their losses, and they looked to the colonies to do so. The author of a book intended to influence lawmakers, however, cautioned against addressing fiscal woes "without the consent of all." They used a historical analogy to clarify the point. When leaders "of a neighboring country" unwisely used force to govern their constituents, "this egregious error caused the revolt of the inhabitants."[90]

Actions by the British Parliament seemed to steadily push Bostonians toward violent resistance. Still, it remains unclear why Crispus Attucks, after being free from enslavement in Massachusetts for twenty years, would protest the tyrannical actions of the imperial government along with white colonists who supported slavery and the tenets of white supremacy. There is no record from Attucks or those who left the tavern to directly inform our thinking. Scholar Douglas Egerton suggests that Attucks died for sailors' and workers' rights.[91] Mitchell Kachun explains Attucks's actions on 5 March through the lens of his life as a sailor, filled with hard work, brutal punishments, and ready exposure to violent brawls aboard ships and in port cities.[92]

Historian Nathan Perl-Rosenthal, along with Julius Scott, locates Atlantic sailors at the center of violent acts within "the colonial resistance movement." The parliamentary laws outraging American colonists like John Adams and John Hancock also adversely affected sailors, subjecting the latter to random searches of their personal belongings by customs officers. Resistance to imperial overreach by men like Adams took the form of learned conversations in taverns, letters in newspapers signed with auspicious pseudonyms, and debates in ad hoc congresses. Like the rebels of color in the 1769 Revolt, seamen presented "a more direct challenge" by "physically assaulting" customs officials and clashing with military units in port cities across North America and the Caribbean.[93] Attucks, Caldwell, and other sailors may have joined outraged colonists on King Street to demonstrate their anger at oppressive imperial legislative action and overbearing British occupation.

The question of why Attucks, or any Black person, would fight on the side of the Americans in the War of Independence is a reasonable one. It acknowledges that the treatment of white colonists toward people of African descent did not warrant the support of Black inhabitants. It remains difficult to understand why an eighteenth-century man, enslaved by another man since birth, sided with people like his enslaver, at the risk of death, against an armed, occupying military force of a white imperial metropole.

Julius Scott's and Jeffrey Bolster's works on the lives of sailors are important for understanding Attucks, the expansion of Black freedom, and the creation of a Black Atlantic identity. Across the eighteenth century, sailors of color established lifestyles and racial dynamics aboard ship that eluded many members of the African diaspora. Three years before Attucks escaped, an enslaved man named Briton Hammon hired himself aboard a ship leaving Marshfield, Massachusetts, thirty miles south of Boston. In recounting his extraordinary adventures in the Caribbean and England, in one of the first publications by an African-descended author, Hammon readily identified as "a Negro man" and referred to his shipmate Moses Newmock as "Molatto." Still, the distinctive atmosphere and spatial limitations of the seaboard workplace, which Bolster masterfully describes, led Hammon to call the crew members of various identities "the people," a multiracial collective of which Newmock and he were also members.[94]

In his memoir, sailor and author Olaudah Equiano, who had been enslaved as a child in present-day Nigeria, made it clear that he understood that working as a sailor enabled him to see other islands and develop a sense of autonomy that enslaved plantation workers did not and could not have exerted. Going ashore in different port cities and interacting with inhabitations from across the Atlantic world empowered him to look white men in the eye and demand respect. On multiple occasions, as he explained, when his ship captain would treat him unfairly, he "used plainly to tell" the white officer that he "would die before" being "imposed on as other negroes were." For Equiano, "life had lost its relish when liberty [freedom] was gone." Scott reveals how the maritime life equipped Equiano to defend his freedom along the Atlantic shoreline, which empowered African-descended workers to negotiate a semi-independent existence with white employers and townspeople.[95]

Working alongside, and extending the limits of "equality" with, white mariners around the clock in confined spaces on vessels floating on the seas led sailors of color to embrace and promulgate a more self-conscious "African," or Black, identity. The eighteenth-century diasporic identity was understood by Black Atlantic populations in New England, Saint Croix, Jacmel, and New Providence. They inhabited a shared existence that was closed to white inhabitants.[96] Scott suggests that the advent of the American Revolution presented a wide range of opportunities for Atlantic people embracing the Black identity "to express their aspirations for freedom and to demonstrate their ability to absorb and transmit the revolutionary excitement in the air."[97] Bolster concludes that those with a diasporic identity expressed "patriotism," demanding to live free as Black people in British America or the evolving United States.[98] Crispus Attucks, born in Massachusetts, left Thomas Symmonds's tavern on the night of 5 March as a man who had found freedom on the waves of the Atlantic and made a life for himself in the Bahamas. He may have still longed for himself and other African-descended people to live freely in the country of his birth.

The body of Crispus Attucks became one of the first emblems of American revolutionary sacrifice. Similar to Jacques Delaunay and the rebels of the 1769 Revolt, Attucks became an Atlantic revolutionary. For the colonists of Boston, the "massacre" on King Street represented more than a riot. It represented a persistent, increasingly agitated protest movement against the British invasion of the city and its shameful quartering of troops from an occupying force.[99]

Silversmith Paul Revere published a print that captures the landing of British troops on Boston's Long Wharf in 1768.[100] Over the next year and a half, the presence of British redcoats, derogatively called "lobster backs" by locals, united Bostonians in their anger against the occupation.[101] The morning after the murders, as the townspeople awoke to "a most shocking Scene, the Blood of our Fellow Citizens running like Water thro' King-Street," a fifteen-member committee, including Samuel Adams and John Hancock, met Acting Governor Thomas Hutchinson at Faneuil Hall. They demanded one thing: "the immediate removal of the Troops."[102]

Printers Benjamin Edes and John Gill, as may be expected of successful newspapermen, seemed to capture the mood and voice of Bostonians correctly regarding British troops in town. In the opening paragraph of a lengthy, full-page exposition, which was reprinted in other papers, they characterized the Boston Massacre as a "melancholy Demonstration of the destructive Consequences of quartering Troops among Citizens in a Time of Peace."[103] According to them, everyone in town understood that, despite suggestions by British officials to the contrary, the Crown had deployed and quartered the troops nearly two years ago "in Reality to inforce oppressive Measures; to awe & controul the legislative as well as executive Power of the Province, and to quell a Spirit of Liberty."[104]

To the people of Boston in the spring of 1770, Crispus Attucks died as part of a revolutionary cause to rid their city of redcoats. They counted him among the martyrs of the "massacre." On 8 March, the town of Boston held a public funeral for the four initial victims, Crispus Attucks, Samuel Maverick, James Caldwell, and Samuel Gray. The soldiers also shot Patrick Carr that night, and he died two weeks later. According to one estimate, fifteen thousand people came out to honor "the unhappy Victims who fell in the bloody Massacre of the Monday Evening preceding!"[105] According to one account, "It is supposed that there must have been a greater Number of People from Town and Country at the Funeral of those who were massacred by the Soldiers than were ever together on this Continent on any Occasion."[106]

Family members and friends accompanied the coffins of Gray and Maverick in the mass procession, and the coffins of Attucks and Caldwell, "who were strangers, [were] borne from Faneuil-Hall, [and] attended by a numer-

84   Chapter 2

Figure 2.1. The bloody massacre perpetrated in King Street, Boston, on 5 March 1770. Courtesy of the John Carter Brown Library.

ous Train of Persons of all Ranks."[107] Revere designed the sketch of the emotionally powerful image of four miniature black coffins that appeared in the center of the *Gazette* story of the public funeral. Above the skull and crossbones on each coffin were the martyrs' initials, including C. A.[108] The four men were buried together in a common grave at the Granary Burying Ground.[109]

The people of Boston and colonists across British America knew Crispus Attucks was not white. Newspapers as far south as Georgia referred to him as "a mulato man."[110] They also knew he was not from Boston. White Bostonians, like John Hancock, were slaveholders, and many subscribed to principles of white supremacy. There is no evidence they knew Attucks had been formerly enslaved. But it is significant that, given these prejudices, they chose not to deny the sacrifice of a man of color. His death raised the death toll and allowed them to portray the British as that much more tyrannical. His death, in short, served their cause.

In that moment, the martyrdom of a person of color helped to shape Atlantic views of the American independence movement. It is curious, then, that artist Henry Pelham, who created the initial drawing of the shooting, chose to depict all the victims as white. He listed Attucks's name alongside those of the other martyrs in the sketch's lengthy title. Paul Revere, a longtime member of the Boston-area Sons of Liberty, plagiarized and altered Pelham's work as an engraving without crediting the artist. In his effort to exploit the political advantages of the 5 March killings, Revere created a readily noticeable, more provocative title, *The Bloody Massacre perpetrated in King Street*. He listed the names of Attucks and his fellow martyrs beneath the picture.

Revere's rendition of the Boston Massacre became and remains the most familiar image of the American Revolution. Scholars have discussed Revere's "distortions" of Pelham's original sketch, but both artists chose to portray all the martyrs as white. Literary scholar Karsten Fitz proposes, "Attucks's ethnic heritage had to be erased, since it was part of the rhetoric of the colonists rebelling against the British crown that *they*—the [white] colonists—were enslaved by a tyrannical mother country."[111] Fitz, however, suggests, "Although there exists at least one rarely printed re-colored version which depicts one of the corpses on the ground as a black man, standard reproductions of Revere's engraving ignore the black presence."[112]

Edes and Gill attached Revere's initial print version to a pamphlet that James Bowdoin, Joseph Warren, and Samuel Pemberton titled *A Short Narrative of the horrid Massacre in Boston*, as part of the town of Boston's attempt to shape public perception of the murders. They published and sold two hundred copies of the pamphlet's first edition. Revere's engraving proved popular. Multiple variants of the original engraving, at least five, including three in London, appeared within months of the original production. Each subsequent version altered the size, wording, objects, and perspective from Revere's first plagiarized edition.[113]

Online, public-accessible renderings of Revere's engraving from the Massachusetts Historical Society, the Gilder Lehrman Institute of American History, and the Library of Congress appear to show Attucks as a victim with a notably brown face.[114] According to the Lehrman Institute, "Crispus Attucks is visible in the lower left-hand corner [of the engraving]. In many other existing copies of this print, he is not portrayed as African American."[115] Scholar Farah Peterson suggests that in the hands of Revere, who showed no scruples about indulging in artistic inaccuracies for the revolutionary cause, "Attucks the hero was white." In 1770, British North Americans did not yet identify themselves as a united people. To spur white colonists to embrace Boston's suffering as their own, Revere or someone else decided the illustration would prove more effective "if the victims were once again 'us,' not 'them' . . . if they were white, not black."[116]

Bowdoin, Warren, and Pemberton cast Attucks and the other victims as central players in the American revolutionary struggle against imperial abuse. In the *Short Narrative*, the authors discussed the tragic night of 5 March within the historical context of the increasingly intense atmosphere that existed between the colonists and the metropole throughout the 1760s after the "end of the late war."[117] They outlined the role of the Stamp Act in interrupting "a happy union [that] subsisted between Great-Britain and the Colonies." In response to the unjust legislation, the colonists, led by Bostonians, assembled at the Stamp Act Congress. The British government repealed the tax and affirmed, by doing so, that resistance by the colonists could be effective.

In 1767, Parliament began passing the Townshend Acts, which included headquartering an imperial board of custom commissioners in Boston. Like the Stamp Act, those measures met stiff resistance from colonists. Instead of repealing the acts, however, the British government deployed military regiments in Boston and "occasioned his Majesty's faithful subjects of this town and province to be treated as enemies and rebels, by an invasion of the town by sea and land." According to the *Short Narrative*, the occupation by commissioners and troops, and their detrimental impact of Boston's commerce within the Atlantic world, represented "the causes of the late horrid massacre."[118] Reactionary policymaking by London officials grappling to rein in an emboldened colonial resistance movement in the years after the Treaty of Paris, had, in part, led to this violence.

Unlike the Stamp Act Congress five years earlier, the violent actions of 5 March 1770 were not organized by an individual or group. But the "happy effect [that had] arisen from this melancholy affair" could not be denied. The troops were removed from town.[119] A military occupation, which had prompted letters and meetings, contributing to souring relationships as well as street altercations over the preceding seventeen months, came to an abrupt end after one night of awful bloodshed that left the townspeople and the troops forever changed. In the capable hands of the authors, the "massacre," a spontaneous, relatively brief, deadly encounter between imperial troops and an indignant crowd of Bostonians and others like Crispus Attucks, transcended the boundaries of King Street to participate in a pivotal moment in the international battles of political will and economic profits in the aftermath of the Seven Years' War.

Six months later, when the trials of the imperial soldiers who had killed the five people began, John Adams described Crispus Attucks and the meaning of his death in terms different from those historians now use to understand it. Adams initiated the process of depicting the Boston Massacre as the localized, unenlightened event many historians describe today. For Adams, 5 March was not part of an Atlantic revolution. In the opinion of Adams, the practiced lawyer, the "massacre" was not special. It was reckless. The people of Boston who turned out at the sound of the bells ringing, including Attucks and the other martyrs, were not patriots. They were irresponsible. Adams, in one of the most principled, professional moves in American history, agreed to represent the British soldiers as defense counsel, and he framed the incident as an unfortunate and preventable accident of self-defense on their part.

The court had charged his clients with murder. Adams crafted a damning portrayal of Attucks as the fulcrum of the defense strategy, deploying unflattering characterizations of artisans, tavern keepers, sailors, ropemakers, cobblers, and others present at the deadly altercation on King Street in the defense of the soldiers who killed them. Attucks was depicted in Adams's narrative as menacing, someone white Bostonians should fear. Attucks and those who followed him, Adams argued, provoked the firing of bullets that struck them down. Despite these negative portrayals, in the fall of 1770, Adams's orations transformed Attucks from an obscure sailor of color about whom people knew little into a hero of a colonial uprising.

The trial of William Wemms, William McCauley, Matthew Killroy, William Warren, John Carrol, and Hugh Montgomery opened in the Superior Court of Judicature on Tuesday, 27 November 1770. Witnesses present on the night the men died agreed that Private Edward Montgomery was the first soldier to fire, killing Attucks. They expressed less clarity about Attucks's motives, words, and actions before and during the encounter.[120] When the bells rang out that night, Adams was dining with friends in Boston's South End, a good distance from the carnage. By the time he arrived at the scene, the deadly fusillade had long ended, and he acquired only second- and thirdhand recollections of events.[121]

Yet Adams entered the Queen Street Courthouse quite certain of the narrative he would construct about what Attucks had done on King Street. He was also confident in the effectiveness of his line of defense. He had good reason. Only a month before, Adams had employed a racialized defense strategy centered on Attucks to achieve the acquittal of Captain Thomas Preston, the Twenty-Ninth Regiment commander. As scholar Farah Peterson suggests, Adams "faced a difficult challenge." The jury must have felt more kinship with the men who had assembled to harass the soldiers than with the soldiers sent by Britain to harass Boston, and this posed a terrible problem for the defense counsel. To acquit the soldiers of murder, the jurors had to see the killings as justified.[122] Racial stereotypes, therefore, factored into Adams's courtroom strategies.

Four years earlier, a similar legal challenge had faced Adams in Falmouth, Maine, when he argued the civil case of Loyalist Richard King. A patriot mob had beaten King and damaged his home. He sued for damages. Adams, to indict the actions of the local population, used resounding rhetoric to evoke the terrors of a mob breaking into a peaceful family home.[123] To depict the King Street participants as a mob and not revolutionaries, Adams used a handy eighteenth-century Atlantic world tool: racial fear. He relied on a collective view of white Atlantic inhabitants that deemed people of African descent as dangerous because they were different from them.[124]

Throughout the trial of the soldiers, lawyers and witnesses referred to Attucks as "the Molatto" at least twenty times.[125] Justice Edmund Trowbridge, on the other hand, referred to "Crispus Attucks" with no color designation in his instructions to the jury.[126] Adams invoked the pejorative racial designation *molatto* five times in his closing, reminding the jury that Attucks was not white and, therefore, was not one of them.[127] The term connoting mixed heritage was levied to conjure in the courtroom "an imagined norm of Negroness." Whiteness, on the other hand, "represented a category of freedom." When evoked, whiteness was generally used as a categorical distinction from non-Europeans. By imposing *molatto* on Attucks, Adams othered him as non-British—and nonwhite. With one word, the lawyer deftly stripped the deceased man raised in Framingham of any life history beyond his apparent association with racial slavery.[128]

Adams called two "Negro" witnesses to assist in his defense narrative. The first Black witness was Newton Prince, a free Boston merchant and homeowner, who left his home that night at the sound of bells, believing there was a fire. According to one historian, "his testimony was not entirely damning for the townspeople," though "he described the crowd as aggressive."[129] Prince testified, "There were people all round the soldiers. . . . I saw people with sticks striking on their [the soldiers'] guns." He also testified he saw snowballs "flung [at the soldiers] by some youngsters," which helped to make an important point during Adams's closing argument. When asked how many people struck the guns, he responded, "I cannot tell you how many of them did it."[130]

Prince's version of events was in stark contrast to that of the second Black witness. Andrew, an enslaved man, testified unequivocally that Attucks attacked Montgomery. Both men agreed people were throwing snowballs at the soldiers. Putting two men of African descent on the stand helped Adams put the visual menace of Blackness in the minds of the jury. In addition to describing their physical presence, Andrew mentioned several times that after the church bells rang, he participated in the evening's event with "[his] acquaintances." Andrew's statements created images of devious Black men conspiring together in the confusion of that night.

Andrew's testimony was the most helpful to Adams's efforts to use a racialized defense. When asked if he also had thrown objects at the soldiers, Andrew responded, "Yes I did." Standing before the white jurors in the courtroom was a Black man who had assaulted white soldiers. The jurors could imagine Andrew and his Black acquaintances hurling snowballs and other objects at the soldiers. The true value of Andrew's testimony to Adams was in its words, which allowed the defense to depict Attucks as a big, menacing African-descended man and *the* leader of the Boston crowd. Earlier, the white witness James Bailey had given testimony that before the shooting, he saw a large crowd around Cornhill, "betwixt twenty and thirty: they appeared to be sailors . . . and the Molatto fellow headed them." Some of them, Bailey added, wielded sticks and "the Molatto fellow, had a large cord-wood stick." He said "the Molatto" was "about fifteen feet" away from Montgomery when he was shot. When asked, "Did you see the person that struck" Montgomery, Bailey responded, "He was a stout man."[131] Andrew testified:

> A stout man who stood near me . . . kept striking on their guns . . . a stout man with a long cord wood stick, threw himself in, and made a blow at the officer . . . the stout man then turned round, and struck the Grenadier's gun . . . and immediately fell in with his club, and knocked his gun away, and struck him over the head. . . . This stout man held the bayonet with his left hand, and twitched it and cried kill the dogs, knock them over; this was the general cry; the people then crouded in.[132]

When asked, "Do you know who this stout man was, that fell in and struck the grenadier?" Andrew responded, "I thought, and still think it was the Molatto who was shot."[133] Because white inhabitants believed African people were prone to lie, the defense called Andrew's white enslaver to affirm the veracity of his testimony against Attucks.[134] In one of the most important trials in early American history, a white defense lawyer used the words of an enslaved Black man, whom the white jurors considered another white man's property, to present the most damning description of a free man of African descent whose death helped to secure political liberty and independence for white American colonists.

Adams connected Andrew's and Bailey's statements in his closing argument to conclude that Attucks "appears to have undertaken to be the hero of the night; and to lead this army with banners."[135] In Adams's skillful oration, Attucks did not warrant inclusion in Paul Revere's inflammatory engraving of the massacre. Instead, a formerly enslaved man "from Framingham" formed the group "in the first place in Dock square, and march[ed] them up to King-street, with their clubs . . . in order to make the attack." Adams associated Attucks with his life of bondage in a nearby rural area known for its plantations with enslaved populations and conflicts with Native Americans. A few years later, white residents of Framingham endured a scare of a slave insurrection, when a cry went out that "the Negroes were coming to massacre them all!"[136] The defense counsel mischaracterized Attucks's home and status though newspapers identified him as "lately belonging to New-Providence," a free Black community in the Bahamas.[137] He was no longer enslaved by Brown. For twenty years, before Adams entered college, Attucks had traveled the seas as a free sailor, lived under the name Michael Johnson, and made his residence among Afro-Caribbeans. The man who died on 5 March was not a field hand but a free citizen of the Atlantic world.

In Saint-Domingue, men of color led the first major attack against French imperial sources during the 1769 Revolt. Likewise, according to John Adams, a man of color led the first colonial attack in North America against British imperial forces after the Treaty of Paris of 1763. Adams told jurors, "Attucks with his myrmidons comes round Jockson's [Jackson's] corner . . . when the soldiers pushed the people off, this man with his party cried . . . kill them! kill them! knock them over!"[138] As legal scholar Farah Peterson suggests, "A critical part of Adams's strategy was to convince the jury that his clients had only killed a black man and his cronies and that they didn't deserve to hang for it."[139]

One of the more important points was to play to the white fear of Black violence. Adams's performance guided the white jurors and judges to imagine the white soldiers, with a crowd bearing down on them "under the command of a stout Molatto fellow, whose very looks, was enough to terrify any person, what had not the soldiers then to fear? He had hardiness enough to fall in upon them."[140] Two years before, many of the court watchers had witnessed firsthand or heard about the "very disagreeable spectacle" of Black infantrymen administering punishment to white soldiers. Drummers of African descent from the Twenty-Ninth Regiment, the same unit as the soldiers in the "massacre" trial, publicly whipped ten white men on Boston Common. Though Bostonians were familiar with whippings and other humiliating punishments, historian Richard Archer suggests, "this role reversal stirred racist fears."[141]

Around that same time, white residents reported to the city's selectmen that they had observed Captain John Wilson, one of the white British officers, right in the city streets, encouraging some enslaved men "to go home, be abusive to their [enslavers], & to cut their throats." According to a petition, also signed by John Hancock, future president of the Second Continental Congress and one of Boston's largest slaveholders, Wilson promised the men that the Twenty-Ninth Regiment had been deployed to Boston "to procure their [the enslaved population's] freedom, and that with their help and assistance they should be able to drive all the Liberty Boys [Sons of Liberty or patriots] to the devil."[142] City officials learned of the threat and worked to allay the citizens' fear of Black violence. The sheriff arrested Wilson, and his bond hearing was held publicly in Faneuil Hall. The selectmen interviewed witnesses and townspeople about "the Wilson affair with the Negroes." In response, they ordered law enforcement officials to increase surveillance of the city's Black population, especially at night.[143]

The fault of the massacre lay not with the soldiers or the white citizens of Boston, Adams proclaimed. In his telling, one man was to blame: "This was the behaviour of Attucks;—to whose mad behaviour, in all probability, the dreadful carnage of that night, is chiefly to be ascribed."[144] Adams used Andrew's testimony to draw out the image of menacing Black men assaulting white soldiers. Of the five times "negroes" were mentioned during the trials, three of them were by Adams during the closing argument. He let the image of dangerous Blackness permeate the courtroom. Robert Treat Paine, in his closing, conceded Adams's argument that "some of this Collection were Boys and Negros drawn there by the Curiosity peculiar to their disposition, and without doubt might throw some Snow Balls, and it's quite natural to believe from the Evidence and the Nature of the thing that there were some there armed with Sticks and Clubbs." He then added, rather lamely, "And many other peaceable people gathered there meerly to see what was going on."[145]

Farah Peterson points out that a lot of white Bostonians who turned out for the event "testified at the trial, proudly describing how they gave [to the soldiers] as good as they got that night."[146] Though there were not many Black people in the crowd, in the minds of the white people in the courtroom, a man of African descent put himself "at the head of such a rabble of Negroes, &c. as they [could] collect together" to incite mob violence and to blame the disturbance of the peace on "the good [white] people of the town."[147] Chief Justice Benjamin Lynde was the last of the four judges to give instructions to the jury. The final thing the jurors and those in attendance heard before the verdict was this: "They say this was done by a large stout man, and describe him in such a manner as we must suppose him to be Attucks." The last deliberative word uttered in the most famous trial in early American history was "Attucks."[148]

In the view of John Adams, Crispus Attucks was *the* leader of American colonists at the Boston Massacre whose aggressive actions sparked the soldiers' deadly response. According to Adams's effective reasoning, the accused killed the five martyrs because "a motley rabble of saucy boys, negroes and molattoes, Irish teagues and out landish jack tarrs" followed Attucks into confronting the British soldiers whom elite, patriotic, white Bostonians decried as having committed "an attack upon the constitution, and a defiance of law; and to be intended to affront the legislative and executive authority of the province."[149] Adams's racialized portrayal of Black men as leading criminals fell on fertile ground in the minds of white Massachusetts residents. The tactic had worked to convict Black inhabitants before, even in recent memory. Two weeks before the judges handed the case to the jury in the Queen Street Courthouse, white jurors of the Superior Court at Salem convicted "a Mulatto Man, named George" for "riotously and tumultuously assembling, with divers other Persons."[150] The men dragged Jesse Savill, a suspected Loyalist in Gloucester, from his home "and then besmear[ed] him with Tar, beating, wounding and otherwise evil entreating him."[151]

The court sentenced George "to be set upon the Gallows with a Rope about his Neck and the other end over the Gallows . . . to be whipped 39 Stripes upon his Back . . . [and] to suffer two Years Imprisonment." The violent actions against Savill were regularly carried out across New England by white mobs, including Sons of Liberty members, against people considered unpatriotic to the cause of American liberty.[152] However, jurors in the Salem court decided the Black man was solely responsible for the violence perpetrated against a white resident. Eight months after the initial incidents, "the other offenders, who were all disguised at the time of the riot, [were] not yet taken."[153] Adams's argument that a man of African descent was responsible for the Boston Massacre had a similar effect in the Queen Street Courthouse. It persuaded the jurors, who deliberated for two and a half hours, to acquit four of the soldiers and to find Montgomery and Kilroy guilty of manslaughter instead of murder. They "were each burnt in the hand, in open Court, and discharged."[154]

In the early nineteenth century, at the Coloured Seamen's Home in New York, "boarders dined under a picture of Crispus Attucks, the seafaring martyr of the Boston Massacre."[155] The memory of Attucks during and after the American Revolution depicted him as a Black man who lived as a sailor and died for liberty to reign in the United States. For twenty years before the moment he was fated to join the ancestors, Attucks used the sea as a cloak of personal freedom. He rode the waves of Atlantic commerce to create a new identity beyond unjust enslavement. However, John Adams's "explicitly racist appeal" to the image of a large, angry Black man causing the Boston Massacre continues to influence our scholarly reimagining and retelling of the event.[156]

Adams's oratory, in essence, convicted Attucks and the other fallen rebels and acquitted the imperial troops who shot them. The insurgents who initiated the 1769 Revolt in Saint-Domingue met a similar legal fate. The Superior Council of Port-au-Prince condemned Jacques Delaunay and the other "authors of the troubles of the colony" to be "hanged and strangled until they [were] dead."[157] The French and British monarchs fortified their colonial holdings with military force in the aftermath of rebel disturbances. On the day after the Boston jury acquitted British soldiers, a New York newspaper reported, "A Man of War was arrived from France, and sailed directly to St. Domingo, with Orders to put all the French West-India Islands, immediately in the best state of Defence."[158] The Fourteenth and Twenty-Ninth Regiments pulled back from Boston but remained in North America. Though often at odds with each other, the British and French Empires faced similar challenges of colonial rule and revolt, and they would each employ force over the years to manage subsequent crises.

The Boston Massacre and the 1769 Revolt yielded similar setbacks for Atlantic resistance movements. Rebels in Boston and Torbeck lost their skirmishes and their lives, while the kings at Windsor and Versailles retained authority and influence in the colonies. Yet, in each instance, the colonial struggles sowed seeds of revolution that eventually secured liberty and independence for both populations.

Chapter 3

"A Natural Right to Be Free"

1773–1775

Three years after the tragic events of the Boston Massacre and the sensational trial, John Adams found himself again invoking the name of Crispus Attucks in reference to the American Revolution. He drafted a letter to Massachusetts Governor Thomas Hutchinson, evoking the menacing characterization of Attucks that he himself had created and made famous.

> Sir:—You will hear from us with astonishment. You ought to hear from us with horror. You are chargeable before God and man, with our blood. The soldiers were but passive instruments, mere machines; neither moral nor voluntary agents in our destruction, more than the leaden pellets with which we were wounded. You was a free agent. You acted, coolly, deliberately, with all that premeditated malice, not against us in particular, but against the people in general, which, in the sight of the law, is an ingredient in the composition of murder. You will hear further from us hereafter. CHRISPUS ATTUCKS.[1]
>
> [also known as John Adams]

Adams likely intended the unpublished letter to the governor for publication in a newspaper.[2] During the period, rebels like Adams commonly wrote and published incendiary missives under pseudonyms. Historians interpret the letter as evidence that, despite his depiction in the Boston courtroom, Adams understood that the British killing of colonial civilians (a group he once described as a "motley crew") on King Street represented a singular revolutionary moment.[3]

Years after the revolution, Adams reflected that none of the famous Anglo-American military conflicts of that time period "were more important Events in American history than the battle of Kingstreet, on the 5th of March 1770."[4] He had defended and achieved the acquittal of most of the soldiers by offering the jury the depiction of an angry Black man who led white people to act riotously. Some scholars view Adams employing Attucks's name in the Hutchinson letter as an indication that Adams changed his mind about Attucks, conceding that the Black freedom-seeker-turned-rebel was indeed the first martyr of the American Revolution. Calling forth his name in 1773 served as a kind of homage to his sacrifice for liberty.[5]

Still, Adams did not allow Attucks to rest in peace. He resurrected the image of the angry, murderous Black man to threaten the governor. In the draft, written at a moment of growing tension within the city of Boston, he tells Hutchison multiple times, "You will hear from us." Parliament passed the inflammatory Tea Act in May. Newspapers published the secret Hutchinson letters in June. And the governor reviewed British military troops at Castle William in early July.[6] In response, Adams warned him to expect "astonishment" and "horror." He used the violent events of 1770 as a threat and concluded the letter with the image of Attucks to remind the governor of the level of volatility the colonists could unleash.[7] His message was clear: if Bostonians had attacked armed soldiers whom they viewed as "machines," they would have no fear of attacking the governor, a "free agent" acting with "premeditated malice" against the people.

Adams used a number of pseudonyms across the revolutionary period to author potentially inflammatory correspondence. Some of his favorites were Novanglus and Humphrey Ploughjogger.[8] Attucks, however, was a publicly identifiable person in recent memory. Scholar Sandra Gustafson offers a distinctive analysis of Adams's use of gothic horror and legal sensationalism in his draft letter. She suggests that the method was intended to mitigate his public role in defending the enemy soldiers by maligning Attucks and "blackening" popular actions by townspeople. The negative press swirling around Hutchinson offered Adams a context in which to adopt the identity of the man he had made responsible for the massacre. He sought to center Hutchinson within a theory of elite conspiracy against American rebellion.

By signing the letter "Chrispus Attucks," conjuring the spirit of a violent nonwhite man, Adams adopted "the mask of resistance common to radical protest in the colonies, where blackface and Indian garb were common strategies of self-concealment" among white American rebels.[9]

The year 1773 ended with Adams's cousins Samuel Adams leading one of the most notable protest events of the American revolutionary era. A newspaper in Port-au-Prince printed a London letter written under a pseudonym to help Saint-Domingue's population understand the imperial-colonial standoff over tea. According to the writer, the process of "raising revenue in America has long been a matter of contention." After Parliament passed the Tea Act, "the East India Company was authorized to send considerable quantities of this commodity to America . . . though it was known that the Americans would constantly refuse to import it." And Bostonians did just that, preventing the ships from off-loading the tea. The writer explained that Americans "will never be convinced by force."[10]

The letter's admonitions went unheeded. The ships sat loaded with tea in Boston Harbor for weeks. After a meeting of about five thousand people led by Samuel Adams on 16 December, the Sons of Liberty led a group of white radicals, dressed and painted to resemble Native Americans, to the docks, where they boarded ships and dumped 342 chests of tea into Boston Harbor. Participants in the Boston Tea Party protest unlawfully trespassed, vandalized, and destroyed over $1 million (in today's currency) worth of British property. An early newspaper report described the event: "A Number of very dark complexioned Persons (dressed like Mohawks or Indians) of grotesque Appearance, approached the Meeting where the People were assembled, with the most hidious Noise, and proceeded immediately to Griffin's Wharf, where three Ships lay that contained the East-India Company's Teas."[11] Dressing up as a violent, destructive band of Native Americans played on the racist tropes of Indigenous peoples as uncivilized and exotically different from Europeans to protect the identities of the white vandals and to shield the Tea Party participants from legal repercussions for their act of resistance.[12]

The inhabitants of Saint-Domingue followed closely the colonial response to the imperial impositions regarding tea in North America. They understood that the Americans' determination to resist the metropole's insistence on East Indian Company tea could "produce the most unfortunate consequences."[13] Britain had negotiated to protect their commercial interests in South Asia against France in the Treaty of Paris of 1763. Article XI of the agreement restored five captured East Indian colonial territories to the

French. It also stipulated that France could not erect military fortifications or maintain troops in the region as the Versailles foreign policy called for across the Caribbean islands.[14] Contemporary writers and modern scholars suggest the treaty gave new life to a floundering British East India Company.[15] Ten years on, efforts by the British Parliament to help the company manage its debts after the Peace of Paris continued to present problems for the Crown and its western Atlantic colonies.

The newspaper *Affiches Américaines* covered the king's position, detailing the tripling of the national debt, with accruing interest, since the Seven Years' War with France. It reported, "The conflict in North America, by everyone's admission, the most important and the thorniest which has presented itself since the accession of the King to the Crown [in 1760], here absorbs almost all the attention of the Cabinet."[16] Dominguans also followed the Tea Party incident with great interest. News subscribers in Port-au-Prince kept up with reports of British colonists resisting King George III through increasingly collective and more violent acts of civil disobedience at a time when—locally, all around them—women, children, and men of the Mondongué, the Congo, and the Nago peoples made nearly daily attempts to achieve freedom by escaping enslavement.[17]

The day after the Boston Tea Party protest, John Adams confided to his diary his sense of excitement and his apprehensions about the resistance action. He considered the action "the most magnificent Movement of all." Upon further reflection, he posed a weighty question: "What Measures will the Ministry take, in Consequence of this?"[18] *Affiches* readers learned that London officials, likewise, waited anxiously to learn if the subsequent departure from Boston of the offending East India Company ships "[would] have restored calm, or if the inhabitants, intoxicated with the spirit of independence," would proceed to resist royal administration. The answer to Adams and the Dominguans was not long in coming. By spring, the *Affiches* reported that the cabinet had decided to send an increased number of troops to American colonies in response to the Tea Party. Ministers, as part of the Intolerable Acts, sent more army regiments and a navy flotilla to occupy Boston and blockade its harbor. The newspaper described the warships heading west to the colonies as "armed, equipped & supplied, as if they were to land on an enemy beach." The writer of the story asked, as had Adams months earlier, a significant question: "What happens, if the King's ships were not better received in the Colonies than those of the East India Company?"[19]

All of England seemed to buzz with a similar anxiety. French colonists learned that talk of the conflict with America transfixed London. "This is the big news of the day," the newspaper reported. "This important affair indeed attracts the most serious attention of the Ministry." The *Affiches* writer considered the conflict as a crossroads. Imperial officials would either give up the king's right to tax the colonies or risk actions that "[would] precipitate the revolt."[20]

Over the two years before the momentous exchange of gunfire across the Concord River that ignited the US War of Independence, Black and white inhabitants debated and contested differing views of freedom in the western Atlantic world. As American revolutionary rhetoric became more inflamed, Black writers and white antislavery allies utilized the tools of print culture to advocate for an end to slavery, and they often used religious ideas as part of their arguments. Ideas around religious freedom evolved as white Protestants questioned the inclusion of enslaved populations in Christian communities. For their part, Black Baptists exercised creative autonomy to establish separate religious spaces to nourish and fortify their spiritual selves. Free people of color in North America and Saint-Domingue formed Freemasonry lodges even when faced with racial hostility from white lodge members. The progress of the American Revolution in the decade after the Treaty of Paris charged the Atlantic environment with the spirit of protest that created opportunities for younger Americans and Dominguans, Black and white, to articulate arguments and to gain leadership experience to be employed later, sometimes collaboratively, during the Haitian Revolution.

The year 1773 began with the march toward freedom in British North America making important strides. In Boston, a man named Felix, like Adams, wrote to Governor Thomas Hutchinson with a grievance. Unlike Adams, Felix submitted his petition for freedom from slavery to Hutchinson, the Massachusetts Council, and the House of Representatives. In the fashion of the American rebels in that day who wrote to government authority and published open letters in newspapers across the colonies, the author sought to amplify his voice by speaking for others like him. Felix wrote on behalf of "many Slaves, living in the Town of Boston, and other Towns of the Province."[21] Scholars remain divided over whether Felix was free or enslaved and whether he was the Felix Holbrook who coauthored a similar petition a few months later.[22] In any case, the author of this first public, Black-authored antislavery petition to the Massachusetts legislature—and perhaps the first in American history—clearly identified with the marginalized population for whom he wrote.[23] The writer explained to the governor and other members that the African-descended population was not monolithic in its response to the cruelties of enslavement and white supremacist attitudes. He then summarized the condition of Black life plainly: "We have no Property. We have no Wives. No Children. We have no City. No Country."[24]

A petition expressing a sentiment common among white colonists printed in the next day's *Massachusetts Spy* made the litany of deprivations all the more poignant. In the fashion of Felix, the white petitioners claimed to speak for "a great number of freeholders and inhabitants of the Town of Salisbury." The white petitioners complained, "Our rights and liberties as Englishmen, and as men . . . have been grossly invaded; and that we have been abused and oppressed." Despite or, more likely, because white residents in the territory around Salisbury enslaved Africans, the petitioners unanimously resolved "that the most essential rights of mankind, are LIFE, LIBERTY and PROPERTY" and "that the only end and design of government is to secure these."[25] Felix, in his petition, attempted to inform and to remind freeholding white men, "How many of that Number [of Black people] have there been, and now are in this Province, who have had every Day of their Lives embittered with this most intollerable Reflection . . . in a Manner as the Beasts that perish."[26] He wrote and submitted his petition in the hope that enslaved people in Massachusetts could join their white neighbors in the enjoyment of these articulated rights for all humankind.

The revolutionary period created a sense of optimism that Felix exhibited in his petition. In the year before the freedom petition, the *Somerset v. Stewart* case involving slavery and race garnered the attention of readers and slaveholders across the British Atlantic world. James Somerset, a thirty-year-old enslaved African, had accompanied his enslaver in relocating from Boston to England. There, he escaped captivity and, with the assistance of white abolitionists, sued for his freedom. Chief Justice William Mansfield ruled that Somerset was no longer considered enslaved. As the laws governing the metropole differed from those of the colonies, the judge decided that because Somerset resided on English soil, he had become a free man.

The petition author Felix likely learned about Somerset's audacious fight for freedom through the Boston newspapers. Throughout the year 1772, publisher Isaiah Thomas covered the progress in the historic court case over multiple issues of *The Massachusetts Spy*, the same newspaper that published the Black freedom petitions. Three times, Thomas featured the case of "the great negro cause" on the front page. In the midst of growing revolutionary fervor, the newspaper argued that "the principle on which the question" of the Somerset case "must be determined concerns the whole British nation." At the end of one article, the publisher chimed in, "We can assure our readers, that the attention of the best men in the kingdom is drawn towards the decision of the very interesting cause of Somerset the negro."[27] Though Mansfield's verdict did not prompt broad moves toward emancipation in North America, Thomas's publication and others like it introduced readers to white inhabitants on both sides of the Atlantic who saw connections between calls for colonial liberty and the freedom of Black people.[28]

According to historian Graham Hodges, "Free and enslaved blacks in Massachusetts petitioned the colonial and later the state assembly to end slavery and include the voice of African Americans in the constitutional debate."[29] The combination of white people like John Adams fighting for greater liberties within a monarchical system and others like James Otis Sr. simultaneously attacking the enslavement of Africans led Felix and other Black Bostonians to believe that white colonists could be persuaded to end the trafficking in Africans.[30] He credited the Christian God with moving white people across the Atlantic world, "on both Sides of the Water, to bear [enslaved Black people's] Burthens," to advocate for the abolition of African slavery. To influence the governor and elected representatives of Massachusetts in his favor, Felix emphasized that some of these early abolitionists "[were] Men of great Note and Influence; who [had] pleaded [their] Cause with Arguments which [they] hope[d would] have their weight with this Honorable Court."[31]

A lengthy newspaper essay published two days before Felix's petition illustrated the necessity and urgency of his effort. In it, a proslavery writer published an attack on the articles appearing in Atlantic world newspapers calling for an end to slavery. Felix and the author S. M. had obviously read the same or similar essays and come to opposing positions. According to the latter, the abolitionists "[were] not well informed about the true state of the Africans in their own country, or in [the] colonies." Characterizing the abolition of the African slave trade as "an infraction upon the liberty of [white] mankind," S. M. argued that "the negroes of the British colonies [were] much more happy and easy" than white laborers in Europe. Despite the Caribbean plantations having some of the highest death rates in the Atlantic world, the writer farcically proposed, "Our colonists, especially those of the Sugar-Islands, are obliged to maintain their negroes in health at a great expense of provisions . . . such as broth, panada made of the same wine, which their owners drink . . . and, in case of death, to take care like care of their children."[32] In Saint-Domingue, because so many white inhabitants agreed with similarly preposterous notions, enslaved children, women, and men of the Cotocoly and the Arada peoples, and those born to white fathers, continued to pursue freedom by running away.[33]

Crispus Attucks and many other enslaved Africans in Massachusetts had secured freedom using the same method, risking recapture and punishment. Felix's hopes for complete abolition, however, remained undaunted. He and others like him were encouraged "that [they] may thus address the Great and General Court of this Province."[34] Dissent and rebellion across the age of revolutions informed and empowered Black people with collective strategies to seek freedom and equal protections through petitions and publishing, even as fellow Atlantic inhabitants of African descent continued to choose self-liberation in the meantime.[35]

In the early 1770s, the revolutionary efforts across Saint-Domingue and British North America began to change the meaning of freedom and liberty in the western Atlantic world. After the Treaty of Paris, as Enlightenment literature proliferated to encourage colonial unrest, enslaved Black peoples found individual and collective means to defy enslavement. Free Dominguan people of color steeled themselves to repel encroachment on their rights from racialized ordinances and actions. White inhabitants in both colonies, joined by neighbors of color, in opposition to royal actions, had challenged imperial military forces and lost their lives. The contagious sense of resistance moved between distant ports on ships manned by multiracial crews carrying goods and news.

The people of Saint-Domingue followed rebellious actions of British colonists, and some on the island took encouragement from those reports to champion similar actions. In one instance, Governor-General Pierre Gédéon de Nolivos ordered the execution of two white planters, "men of immense fortune in the issland of St. Domingo," for translating across the colony newspaper stories from Boston and Virginia.[36] During that period, Massachusetts writers using pseudonyms filled newspapers with lengthy letters against British tyranny. In one, Candidus supported popular resistance, arguing, "What has been commonly called rebellion in the people, has often been nothing else but a manly & glorious struggle in opposition to the lawless power of rebellious Kings and Princes."[37] Similar language appeared in the press in Virginia. The interests of Virginian colonists revolved around the new governor, John Murray, 4th Earl of Dunmore, and the unrelated arrests and persecution of Baptist preachers accused of participating in rebellious, mutinous practices across the southern colonies.[38]

According to Governor-General Nolivos, the Dominguan planters circulated the stories of Atlantic rebellion "to excite the people to support their liberties after the example of the British American subjects."[39] The stories alone may not seem dangerous enough to warrant the death penalty. However, the distribution of seditious literature coincided with the Versailles government's discovery of a plan to break up the French Empire. Five provinces in France—Guyenne, Aquitaine, Languedoc, Dauphiné, and Lyon—reportedly were preparing to declare independence from Versailles. French officials feared that the disgruntled inhabitants of Saint-Domingue would ally with the newly independent republic and play a significant role to secure for that nation "the friendship and protection of Great Britain."[40]

Nolivos also likely ordered the executions of rich white inhabitants to quell the lingering sparks for liberty that the multiracial rebels of the 1769 Revolt had ignited. A letter written in 1773 spoke to the endurance of seditious ideas left over from the revolt. The author, a militia officer loyal to the metropole, assessed that "the disturbances were too widespread and last[ed] too long for anyone to doubt" their importance to the people. Similar to the defiant atmosphere across British North America, the sentiments toward rebellion, which the author deemed "fanaticism," secretly existed in the hearts of the French colonists.[41]

Fighting for freedom in the western Atlantic world was not without intellectual inconsistencies. When the participants of color risked and lost their lives in the 1769 Revolt, the objectives for which they fought did not include the emancipation of Hispaniola's enslaved Africans. Some of the martyrs were themselves slaveholders who were not interested in freeing Black people from bondage. The main objective for free Afro-Caribbean rebels was equality with white Dominguan inhabitants. They wanted French royal decrees to apply to elite white colonists and themselves equally. Newly arrived *petit blanc* migrants generally resented *gens de couleur* because of their wealth and prominence. Yet, in the violence of 1769, Afro-Caribbean leaders found common cause with poorer white colonists. Both groups aspired to secure greater equality and closer ties with their wealthy white brethren.

In their efforts to preserve their freedom and secure equality, free Afro-Caribbean rebels did not readily identify with the plight or the demands of people of African descent in bondage. In this regard, the contested views of freedom and slavery held by rebels of colors in Saint-Domingue were similar to those of white British American rebels. The most influential white men from the thirteen colonies assembled, debated, and strategized with one another to seek liberty from monarchical overreach. Yet, throughout their deliberations and exchanges of correspondence, few of them gave little serious thought to the emancipation of the tens of thousands of Africans enslaved in homes and on plantations from New Hampshire to Georgia.

Instead of including freedom from slavery in their protestations, some white rebel leaders, like Adams, used words like *slavery* as hyperbole to accentuate their grievances against the king's oppressive measures.

Accelerating movements for freedom and liberty among wealthier colonists, however, also intensified calls for abolition. As white colonists in Saint-Domingue and British North America contemplated open rebellion against their respective metropoles, the enslaved members of the African diaspora took charge of seeking freedom from slavery through self-liberation or self-advocacy. In the weeks after Felix's petition in Boston, which did not move its white recipients toward abolition in that moment, members of the Sénégaloise, Congo, and Tapa peoples in Africa, named Therese, Jean-Pierre, and Lajoie respectively, decided to join the hundreds of Black people across the Caribbean who were choosing escape and marronage over enslavement.[42]

Editors dedicated lengthy sections to naming children, women, and men who eluded their white captors on the front page of the weekly newspaper and listed maroons whom bounty-hunting parties had arrested and jailed on the last page. Self-emancipation became so popular, and maroons resisted return so fiercely, that apparently the white bounty hunters killed freedom seekers during their recapturing efforts. In March 1773, enslavers, including a Mr. Texier, sought and received from the Superior Council of Cap-Français a regulation, not to protect Black lives, but rather to allow them to seek compensatory restitution from bounty hunters for "Negroes who may be killed during the pursuit."[43] Enslaved Africans were regarded as valuable property by Dominguans as much as in British North America.

A month later in Massachusetts, four Black men, perhaps including Felix from the January petition, submitted a second petition to the colonial legislature, congratulating its white male members for their efforts "to free themselves from slavery" and calling for the abolition of African slavery in the province.[44] In June 1773, a third petition, so beautifully written, represented the first collective act by people of African descent in US history to prompt a governing body to reconsider the question of enslaving fellow human beings. The petitioners argued, "They have in common with other men, a natural right to be free." They employed the language popular with the American revolutionary community, including *Cato's Letters*, declaring that there existed a "natural right of men to liberty," meaning, in this case, freedom from enslavement.[45] They embraced the revolutionary climate to propose that Black people deserved equal opportunities in the burgeoning American republic.

In some of the most moving prose of the age, the writers explained, "The endearing ties of husband, wife, parent, child and friend, we are generally strangers to: And whenever any of those connections are formed among us, the pleasures imbittered by the cruel consideration of our slavery."[46] The petition, perhaps inadvertently, mocked the American rebels, including John Adams. British Americans enslavers inflicted suffering and humiliation on Black people "to Render [them] the most Sordid and forlorn Slaves."[47] Yet, revolutionaries (mis)appropriated the imagery of "slavery" to express their political struggles with King George, like the Stamp Act.

Publisher Isaiah Thomas printed the petition against slavery in the column next to a letter from one white "gentleman" lamenting to another "that we [white men] have been so unreasonably loaded with burthens so heavy to be borne, so long groaned under unconstitutional and oppressive parliamentary and ministerial impositions, have been treated as slaves, and denied the common rights of English subjects." To these gentlemen and other white rebels like Adams, the Black writers suggested, "We are deprived of every thing that has a tendency to make life even tolerable. . . . How can a slave perform the duties of husband or parent, wife or child? . . . So inimical is slavery to religion!"[48]

In response, the Massachusetts legislature formed a "Committee on the Petition of Felix Holbrook, and others; praying to be liberated from a State of Slavery."[49] According to historian Chernoh Sesay, across the early revolutionary period, people of African descent in Massachusetts "wrote more abolitionist petitions to their state government than in any other state."[50] Though the tradition of Black resistance to slavery through writing begun by Felix in 1773 did not directly end slavery, his efforts and those that followed proved important to the eventual abolition of slavery in Massachusetts a decade later.

In that same year, 1773, several important events occurred in the life of the twenty-year-old enslaved writer Phillis Wheatley. The native-born African circulated her poems broadly, embraced the white colonists' revolution, and directly engaged the rebellious actions of fellow Bostonians against the Stamp Act in her poem "To the King's Most Excellent Majesty." A week after the Boston Massacre, her words pledging to the martyrs "Dear to your Country shall your Fame extend" appeared in a local newspaper.[51] Still, Wheatley and her supporters failed to secure investment from the three hundred subscribers in the colonies that publisher Ezekiel Russell required before he would publish a book of some thirty collected poems. Between the time that four Black men petitioned Massachusetts lawmakers to abolish slavery and the time John Adams took Crispus Attucks as a pseudonym, she traveled with her enslavers' son Nathaniel to London, where literary interest in Wheatley and financial support to publish her volume grew. Selina Hastings, Countess of Huntingdon, a big supporter of Wheatley's poetry, underwrote the publication of *Poems on Various Subjects, Religious and Moral* and urged the publisher to include the extraordinary, now-famous frontispiece portrait of the author.[52]

Religion was an important component of Wheatley's success as an author. While enslaved, she was baptized into the Christian faith at Boston's Old South Church. Her enslavers were intensely pious within an evangelical circle that connected them to coreligionists across the Atlantic world. Many of the connections she made within the white Protestant community, in fact, led to the publication of her poems. In September 1770, Wheatley likely met the famous evangelist George Whitefield during his visit to the home of her enslavers. When he died only a few weeks later, she penned "An Elegiac Poem, On the Death of that Celebrated Divine, and Eminent Servant of Jesus Christ, the Late Reverend, and Pious George Whitefield." Newspapers around the region, on the same page as they promoted the sale of a twenty-one-year-old Black man, advertised the sale of the poem "Wrote by Phillis, a Servant Girl of 17 Years of Age, belonging to Mr. Wheatley, of Boston. She has been but 9 Years in this Country from Africa."[53] The Whitefield elegy gained the attention of the Countess of Huntingdon, a devout Calvinist, and eventually led to the publication of *Poems*.[54]

As the American colonies moved closer to conversations of national independence, enslaved Black Baptists in Georgia took a major step to acquire a level of religious freedom. The evangelist efforts of the Great Awakening across the mid-eighteenth century attracted many people of the African diaspora to the Protestant Christian faith. Notably, Whitefield influenced the spiritual worldview of African descendants in the North and the South. The impact of the slaveholding preacher in the South was especially profound. He pastored Christ Church in Savannah in the 1730s and held popular revivals around Georgia over the next quarter century. Despite being "impeach'd" by the Anglican Commissary Court in South Carolina "for not using the Liturgy of the Church of England," Whitefield and other Awakening theologians like John Edwards proved powerful proponents of slavery.[55]

Whitefield, to fulfill a life's calling to build an orphanage in Savannah (today Bethesda Academy), encouraged Georgia leaders to adopt slavery after they had banned the trafficking of Africans into the colony.[56] In a letter to white slaveholders across the South, he sanctioned the buying, selling, and owning of African children, women, and men. In chastising the enslavers' unusually cruel treatment of enslaved people, Whitefield did not refer to their acts as immoral or unchristian; rather, he reminded the enslavers of the Stono Rebellion in South Carolina and suggested that more slave insurrections could happen across the region if they did not change their ways.[57]

Some white slaveholders were reluctant to permit enslaved peoples to hear or learn of the Christian Gospel, fearing it would fuel their desire for liberation. The work of scholar Katharine Gerbner explains the conflict between white Protestants of the Atlantic world. One group worked to exclude enslaved peoples from the tenets of Christianity. Others sought to include the enslaved populations as unequal members of the Protestant faith. The evangelist Whitefield was a strong proponent of the latter, Christian slavery, perspective.[58] In his view, enslavers incorrectly believed that "teaching [enslaved people] Christianity would make them proud and consequently unwilling to submit to Slavery." To the contrary, he suggested that Protestant Christianity, particularly purposefully selected biblical passages from the Pauline letters, would make them more inclined to obey white authority. In fact, he strategized, with a touch of cruelty, "Your present and past bad Usage of them, however ill-designed, may thus far do them good, as to break their Wills, increase the sense of their natural Misery, and consequently better dispose their Minds to accept the Redemption wrought out for them, by the Death and Obedience of Jesus Christ."[59]

The noted revolutionary writer Thomas Paine, addressing the topic of religion and slavery, suggested, "The past treatment of Africans must naturally fill them with abhorrence of Christians."[60] However, thousands of enslaved people across the South responded positively to the emotion-filled, evangelical preaching, showing their engagement with a religion that white inhabitants had used to rationalize slavery. In their bondage, they found the hope of Jesus as a means to a new birth or new light. Yet the Christian beliefs of Whitefield and other white religious leaders could not move the clergy to see Africans as equal children of God. White enslavers established laws and proslavery residents created social norms to convince Black inhabitants of their inherent inferiority. As scholar Monica Najar put it, Baptist theology's principle of "the equality of souls conflicted with the social practices of their communities, churches, and, for slaveowners, their homes."[61] White Baptist preachers taught and laypeople believed that God was a respecter of persons, favoring white Protestant colonists.

The Black congregants disliked the Christian teachings offered and encouraged by the white preachers. They wanted more from the Bible than Paul's misused admonition "Slaves, obey your masters." Enslaved community members wanted one of their own to serve as a spiritual leader.[62] Similar to sailors of color who adopted more prominent ways of being African as they lived and worked in close proximity to European descendants across the Atlantic world, Christians of the diaspora wanted a place within the racist, dehumanizing South to be unabashedly Baptist and Black.

George Liele, an enslaved Black man, received a license from the white American Baptist church in Burke County, Georgia to preach the Christian Gospel.[63] In the same year, John Benjamin Deveaux, an enslaved child of mixed-race parentage, was born in Savannah.[64] Though Deveaux's birth records are not extant, it is believed the planter-enslaver fathered the child with an enslaved woman.[65] According to historians Walter Fraser and Charles Hoskins, an earlier generation of the Deveaux family emigrated from Saint-Domingue during the eighteenth century.[66] Deveaux later joined the Protestant faith community Liele had established and made important contributions to its expansion.

Liele was enslaved at birth in Virginia around the time Crispus Attucks escaped slavery in Massachusetts. Liele's enslaver manumitted him before the American Revolution, and, despite the arguments of the American rebels against the monarchy and the tyranny of taxation, he decided to remain loyal to the British Empire.[67] For the next eight years, Liele traveled along the Savannah River, preaching to enslaved populations at plantations around Brampton, Savannah, and Yamacraw. Historian Edgar Thomas explains, "Many white owners encouraged this work, seeing the good effects of Christianity upon slaves."[68] As scholar Albert Raboteau notes, enslavers understood the religion's "good effects" on people of the African diaspora as making those in bondage "better slaves."[69] Liele's Christian exhortations attracted many enslaved people to the Baptist tenets of Christianity. Andrew Bryan was one of the men Liele converted at the Brampton plantation, about three miles outside Savannah. Within a year of his baptism, Bryan began preaching to fellow enslaved people "and a few white persons who would assemble to hear him."[70] When Liele and thousands of other Black Loyalists departed the United States with the British military, Bryan continued to minister to people around southern Georgia. Under Bryan's leadership, the congregation would later relocate to Savannah and take the name First African Baptist Church.

The First African Baptist Church of Savannah is considered popularly as the first Black Baptist church in the United States. Popular storytellers date its beginnings, and the birth of an African Protestant movement in America, to the ministerial work of Liele and Bryan during the US revolutionary era.[71] There are

Figure 3.1. Andew Bryan. Courtesy of the New York Public Library.

other contenders that claim to be America's "first" Black Baptist church. Historians Carter G. Woodson, C. Eric Lincoln, and Albert Raboteau date the establishment of the Silver Bluff Church organized in South Carolina by David George and fellow enslaved people to 1773 and consider that congregation the first Black Baptist church.[72] George and Liele had been friends since their days as enslaved children in Virginia. They both became Baptist preachers, and, in part because the British secured both men's freedom from slavery, they were Black Loyalists.[73]

Recent archaeological and historical research has renewed interest in the establishment of a Black Baptist Church in Williamsburg, the capital of Virginia until 1780, during the revolutionary era. The church and its leaders are not new to US history. As early as the 1920s, Carter G. Woodson wrote about Reverend Gowan Pamphlet, who pastored "a progressive Baptist Church in Williamsburg, some members of which could read, write and keep accounts."[74] Writer Ella Wall Prichard describes recent archaeological exploration that uncovered the location of the church's foundation, along with grave sites, sparking greater public and scholarly interest in Black colonists, who, in the 1770s, made up the majority of the town's 1,800 residents.

Despite the enslaved status of most of the Black population, they braved Anglican scorn and flouted restrictions on their movements to establish the capital city's first Baptist congregation of any color.[75]

Before Pamphlet, who has gained fresh attention, a Black preacher named Moses began ministering to the free and enslaved people of the African diaspora who risked harsh punishments from white Protestant enslavers to meet secretly in the woods to worship Jesus Christ together as a Christian community.[76] Moses also led congregations of color across Virginia in Charles City, Petersburg, and Lunenburg Counties.[77] For leading these Christian meetings, he endured much physical violence such as humiliating whippings, "as prescribed by law, to be any number of lashes, not exceeding thirty nine," at the hands of white Virginians who likely empathized with white Baptist preachers in the colony claiming persecution in newspaper stories across British North America.[78]

White Virginians were fearful of enslaved people revolting. In a period of mounting colonial acts of resistance against British tyranny, it was considered dangerous to the white population for Black people to gather in numbers anywhere, including places of Christian worship. But, in the spirit of the revolution, according to nineteenth-century Virginia writer Robert Baylor Semple, "many of the blacks were rebellious and continued still to hold meetings."[79]

The work of historian Linda Hunter Rowe indicates that, like fellow African-descended Baptists in South Carolina and Georgia, Williamsburg's Christians of the diaspora, under the spiritual leadership of Moses, did not have a designated edifice in which to gather. They met in the woodlands around the Green Spring plantation and later near a place called Raccoon Chase on the outskirts of town. Unlike their cross-colony coreligionists of color, who possessed the consent of enslavers, Black Baptists of Williamsburg met secretly in worship as white Virginians prepared to openly declare their independence from Britain.[80] Across the southern colonies, the revolutionary fervor of white Americans in the making inspired and empowered Black Baptists, with and without white consent, to establish separate, foundational, and racialized worship spaces, under the leadership of Black preachers David George, Moses, and George Liele.

Religion played an important role in the worldview and lived experiences of leaders and subjects across the eighteenth-century Atlantic world. Ecumenical Christianity emerged on display in the resulting settlement from the negotiations in 1763 to end the Seven Years' War. The Treaty of Peace, according to its first sentence, was issued, signed, and ratified by the leaders of three Catholic kingdoms and one Protestant empire, "In the name of the Most Holy and Undivided Trinity, Father, Son, and Holy Ghost." The complete royal styles of address for the British and French monarchs in the final copy of the seismic diplomatic document included, respectively, "Defender of the Faith" and "His Most Christian King."[81]

The Franco-British bilateral negotiations reveal signs of religion's importance to the talks. In the resolution of Article IV, the crestfallen French negotiators ceded most of France's territory in Canada to Britain. Yet they still found it imperative to secure in the treaty the religious freedom for inhabitants there to practice "the Catholick Religion."[82] Writing later of the treaty negotiations, one commentator employed Christian reasoning to defend the British diplomats in Paris for seeking a just peace in lieu of vengeance. The author suggested that "the Christian law" to "Love your neighbour as yourself" remained an obligation of monarchs and sovereign nations once the "universal right of war" had been satisfied.[83]

Religious practice and theology remained interesting to John Adams when, in 1774, he represented Massachusetts at the First Continental Congress. Twenty years before, he had attended Harvard College with his father's hope that he would graduate as a Congregational Church minister.[84] In Philadelphia, on one Sunday afternoon, he attended a Baptist church. In his diary, Adams had little to say about the congregation but seemed intrigued by the preacher, Reverend William Fristoe. Raised in the Congregational Church, he found the ninety-minute sermon by an untrained preacher to be laborious. To his ears, the speaker had "no grace of action or utterance." Adams admitted that Fristoe possessed "an honest zeal," exemplified through a vignette during the sermon of religious persecution in Virginia. Contrary to established Anglican doctrine there, Fristoe preached the Baptist belief that spiritual salvation was granted through grace, not through good works or rote obedience. Authorities arrested him "for reviling the Clergy of the Church of England."[85]

The Christian homiletical style and theological teaching of the "trans Alleganian," or Southern, preacher garnered much attention in Adams's diary. Given his descriptions of Reverend Fristoe's education, religion, and region, he seemed to regard his fellow British subject "from the back Parts of Virginia, behind the Allegheny Mountains," as the other.[86] The Baptist faith was prohibited in Massachusetts, where Congregationalism was the established form of Christianity. During his sojourn in Philadelphia, Adams admitted to a gathering of Baptists and Quakers that he had helped to prosecute Massachusetts Baptists for illegal worship practices and religious tax evasion. As a lawyer, he saw "no oppression or injustice" in legal actions hostile toward Baptists and other religious minorities.[87] Historic Baptist foundations and evangelistic movements spread across the North during the era of the American Revolution, led by noted preachers Isaac Backus, Hezekiah Smith, and John Gano. Yet the expression of religious freedom through a distinctive African Baptist movement, with separate, Black church communities, did not take root in the region until the following century.

Prince Hall, a free man of color, had been a member of Boston's predominantly white New North Church for over a decade when Black Baptists began establishing African Baptist churches in Virginia and Georgia.[88] By the spring of 1775, segments of the British colonial population began preparing openly for the Anglo-American military conflict. A number of Black inhabitants like Wheatley and Attucks had embraced the American revolutionary cause. The meaning of liberty in the emergent United States held different connotations for Black people than for their fellow white rebels. Prince Hall, therefore, made different sets of decisions about how to best achieve freedom for himself and his family.

During the American Revolution, Hall established one of the most enduring Black civic institutions in US history. His path to rebellion and prominence proved very different from that of John Adams. Hall and Adams were both New Englanders born in 1735. Adams was born to a fourth-generation Massachusetts farmer, deacon, and militiaman on thirty-five acres of land in Braintree. Continuing the legacy of generational wealth among white colonists, he later purchased his father's land outright and bequeathed it to his children.[89] Less is known about Prince Hall. Though a burgeoning historical literature and popular interest exists around Prince Hall's impact on American society and culture, his origins, vital statistics, and personal history beyond historic achievements, like those of so many Black members of the founding generation, remain unclear and disputed.[90] Hall was born likely in Boston to at least one parent of African descent. White Bostonians William and Margaret Hall enslaved an adolescent Hall as a tanner apprentice.[91]

In 1756, the year a Franco-British battle on the Mediterranean island of Minorca touched off the Seven Years' War, a twenty-one-year-old Hall, still enslaved, sired a son named Primus with Delia (no known last name), a servant. In that same year, Adams began reading the law and, like his father, was elected a selectman in Braintree.[92] In April 1770, a month after Crispus Attucks's martyrdom on King's Street, Hall secured a certificate of manumission from the couple who had enslaved him for two decades. As John

Adams prepared to defend the accused Boston Massacre soldiers at trial, Hall's enslavers decided "that he [was] no longer to be Reckoned a slave," and he began, for the first time, to experience life in the British American colonies as a free man.[93]

Gaining freedom at age thirty-five seemed to propel Hall with a sense of urgency to free others. In March 1775, he and fourteen other free male colonists of color sought to become the first Black members of the brotherhood of Freemasons in North America. They joined the authors of abolitionist petitions and the creators of Black churches in embracing the opportunities presented within the Atlantic revolutionary era to redefine Black existence in America. Hall, Peter Bestes, and other members of his cohort wanted the capacity to become Freemasons, a fraternity that, according to historian James McClellan, "embodied that noble search after brotherhood and Enlightenment that knew not class or nation."[94]

Freemasonry in the colonies began in Philadelphia in the 1730s, around the time of Hall's birth. Similar to their progenitor in England, Masons in North America came from the elite classes. White men of rank embraced the organization's tenets of love and honor as a means to sew solidarity and shared identities among themselves across colonial regions. American rebel Freemasons like George Washington and printer Isaiah Thomas reoriented Freemasonry in the colonies toward a more democratic organization that represented the principles with which they resisted British monarchical control. The atmosphere of the revolutionary period created for white Masons new social groupings and gathering spaces to assemble as brethren collectively learning, adopting, and propagating a new, dynamic worldview.[95]

For Black men like Hall and Bestes, the latter of whom had petitioned the Massachusetts government to abolish slavery in 1773, Freemasonry provided an infrastructure for mutual aid and more coordinated advocacy for freedom within the community of color.[96] Becoming Freemasons would allow them to assert the concerns of Black people in the expanding public sphere and, in the aftermath of freedom petitions and Wheatley's success publishing a book, encourage free people of color to engage with, at some level, the widening channels of political power and social influence. According to historian Chernoh Sesay, "The ideas of Freemasonry reconciled the patriotism that inspired cries for colonial independence with a genteel sophistication developed by acquiring a broad perspective on human experience."[97] In Boston, famous American revolutionaries John Hancock, Joseph Warren, and Paul Revere were Masons. Black people with an eye toward freedom and equality with their white neighbors wanted to gain membership in this prestigious network. With an unfettered sense of ambition, Hall and his cohort petitioned a lodge for admission and were denied acceptance within the white-only brotherhood.[98]

As became a regular feature during the American Revolution, Black people seeking freedom sought recourse and assistance from the protectors of British tyranny when white American colonists refused to expand their transitioning ideals of freedom and liberty to include their fellow Black colonists, free or enslaved. Phillis Wheatley had to travel to London to secure subscribers and supporters for her book of collected poems after her fellow Bostonians refused to support the effort. Foreigners, in short, were often more open-minded about Black potential than American colonists.

Similarly undaunted by the prejudiced rebuff, Hall and his colleagues approached an Irish contingent of the British Thirty-Eighth (First Staffordshire) Regiment of Foot garrisoned at Castle William (now Fort Independence) in Boston Harbor, stationed there with a mission to stamp out the colonial revolutionary embers spreading across Massachusetts.[99] It is telling that the white Bostonians' rejection of their Black neighbors led the latter to petition the city's imperial occupiers in search of brotherhood. In the midst of a revolutionary era auguring the liberation of white British subjects from imperial tyranny, inhabitants of African descent trusted their aspirations for collegiality, education, and advancement to men from three thousand miles away over the white men around whom they lived, worshipped, and worked daily. In one scholarly estimation, perhaps "they determined that the British might serve the enslaved and marginalized free blacks of Boston better than had the white Bostonians, who, after all, had subjugated them. . . . If this conjecture informed the black men's actions, then they were spot on."[100]

Within the camp of the counterrevolutionary forces, the aspiring Freemasons found affirmation and fraternity. The Irish soldiers and the Black Bostonians, though different, were all imperial subjects and shared the inferior position as members of marginalized groups within a highly racialized British Empire. It is likely the Irish appreciated the common sense of disenfranchisement endured by the African-descended aspirants. Without the approval of and in opposition to the Premier Grand Lodge of England, presumably because of rejection or alienation, Irishmen established their own lodge. The expanding deployment of British imperial troops, requiring increased numbers of Irish enlistees, throughout the realm across the eighteenth century allowed Irish lodges to spread rapidly. Over fifty military lodges were stationed in the North American colonies, facilitating the formation of fraternal bonds among lower-ranking, often mistreated soldiers.[101]

Hall approached Army Lodge 441 in his efforts to gain repute and status while questions of greater liberty and citizenship fueled debates among the white leaders of the emerging new nation. There are no existing records from the Bostonians or the Irish that detail the conversations or sequences of events surrounding the encounter with Black candidates for lodge membership. Little is known about John Batt, a sergeant in the Thirty-Eighth Regiment and master of Lodge 441, outside of histories on Black Freemasons. Yet Batt did what John Hancock and Paul Revere refused to do: He presided over the ceremony in which Irish Freemasons invited Hall and fourteen fellow Black initiates and received them into the Ancient and Accepted Order of Freemasons as brothers. The unprecedented event gave people of African descent another avenue to achieve social status and networking opportunities outside of heavily racialized Christian church circles.

Freemasonry took root in Saint-Domingue around the same time as it did in British North America, when English merchants from Jamaica established the French colony's first lodge in the southern city Les Cayes in the 1730s. Similar to their British counterparts, Dominguan lodges maintained colonial connections stemming from the imperial metropole in London and Paris. Some later lodges were affiliated with the Grand Lodge of Pennsylvania. The order became fairly popular, setting up lodges in cities across the colony, including Môle Saint-Nicolas and Cap-Français in the north, Fonds-des-Nègres and de Léogâne in the south, and Saint-Marc and Port-au-Prince in the central region. Freemasonry attracted several thousand Dominguan members across the eighteenth century.[102]

French and British colonists spread Freemasonry across the western Atlantic world in the decades after the Seven Years' War.[103] In a Saint-Domingue influenced by Enlightenment thinking, lodges served as one of several "sites of social compromise," including theaters and reading circles, that facilitated the creation of societal refinement and collegiality outside the metropole. Like the British colonial Masons, colonists on Hispaniola established a fraternal organization that sought to embrace an equality, akin to a brotherhood, among its members across different social ranks. Also like their British American counterparts, the lodges tended to create spaces for elite sociability that welcomed the wealthy planters, more affluent merchants and shippers, military officers, and members of the Catholic clergy.[104]

Like the lodges in Boston and Philadelphia, the Dominguan lodges were welcoming to only white men. As Freemasonry spread across North America and the Caribbean, its leaders created spaces that drew connections to their European hubs yet strove for distinctions. A buffer created by thousands of miles of Atlantic Ocean gave them the possibility of defining who the members of their "universal family" would be differently from their brothers in the Old World. Still, they decided to ban fellow colonists of color from becoming members. As revolution and rebellion spread across the Atlantic world, white Masons, like other racist colonial elites, refused to share newly gained status and power with Black people seen as inferior. Regardless of repeated efforts to assimilate and cooperate, their white neighbors created new ways to exclude them from the emerging definitions of citizenship and status. Many of the Masons became or remained wealthy and powerful through their participation in the trafficking of African children, women, and men. To accept Afro-Caribbean men with white fathers as equal members of their exclusive fraternity could have cast doubts on their definitions of Black people, which buttressed their foundation of slavery and disenfranchisement.

Despite the exclusivity of western Atlantic world Freemasonry, Afro-Caribbean men of Cap-Français, like Black Bostonians, sought to enter the lodges. They saw and desired the benefits of being a part of an organization that claimed universalism and enlightened ideas. Black men, particularly enslaved men, lived with their backs pressed against the white colonists' system that practiced the "politics of difference." Particularly as racism-inspired changes swept Saint-Domingue across the 1760s and 1770s, they navigated non-Masonic hierarchies and forms of exclusion in most parts of their lives. As lodges in North America and the West Indies followed patterns of racial segregation, Black men refused to concede their value or to permit their contributions to society to be demeaned. They continued to demand acceptance to the affirming, collegial, and empowering environment of Freemasonry.[105]

Some, but not many, of these men succeeded in entering Dominguan lodges despite the resilient exclusivity of the white brothers. An explanatory history of the broader effects of Prince Hall Freemasonry and Dominguan Freemasonry across the Atlantic world has yet to be written. French author Alain Le Bihan, however, argued that lodges in Les Cayes, Saint-Marc, and Môle-Saint-Nicolas did include some Afro-Caribbean men, free and enslaved, who later led the revolution that eradicated slavery in Hispaniola and established an independent Haiti.[106] In any case, their general exclusion from white organizations and elite institutions likely helped inspire their decision to fight for more radical changes in western Atlantic societies.

Historians suggest that Haitian Revolution leader André Rigaud was a Freemason in Saint-Domingue.[107] He was born free in Les Cayes in 1761 to Rose Bossy Depa, an enslaved woman from the Arada people of Benin, and André Rigaud, a wealthy white French planter. His given name at birth was Benoit Joseph André Rigaud.[108] His parents, like those of his Caribbean counterpart Edward Stevens, sent their son to Europe for education and professional advancement. According to Michel-Rolph Trouillot, around the time that Felix Holbrook petitioned to abolish slavery in Massachusetts and his white townspeople initiated the Boston Tea Party, Rigaud's parents sent him to obtain "a very good classical education" and to train as a goldsmith in Bordeaux.[109]

Goldsmithing proved to be a popular profession for affluent young Dominguan men of color. Vincent Ogé, a future rebel leader and revolutionary martyr, was born free around 1757 in Dondon to Angélique Ossé, a free woman of color, and Jacques Ogé, a white colonist. He also trained as a goldsmith in Bordeaux.[110] In the mid-1770s, Rigaud returned to Les Cayes to begin a professional life.[111] According to one biographical sketch, André Rigaud later emerged as "one of the great figures in the struggle for freedom in Saint-Domingue and perhaps also one of the most fervent supporters of the idea of French citizenship for the inhabitants [of color] in the former French colony."[112] Haitian poet and essayist Michel R. Doret, in the only book-length biography of Rigaud, suggests he served in a colonial military unit of Afro-Caribbean men after returning from France.[113]

In Cap-Français, thirty-year-old Jean-Baptiste Belley, a free Black man and future Haitian revolutionary, employed his skills as a wigmaker to become financially independent. He had been born in Senegal, trafficked across the Middle Passage, and raised as an enslaved child in Cap-Français. In the late 1760s, he achieved freedom. During the Haitian Revolution, residents of the northern region of Saint-Domingue elected him to the French National Convention, making Belley the first Black deputy to take a seat in the convention. He joined one of the five militias of color that existed in Cap-Français in the 1770s. Scholar Christine Levecq suggests that Afro-Caribbean men in Saint-Domingue "associated with the military not only knew each other but formed a sort of pseudo-kin family that provided support and also participated in many of the other members' important life events."[114]

As Rigaud made his way as a young professional, Jean-Baptiste Chavannes was likely working on and learning the business of his family's plantation in northern Saint-Domingue. Chavannes, the future Haitian revolutionary martyr, alongside Ogé, was born around 1748 into a wealthy family of color who owned a coffee plantation.[115] Louis Jacques Beauvais was born into a rich family of color in the Croix-des-Bouquets, near Port-au-Prince. Like Rigaud, he received "a good classical education" in France. His parents sent him to study at the *Collège Militaire de La Flèche* (known today as *Prytanée National Militaire*) in the Loire region. Established as a military institution after the defeat in the Seven Years' War, the school was reserved to a limited number of students of noble extraction, as well as sons of officers who were wounded or died in combat. Beauvais, a future general in the Haitian Revolution, entered military service there and, after returning to Saint-Domingue, pursued a successful military career until the end of his life.[116]

Rigaud, Belley, and other men of varying degrees of African ancestry, who could not easily join elite organizations like Freemason lodges, performed colonial military service in the hope of acquiring respect and acceptance from white colonists in a Dominguan society increasingly committed to racism and white supremacy. By the close of the decade, each of the noted Dominguan free men, before achieving historical fame in the Haitian Revolution, would choose to fight in the French army on the side of the colonists in the American War of Independence. They were willing to risk their lives and their fortunes in a war for white North American freedoms in the hope of realizing their collective dream of being treated as equal citizens in their own country.

As free Afro-Caribbean men sought education abroad, accumulated financial fortunes, and accomplished military service to better assimilate into the dominant white Dominguan society, little movement was made by anyone of any racial group to abolish slavery or ameliorate the lives of the enslaved. The government and elite planters united to restrict racial equality and to stunt the socioeconomic aspirations of free Afro-Caribbeans in the aftermath of the Seven Years' War. To constrain and dash the hopes for freedom among enslaved Africans, Saint-Domingue's plantation economy persistently and relentlessly exerted and manipulated all levers of power. As historian John Garrigus points out, "except for the work focused on slave escapes, very little has been written about how enslaved men and women resisted captivity in Saint-Domingue" before the Haitian Revolution. For Garrigus, the enslaved people's resilience and efforts to survive represented resistance.[117]

Black women and men continued to live, to love, and to nurture successive generations of Africa's children in diaspora despite overwhelming white planter dominance, brutality, and oppression. They also persisted in escaping, slowing or stopping work, and poisoning. In one instance, the Superior Council of Cap-Français condemned Jacques, an enslaved Black man, for reportedly poisoning one hundred animals belonging to his enslaver over the span of eight months. Jacques, similar to Makandal, was sentenced to being burned alive on the evidence that he was found carrying a bowl of arsenic.[118]

There were some white revolutionaries who called out the racial hypocrisies of colonists. Thomas Paine, a newcomer to the revolutionary movement in the mid-1770s, condemned his fellow white insurgents for their insistence on enslaving African peoples. Before the release of his seminal publication *Common Sense*, Paine, within a month after emigrating from London to North America, addressed a letter "To Americans" that was published in a March 1775 Philadelphia newspaper. In the clear, straightforward style that characterized his most famous pamphlet, the letter's first sentence declared, "That some desperate wretches should be willing to steal and enslave men by violence and murder for gain, is rather lamentable than strange." The following sentence was no less potent, exhorting, "That many civilized, nay, Christianized people should approve, and be concerned in the savage practice, is surprising."[119]

For Paine, and a growing number of revolutionaries, white American liberty was incompatible with African slavery. He asked his readers to consider the brazen duplicity of white colonists to "complain so loudly of attempts [by the Crown] to enslave them, while they hold so many hundred thousands in slavery; and annually enslave many thousands more." Paine argued that because people of African descent had never forfeited their freedom, "they have still a natural, perfect right to it."[120] But he did more than write about the inconsistency of slavery in the revolutionary moment. Five days before patriot blood was spilled three hundred miles to the northwest at Lexington and Concord, Quaker abolitionist Anthony Benezet led the establishment of the Society for the Relief of Free Negroes Unlawfully Held in Bondage (better known as the Pennsylvania Abolition Society) in Philadelphia. A month after publishing his letter, Paine became a founding member of the abolitionist organization.

Another recent arrival to North America was making a name for himself as an up-and-coming revolutionary. Alexander Hamilton left the Caribbean island of Saint Croix to seek his fortune in New York. He followed fellow Cruzan Edward Stevens to King's College, beginning as a private student there in 1773. Like his lifelong friend, he had initially aspired to study medicine, but he quickly became interested in ideas circulating outside the academy.[121] Hamilton and Stevens formed a literary society for debating pertinent topics of the era. Their group is considered a forerunner to the Philolexian Society, the oldest student group at today's Columbia University (the name King's College took in 1784).[122] The university experience on the continent provided the two young men a solid classical education in Greek and Latin literature, rhetoric, history, and math, similar to the studies other Caribbean students—like André Rigaud and Louis Jaques Beauvais—left Saint-Domingue to receive in France during roughly the same period.[123]

Stevens graduated in 1774 and began studies at the University of Edinburgh to become a physician. In that same year, Hamilton attended a mass meeting organized by the Sons of Liberty (New York) at the commons near King's College. As if he had met the moment for which he had left his home island, Hamilton mounted the platform and spoke with great command and moving fervor in support of the Boston Tea Party. He predicted that similar actions promoting intercolonial collaboration "[would] prove the salvation of North America and her liberties." New Yorkers had never heard of Alexander Hamilton. While applauding the teenager's oration, attendees murmured, "It is a collegian."[124]

King's College president Myles Cooper held Loyalist leanings and was no fan of the Sons of Liberty. He would have been appalled to learn that one of his students aligned so closely with that group. According to biographer Ron Chernow, "Hamilton had immigrated to North America to gratify his ambition and successfully seized the opportunity to distin-

Figure 3.2. Alexander Hamilton. Photograph of painting by artist John Trumbull, 1900. Courtesy of the Library of Congress.

guish himself."[125] The American Revolution provided him ample chance to achieve his goals.

Back home in Saint Croix, Hamilton's white benefactors and friends remained committed to African slavery. Still, the island's Afro-Caribbean population refused to accept life under white supremacy as a fait accompli. Military service was compulsory for all free Cruzan men, Black and white. However, authorities racially segregated the units. Men with any African ancestry were consigned to a Free Negro Company in Christiansted and across the Danish West Indies. Similar to Dominguans, Cruzans in power considered a person of African and European parentage, despite the varying percentages, to be unfit for the white units. In terms of military placement, as with many things in Caribbean society, there were white companies and nonwhite companies. Officers of African descent, uniformed and armed with swords, staffed Black units. Company troops, who attended civilian jobs when not in service, carried wooden sticks when called up for guard duty or other military deployments. Across the 1770s, members of the Free Negro Company developed and executed a variety of strategies to challenge the socioeconomic order that constrained their movements and advancements within a racialized society. Similar to their Dominguan counterparts Rigaud, Beauvais, and Belley, company members attempted to use their service records to persuade white Cruzans that they should be treated as equals and, at the same time, to distinguish their status apart from that of the enslaved population.[126]

Saint Croix's enslaved peoples also devised means of resistance against the island's racist regime. Joe, a sixteen-year-old boy of mixed parentage, just a few years younger than Hamilton, escaped enslavement at the hands of merchant Nicholas Cruger, the King's College student's former employer, who offered a reward to entice Cruzans to "apprehend and bring him home." Other enslaved people continued to seek freedom in the Danish West Indies. Around the same time, "a young Creole Negroe woman, called Jinny Diver," "an old Negroe man, named Febula," and "a young Negroe man, named Adam," escaped separately at opposite ends of the twenty-two-mile-wide island.[127] Despite these regularly publicized courageous acts of self-liberation, white Cruzans continued to enslave African people until abolition spread across Saint Croix in 1848.

In December 1774, a merchant in Frederiksted posted the sale of "100 Prime Gold Coast Slaves," profiting off the bodies of Black people trafficked from communities and wrenched eternally away from those who loved them.[128] In that same month, some 1,700 miles to the north, the Cruzan college student Hamilton penned a lengthy newspaper article defending the seating and the deliberations of colonial delegates at the Second Continental Congress in Philadelphia. In it, Hamilton declared, "I wish well to my country," meaning New York. Hamilton never returned to Saint Croix. In February 1775, he published a second newspaper article, twice the length of the first, exhibiting an impressive grasp of politics and economics. In addition, the essay made a grand appeal to the natural rights of mankind in the cause of American liberty. He condemned the British government for not respecting, in the case of the colonies, that all men were, "by nature, entitled to a parity of privileges."[129]

The collegiate Hamilton's writing was reminiscent of that by Felix Holbrook and Black Bostonian abolitionists from a couple of years earlier. They had sought to move the Massachusetts government toward the emancipation of African people held in bondage. For Hamilton, "natural liberty is a gift of the beneficent Creator to the whole human race, and that civil liberty is founded in that; and cannot be wrested from any people, without the most manifest violation of justice."[130] Published in a Boston newspaper, the early Black abolitionists petition, similar to Hamilton's reasoning, argued that natural rights were provided for Black people as well as white colonists. Therefore, the writers requested that enslaved Africans "be liberated and made free-men of this community, and be entitled to all the privileges and immunities of its free and natural born subjects."[131] Hamilton concluded his treatise by proposing, "The best way to secure a permanent and happy union, between Great-Britain and the colonies, is to permit the latter to be as free, as they desire."[132] Both writings ground their petitions for the advancement of their people in an unwavering belief in the natural rights of humankind. Though written and published in British North America, albeit in different cities, the essays promoted freedom for different populations—one Black, one white.

In the era of the American Revolution, fueled in part by the dynamic energy of the moment itself, colonial inhabitants sought determinedly to transform the conventional meanings of freedom and liberty. The two states of being continued to be contested, and with increasingly greater intensity—between kings and colonists and among the colonists themselves—in the years after the first Treaty of Paris. People of the African diaspora and white imperial subjects sought to actualize Enlightenment ideals beyond the pages of popularized tomes. Inhabitants of the western Atlantic world—Black and white, free and enslaved, affluent and poor—employed a myriad of ways to experience life beyond the imposed strictures of shackles and chains, demoralizing poverty, racialized demarcations, and loyalty to a crown.

Enslaved Africans across North America and the Caribbean became fugitives to escape bondage. Young people from both regions, Black and white, pursued academic and military training as prospective avenues to greater access to status, affluence, and leadership. Writers from different racial and socioeconomic backgrounds entered the expanding public sphere to register their views on slavery, taxes, and collective resistance. These diverse populations undertook relocation, education, petition, and oration, with a belief in their appeals to universal, natural rights to act as effectual catalysts for change. They may not have fully realized that their objectives would be won not by words but, rather, by war. The gunfire at Lexington and Concord helped to convince rulers and rebels across the Atlantic world that the price of racial freedom and colonial liberty would be nothing less than blood.

Part II

THE DAWN OF A NEW TREATY IN PARIS

1776–1783

His Britannick Majesty acknowledges the said United States to be Free, Sovereign, and Independent States.

—Article I, *The Definitive Treaty of Peace and Friendship, between His Britannick Majesty, and the United States of America, 1783*

Chapter 4

"No More Talk of Reconciliation"

1775–1776

A month after Irish members of the Thirty-Eighth Regiment helped Prince Hall and other Black Bostonians establish the first Freemasonry lodge in the western Atlantic world to welcome and affirm brothers of color, in April 1775, the minutemen of Concord, Massachusetts, fought in one of the most memorable battles in American political and military history. Irish Masons of the Thirty-Eighth Regiment fought as part of the British counterrevolutionary redcoats. Hall and North America's only lodge of African-descended Freemasons likely remained appreciative of their new Irish brothers of the Thirty-Eighth Regiment. The transnational Masonic bond, however, did not supplant the Black Bostonians' loyalty to the patriots' cause when the Thirty-Eighth Regiment deployed in the first military-to-military engagements of the US War of Independence.

Paul Revere, whose widely popular prints five years earlier had helped transform the image of Crispus Attucks from a fugitive freedom seeker into an icon of the American Revolution, made his famous ride from Boston on the night of 18 April 1775 to alert the militia at Concord. The next morning, armed Massachusetts rebels fatigued after a decade of newspaper fights and relatively fruitless Continental Congress petitions met imperial troops, first at Lexington and later in Concord, to check the capacity of the British

Crown to rule over them absolutely. By the end of the day, some 120 men from both sides lay dead and 215 more were wounded. The Freemasons and many other Black residents of Massachusetts, like Crispus Attucks, supported white Americans as militia members and civilians. Across the revolutionary period, adjacent to their white neighbors, free and enslaved Black inhabitants asserted themselves in their engagement with the rebellious actions and civic society. Hall, a leatherworker with a shop across from the Quaker meetinghouse, created drumheads for the Massachusetts artillery regiment.[1]

Two days before the momentous skirmish, John Adams, writing under the pen name Novanglus, made a bold case, grounded in English history and law, later published in newspapers, which concluded that from the arrival of the earliest English migrants, "America was not any part of the English realm or dominions" and, therefore, was "out of the legal jurisdiction of parliament."[2] Adams and his fellow Americans did not know their quest for the acknowledgment of rights and parliamentary representation would touch off decades of revolutions elsewhere in the world.

When the United States' position as a revolutionary beacon became clear, some Americans relished in their accomplishment. In the nineteenth century, after the conclusion of the Haitian Revolution, the Napoleonic Wars, and the Congress of Vienna, Abraham Hews Jr. and Sylvester Goss reissued the letters of Novanglus and his public opponent Massachusettensis in a collected volume to celebrate the influence of the American Revolution on political transformations in the Atlantic world. Hews and Goss suggested to the reading public, "In reflecting on the CONSEQUENCES of that glorious revolution . . . the mind is imperatively drawn to a contemplation of the present political condition of Europe. Representative governments are gradually introducing themselves into every part of that country; and we hope the day is not far distant, when the whole world shall be emancipated from tyranny. As AMERICANS we feel a *conscious* pride, that the resistance which our ancestors made . . . will terminate in the civil and political freedom of ALL MANKIND."[3]

A much older Adams was a bit more circumspect in his reflection on the impact of the American Revolution in the Atlantic world. Throughout the 1810s, around the time his Novanglus letters were republished, revolution advanced across Latin America as subjugated peoples, many of Indigenous and African descent, overthrew Spanish rule. Writing to Hezekiah Niles, Adams acknowledged the US's role as a revolutionary lodestar for Atlantic political upheavals. "The American Revolution was not a common Event. It's Effects and Consequences have already been Awful over a great

"No More Talk of Reconciliation"   127

Figure 4.1. John Adams. Engraving by James Smither, 1797. Courtesy of the Library of Congress.

Part of the [whole] Globe," he wrote. However, Adams, like others of the founding generation, came to believe revolutions, though laudable on some level, were uncontrollable and could easily lead to excesses of liberty. In the same letter, he urged caution: "Revolutions are no Trifles; they ought never to be undertaken rashly; nor without deliberate Consideration and Sober Reflection; nor without a Solid, immutable, eternal foundation of Justice and Humanity; nor without a People possesed of Intelligenc, Fortitude and Integrity Sufficient to carry them with Steadiness, Patience, and Perseverance, through all the Vicissitudes of fortune, the fiery Tryals and Melancholly Disasters they may have to encounter." Once revolutions begin, he asked, "When and Where are they to cease?"[4]

Adams's query provides an important point of departure in the history of US diplomacy in the age of Atlantic revolutions. Race served as a lens through which early Americans perceived and reacted to the unfolding of later revolutions in the western Atlantic world. As historian Alan Taylor suggests, "Before the slave revolt in Saint-Domingue, Americans had celebrated their revolution as a 'contagion of liberty.'" They congratulated themselves on providing a model for expanding political freedom. However, during the

Haitian Revolution, which began fifteen years later, "when black people became revolutionaries, white Americans recoiled."⁵

In 1775, as George Washington took command of colonial militia units and the Continental Congress debated the intellectual foundations of their prospective republic, a steady exchange of information through newspapers helped to fuel a current of transcolonial cultures of resistance between British North America and Saint-Domingue. White American leaders convened in Philadelphia to move American colonists toward independence from the British Empire. In Cap-Français and Port-au-Prince, Afro-Caribbeans, including future leaders of the Haitian Revolution, achieved freedom through creative means and determinedly advocated for equity in a racialized society. Armed with muskets and quills, Black inhabitants joined their white neighbors of Massachusetts in fighting and framing the US War of Independence. In Virginia, Lord Dunmore successfully encouraged enslaved peoples to join British imperial forces with a pledge of freedom, which enlightened American patriots steadfastly refused them. Meanwhile, Washington and other revolutionary leaders considered the controversial question of whether to include Black patriots in their fight. Most did not encourage the idea. During and after the American Revolution, white American colonists, and later citizens, believed resistance was the privilege of European descent although they were surrounded by Atlantic revolutionaries of Indigenous and African descent. There were clear limits on white American notions of liberty.

Americans in 1775, however, were serious about defending and asserting their own liberties. After "the militia companies had shown themselves ill-equipped to meet an emergency," the townspeople of Concord voted to establish a special force of one or more companies, from which the officers would be chosen, to "stand at a minute's warning in case of an alarm." In January, the town began signing up soldiers to serve as minutemen. The Concord companies "reached out into nearly every neighborhood of the town." Enlistments, though, fell short of expectations. The Concord minutemen numbered just over one hundred men, a mixture of farmers, mechanics, selectmen, and militiamen. Early on, Massachusetts rebel leaders reconciled themselves to participating in acts of resistance with poorer, white colonists, some of whom did not own a musket.⁶ With the abundance of white volunteers, the townspeople and militia leaders saw no need to enlist the help of their fellow Black Congregationalists and neighbors.⁷

During the military spring in 1775, the rules of inequality and privilege across races, genders, and classes continued to solidify Concord's cohesive white, Calvinist-centered societal fabric, interwoven with the New England sense of responsibility and duty. For the townspeople, according to historian Robert Gross, "there was to be no social revolution." The patriots' opponents in town recognized the hypocrisy. One Black Concordian, John Jack, entrusted his white Loyalist neighbor Daniel Bliss to serve as his executor to handle his affairs after his death in December 1772. Bliss, with or without his client's knowledge or permission, used Jack's headstone to send a message to his neighbors regarding their contradictory views on white liberty and Black enslavement. The stone marker, still legible in Concord's Old Hill Burying Ground, reads, in part, "Here lies the body of JOHN JACK a native of Africa. . . . He was born free. Tho' he lived in a land of liberty, He lived a slave." Bliss pointed out that despite the townspeople's rhetoric around freeing themselves from slavery under King George, it was not they, but rather "Death, the grand tyrant," that granted John Jack "his final emancipation."[8]

The colony's inhabitants of African descent wanted freedom as much as the Concord townspeople sought liberty. And they were ready to take up arms for the cause. Eighteen Black men deployed to the battle sites on 19 April. Thirty-five-year-old Prince Estabrook, an enslaved African of Lexington, stood and faced the imperial army on the Lexington Green as a member of Captain John Parker's Lexington militia with his white enslaver and neighbors. He was wounded during the fight, becoming the first militiaman of African descent to be wounded in the Revolutionary War. On the first anniversary of the battle, Reverend Jonas Clarke, the pastor of the Lexington church and an eyewitness to the battle, reminded his parishioners that "Prince, a Negro, of Lexington," was wounded in the cause of American liberty. Black men from Framingham, Middlesex, Worcester, and Essex Counties marched to assist the white rebels in arms, but their units arrived too late to join the fight that day.[9]

On the day after the battles of Lexington and Concord, Lemuel Haynes, a man of color from Granville, marched with forty-two of his neighbors as a private in Captain Lebbeus Ball's company of minutemen to join other units at Roxbury to pin down British forces holding Boston.[10] He joined other free soldiers of color there, like Luther Jotham and Elias Sewell of Captain Josiah Hayden's minute company out of Bridgewater.[11] Haynes was twenty-two years old and had known freedom from indenture for only months when he marched one hundred miles to secure the liberty of white Americans. Both Haynes and Phillis Wheatley were born in 1753, he in Connecticut and she in West Africa. Haynes's Black father and white mother, the identities of whom remain elusive to scholars, made the choice to give up the child. The

Rose family of Granville, Massachusetts, raised the infant as an indentured servant within their household. David Rose was a farmer and Congregational deacon, and Lemuel Haynes provided agricultural labor for the family.

Haynes encountered and accepted the New Divinity Calvinist theology popular at the time across New England. Influential proponents of post-Edwardsean Calvinism Reverends Joseph Bellamy and Samuel Hopkins both led congregations within forty miles of Haynes's home and workplace. One evening, Haynes read to the family one of his own sermons, which Rose compared to those of George Whitefield.[12] With the education provided under the Roses' care, he began to write and prepare for the ministry, studying Latin, Greek, and hermeneutics. In 1774, he completed his indenture to the Rose family at age twenty-one and became a free man.[13]

During the month or so Haynes was garrisoned at Roxbury, he composed the ballad "The Battle of Lexington," a composition that certainly belongs in the canon of poems and songs of American resistance that had been circulating across the colonies for over a decade.[14] Wheatley had offered the poem "To the King's Most Excellent Majesty" seven years earlier to remark on King George's repeal of the Stamp Act. Despite knowing servitude at the hands of white colonists and acknowledging that thousands of other Africans in diaspora remained enslaved and disenfranchised, Haynes and Wheatley chose to lend their literary skills to the American revolutionary cause. Scholar John Saillant describes Haynes's hymn and Wheatley's writings as republican works that exerted "the Puritan heritage and classical heroism on the patriot and abolitionist causes."[15] In his own words, Haynes described his efforts as a "Poem on the inhuman Tragedy . . . shocking Displays of ministerial & tyrannic Vengeance."[16]

The newly freed poet wrote his ballad in the style of white rebel lyricists around him, employing revolutionary rhetoric of righteous anger yet remaining open to redemption and reconciliation, language that was common across Massachusetts. Like Wheatley in her 1773 published book and Briton Hammon fifteen years prior, Haynes clearly identified himself as a writer of the African diaspora. The author dithered about letting readers know the poem was "composed by Lemuel a young ~~Mollatto Man~~ Mollatto." Haynes's indecision about projecting himself as a man likely derived from youthfulness or a learned anxiety about how white readers would perceive him. However, he possessed no reticence to display his education, which was an important status indicator in Massachusetts. He informed them that the poem was written from the "knowledge he possesse[d], by his own Application to Letters."[17]

LEMUEL HAYNES

Figure 4.2. Lemuel Haynes. Courtesy of the New York Public Library.

Across thirty-seven stanzas, Haynes embraced the liberty sought by his Massachusetts neighbors and fellow British colonists across the continent. He invoked the awfulness of slavery—in the way white writers regularly did—to emphasize to the king that "We," American rebels, would rather die "than to live as slaves to You."[18] Soon after obtaining his personal freedom, Haynes had embraced the cause of American liberty and offered his physical service, his faith, and his pen to advance the ideals of white revolutionaries who saw no duplicity in enslaving and demeaning people of African descent.

Phillis Wheatley, Lemuel Haynes, Edward Stevens, and Alexander Hamilton were all young adults, just about twenty years old, in the mid-1770s. One had been born in Africa, one in North America, and two in the Caribbean. The Atlantic world into which they were born was rapidly and irrevocably transforming. By this point, all four of them were living as free people within the thirteen colonies, with the two white students residing about two hundred miles from the two New England writers of color. As they looked into their futures, the American Revolution opened new possibilities and challenges. After years of indentured servitude, Haynes, for one, entered American military service as a minuteman in Roxbury and wrote patriotic songs to support the cause. Stevens, however, possessed no affinity for offering his energies to the American Revolution. After graduating from King's College, he left British North America to begin his medical studies in Scotland. Stevens was not a Loyalist. Neither was he a patriot. He viewed education and profession as the means to greater access to status and wealth in the Atlantic world.[19] Living amid revolutionary fervor did not alter his ambitions.

Hamilton followed his friend to New York and enrolled at the same university. Their paths diverged from there. Shortly after the battles of Lexington and Concord, Hamilton, like Lemuel Haynes, joined the militia, a New York volunteer unit. He drilled with the unit each morning before classes. Later, Hamilton and fifteen King's College student militiamen volunteered to transport more than ten heavy artillery guns to the liberty pole on the commons near campus while under fire from British ships in the harbor.[20] Wheatley, unlike Hamilton, did not actively assist in the war-making efforts of the revolution. Instead, she employed the quill to contribute to the American cause. In addition to writing poetry, she engaged in her own form of battle: a verse dialogue with British officers. "Like Virgil, Horace, and Alexander Pope," asserts historian David Waldstreicher, "she retailed [African] pastoral nostalgia in part to be able to comment on the effects of war, including enslavement."[21]

Around the time Hamilton and his classmates were performing military logistics in New York, Wheatley took up residence in Providence, Rhode Island. She, like many others, evacuated Boston, which languished under the British occupation.[22] In Providence, Wheatley composed the poem "To His Excellency General Washington" to commemorate his appointment, in her words, "by the Grand Continental Congress to be Generalissimo of the armies of North America."[23] Written in iambic pentameter using heroic couplets, Wheatley's verse honoring the man who embodied the embryonic nation's aspirations demonstrated her loyalty as a person of African descent to the American revolutionary endeavor. The poet mailed a copy of the poem to the general at his headquarters in Cambridge, Massachusetts. Thomas Paine later published the poem and the letter in the *Pennsylvania Magazine*.[24] Biographer Vincent Carretta posits that Wheatley sending her words to Washington exhibited a hope "that even the most eminent slave owner in the colonies would ultimately apply the revolutionary ideology of equality and liberty to people of African as well as European descent."[25]

In 1775, Wheatley and Hamilton engaged separately with the general from afar. Later, the African and the immigrant, given their humble origin stories and upbringings, likely enjoyed personal meetings with the man Wheatley crowned America's "great chief."[26] Hamilton, an indistinct figure in a boisterous throng of onlookers, first glimpsed Washington when the commander in chief made a triumphant procession past King's College in a carriage pulled by a team of white horses during a stop in New York en route to assume command at Cambridge.[27] The poet connected with Washington through ink and literature from forty miles to the southwest of his military command center. She received a positive, surprisingly lengthy response to her poem. In the finest fashion of gentlemanly respect, he commented that the poem's "style and manner exhibit[ed] a striking proof of [her] great poetical Talents." He also invited Wheatley to visit him in person.[28]

The incongruity of Washington's reply and invitation cannot be overlooked. The general accepted praise from a woman born in Africa and proposed to meet her as he made the strategic decision to discourage the recruitment of men of African descent into the Continental Army. Also around the same time, a Black man named Harry, whom Washington enslaved on his Mount Vernon plantation, escaped slavery to fight with the British army in Virginia.[29] It is most likely that the African poet and Virginian general met in Providence, where Washington stopped during his march to New York to face the British there.[30] Shortly after his encounter with Wheatley, Washington and Hamilton met for the first time during the Battle of New York.

At a younger age, in a letter to Stevens, the precocious Hamilton understood himself and clearly and confidently wrote words that offer prescient insight into the man and legend he would become. He expressed his aspirations to Stevens, who had already left Saint Croix for King's College, writing, "To confess my weakness, Ned, my Ambition is prevalent." The two Cruzan boys, like so many young Afro-Caribbean and European men from the Caribbean, left the islands in search of education and professional advancement. Hamilton, his youthful passions on full display, wrote Stevens, "I mean to prepare the way for futurity." He closed the letter with a prescient desire: "I wish there was a War."[31]

The US War of Independence provided the enterprising lad with the opportunity of a lifetime. And he did not dare let it slip away. Hamilton dropped out of college to pursue his fortune with the military. He helped New Yorker John Jay recruit sixty patriots for the New York Provincial Company of Artillery and was made a captain. Exhibiting a mature level of gratitude and a measure of youthful grandeur, he posted a dispatch to a Saint Croix newspaper to inform the folks back home of his decision. Given that Hamilton had endured a difficult childhood with little family help, residents of Christiansted, including Stevens's father, had generously contributed money to fund his university education. He explained, "I am going into the army and perhaps ere long may be destined to seal with my blood the sentiments defended by my pen." He proved a worthy soldier during the Battle of New York. With a steady head and decisive leadership, Captain Hamilton commanded several raids against British foes. Hamilton's organizational skills at leading his company in building an earthwork caught the attention of Washington, who, according to Hamilton's son John, "entered into a conversation with him, invited him to his tent, and received an impression of his military talent."[32] Their first meeting laid the foundation on which Alexander and Washington built one of the greatest, most influential professional partnerships in American military and political history.

Afro-Caribbean and white readers across Saint-Domingue learned about the appointment of George Washington as commander in chief of the Continental Army from a lengthy, two-page feature story in the *Affiches Américaines*. The newspaper reported on Washington's procession through New York on his way to take command at army headquarters in Cambridge. It informed Dominguans that the Virginian marched through the city at the head of one thousand cavalrymen and two thousand infantrymen. During that spectacle, from the university campus, Alexander Hamilton caught a glimpse of the man whose stature and decision-making would change the entire direction of his life. Members of New York's patriotic provisional congress addressed the gathered spectators, describing Washington as "a general whose talents & virtues offer us the prospect of a happy & peaceful future."[33]

The French-language *Affiches Américaines* was established in the year after the Treaty of Paris of 1763 as part of the reforms meant to cultivate the colony's postwar commercial versatility. Closely monitored by officials, the paper began and served as a communication tool for the planter class and the colonial administration. Its primary role was to publicize official edicts and commercial news, not to serve as a vehicle to challenge royal authority. However, the paper was not simply a propaganda organ. Beginning with reporting news of the Stamp Act crisis in North America, the editors, who were nameless functionaries of the state, fostered public conversation with news from and about other colonies of the western Atlantic world, regarding the needs of the colonists. Early on, the primary sources of news on the American Revolution were contacts and dispatches in London. The historical literature, unfortunately, offers no indications of the newspaper's subscriber or readership levels, making it difficult to gauge its reach.[34]

Yet with its two printing presses located in Port-au-Prince and Cap-Français, the *Affiches Américaines* kept colonists in Saint-Domingue abreast of the political unrest and rebellious stirrings in North America. The reports about mounting colonial dissent in the thirteen colonies may have cultivated a sense that Versailles's capacity to oversee post-treaty reforms and rebuilding efforts faced limitations and challenges.[35] In response, the colony's white population, exhibiting *"l'esprit autonomiste,"* an "independent spirit," consistently pushed for more rights and less imperial oversight.[36] The *Affiches* stories of the developing American Revolution may have shaped Afro-Caribbean and European inhabitants' perceptions of the plausibility of enduring an armed conflict between the colony and the king.[37] News from the north of protests, riots, and ideological arguments against imperial rule supplied Dominguan colonists with contemporary examples of colonial agitators willing to risk wealth and reputation to put the Enlightenment theories of expanded freedom, liberty, and equality into practice.[38]

The individual and collective impact of the Dominguan-American exchange of information on transcolonial resistance and rebellion remains undetermined. Beyond a shared commitment to African slavery, the concerns of planters and merchants in Saint-Domingue were not strictly the same as those of their American counterparts. The Dominguan planter class would have supported American calls for free trade and the fight against the monarchical metropole. Yet fears of slave rebellions would have tempered their protests, which tended toward petitions and political lobbying in lieu of open armed conflict. The news coming into Saint-Domingue and the editorial decisions about what to distribute helped to gradually expand the colony's public sphere as it, according to one scholar, "provided raw material for colonists across the color line to shape their geographic imaginings and political views." Reports of riots in reaction to protests and the Stamp Act likely influenced the Afro-Caribbean and *petits blanc* rebels of the 1769 Revolt. Rebels in Boston likewise may have found encouragement in Saint-Domingue's 1769 Revolt to step up violent attacks against the military forces occupying their city. The steady increase after the Treaty of 1763 in the number of individual acts of defiance and the intensity of collective acts of protest in both colonies is too significant to be reduced to coincidence. Parallel movements offer glimpses into the "current" of transcolonial "cultures of resistance" early in the age of revolutions.[39] Though news of rebel acts traveled by word of mouth as well, newspaper accounts helped bring stories of resistance to light for readers, who disseminated the information to their acquaintances more widely.

In the fall of 1775, the *Affiches Américaines* reported on preparations across the thirteen colonies to open the Second Continental Congress in Philadelphia. The Massachusetts Provincial Congress, meeting at Concord before the outbreak of April 1775 hostilities in that town, had passed a resolution calling on "the people to intensify their efforts and their resistance against the schemes of the common enemy, regardless of the risks there was to run." It also reported that France was sending a larger than usual number of fishing vessels to Newfoundland in the hope of exporting more fish to Spain and Portugal in the event of an Anglo-American war.[40]

Only a few weeks later, the newspaper quoted the Speaker of the House of Commons Fletcher Norton as suggesting that "the unfortunate disputes in America [had] been the main cause" of increased budgetary expenses. The next paragraph cited dispatches from the office of British Secretary of State for the Colonies William Legge, Earl of Dartmouth, to inform Dominguan readers, "We learn that hostilities have finally begun in New England, where blood has been spilled on both sides." The report detailed moves and countermoves between colonial militiamen and the king's troops over the course of 18 and 19 April, along with casualty counts and the redcoats' retreat to Boston. The newspaper's source, likely for the benefit of French colonial readers, thought it important to weigh in on France's scheme to encroach on British Atlantic trade while the empire battled its colonies: "The trade of Portugal, which for the past seven years has yielded nearly a million pounds annually in favor of Great Britain, was worth to our merchants last year only 89,740 pounds."[41]

The newspaper also reported on the public war of words each side carried on in the wake of Lexington and Concord. Two months after the conflict, the writer lamented that neither side had provided accurate information about the battles beyond British government reports and Massachusetts assembly proceedings. One partisan voice suggested, "The stupidity of the American rebels equals their fury." To offer readers a firsthand account, the correspondent translated and published a report by British Lieutenant Edward Thoroton Gould, an injured prisoner of war, who complimented the medical care and humane treatment provided by his Americans captors. Newspapers in North America also widely reprinted Gould's firsthand account. The Massachusetts Provincial Congress's meeting at Watertown addressed an open letter to the people of England, blaming the fighting on British military aggression while pledging their continued loyalty to the Crown. Yet the rebels remained clear that "they [would] never possess the cowardice to submit to the persecution and to the tyranny of [the king's] cruel administration; and appealing to heaven for the justice of their cause, they [were] determined to die or to be free."[42]

The *Affiches Américaines* provided Dominguans, free and enslaved, Afro-Caribbean and white, who could read or listen, with regular news updates regarding the increasing political instability in North America. The newspaper and other carriers of news, like ship captains and crews from across the Atlantic world, dispersed rumors and verifiable reports that shaped what Dominguans heard and thought about the American Revolution. A steady exchange of information in print and in port cities between French colonists in Saint-Domingue and their British continental counterparts to the north had existed since at least shortly after the Treaty of Paris of 1763. Dominguans had remained well informed of American unrest since the Stamp Act. Transcolonial communications across the Caribbean Sea during this dynamic revolutionary period spanning the US War of Independence proved critical to shaping the perspectives of the Dominguan population on why western Atlantic rebellions occurred and what they themselves might achieve in similar conflicts over political liberty and racial equality vis-à-vis the colonial government and the French metropole.[43]

As late as October, months after the Battle of Bunker Hill and the commissioning of George Washington as Continental Army commander, the *Affiches* dedicated a full page to an open letter by the Massachusetts Provincial Congress president, General Joseph Warren, to "friends and fellow citizens" of Great Britain. Warren also presided as the grand master over the Grand Lodge of Massachusetts, which had likely rejected the petition of Prince Hall and other Black Bostonians to become Freemasons earlier that year.[44] Pointing out the barbarity of the British tactics during the battles, he reported soldiers chasing women naked in the streets and "killing old men in cold blood inside their homes." He cited those actions as "the effects of a vengeful administration against this Colony [Massachusetts], because she refused with the others to suffer the yoke of slavery."[45] After the rebel victories, Warren organized plans and personnel for the Siege of Boston and spread the patriots' version of events through writings like the one in the *Affiches*. As a high-ranking rebel political leader, he also negotiated with General Thomas Gage throughout the siege. By the time Dominguan colonists read Warren's letter, the thirty-four-year-old physician-politician-general was dead, killed in action at Bunker Hill.[46] His words of protest, however, would carry on and influence others in the coming years.

In November 1775, as the patriots' fervor grew and the imperial position weakened, John Murray, the Earl of Dunmore, the royal governor of Virginia, established martial law, requiring all abled persons to support the king's troops "to the end that *peace and good order* may the sooner be restored."⁴⁷ Such actions were not extraordinary to counteract rebellion in the Atlantic world. However, one sentence in particular from the Dunmore Proclamation garnered enormous attention from the contemporary American insurrectionists and, since the revolution, from writers and scholars: "I do hereby farther declare all *indent[ur]ed servants, Negroes*, or others (appertaining to rebels) *free*, that are able and willing to bear arms, they *joining his Majesty's troops*, as soon as may be, for the more speedily reducing this colony to a proper sense of their duty, to his Majesty's crown and dignity."⁴⁸ Dunmore offered freedom to enslaved Africans in Virginia who would join the British army and take up arms against liberty-loving, patriotic slaveholders.

Newspapers reported that within a month of the proclamation, Dunmore had raised an "Ethiopian Regiment" numbering some one thousand Black Loyalist soldiers. Rumors spread that the Black troops wore on their chests an inscription reading "Liberty to Slaves."⁴⁹ The unit under Dunmore's command engaged white American patriots in a minor British victory at the Battle of Kemp's Landing. During the fight, formerly enslaved African privates captured a white Virginian commanding officer.⁵⁰ The skirmish, which occurred before the Declaration of Independence was announced, was likely the first of what would become many battles in which inhabitants of color fought against their white colonial neighbors who adamantly refused to abolish African slavery even as they sought greater liberties for themselves.

The Dunmore Proclamation applied only to Virginia, but newspapers across the colonies reprinted it.⁵¹ Americans committed to the enslavement of African people seemed to grasp the immediate impact of Dunmore's call for Black liberation. They rightfully understood that people of the African diaspora, abused and dehumanized under the guise of racist ideologies to secure profits, would kill to secure freedom for themselves and their families. The determination of Black inhabitants to achieve freedom resembled that of white American rebels to secure fairer taxes and rid their cities of occupying forces.

Dunmore's act and the British collaboration with African comrades in arms seemed to insult Americans and caused popular indignation across the colonies. After the Battle of Great Bridge, a minor American victory at which Ethiopian Regiment members were killed in action, Americans took some pride in humiliating white British prisoners of war by coupling "them to a Negro with hand cuffs."⁵² In the weeks after enslaved Africans became soldiers in the royal army, American writers became obsessed with people of color across the colonies. They feared Black liberation. More importantly, they fretted over how the new capacity of unjustly treated men to exist unfettered at the operating end of a musket would elevate self-esteem and inspire greater self-worth among African-descended people from Boston to Savannah.

In an article from a Connecticut newspaper, the writer showed no restraint in recording his disgust of the new state of Black lives in the colonies. One evening, after a white woman berated a man of color on the streets of Philadelphia "for his rude behaviour," the target of her scorn reportedly responded, "Stay, you'd----d white bitch, till Lord Dunmore and his black regiment come, and then we will see who is to take the wall." Two white men came to defend the woman's honor by apprehending the man, but he escaped.[53] The intent of the story, whether real or apocryphal, was clearly to antagonize white colonists and mobilize the white populace against the slightest move to liberate or improve the lives of Black people.

American leaders took a different approach to questions of enlisting the assistance of the African-descended colonists in the fight that was clearly leading toward war. Revolutionary colonists could not countenance the idea of needing the assistance of Black men—particularly those men they had kidnapped, beaten, and demeaned—to secure the liberty of white people from British rule. Some of the brightest minds of the eighteenth-century Atlantic world were closed to the thought of arming Black men or the idea that those men could actually augment the American rebels' chances for victory. The intellectuals understood the danger that a British offer of freedom to oppressed Black people posed to American strategic military goals. They had worried for some time about such a development. Still, they refused to make a preemptive move or counteroffer toward freedom from bondage to people of the African diaspora. Instead, for over a decade they keenly focused attention on crafting and refining the political, economic, and religious ideals of liberty and prosperity for the white inhabitants of North America.

American leaders perceived threats of Black liberation as all the more real for proslavery colonists across the South, particularly in Georgia. There, since the instatement of slavery championed by George Whitefield, the forced migration of Africans had resulted in African-descended people constituting nearly half of the population.[54] During this period, John Adams was resident in Philadelphia, representing Massachusetts at the Second Continental Congress. One evening, after smoking and chatting with two delegates from Georgia, he recounted in his diary, "These gentlemen give a melancholy account of the State of Georgia and South Carolina. They say that if one thousand regular troops should land in Georgia, and their commander be provided with arms and clothes enough, and proclaim freedom to all the negroes who would join his camp, twenty thousand negroes would join it from the two Provinces in a fortnight."⁵⁵ Freedom for Black people did not represent a comforting thought for most white revolutionaries.

The Georgians were pretty accurate in their predictions about Africans choosing freedom with the British instead of perpetual enslavement. The sentiment and promise behind the Dunmore Proclamation inspired thousands of African-descended people throughout the Revolutionary War to escape slavery under the cover of British might. Enslaved people had long sought freedom across Virginia, North America, and the Caribbean. Three days before Dunmore signed the proclamation, a newspaper published an advertisement reporting that a short, twenty-year-old Black man named Sampson, from Fauquier County, Virginia, was three months into a freedom-seeking venture. Like Crispus Attucks and many others before and after the Dunmore Proclamation, Sampson chose to risk the travails and suffering of fugitive life rather than languish until death under white oppression.⁵⁶ At the time men were falling at Lexington, Concord, and Kemp's Landing, white American patriots enslaved some half a million descendants of Africa. As the guns of war came to life throughout the thirteen colonies, roughly one hundred thousand African-descended inhabitants, some 20 percent of British North America's Black population, refused America's promise of continued abuse, enslavement, dehumanization, and exploitation for themselves and their progeny. They chose instead to fight for the opportunity to live as free subjects of the king in British territories across the Atlantic world.⁵⁷

White Virginians took great offense at Dunmore's effort to usher toward freedom the people whom they had systemically enslaved for generations. Members of the General Convention, who assembled to strategize about effective ways to increase liberty for white colonists, refused to appreciate the attractiveness of Dunmore's offer of freedom from slavery for Black inhabitants. The well-read, highly informed gentlemen refused to consider persuading enslaved Africans to support the white American cause by employing humane, Enlightenment-inspired means. Instead, true to their commitment to white supremacy, they decided to threaten with execution those Black inhabitants who dared to seek freedom under Dunmore's protection. The convention issued a declaration, signed by its slaveholding president Edmund Pendleton, "that all Negro or other slaves, conspiring to rebel or make an insurrection, shall suffer death, and be excluded all benefit of the clergy."⁵⁸ The Pendleton Declaration exhibited an appalling dearth of imagination regarding the consideration of Black lives in the revolutionary era. White Virginians, civilians and law enforcement officials, harassed, arrested, wounded, and killed Black people fleeing to Dunmore's army in search of freedom.[59]

The Continental Congress established the Continental Army with George Washington as its commander in chief in June 1775. Its first sustained campaign was the Siege of Boston, which dragged on through the summer and into the fall. The soldiers' will to fight waned steadily across the months because of a constant need for provisions, clothes, and pay. The poor esprit de corps weakened the officers' capacity to recruit, replenish, and retain troops. In October, Washington met at his headquarters in Cambridge with a Congress committee chaired by Benjamin Franklin to discuss means of strengthening the army's supplies and resolve. One question was "Ought not Negroes to be excluded from the new Inlistment especially such as are Slaves?" The group and the Council of Officers agreed that Black men, free and enslaved, should not be permitted to enlist in the Continental Army.[60]

Therefore, five days after the Dunmore Proclamation, Washington took the opposite approach, ordering, "Neither Negroes, Boys unable to bare Arms, nor old men unfit to endure the fatigues of the campaign, are to be inlisted."[61] But Massachusetts patriots of color refused to let Washington's racist recalcitrance prevent them from serving their country. Men like Peter Salem of Framingham had fought the British throughout 1775.[62] While their white neighbors deserted or chose not to reenlist to advance the revolution, free and enslaved Black men refused to stop serving, even when their commander in chief did not want them. In ways that reached General Washington, veterans of the previous campaigns made it known that they were "very much dissatisfied at being discarded" after honorably enduring months of drudgery as disaffected white soldiers deserted all around them. Washington's thinking, unlike that of his fellow Virginians who passed the Pendleton Declaration, changed in light of Dunmore's act of abolition. He understood the threat of notably seasoned soldiers who had killed men in battle seeking "employ in the ministerial Army" if he refused their service in the Continental Army.[63]

Similar to Dunmore's move, Washington's was not motivated by abolitionist zeal. His racialized views toward Africans took a back seat to the tactical necessity of enlisting soldiers of color to secure military objectives. Therefore, after being advised in late December that "numbers of Free Negroes [were] desirous of inlisting," despite his previous orders, Washington gave "leave to the recruiting Offices, to entertain them, and promise[d] to lay the matter before the Congress, who he doubt[ed] not [would] approve of it."[64]

Figure 4.3. George Washington, commander in chief of the armies of the United States of America. Engraving by Noël Pruneau, 1770s. Courtesy of the Library of Congress.

Yet, only a few weeks later, in his commission to Robert Breck to raise a regiment in western Massachusetts, near the hometown of Lemuel Haynes, he renewed previous orders: "Neither Negroes (being Slaves) old Men, or Boys, unable to bear Arms, & to endure the fatigues of the Campaign, nor Persons labouring under any bodily infirmity whatsoever are to be allowed to pass Muster, of which you are to take due Notice."[65]

Figure 4.4. Engraving of Toussaint Louverture. Unknown artist, 1801. Courtesy of the John Carter Brown Library.

While Black men of Massachusetts negotiated the dynamics of freedom created by their participation in an evolving Atlantic revolution, one Afro-Caribbean man on the island of Hispaniola experienced the transition from enslavement to liberation. Based on records detailing the lives of other people, historians agree the enslaved man named François Dominique Toussaint, commonly referred to as Toussaint—who later took the surname Louverture—lived as a free man in 1776.[66] In the year Americans proclaimed independence, Toussaint Louverture began to build an extraordinary life on his way to becoming one of the greatest military leaders in the eighteenth century.[67]

The evolution of the historic figure Toussaint Louverture began with some relatively ordinary life events, but by the 1790s, he would wield power and influence comparable to those of the new leaders in the United States, such as John Adams, with whom he forged an extraordinary diplomatic relationship at the turn of the century.[68] In 1776, however, Louverture was learning how to live as a free Black man in a slave society as Adams employed intellect and oratory to design the first republic in the western Atlantic world. In the spring before American independence, Adams resided temporarily in Philadelphia as a delegate to the Second Continental Congress. While there, he wrote to one of his former law students, offering a checkered review of Paine's most popular pamphlet. He considered *Common Sense* "a very meritorious Production," although "in Point of Argument there [was] nothing new." In brash language that became a hallmark across his political career, Adams concluded, "I believe every one [argument] that is in it, had been hackneyd in every Conversation public and private, before that Pamphlet was written."[69] During that period, Louverture, only eight years younger than Adams, performed more mundane activities in Saint-Domingue. For instance, he stood as godfather at the baptism of Marie-Josèph, the one-month-old baby girl of François Lazare and Marie-Rose, at the church in the northern commune of Le Borgne.[70]

Louverture lived, worked, and prospered within the ranks of Saint-Domingue's free Black men and men of color. The population of free *gens de couleur* was more numerous in the southern part of the colony. One estimate puts only 750 free Afro-Caribbeans at Cap-Français and Port-au-Prince during this period. Problems of educating and employing liberated Africans remained a persistent challenge in Saint-Domingue, in the United States, and across the Black Atlantic over the next century. Louverture's emancipated status, therefore, did not immediately change his economic or social lifestyle. Despite being regarded as a diligent worker as an enslaved and free person, he did not readily obtain affluence or acquire large landholdings. White colonists viewed Louverture, like freeborn Afro-Caribbean men possessing greater wealth than he, including Julien Raimond and Jean-Baptiste Chavannes, as inferior beings underserving of political enfranchisement or social equality. On the plantation where Louverture lived in Haut-du-Cap, just outside Cap-Français, life for the African captives was brutal and unstable during the early 1770s.

During this period of unrest, many bonded Africans on the plantation escaped to freedom from enslavement and rampant physical violence at the hands of an especially cruel white overseer.[71] White enslavers and guarantors of white supremacy in Saint-Domingue gained a reputation for their brutal treatment of African people. They inflicted on Black captives barbaric physical and emotional trauma that went well beyond the absurd attempt to humanize slavery in the Code Noir of 1685. Violence, dehumanization, and fear were normal experiences in the daily lives of the enslaved people across the colony. According to one estimate, white people made life so harsh for Africans in Saint-Domingue that half of them died within a few years of disembarking from the ships that trafficked them from their homes.[72] Like so many Black children of the Atlantic world whom white inhabitants viewed as expendable, young Toussaint experienced the "sell" of his especially close half sister Geneviéve to another white planter.[73]

According to one biographer, four years before he lived in freedom, Toussaint ran away from the horrid plantation life as a fugitive.[74] In this rebellious effort, he joined thousands of African-descended people across the Atlantic world, like Crispus Attucks, the maritime maroons from Saint Croix, and the soldiers in Dunmore's Ethiopian Regiment. Black people in search of freedom, decades before Americans pondered independence, were forced to risk physical retribution by white enslavers to escape the bonds of inhumanity. An autumn 1772 edition of the Dominguan newspaper, in the *Esclaves en Maronage* section, reported that "Un Negre Créole, nommé Toussaint, agé de 30 ans," (a thirty-year-old Black Creole man named Toussaint) had escaped to freedom. The same print edition also reported that a forty-year-old woman from the Congo named Magdeleine and a twenty-five-year-old woman of mixed parentage born in Saint-Domingue had both fled from slavery.

Earlier that year, an English court ruled that a Black man named James Somerset could not be reenslaved after he escaped to freedom in London. The *Affiches Américaines* did not report on the remarkable legal verdict in the British Empire. Yet, in just about every edition, the editor listed for Dominguan readers the names of children, women, and men who, like Somerset, hungered so fiercely to be free that they escaped their enslavers. On the day Toussaint's flight became public, the newspaper detailed how "Deux Negres Créoles" men named Jean-Baptiste and François slipped away from the clutches of a Mr. Leclerc in Cap-Français while still wearing collars around their necks and carrying the actual four-foot-long iron chain that had bound them.[75] Four days later, the Port-au-Prince edition of the newspaper informed readers that recently kidnapped Africans, in the process of being trafficked aboard the British slave ship *Exeter*, "off the coast of Africa," had killed the crew of white human traffickers to rescue themselves from a life of perpetual bondage and inhumane cruelty in the western Atlantic world.[76] It was within this dynamic atmosphere of self-liberation on Saint-Domingue that the future leader of the Haitian Revolution was first known to become an escapee. By the time the newspaper ran the runaway advertisement, Toussaint had been *en maronage* for two months.

Across the western Atlantic world, newspapers printed accounts of the varying means Black and white inhabitants used to achieve greater access to freedom and liberty during a contagion of revolution. Weeks before the

Dominguan newspaper first printed publicly the name of Toussaint Louverture, the *Essex Gazette* informed readers of the escape of a twenty-year-old man called Cato from the bondage of his enslaver in Ipswich, Massachusetts.[77]

On Saint Croix, the *Royal Danish American Gazette* reported that two Black men named George and Frank had fled the degrading life their enslaver had prescribed for them near Frederiksted.[78] A month later, the Cruzan newspaper published its most renowned feature among modern readers, the letter by Alexander Hamilton. The famous essay by "a Youth of this Island" described the fifteen-year-old's experience in the hurricane that had hit the island and changed the course of his life. In the letter, the brilliant future US treasury secretary asked, "Hast thou no feelings for the miseries of thy fellow-creatures?" He referred to the white residents to whom the storm had delivered "ruin and confusion on every side."[79] Hamilton's writing inspired people in Christiansted to invest in his university education in New York.

The editor Daniel Thibou considered Hamilton's letter as a human-interest story that would find resonance with the newspaper's white subscribers. He did not hold the same expectations for the articles he featured about members of the African diaspora. The same edition informed the Cruzan population that three unrelated men, named Mocco Sam, Superbus, and Quamina, had escaped enslavement on three different estates. Similar to Hamilton, the three African-descended colonists took a risk on relocation in pursuit of better lives. Thibou headlined the front page with pitiable accounts of a Black woman named Sara, "several very good House Negroes," "several very good Negroes," and "thirty to forty very valuable Negroes."[80] The presentation evoked no empathy from the white readership. As cries for liberty spread across the Atlantic, commercial brokers used advertisements in the periodical to traffic African bodies to their white neighbors through public auctions in Christiansted and Frederiksted.

Back on Saint-Domingue, the fugitive freedom seeker Toussaint was eventually returned to the plantation. Two years later, in 1774, Toussaint endured the painful grief of being orphaned as an enslaved adult after the death of his father, named Hyppolite, and his mother, named Pauline. They were members of the Allada nation (today, in Benin). Both parents died months apart from a chest infection.[81] It remains unclear how Louverture, four years after his escape, achieved freedom by the year of American independence. His cohort of free Dominguan men of color in the 1770s included future Haitian revolutionary and state leaders like André Rigaud, Henry Christophe, Jean-Baptiste Chavannes, and Jean-Baptiste Belley.[82] These three men and the teenage Christophe later traveled north during the US War of Independence to augment the white American military campaign during the Siege of Savannah. During that period, Louverture purchased his first parcel of land, a small lot in Haut-du-Cap, in the same general area where he had been born and enslaved. It was his home. His parents had died there, and his siblings still lived there. On that land, a free Louverture enslaved Jean-Baptiste, a man from West Africa. He later manumitted Jean-Baptiste to allow the latter to begin his married life as a free husband. The future leader of the Haitian Revolution also rented from another free Black man, Philippe-Jasmin Désir, a coffee plantation on which he enslaved thirteen African-descended people.[83]

The spirit of rebellion across the 1770s nurtured dynamic aspirations toward personal freedoms and collective liberty and equality across the western Atlantic world. White Americans transitioned from a rebellion in print to armed continental warfare as enslaved people creatively gained freedom in Saint-Domingue and free gens de couleur negotiated the fluctuating racist strictures on racial equality. Within a generation, the scenes of revolutionary violence that unfolded in Boston, New York, and Savannah occurred similarly in Cap-Français, Port-au-Prince, and Léogâne. Important Atlantic military generals with American names like Washington, Henry Knox, and Benjamin Lincoln would be joined by Haitian revolutionary counterparts Louverture, Rigaud, and Christophe.

Around the time church records in Le Borgne described Toussaint Louverture as a free Black man of the Atlantic world for the first time, white British patriots, including John Adams, arrived in Philadelphia representing their respective colonies at the most significant session of the Second Continental Congress.[84] The topic of discussion involved the method of achieving a collective liberty for portions of the North American population. As a result of their decision in what Joseph Ellis has termed the "Revolutionary Summer," many of them soon became national leaders.[85] The future of the American nation weighed on them. On Wednesday, 3 July 1776, from Philadelphia, Adams wrote to his wife, Abigail, "Yesterday the greatest Question was decided, which ever was debated in America, and a greater perhaps, never was or will be decided among Men." The delegates passed a unanimous resolution—with the New York delegation's abstention—"that these united Colonies, are, and of right ought to be free and independent States." Since the Stamp Act, white colonists from Savannah to Portsmouth had protested, assembled, written, boycotted, vandalized, and died, increasingly as a collective, in resistance against British imperial efforts to impose its fiscal, political, and military will on the North American territories. Finally, in Philadelphia, the colonial delegates decided independence from monarchical rule offered the best hope to achieve liberty for free Black and white people who onward would be identified as Americans. As John Adams informed Abigail, "You will see in a few days a Declaration setting forth the Causes, which have impell'd Us to this mighty Revolution."[86]

Adams served as a Massachusetts delegate to the Second Continental Congress, an unsurprising choice given his involvement in events leading up to the break of independence. For a year, he and his fellow delegates had debated the question of a national identity for white subjects living in the thirteen British North American colonies. On Tuesday, 2 July 1776, the Congress voted "That these United Colonies are, and, of right, ought to be, Free and Independent States; that they are absolved from all allegiance to the British crown, and that all political connexion between them, and the state of Great Britain, is, and ought to be, totally dissolved."[87] The vote for American independence gave birth to a new nation-state in the Atlantic world. Adams suggested to his wife back home in Braintree that the unprecedented moment in international history "[would] be celebrated, by succeeding Generations . . . as the Day of Deliverance . . . solemnized with Pomp and Parade . . . from one End of this Continent to the other from this Time forward forever more."[88]

Adams possessed every right to be "transported with Enthusiasm" regarding independence. From the time of the Stamp Act, Adams had given much thought and lent his superior intellectual and writing skills to advancing the arguments against excessive taxation toward the creation of a new nation. According to an early biographer, by the spring of 1776, on the question of independence from England, "Mr. Adams knew no middle course."[89] In May, Congress took actions that Adams later "considered as an Epocha, a decisive event." Congress adopted a resolution to "best conduce to the Happiness and Safety of their Constituents in particular, and America in general." Several days later, Adams presented, and Congress adopted, a preamble to the previous resolution that advised throwing off loyalty oaths and revoking imperial authority in any colonial government. James Duane of New York described the resolution and Adams's preamble as "a Machine for the fabrication of Independence." To Adams, the two votes "were independence itself."[90]

John Adams had given many speeches during the sessions on the floor of the Congress in Philadelphia. But on Monday, 1 July 1776, "the greatest and most solemn debate was had on the question of Independence." He

Figure 4.5. Signing of the Declaration of Independence, 1817. Painting by John Trumbull. Courtesy of the New York Public Library.

confided to his diary that John Dickinson of Pennsylvania "had prepared himself apparently with great Labour and ardent Zeal, and in a Speech of great Length, and all his Eloquence," to oppose independence. Adams, "after waiting some time, in hopes that some one less obnoxious than [himself]" would rise to answer Dickinson, "determined to speak."[91] He felt "ashamed to repeat what [he] had said twenty times before, and [he] thought nothing new could be advanced by [him]."[92] He considered the entire debate "an idle mispence of time, for nothing was said but what had been repeated and hackneyed in that room before, a hundred times, for six months past."[93] He felt that repetition likely diluted the power of his statements.

Adams's Congress colleagues viewed his performance differently.[94] Thirteen years later, George Walton of Georgia vividly recalled Adams's speech for independence as "a scene which [had] ever been present in [his] mind." Richard Stockton, upon his return to New Jersey, described Adams to his twelve-year old son as "the Atlas of American independence. He it was who sustained the debate . . . by the force of his reasoning."[95] Thomas Jefferson, commemorating his former colleague's floor speech, remembered Adams as "[their] Colossus on the floor. Not graceful, not elegant . . . he yet came out with a power, both of thought and of expression, which moved [them] from [their] seats."[96] According to biographer David McCullough, when American independence was ultimately decided in Philadelphia in July 1776, "it was John Adams, more than anyone, who had made it happen."[97] Decades later, Adams himself conceded, "I wish Some one had remembered the Speech, for it is almost the only one I ever made that I wish was literally preserved."[98]

To the south of Philadelphia, in Port-au-Prince, the *Affiches Américaines* had followed and reported on developments of protest and rebellion in British North America. In the latter half of 1776, the *Affiches* concluded that the American rebels had achieved dominance across the continent. On 3 July, the newspaper quoted a London source who shared that in the metropole "there was no more talk of reconciliation with the Americans." The day before, although the Dominguan population did not yet know it, the Continental Congress delegates had voted to fight for the liberty they reasoned could only be achieved through independence. The same print edition also reported that thirty men and women of the African diaspora had recently liberated themselves by fleeing enslavement across Saint-Domingue.[99] Even for a colony with one of the larger enslaved populations in the Caribbean, the reporting in a single newspaper issue of thirty Black people who exercised self-liberation was remarkable.

Two weeks after the Continental Congress published the US Declaration of Independence, the Cap-Français edition of *Affiches* wrote about the publication and popularity of Thomas Paine's pamphlet *Common Sense* while incorrectly crediting authorship to John Adams.[100] Earlier that year, Adams had lamented to William Tudor, "It has been very generally propagated through the Continent that I wrote this Pamphlet."[101] However, he could not help but to boast unabashedly to his wife, "Altho I could not have written any Thing in so manly and striking a style, I flatter myself I should have made a more respectable Figure as an Architect, if I had undertaken such a Work."[102]

There is no record in the Caribbean newspaper of the US Declaration of Independence. It did, however, detail the spring 1776 movements to encourage local governments across the "united-colonies" to throw off monarchical legitimacy and create representative governing bodies. The paper also detailed resolutions passed in Massachusetts and South Carolina to support moves in the Continental Congress. The Southerners resolved not to negotiate separately with British officials. Their fellow revolutionaries in New England lamented, "The hopes we had of the king's help [toward reconciliation] have long vanished." The *Affiches* writer concluded that as the years of tension advanced and mutual angst escalated, the greatest, irreparable insult the British made toward the Americans was in responding to grievances by trying to put "things back on the footing where they were in 1763." He recognized that relations between the colonists and the metropole had deteriorated irrevocably since the Treaty of Paris, and he correctly concluded, "The colonists were fighting for independence and would not put down their weapons until they had achieved it."[103] This analysis would later apply to the Dominguan revolutionary events in the 1790s that established an independent Haiti.

In 1776, however, the people of Saint-Domingue were trying to keep up with the pace of events thousands of miles away. The paper recorded in French the important resolution passed by the Fifth Virginia Convention, presided over by Edmund Pendleton. On 15 May, the convention "resolved unanimously that the delegates appointed to represent this colony in General [the Continental] Congress be instructed to propose to that respectable body to declare the United Colonies free and independent states absolved from all allegiance to or dependence upon the crown or parliament of Great Britain." More than a recitation of revolutionary rhetorical fervor, the resolution assented to proper and necessary actions "by the Congress for forming foreign alliances." The Virginians understood that the survival of their new nation required Atlantic world allies. In the expectation that Congress would declare independence, they formed a committee to prepare a state-level declaration of rights "to secure substantial and equal liberty to the people."[104] The optimism was rewarded a few weeks later, when their delegate Richard Henry Lee, on their instructions, moved Congress to declare the colonies free and independent, to form foreign alliances, and to develop a plan of government. The Virginia resolution laid the foundation for the eventual draft of the Declaration of Independence that John Adams would champion to a unanimous affirmative vote. The Dominguan newspaper ensured that its Afro-Caribbean and white readers stayed current regarding American moves toward throwing off British imperial rule. Stories of the American Revolution circulated among Saint-Domingue's free and enslaved population from its rhetorical beginnings in the 1760s through military advances toward independence until, finally, the diplomatic conclusion with the Treaty of Paris of 1783.

After the pivotal year of 1776, colonists in Saint-Domingue continued to read about the developments in the US War of Independence. Early the following year, the *Affiches* dedicated two full pages to the military clashes between imperial forces and the Continental Army occurring across North America.

In one battle along the Potomac River separating Virginia from Maryland, a patriot unit scored a victory over troops led by Lord Dunmore. In relaying details of the British defeat, the story noted the abandonment of artillery and munitions, as well as of the formerly enslaved Africans who had fought with the redcoats in the hope of achieving freedom. Instead of escaping aboard ships alongside the evacuating army, the Black Loyalist soldiers were taken into custody by American soldiers.[105]

The newspaper writer dedicated a large section of the story—spanning an entire column—to the American war's residual effects on the Caribbean. The assembly of Barbados expressed to King George "the difficulty of the suffering white inhabitants of the island, who in great numbers" found it difficult to support their families.[106] A decade before, the white colonists of Barbados had refused to support the Stamp Act Congress assembled by the North American rebels. Their refusal to join fellow colonists in resistance to royal actions drew the ire of John Adams's quill. He unflatteringly described the decision by the island's white colonists to surrender their rights for their loyalty to the Crown as a "base Desertion of the Cause of Liberty."[107] After the Declaration of Independence, the British rules and navy prohibited the planters in the Caribbean from trading with their once fellow subjects of the realm in the previous thirteen colonies. Because North American commercial ties were so important to Barbados, the planters "had no other resource for provisions, which, for some time, arrived most irregularly, and in very small quantities." Therefore, they could not provide the Black people they enslaved with adequate food supplies and had to endure watching them starve to death.[108]

The paper's reporting assured Dominguan residents that American citizens would never again return to the status of subjects. According to the *Affiches*, "The hope of a reconciliation of Great Britain with its Colonies, which the widespread rumors have given birth to, is absolutely illusory." To secure this sentiment in law, the Continental Congress, as the newspaper reported, "declared as traitors to the country, and enemies of the freedom of America, all who would put forward the slightest proposal for accommodation with Great Britain." It was also in this *Affiches* edition that the people of Saint-Domingue first saw the name of their new, and only, nation-state neighbor in the western Atlantic world: "the United States of North America."[109]

Edward Stevens, the King's College alumnus, delighted in the use of the new nation's name. In a letter from Edinburgh, by way of France, he congratulated his fellow Cruzan and lifelong friend Alexander Hamilton "on the late successes of the United States against their tyrannical adversaries." Some three thousand miles away from the fighting in New York, Stevens composed a missive that benignly expressed a longing to return to the US, informing Hamilton of his achievement in September 1777 of "the degree of M.D." and offering praise to his friend, also twenty-two years old, on being "exalted to the Rank of Col[onel] and Aid de Camp to general Washington" to work alongside John Laurens of South Carolina and Marquis de Lafayette. Stevens and Hamilton had left Saint Croix as teenagers to pursue professional achievements and elevated social status in the United States. Within short order, educational pursuits and the American war had propelled the ambitious Cruzans toward their objectives. Still, Stevens criticized Hamilton for not writing: "Has your Anxiety for publick Affairs entirely eradicated from your Mind all remembrance of your private Concerns?"[110] He could not appreciate the deprivations of the combat theater from his academic environment in Scotland, where he completed an influential dissertation on gastric digestion and a prize-winning research paper on the color of blood.[111]

Stevens had heard about the "capitulation of Gen[eral] Burgoyne" in October 1777 at the decisive Battle of Saratoga. Diplomatic historians consider the Saratoga victory to be crucial in convincing France to recognize an independent United States and ally militarily with the new nation against its Atlantic nemesis Great Britain. By the time Stevens's letter arrived, his friend was encamped at Valley Forge, Pennsylvania, where over the brutal winter, as many as two thousand Continental troops died from disease and malnutrition, giving Washington's army there the highest mortality rate of any Continental Army encampment. Stevens's letter articulated pride in Hamilton's military service "in Defence of the glorious Cause" and communicated his "hope to see America (one of the) most flourishing Republics in the World."[112]

The aspirations for the infant United States articulated by the Caribbean native echoed those of Thomas Paine, whose writing the year before had inspired British subjects across the thirteen colonies "to form the noblest, purest constitution on the face of the earth." He argued compellingly, "We have it in our power to begin the world over again." White American colonists had worked together since the Treaty of Paris of 1763 to usurp their imperial masters, from whom they had inherited economic strength, cultural foundations, racialized perspectives, and the revolutionary thoughts that inspired their independence movement. They established a lone Atlantic republic in an international regime that European monarchies controlled using military might and economic leverage. They pushed Enlightenment ideas to the very brink of truly extraordinary revolutionary action. Paine, suggesting US independence as an Atlantic exemplar, urged the revolution's leadership toward greater social progress. He wrote, "The birthday of a new world is at hand, and a race of men, perhaps as numerous as all Europe contains, are to receive their portion of freedom."[113]

The American Revolution endowed US leaders with the power to abolish the enslavement of African people in the new republic, grant citizenship to free people of color, and expand the rights and political standing of women of all complexions. John Adams in the summer of 1776 contributed his exceptional writing and oratory skills to the efforts to secure a passage of the Declaration that signaled to Atlantic world nations that the United States "have, and of Right ought to have full Power to make War, conclude Peace, establish Commerce, and to do all the other Acts and Things, which other States may rightfully do."[114] Unfortunately, white American leaders, on the threshold of a revolution, chose instead to retreat to the safer confines of traditional racialized and patriarchal power structures.

Chapter 5

"Articles of Entangling Alliance"

1776–1778

US diplomacy during the American Revolution endeavored to be revolutionary. John Adams and members of the Continental Congress sought to break from the European balance-of-power model that dominated the Atlantic world's economic and military affairs throughout the eighteenth century. Adams later told the Dutch government that, on 2 July 1776, he and fellow Continental Congress delegates "pass[ed] that memorable Act, by which they assumed an equal Station among the Nations."[1] The Americans challenged the methods and modes of Atlantic diplomacy at the moment of independence. But the harsh realities of the United States' desperate need for diplomatic recognition and its fledgling position as an embryonic nation enticed American leaders toward the familiar European balance-of-power foreign policy.

The Declaration of Independence was as much an international statement to Atlantic world powers as it was a statement of rights to its domestic population. Since at least Lexington and Concord in April 1775, if not before, the thirteen colonies of British North America, connected by the Continental Congress, had waged open rebellion against the European imperial structure. Throughout the remainder of that year, each side scored military victories and suffered setbacks. In the minds of many colonists, there was only one viable way forward: separation from the metropole. That perilous route required foreign alliances and international commercial partnerships to establish and maintain national sovereignty. In *Common Sense*, Thomas Paine urged his fellow dissatisfied colonists to declare independence. In the pamphlet's penultimate sentence, he concluded, "Under our present denomination of British subjects, we can neither be received nor heard abroad: The custom of all courts is against us, and will be so, until, by an independence, we take rank with other nations."[2] For Paine, independence and diplomacy were inseparable. Once unfettered from Britain, Americans would need to fend for themselves among empires.

Members of the Congress in Philadelphia shared the writer's view regarding the importance of an effective foreign policy on their march toward liberty. Three months before Paine published his famous essay, Adams, as a congressional delegate from Massachusetts, addressed the important questions of diplomacy and trade in a letter to a trusted friend back home. His written inquiries and analyses exhibited a solid grasp of the diplomatic challenges that faced a colonized people proposing to live in defiance of an Atlantic hegemon. If Congress dared to send foreign representatives to European governments, he asked, "is there a Probability, that Our Ambassadors would be received, or so much as heard or seen by any Man or Woman in Power at any of those Courts." Congress and colonists were yet unclear about what an American foreign policy would encompass. He posed other pressing questions: "What then can We offer? An Alliance, a Treaty of Commerce?" Of one thing Adams was certain: prospective allies, specifically France, would require American sovereignty, a commitment to live free of British power.[3]

The move toward American independence, from the vantage point of contemporary congressional documents and correspondence, had proceeded across the early 1770s deliberately without haste. In Saint-Domingue during that period, the French king offered gestures of reconciliation toward colonists to tamp down the lingering tension from the 1769 Revolt. The British king, by contrast, made no effort to mend the broken relationships with the thirteen colonies. Consequently, the Continental Congress assembled in the summer of 1776 to establish an independent nation with bilateral alliances and free trade relationships.

As American leaders looked to diplomacy and warfare to secure liberty, their Dominguan counterparts resorted to primeval punishments to deter collective acts of Black resistance. In Philadelphia, Adams constructed a foreign policy model to win France's alliance and to protect his nation's sovereignty. Throughout the year 1777, newspapers across the western Atlantic world covered the innovative and intriguing diplomatic maneuvers of Ben-

"Articles of Entangling Alliance"   157

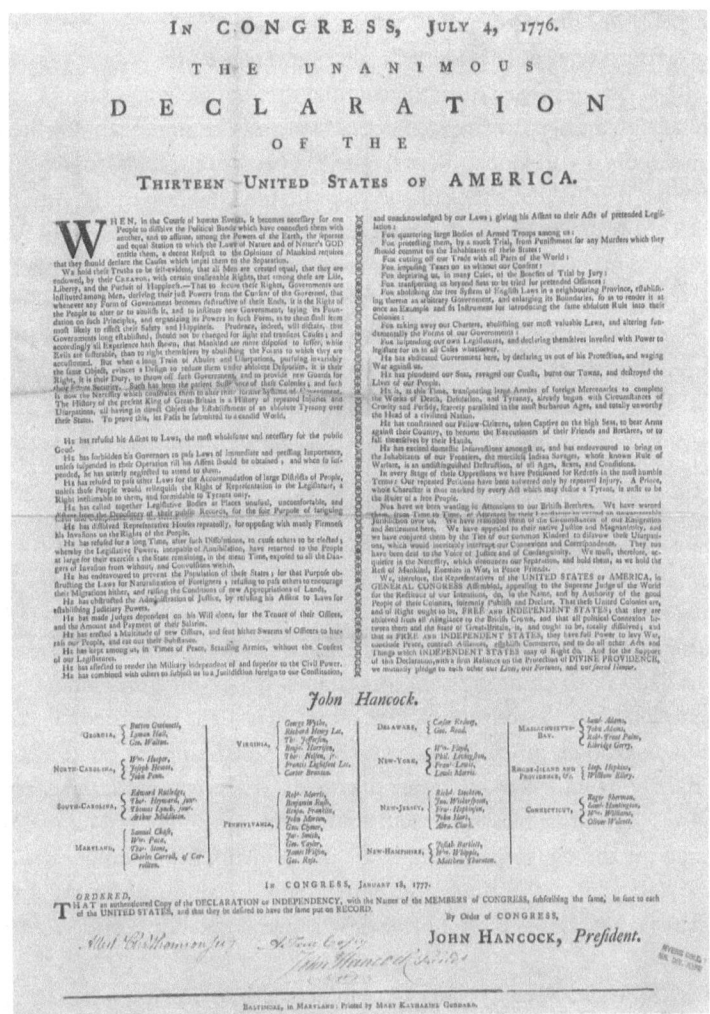

Figure 5.1. Declaration of Independence, 1776. Courtesy of the New York Public Library.

jamin Franklin, who served as the chief US negotiator in Paris. Fifteen years, almost to the day, after the Treaty of Paris of 1763, which ended the Seven Years' War, the United States and France signed an accord that effectively reignited hostilities between Britain and France, as an indispensable means to safeguard the independence of the United States. In the process of asserting their independence, leaders in the United States debated how best to convince France to take their side. They weighed France's insecurities and desires, all stemming from the 1763 Treaty of Paris, into their calculations about what to offer or exclude in an alliance agreement.

John Adams emerged from the summer of independence and diplomacy in Philadelphia as a powerful intellectual leader of the American Revolution. Up until then, his provincial New England appearance and his candid, sometimes disagreeable demeanor did not capture the attention of the American public (or historical scholarship) as much as fellow founders George Washington, Thomas Jefferson, and Benjamin Franklin did. No extant record has been found of Adams's extraordinary "Atlas of American independence" speech given to the Continental Congress on 1 July 1776. Therefore, his accomplishment in pertinaciously advocating for the passage of the Declaration of Independence is eclipsed by Jefferson's eloquently written words that continue to be read by thousands each year in the rotunda of the National Archives in Washington, DC. Becoming the nation's second president, in Washington's shadow, is not as remarkable as being the first.

Regarding diplomacy, Franklin's flamboyance and adeptness always outshone Adams's intellectual depth in the field. Still, scholars acknowledge John Adams's foundational and lasting achievements in American foreign policy. According to one biographer, "The 'Plan of Treaties' constitutes Adams's greatest and most enduring congressional work."[4] Noted diplomatic historian Samuel Flagg Bemis suggested that his treaty plan "furnished the model for all, except one, of the eighteenth-century treaties of the United States, and may be regarded as a charter document of early American maritime practice."[5] The principles, spirit, and tenor of foreign policy that John Adams outlined for the United States in 1776, at the nation's founding, remained critical determinants in the establishment and execution of US diplomacy across two centuries and multiple conflicts until, arguably, World War II.

Adams's forays into foreign policy began before 1776. In November 1775, he seconded a floor motion for the Congress to send envoys to France with conditional instructions. The proposal, made by Samuel Chase of Maryland, came well before the American rebels had determined to pursue irreversibly the path toward sovereignty. A vigorous debate led to the motion's defeat.[6] On the same day, Congress formed the Committee of Secret Correspondence to actively answer Adams's questions about what European nations would need in order to form the necessary alliances for the colonists to achieve their revolutionary objectives. The committee members were Benjamin Franklin, John Dickinson, Benjamin Harrison, John Jay, and Thomas Johnson.[7] From the questions raised by Adams and Congress's investigatory endeavor came the US diplomatic corps.

Both Congress and France moved purposely to establish a clandestine alliance. Several months earlier, the French foreign minister Charles Gravier de Vergennes had dispatched Julien-Alexandre Achard de Bonvouloir as a government agent to open secret communications with the Congress.[8] Before this assignment, Bonvouloir had served in a French military unit stationed at Cap-Français. During a trip to the colonies, American officials unsuccessfully sought to enlist his services in the rebel army.[9] Within a few weeks of the committee's creation, Franklin and his colleagues met three times with Bonvouloir.[10] During the same period, two French officers, Pierre Penet and Emmanuel de Pliarne, arrived in Providence, Rhode Island, from Cap-Français to meet with American leaders about aiding the rebel cause. They met with General George Washington in Boston before making their way to Philadelphia. There, Congress received the French agents and accepted their offer of arms and munitions.[11]

The international audience and resonance of the Declaration of Independence was not an afterthought. Well before taking the formal, irreparable step of independence, Congress understood the need for international support of its cause. The members consciously and consistently assigned Adams and Franklin to committees that created the foundations of American foreign policy. Adams understood the French as the key foreign ally needed to secure American independence. But the colonists, including Adams, suspected French intentions toward their revolution, especially since officials in Paris had long held territorial interests in North America. Congress and General Washington considered the potential threat of France using the revolutionary upheaval in North America as cover to invade and overtake the thirteen colonies from its Caribbean territories.[12]

American fears of a French invasion were not without foundation.[13] Newspapers reported that France had stationed twenty thousand soldiers in Saint-Domingue. Since its defeat in the Seven Years' War, the French king had fortified French West Indian colonies with a greater military presence to deter attacks from the British. Uncertain of French intentions, Washington asked if the French would act as a friend or foe of the revolutionary cause. No assurances from France relieved the suspicions of the military commander or the Congress. Americans lived with the fear of a French invasion from Saint-Domingue along their southern coast for the next half century.

Beyond the fear of France, Adams also understood the importance of the western Atlantic world to French imperial ambitions. Caribbean colonies like Martinique, Guadeloupe, and Saint-Domingue provided great wealth and military leverage to the Parisian metropole. To his diary, he posed a question regarding how war between the American colonies and Britain would affect French interests in the Caribbean.[14] Would the military buildup and modernized fortifications that successive French governments had foisted on Saint-Domingue since 1763 prove adequate to preserve French power and authority in the region? Versailles was concerned about the readiness of its Caribbean territories to withstand a British invasion.

The American example of open rebellion gave the monarchy additional concern about the loyalty of French colonists in the western Atlantic world. King Louis XVI took a curious step to ease colonial-imperial tensions in Saint-Domingue. He pardoned Jean-Pierre and François Mallet and vacated their convictions for the crime of sedition.[15] Seven years earlier, the Royal Council of State in Port-au-Prince had characterized the white Dominguan brothers as leaders of the 1769 Revolt.[16] In fact, Afro-Caribbean leaders, including Jacques Delaunay and François Boisrond, and white inhabitants shared command authority throughout the rebellion.[17] Dominguans across races and economic statuses fomented and fought in the revolt, which was sparked in part over colonists' opposition to imperial changes to the structure and service obligations of West Indian militias.

Governor-General Charles Henri Hector d'Estaing had implemented the changes on behalf of the king after the first Treaty of Paris. The interracial insurrection shook royal officials and disconcerted colonial administrators. Jean-Pierre and François Mallet, along with their Revolt coleaders, were convicted of treason and condemned to be hanged publicly.[18] The Mallet brothers, unlike the leaders of color, had escaped the island and were sentenced in absentia. They witnessed their coleaders being sentenced to death before fleeing to Jamaica, continuing to other foreign colonies, and then living as fugitives abroad into 1776.[19] Delaunay and others were hanged in accordance with the judgments.

The king's writ of pardon acknowledged that, indeed, the Mallet brothers had committed treason against the crown. It reasoned, however, that the rebels' actions, in some ways, reflected the sentiments of "the Inhabitants of the Colony generally opposed to the re-establishment of the Militias." King Louis XV had authorized the militarization plans after the humiliating negotiations for the Treaty of Paris of 1763. His power in Saint-Domingue survived the 1769 Revolt. He punished the leaders brutally and conspicuously in France and across Saint-Domingue. American newspapers printed stories of his retribution. In 1773, perhaps as he saw the advent of renewed warfare with Britain, Louis XV imposed on his prosecutors general and his judges in Saint-Domingue a gag order regarding all actions relative to the 1769 Revolt.

The actions of Louis XVI continued his late father's strategy. The writ of pardon suggested he preferred to bestow "mercy" instead of adhering "to the rigor of the Law." The order also stated rather clearly the king's overall intent. He wished to erase in Saint-Domingue "the slightest memory of the mentioned unrest, as well as the damage caused by its occurrence." The king also intended the pardon of the insurrectionists to express royal appreciation for the subsequent healing effected "by the zeal that the Inhabitants of the said Colony [had] shown over the past several years in the service of the Militias."[20]

By the mid-1770s, the outrage and bloodshed of the 1769 Revolt had given way to a renewed commitment to patriotic militia enlistments. In particular, Afro-Caribbean men pursued military service as an opportunity to prove that they deserved to be treated equally as citizens of the realm. In some ways, moves by Dominguan administrators toward increasingly racist changes to societal norms heightened support among the population of color for the king's colonial militias. He, therefore, chose to mitigate the risk of lingering embers of bygone strife that could disrupt colonial cooperation with the metropole.

Saint-Domingue, the French Caribbean colony closest to North America, lay one thousand miles from Savannah, Georgia, four hundred miles from the British-held Bahamas, and just over a hundred miles from Jamaica, the crown jewel of the British West Indies. Adams reasoned that if the North American colonies and the Crown reconciled their differences, "a British Fleet and Army united with an American Fleet and Army . . . might conquer all the French Islands in the W. I. in six Months." Moreover, a combined expeditionary force would take less time "to destroy all their Marine and Commerce."[21] France would consider such a development catastrophic to its strategic outlook. French officials desired desperately to increase their standing in Atlantic world power and trade vis-à-vis Britain. The territorial and commercial losses incurred at the hands of the British in the Treaty of Paris concessions remained fresh in their minds and shaped their global strategy.

The separation of the rich North American colonies provided French strategists a prime opportunity to shift the balance of power in Atlantic trade and military supremacy. In the spring of 1776, Congress debated making more direct overtures to the French. Adams calculated how to establish a Franco-American diplomatic alliance and enlist the French navy and military against Britain forces without suffocating American sovereignty in its infancy. He asked the existential question for a band of colonies seeking to depart one imperial power structure with the aid of another: "What Connection may We safely form with her?" In response, he scribbled the foundations of a plan to approach France, which was substantially more militarily powerful and more diplomatically skillful, with an offer of alliance. Adams's first rule was straightforward: "No Political Connection. Submit to none of her Authority." This priority exhibited his—and the colonists'—desire to safeguard the sovereignty Americans were attempting to secure. Second, Adams sought that there be "No military Connection," that the colonies "Receive no Troops from her." Third, and probably the most clearly articulated and explained plank of his musings on foreign policy, Adams wanted Congress to seek "Only a Commercial Connection, i.e. make a Treaty, to receive her Ships into our Ports." According to his reasoning, the Americans would provide only commercial goods to France, and the French would furnish [the US] with Arms, Cannon, Salt Petre, [and] Powder."[22]

A review of his diary reveals that Adams likely wrote down the notes on foreign policy as draft remarks for a congressional speech of which no record was made. These top principles that Adams defined for avoiding political and military connections with prospectives allies in the eighteenth century would eventually serve as a bedrock objective of US foreign policy for nearly two centuries. He envisioned the Congress offering France its long-sought-after moment to strike a blow against Britain in return for a treaty of diplomatic recognition and a commercial partnership with the Atlantic world's newest nation-state, which held immense resources and had proved its capacity to generate wealth. His plan would supply General Washington with many military materials, provide international standing for the would-be national leaders, and protect American sovereignty. George Washington's famous stance against foreign entanglements, expressed in his Farewell Address, had precursors in Adams's revolutionary thought.

In June 1776, the work of establishing the principles of independence and articulating a national foreign policy doctrine began in earnest. The Continental Congress resolved to appoint a committee "to prepare a declaration to the effect of the said first resolution" presented by Virginia delegate Richard Henry Lee.[23] The month before, the Virginia Convention advised Congress to declare the colonies free and independent, to form foreign alliances, and to develop a plan of government. The committee to prepare the foundational document of US sovereignty, on which sat Adams, Franklin, and Thomas Jefferson, drafted a declaration that underscored the importance of international affairs to American independence, basing it on language in the Virginia resolution.

On 1 July, when Congress debated the committee's draft, Pennsylvania delegate John Dickinson argued against the supposition of the necessity of American independence as a prerequisite to gain foreign alliance and aid.[24] Adams's rebuttal framed the proposed declaration, in part, as a foreign policy document necessary to secure the French alliance to achieve a US victory in its war for survival against Britain. As a member of the special Committee on Treaties, he had demonstrated that he possessed as adept an understanding of Atlantic foreign policy, and particularly of the interests of France, as that of any other delegate. Adams's argument won the day. The penultimate sentence of the Declaration that Congress approved on 2 July 1776 announced that the United States of America, "as Free and Independent States, they have full Power to levy War, conclude Peace, contract Alliances, establish Commerce, and to do all other Acts and Things which Independent States may of right do."[25]

Modern scholars of the early American republic and of international affairs concur with Adams's grasp of the diplomatic necessity of the Declaration. Without diminishing the importance of the document's commitment to inalienable rights, recent historical literature discusses the Declaration as a mover in revolutionary diplomatic alliances and as an international model across the age of revolutions. Foreign policy expert Robert Kagan describes the Declaration as "America's first foreign policy document."[26] The Declaration, as its drafters had hoped, provided France a necessary international legal basis to recognize the colonists' revolution and establish a lucrative bilateral trade partnership. The unanimous vote in Congress to separate from Britain launched the rebellious colonists into the Atlantic arena of war, politics, and trade. The American leaders braved the storm of war and diplomacy, but not "in a skiff made of paper," as John Dickinson had portended. Rather, their decision to evoke independence exhibited a shrewd understanding of the European balance-of-power structure.[27] Adams later told a Dutch merchant he had been "educated from the Cradle" to determine Britain's "important Weight in the Ballance of Power in Europe against France."[28]

Congress's vote transformed a local skirmish of disgruntled colonists into a war with international ramifications waged by citizens to repel the brutality and excesses of an invading power. For historian David Armitage, the global impact of the 2 July decision was immediate: "It announced the entry of the United States into international history. The very term, 'United States of America,' had not been used publicly before its appearance in the Declaration." Armitage argues further that the work of concurrent committees to draft the Declaration, the Model Treaty, and the Articles of Confederation reveals Americans' intent "to set up central institutions for the conduct of vital domestic and foreign affairs." Congress's appreciation for the diplomatic implications of independence can be seen in its prioritization of establishing a US foreign policy. Again, Armitage suggests that placing the 2 July vote in Congress in conversation with the longed-for Franco-American treaties provides a more adequate method "to grasp the original meaning of the Declaration."[29]

The Declaration's publication yielded immediate strategic and economic dividends for the new country. As early as 19 July, newspapers across the United States began reporting, "By a Vessel from Cape Francois, we learn that the French at Hispaniola are determined not to suffer any American Vessels to be seized within their Limits, by any English ships."[30] In preparation to exploit the geopolitical ripples to be made across the Atlantic world by the US War of Independence, French military leaders deployed thousands of troops to Saint-Domingue.[31]

American newspapers printed the narrative from an Englishman on the island: "The French are mounting their guns everywhere, and building new fortifications in several places. . . . Powder is now in great plenty." France revived and augmented its plans from the 1760s to fortify and militarize its Caribbean territories to prepare for a subsequent war with the British. The American Revolution set the stage for a rematch of the warring European powers. According to the Englishman, "The people here are all for the Americans, and last week the [governor] general ordered all the ports of this island to be opened to ships of every kind."[32]

To secure a formal diplomatic alliance with France, Congress appointed a committee "to prepare a plan of treaties to be proposed to foreign powers." The Committee on Treaties members were Adams, Benjamin Franklin, John Dickinson, Benjamin Harrison, and Robert Morris.[33] Adams and Franklin emerged as two of the more important individuals in the history of the early United States' foreign policy and diplomacy overtures. In the previous year, Franklin had served on the Committee of Secret Correspondence and met with French agents as Adams sketched a plan for American engagement with France. The two men worked together on the Committee of Five to draft the Declaration at the same time they were collaborating on the plan of treaties.

The Committee of Five had chosen Jefferson to take the lead role in drafting the Declaration. In similar fashion, Committee on Treaties members selected Adams for the task of drafting America's first foreign policy strategy. He was acknowledged, even by opponents like Dickinson, as one of the new country's finest minds in the study of international affairs.[34] As he wrote, Franklin made some notes on "a printed Volume of Treaties" and offered them as suggestions.[35] Two weeks after Congress published the Declaration, Adams submitted to Congress a first draft of the Model Treaty "between the most Serene and mighty Prince, Lewis the Sixteenth, the most Christian King his Heirs and Successors, and the united States of America."[36] The committee's mandate was to prepare a plan of treaties for all nations. But the author and fellow committee members understood their primary audience to be the king of France. Over the next two months, Adams, the Committee on Treaties, and Congress debated different points and revised drafts of the plan.

Adam was the lead author of America's first draft diplomatic treaty. His vision embodied only minimal terms of connection with France. His written proposition seemed to follow the three principles he had laid out as notes for a floor speech on foreign policy earlier in the spring. Despite its humiliation from the Treaty of 1763, France remained the Atlantic world's second most powerful nation. US leaders, appreciating their precarious position, feared the prospect of throwing off one king only to become subject to another. But they also needed a powerful ally. Better than most, Adams understood how much the United States depended on French diplomatic recognition, steady financial assistance, and naval support. In exchange for these elements essential to his country's survival, Adams offered King Louis only a commercial connection between their two states, hoping that would strike the right balance between alliance and autonomy. Congressional members, however, opposed the treaty draft because it "held out no sufficient temptation to France, who would despize it and refuse to receive [the US] Ambassador."[37] They believed France would require some significant diplomatic or military assistance from the United States, beyond commercial agreements, to achieve its objectives in financing, recognizing, and securing American independence. Adams had emerged as "our Colossus on the floor" of Congress when advocating for the drafted Declaration of Independence.[38] In debates over the Model Treaty, he recalled, "it was chiefly left to [him] to defend [his] report."[39] He remained steadfastly confident in the emergent power and undeniable commercial richness of the new republic as sufficient lures to French diplomatic compliance.[40] He was proud that his argumentative and oratorical skills repelled the "Many Motions [that] were made to insert Articles of entangling Alliance" into his simple proposal. Adams defended his work "with so much Success that the Treaty passed," on 17 September 1776, "without one Particle of Alliance, exclusive, Priviledge, or Warranty."[41]

Though Adams prevailed in the debates over the treaty, members of Congress remained unconvinced that his design, without an entangling alliance, would achieve US diplomatic objectives. Therefore, a week after accepting the Model Treaty, members of Congress agreed to diplomatic instructions authorizing its commissioners "to use every Means in [their] Power for concluding" a treaty with France. They understood, as Adams had argued for the last year, that the survival of their national independence was dependent on France and its active involvement in the revolutionary experiment. Congress expected the envoys to advocate for an alliance based on the Model Treaty. However, they left the door open for modifications, saying, "If you shall find that to be impracticable, you are hereby authorised to relax the Demands of the United States, and to enlarge their Offers."[42] The Committee on Treaties took the lead in constructing the instructions for the commissioners. Debates and revisions continued between committee members and Congress until the approval of the instructions on 24 September.

Article 8 of the adopted treaty language remained a major area of contention and became a singular target for discussion. Revised during earlier debates with Adams, the resulting Article 8 that the envoys were instructed to present to the French during the treaty negotiations stated, "If, in Consequence of this Treaty, the King of Great Britain, should declare War, against the most Christian King, the said United States shall not assist Great Britain, in such War, with Men, Money, Ships, or any of the Articles in this treaty denominated Contraband Goods."[43] In essence, if, after the French king signed the treaty and recognized the United States, to Britain's detriment, Britain declared war on France, the US would not aid Britain, but it also would not aid France. In return for international legitimacy, the United States promised its most significant partner military neutrality. Some members remained unconvinced—as Adams was confident—that neutrality provided an attractive enough incentive to secure the necessary Franco-American alliance. Adams kept the United States from offering too much too soon.

The final instructions acknowledged to the commissioners, with some understatement, "The eighth article will probably be attended with some difficulty."[44] During the debates, members offered several follow-up suggestions for the commissioners in the event that the king refused to agree to the article. One proposal, from Richard Henry Lee, exhibited appreciation for France's long-held desire to regain the territories ceded after its humiliating military defeat and the resulting Treaty of Paris of 1763. He proposed, "These United States will wage the war in union with France, not make peace with Great Britain until the latter France shall gain the possession of those Islands in the West Indies formerly called Neutral, and which by the Treaty of Paris were ceded to G. Britain; provided France shall make the conquest of these Islands an early object of the War and prosecute the same with sufficient force." Lee's option went well beyond Adams's threshold of entangling alliances and was defeated. Another, more restrained suggestion proposed, "If [France] should undertake an Expedition to recover what she lost in the West Indies during the last War with G. Britain the United States will, in that Expedition, supply France with Provisions if required, and will not supply G. Britain with any."[45] Congress rejected that proposal as well.

Adams again won the debate over the diplomatic instructions. The final version of the instructions to the commissioners for Article 8 represented a return to Adams's original intention as expressed in his first draft, which had been altered during the congressional debates. If France did not accept American neutrality—in response to an inevitable Franco-British war—as an incentive for bilateral relations, the wordy suggested alternative, written by George Wythe, pledged, basically, that the United States would not give up its fight for independence or enter into a peace treaty with Britain without notifying and including France. In the end, however, the concerns of the Continental Congress about the limitations of the Model Treaty proved to be well founded.

Adams had debated congressional colleagues throughout the summer of 1776 to secure passage of the Declaration of Independence as an effective foreign policy document and to protect the integrity of his draft language laying the foundation of US diplomacy. Congress deliberated, and Black inhabitants across the Atlantic world worked to expand access to freedom in the revolutionary era. As white men in Philadelphia argued over white colonists' liberty, white men in Cap-Français decided the freedom status of a Black woman. According to legal records, Ahyssa had been born free in Senegal and had been "kidnapped and trafficked" from there to the Caribbean island of Grenada. A European man named François C. took part in the kidnapping and brought Ahyssa illegally to Saint-Domingue. Her enslaver died from self-inflicted wounds in 1774, but he left a will that granted freedom to Ahyssa. However, the estate executor sought to sell her as a mixed-race concubine. The council in Cap-Français ruled that the white executor had the authority to sell into concubinage a free African woman whom a deceased Dominguan resident had kidnapped, trafficked, and mistreated. Ahyssa appealed the decision, claiming her freedom as a Moor, a member of the North African Muslim peoples. Médéric Louis Élie Moreau de Saint-Méry, a twenty-five-year-old racist, slaveholding, white French Freemason, acting as Ahyssa's lawyer, appealed the case directly to Governor-General Victor-Thérèse Charpentier.[46] The day before Bostonians were informed of American independence as Tea Party participant Thomas Craft read aloud the Declaration from the State House, Ahyssa learned that Governor Charpentier had rewarded her relentless legal efforts by declaring her a free woman and ordering her captors to set her free.[47]

One hundred miles west of Boston, Lemuel Haynes learned of the Declaration and its far-reaching implications for the Atlantic world. The words of Thomas Jefferson regarding liberty and happiness in life moved Haynes deeply. John Adams passed the revolutionary summer in Philadelphia drafting and defending the Model Treaty. Haynes spent that summer writing a declaration of freedom for enslaved peoples. As a Christian man of color and former indentured servant, he empathized with the suffering of African-descended people whose personal freedom and human dignity white Atlantic inhabitants routinely abused and violated.

Across the United States, people of the African diaspora, free and enslaved, made a myriad of personal choices about how to pursue personal and collective freedom as the American Revolution evolved. Haynes chose to continue contributing his intellectual and literary talents to the American cause. In 1775, in addition to serving in the military, he penned the song "The Ballad of Lexington" to commemorate the efforts of his fellow colonists to resist with collective force British imperial domination. A year later, after the publication of the Declaration, Haynes, a revolutionary militia veteran, cited the founding document's claim to a self-evident truth "that all men are created equal" as the basis for his manuscript *Liberty Further Extended*. In the volume, Haynes went beyond Thomas Jefferson's most memorable phrase to suggest, "I think it not hyperbolical to affirm, that Even an affrican, has Equally as good a right to his Liberty in common with Englishmen."[48] Within only weeks of Congress's vote for independence, the Declaration transcended the bounds of parchment to become the symbol of universal freedom in ways its slaveholding author likely never imagined. As John Adams solidified the Declaration's importance as a foreign policy document in his construction of the Model Treaty, Haynes interpreted its theories of individual freedom to argue that there existed no distinctions in human freedom.

For Haynes, there was no white freedom without Black freedom. In fact, he used neither parable nor metaphor to state clearly, "Therefore we may reasonably Conclude, that Liberty is Equally as pre[c]ious to the *Black man*, as it is to a *white one*, and Bondage Equally as intollarable to the one as it is to the other." He and fellow African-descended writer Phillis Wheatley had grown up in Massachusetts in differing forms of Black servitude, and both held strong Calvinist beliefs. In the ballad, Haynes contrasted freedom to bondage and argued strongly that honor lay in dying for freedom over enslavement. He and Wheatley both viewed the American interpretation of natural rights as a biblical precept. Haynes's theology empowered his reasoning that "Liberty is a Jewel which was handed Down to man from the cabinet of heaven, and is Coaeval with his Existence." To those who sought to employ the Bible to justify slavery, he responded, "There is Not the Least precept, or practice, in the Sacred Scriptures, that constitutes a Black man a Slave, any more than a white one." He considered it an act against God's sovereignty for one human being to deprive another of their freedom. For him, Christianity held no place for white supremacy or enslavement based on ethnicity. He asserted: "God has been pleas'd to distiungs [distinguish] some men from others, as to natural abilitys, But not as to natural *right*, as they come out of his [God's] hands."[49]

By all accounts, Haynes received relatively fair treatment as a servant in the Rose household and had access to education, which was atypical of the lived experiences of many servants and enslaved peoples of African descent across North America. The area where he lived, western Massachusetts, revolved around an agricultural and labor-intensive economy. He witnessed the cruelties of slavery and the racist indignities that the region's 250 residents of color endured. The lines of inquiry throughout his manuscript exhibited an inclination to identify with Black people and a capacity to empathize with the pitiable harms European inhabitants committed against them. Haynes comprehended slavery as an inherently racist endeavor. Therefore, he asked, "Shall a mans Couler Be the Decisive Criterion whereby to Judg of his natural right? or Because a man is not of the same couler with his Neighbour, shall he Be Deprived" of basic human dignities, courtesies, and freedoms? He refused to accept Blackness as a marker of natural inferiority. He boldly posed a fundamental query: "Whence is it that an Englishman is so far Distinguished from an Affrican in point of Natural privilege?" Haynes asked the basic question at the heart of racists' unfortunate beliefs: What made (or makes) any white person better than any Black person? In the response to his question, he diagnosed the root problem of slavery: the assumption of white supremacy. As he saw it, the proponents of slavery lived by an unholy "Bost of some hygher Descent that gives [them] this pre-heminance." He considered it "Lamentable" that proslavery people "[had] an insatiable thurst after Superorety [Superiority] one over another."[50]

Liberty Further Extended unequivocally condemned wholesale trafficking by Europeans of human beings from the African continent. Imperial and colonial assemblies passed laws and regulations to provide a semblance of legality to the international practice of kidnapping and transporting African children, women, and men across the seas. White newspaper editors across the Atlantic offered legitimacy to the sale, purchase, and leasing of Black bodies as if they were animals or inanimate commodities. Yet Haynes gave no quarter to the racist normalization of the slave trade. He characterized the European systemization of physical, emotional, spiritual, and cultural destruction of Black persons and societies as "man-stealing." Those who participated in, supported, and benefited from slavery, according to his understanding of the Bible, were "to Be punished with death." God did not create people from Africa and their progeny to be enslaved. To be most clear in his argument, Haynes reminded the reader that "the main proposition" was "that an African, or, in other terms *that a Negro may Justly Chalenge, and has an undeniable right to his Liberty: Consequently, the practice of Slave-keeping, which so much abounds in this Land is illicit.*"[51] Haynes put forth some of the first, strongest, most direct writing against slavery by a man of color in the eighteenth-century United States. However, the treatise inexplicably remained an unpublished manuscript until recovered in the late twentieth century.[52]

After drafting his abolitionist declaration, Haynes reenlisted in the American military. He joined the Continental Army as a private and marched northward with the Hampshire County regiment to reinforce American troops at Fort Ticonderoga in upstate New York.[53] Disappointed with his nation's crimes of slavery and its racist restrictions on freedom, he remained simultaneously patriotic and critical. Just over a year apart, between his military deployments to Boston and then Ticonderoga, Haynes wrote "The Ballad of Lexington" and *Liberty Further Extended*. An examination of the two writings allows scholars, as historian Rita Roberts puts it, "to trace the progression of one Black Revolutionary War soldier's political consciousness from seemingly uncritical patriotism as a Minuteman in 1775 to virulent criticism when he became a Revolutionary War soldier in 1776."[54]

Haynes served on station at Fort Ticonderoga in October and November 1776. His military service to the American Revolution ended when he contracted typhus, as many US soldiers did, and returned to Granville.[55] During the period of Haynes's deployment, a council of European men in Saint-Domingue convicted and condemned five Afro-Caribbean men and women for an alleged conspiracy and murder of their white enslaver, named

Poncet. The alleged conspirators came from different communities within the African diaspora. Saintonge, deemed the group leader, and Boussole were Black men. Sannitte, the cohort's only woman, was classified as *quarteron* (or quadroon), signifying mixed-race parentage, with one-quarter African ancestry. Paul and Etienne had recently been forcibly brought from Africa.[56] The manner of and motive for Poncet's death were not reported. Earlier in the year, as John Adams, in Philadelphia, drafted his personal notes on US relations with France, enslaved people had escaped on separate occasions from Poncet's grasp. The *Affiches Américaines* newspaper reported that a Black man, Valentin, fled the plantation in the northeastern region around Fort-Dauphin (today Fort-Liberté). A month later, a Black woman, Jeannette, escaped bondage from the same estate. Both freedom seekers were members of the Nago (Yoruba) people. Before their flight from captivity, Poncet had had his name branded into their skin with a hot iron.[57]

In fall 1776, the Superior Council of Cap-Français sentenced the Afro-Caribbean people condemned of murdering Poncet to extraordinarily cruel and unusual punishments. Saintonge and Boussole were ordered, first, to confess and ask forgiveness before having their hands cut off. Then, their bodies were broken on the wheel while they remained alive. After they died from the torture, their bodies were exposed publicly along the road leading to the Poncet plantation. Sannite received a small measure of grace in her sentence. When officials determined she was pregnant, they suspended her sentence until after she gave birth. The council ordered "that the Sacrament of Baptism will be administered to the infant before the execution" of the mother. Sannite was then publicly hanged at Fort-Dauphin.[58]

Alleged coconspirators Paul and Etienne received relatively light sentences. Still, the judicial guarantors of the slave system ensured that psychological trauma was inflicted on the accused Africans. They were forced to attend the executions of their codefendants with a noose tied around their own necks. The high executioner then branded the letters G A L into the skin on their right shoulder, before locking them away to serve as convicts for life. The branding of letters G A L into the skin of French prisoners signified the status of *galérien*, a galley slave. Ancient Mediterranean countries customarily sentenced condemned criminals to row in the war galleys of the state. In the sixteenth century, France adopted the practice.[59]

The horrific methods of punishment meted out to members of an Afro-Caribbean group condemned for murdering one white slaveholding planter were comparable to penalties for crimes involving mutiny or treason against the crown. The severe nature of the sentences resembles what had been perpetrated on the condemned leaders of color from the 1769 Revolt. Nearly two decades before, the Cap-Français council sentenced the self-liberated African-descended spiritual leader Makandal to be publicly burned at the stake for suspicion of leading an insurrection against white colonial rule. More famously, fifteen years after the Declaration of Independence, the Superior Council of Cap-Français convicted Vincent Ogé and Jean-Baptiste Chavannes, free men of color, of insurrection and ordered their bodies to be publicly dismembered and dishonored. After the rebels of color died by hanging and were made the first martyrs of the Haitian Revolution, the executioners severed their heads and placed them on spikes in a prominent section of the city.[60] In the fall of 1776, as Americans committed more fully to global diplomacy and armed conflict in their bid for independence from imperial subjugation, officials in Saint-Domingue brutally punished Afro-Caribbeans who defied the colony's slavocracy. The heinous acts, under the cloak of justice, were carried out publicly as a conspicuous deterrent against Black resistance to the rule of white supremacy in the Atlantic world.

This was a widespread Atlantic world issue, as slavery and its brutal consequences affected colonists in the Caribbean and North America. In his writing, Lemuel Haynes underscored the horrific cruelties that slavery sanctioned Europeans to exact with impunity on African descendants. He lamented that when Black people "have manifested a Diposision [Disposition] to rise in their Defence, they have Been put to the most Cruel torters [tortures], and Deaths as human art could inflict." Haynes also argued that enslaved people "had as a good a right to rise in Defence of their own Natural rights and Libertyes as a man would have to repel the assaults of an hyghway robber."[61]

In December 1776, five months after the Continental Congress published the Declaration of Independence, Benjamin Franklin, one of the most formidable citizens and astute diplomats the United States has ever produced, landed in France.[62] The United States government, in its first major foreign policy endeavor, appointed three commissioners, Franklin, Silas Deane, and Arthur Lee, to negotiate the Model Treaty with France.[63] Besides Franklin and a few others, most US leaders had never traveled outside the continent. With their actions, influential founders like John Adams worked to put into practice theories and principles they had heretofore studied in books. For instance, the Swiss international affairs thinker Emmerich de Vattel was a favorite of American leaders. His 1758 book *The Laws of Nations* had informed the tense debates between Adams and Congress members over the construction of American foreign policy.

Not everything, however, could be decided by the book. In an attempt to prevent precipitous hostile action between Britain and France, Congress members decided to manage the diplomatic mission as a covert operation. They resolved that "until permission be obtained from Congress to disclose the particulars of this business, no member be permitted to say anything more upon this subject, than that Congress have taken such steps as they judged necessary for the purpose of obtaining foreign Alliance." Carrying out the ad hoc dictates of the nation's first official diplomatic mission, Congress formally granted the commissioners "full power to communicate, treat, agree and conclude with his most Christian majesty, the king of France . . . a firm, inviolable, and universal peace" and resolved that they, as representatives of the United States, "would live in such stile and manner at the court of France, as they may find suitable and necessary to support the dignity of their public character" at the expense of Congress.[64] After weeks of rigorous debate over the Model Treaty's instructions to the commissioners, Congress members proved astute enough to understand that the on-the-ground situation in Paris would unfold much more dynamically than the theorized models of diplomacy they had discussed in Philadelphia.

Within days of Franklin's arrival, one year after he first met secretly with French agents in North America, he met French foreign minister Charles Gravier, comte de Vergennes, at a secret session in Paris. Deane and Lee also attended the meeting, but it was clear from the outset that Franklin served as America's chief representative abroad. The opening session, unfortunately, yielded little for the US mission. Franklin presented the minister with a copy of the Model Treaty that proposed a bilateral relationship anchored in commercial connections. The French were recognized leaders in eighteenth-century international diplomacy. Vergennes, a seasoned negotiator dating to the 1740s, would not surrender France's valuable leverage—recognition and alliance—to America's relative neophytes after one meeting. He complimented Franklin on his presentation and demeanor during the conversation. The Americans, however, left the meeting with only Vergennes's pledge to consider the US position more fully when it was submitted in writing.[65]

The following week, the commissioners secured a second meeting. Acknowledging that the Model Treaty had not garnered French interest, Franklin acted on Vergennes's suggestion to prepare a written memo. In it, Franklin requested thirty thousand muskets, ammunition, and artillery, plus the loan of French navy ships. The memo also proposed that, in exchange for France joining the American cause, the US would support France in retaining all its Caribbean territories and, more importantly, augmenting its

Figure 5.2. Charles Gravier de Vergennes. Portrait by Edme Bovinet, 1785. Courtesy of the Library of Congress.

empire with territories there that Britain would lose in the war. Franklin was well aware of French ambitions to use the US War of Independence to shift the post-1763 balance of power in the western Atlantic world. He sought to advance Franco-American talks beyond pleasantries and platitudes by offering US support for French territorial expansion in the Caribbean. Franklin's move well exceeded the diplomatic instructions Congress had spent weeks debating and amending.[66]

Franklin, with a sense of urgency for the plight of his country, pushed the French a bit too fast and forcefully. His memo contained a clumsily worded threat that if France did not ally with the United States, the precarious position of the new nation would force the Americans to seek an accommodation with Britain. Such a scenario would deny France its best opportunity since the Seven Years' War to gain a strategic advantage over its European nemesis. The latter move proved to be a tactical overreach. In response, Vergennes gave Franklin what one historian describes as "a schoolboy's lesson in diplomacy." The foreign minister understood, likely better than anyone, the Americans' desperate military and economic needs in the war they had waged with the Atlantic superpower. As the quintessential diplomat, Vergennes used his undersecretary Conrad-Alexandre Gérard to explain the naivete of American demands for traceable means of assistance, such as artillery and ships. Such a move on France's part would be interpreted by Britain as a declaration of war.[67]

Despite the verbal setback, Vergennes recommended that King Louis XVI approve the American commissioners' request for financial assistance. The secret payment of two million French livres (roughly $300,000) kept the negotiations going.[68] The Americans, however, continued to push the French for more decisive action. Franklin wrote to Vergennes with renewed requests for an open alliance. He also restated the threat that America's weakness could lead its leaders to reconcile with Britain.[69] Louis and Vergennes were unmoved.

Back home, Congress's plan to keep the US diplomatic mission a secret fared as poorly as its initial overtures to the French. By early February 1777, American newspapers were reporting the arrival of Franklin in France. Rumors about the nature and scope of his visit began circulating immediately thereafter. Citing a letter from Bordeaux, the *Essex Journal* reported that his "business, which must certainly be very important, [was] matter of great speculation among the French."[70] One newspaper listed Franklin's first Paris residence at "the Hotel d'Entragues, in Tournon street."[71] Another reported that Lee, Deane, and Franklin—evidently not so secretly—"[had] already negotiated a loan of two million of livres, for and on account of the United States."[72] It was unlikely that the most famous American would enter the French capital unnoticed. Some one hundred stories about Franklin in France appeared in newspapers across the United States during the spring of 1777.

Franklin was, from one account, "most graciously received by His Majesty and the Nobility in general."[73] The mention of the French aristocracy helped to ease the concerns of some Americans about how Europeans would perceive their new status as independent, national citizens. A Pennsylvania publication went even further, informing readers that their chief diplomat in Paris "[was] visited by many of the first rank of all nations" and "and treated with all the respect shewn to European Ambassadors."[74] The *Providence Gazette* printed an unpublished excerpt from the Bordeaux letter saying, "The people at large here are all our friends," and the correspondent asserted, "The government of France are disposed to favour us."[75]

The *Affiches Américaines* in Saint-Domingue also covered the diplomatic mission of Franklin. The editors put stories together from London

Figure 5.3. Franklin's reception at the court of France, 1778. Lithograph by Anton Hohenstein. Courtesy of the Library of Congress.

dispatches, letters from France, and the spread of news by word of mouth in Dominguan port cities. The Port-au-Prince edition followed Franklin from his arrival at the western French city of Nantes through his sojourn in Paris. It portrayed Franklin as an effective emissary for the American states. It addressed him consistently with the honorific "docteur Franklin" and informed readers about his multilateral correspondence and official actions around Paris.[76] In one issue, the newspaper reported that the Marquis de Lafayette had met with Franklin before his departure to join American forces in the US War of Independence. The two men agreed the "young officer," upon arrival at American shores, should plan to raise and lead an infantry corps, "which would bear his name."[77]

The Cap-Français edition of the *Affiches* offered its readers a British view of Franklin in France. Not surprisingly, little about his diplomacy was reported from that perspective. Instead, one English story lampooned the dress and coiffure of French women to take a swipe at the flamboyant American. The writer referred to "le *Solon* de l'Amerique (Franklin)" (the wise legislator of America [Franklin]), to mock the chief US diplomat's reputed penchant for frequenting the country's elaborate fetes.[78] Another story featured a pamphlet from a British author addressed to King George, expressing the futility of attempting to recolonize an independent United States. The report suggested, "France is entirely determined a make with the Americans treaties of alliance & commerce." When that happened, the pamphlet argued, the American people would gravitate toward France and away from Britain: "They will send their children to France to be raised and to learn French, as Franklin already did." The English writer, instead of acknowledging Franklin's diplomatic prowess in moving the French government toward a bilateral alliance, chose to focus on Franklin's famous social and cultural presence in France.

Even in American newspapers, British perspectives attempted to downplay Franklin's popularity or undermine publicly the American mission in Paris. One US newspaper's characterization that "the English ambassador look[ed] on him [Franklin] with a jealous eye" may have been exaggerated.[79] But British correspondents, indeed, misrepresented Franklin as "promising not to trouble himself with any public affairs, and declaring that he [was] entirely devoted to the King of England."[80] Another article alleged, "We have the strongest Assurances, that Dr. Franklin's Residence in Paris, is merely an Act of Self-Policy."[81] In fact, Franklin's residence served as the first American embassy in Paris. The more moderate *New-York Gazette* readily gave voice to British correspondents who "believed that Dr. Franklin [would] not succeed in the object of his coming to Paris,"[82] as "the French Court, so far from treating with him, look[ed] down upon him with the most sovereign Contempt."[83]

American writers also produced their share of embellishment. Clearly intending to enflame anti-British sentiments, a Boston newspaper alluded to an uncorroborated letter that "mention[ed] that the British ministry intend[ed] totally to destroy the New-England States, and make slaves of the southern."[84] Much of the press's aggrandizement centered on Franklin's capacity to move the French. One correspondent rightly expressed confidence that Franklin's "superior abilities and experience [would] probably at this juncture be of the greatest advantage to America."[85] As one journal reported, "Great respect is paid him." But a general belief articulating "that whatever the Doctor ask[ed] of the court of France, [would] be readily granted him" proved unfounded.[86] An early prediction was that "the arrival of Dr. Franklin [would] probably hasten" France's entrance into the war against Britain.[87] The collective impression from the newspapers of Benjamin Franklin's diplomatic prowess raised American hopes regarding French involvement in the US War of Independence.

However, as many in Congress had predicted, the king and foreign minister balked at the Americans' offer of French military assistance in exchange for neutrality and access to American commerce only. The Model Treaty that John Adams had drafted and defended proved inadequate to achieve America's strategic objectives. This setback, along with successive British military victories and the deteriorating state of the Continental Army, pressed Congress to reexamine its foreign policy.

American leaders became progressively more desperate to secure a Franco-American pact. In March 1777, the commissioners received expanded instructions from Congress empowering them to offer the French direct US assistance in conquering the British West Indian islands in exchange for military assistance. The change shifted US diplomacy well beyond the scope of the Model Treaty. The alterations also vindicated legislator Richard Henry Lee. He had argued in September 1776 that Congress should offer American support for French ventures in the Caribbean. Yet the French government continued to rebuff US overtures toward bilateral relations even after the envoys presented the amended proposals. Franklin and his fellow commissioners settled in for the long game. The talks stalled, and news from North America offered few reasons to hope for progress.[88]

Throughout his time in France, Franklin understood that his physical presence, professional achievements, and cultural persona created for the Parisian court and population a tangible image of the newly created United States, its novel republican government, and those curious Atlantic world inhabitants known since July 1776 as Americans. As diplomatic negotiations came to a standstill, Franklin leaned on his personal renown to garner goodwill for his country. A major impediment to US diplomacy in the nation's first year was the Continental Army's inability to convince European powers that it could muster more than temporarily sensational guerrilla attacks against the Atlantic world's most formidable army. Its debilitating defeat at the Battle of Long Island and its leaders' sustained tendency toward retreat lowered the French public's already skeptical opinion of the American cause. Steady reports of the army's dismal performances, carried in newspapers aboard ships crisscrossing the seas, drained needed political capital from the commissioners as they approached French foreign ministry officials. Eschewing humility, Franklin embraced his standing as the best-known person in the Atlantic world, besides French writer Voltaire, to salvage the US's prestige. He exploited the Parisian fascination with his life as a venerable printer, philosopher, philanthropist, and patriot to the advantage of his country's ailing foreign policy campaign.[89]

John Adams had provided the document to initiate the Franco-American negotiations, which ultimately proved fruitless. With little help from George Washington's lackluster battlefield results, Franklin pivoted to an ad hoc, eighteenth-century form of public diplomacy to cultivate French opinion. He activated the dinner table at the US embassy as an instrument to sustain perceptible forward momentum in the talks toward a bilateral alliance. He hosted seemingly endless rounds of dinner parties to transmit his message that the US could win the conflict and stood poised to privilege France in a robust postwar commercial relationship. His primary audience included members of the French nobility who calibrated their attitudes in connection with the relationships they cultivated. Franklin transformed embassy soirees into living theater for noblemen, like Jacques-Donatien Le Ray de Chaumont, with access to the court. He played the principal actor before aristocratic influencers of public opinion.[90]

As the year advanced with no movement in the Paris talks, the American financial situation weakened and the public's outlook for success dimmed. The US commissioners' appeals to Vergennes for monetary assistance went unheeded. In the fall, Arthur Lee related to Chaumont his frustration over the slow French responses to American entreaties. He voiced his concern over "how they [the United States] could go to war without money."[91] Lee later shared with Franklin and Deane a paragraph in a letter from his brother, the influential Congress member Richard Henry Lee, affirming his fears that unless they secured an alliance with France and, more immediately pressing, "a considerable loan to support their funds, it would be difficult to maintain their independence."[92]

In December, Franklin's public diplomacy campaign and American outlooks for victory received a significant boost when news arrived in Paris that the Continental Army had won its first major victory over the British military. Seven weeks earlier, 3,500 miles west of the French capital, in the woods of upstate New York, US forces under General Horatio Gates had forced General John Burgoyne to surrender an imperial army for the first time in British history. The Battle of Saratoga victory dramatically transformed the bargaining position of the US commissioners in Paris almost overnight. Two days after hearing the news, Vergennes, after tabling the Model Treaty for a year, asked the American diplomats, through his undersecretary Gérard, to resubmit their proposal for a bilateral alliance.[93]

The US victory at Saratoga ranked as newsworthy across the Atlantic world. The editor of the *Affiches Américaines* in Port-au-Prince used an American-based source to publish a story on the important moment in the long progression of the American Revolution. Though the newspaper offered Dominguan readers extensive coverage of the US War of Independence, most related articles were based on dispatches from London, Paris, Brussels, or Amsterdam.[94] Therefore, much of what the Dominguan population learned from the newspaper about the American Revolution, whether positive or negative, was gleaned from a European perspective.

After the Declaration of Independence, the United States began trading directly with Saint-Domingue. Merchants in North America quickly began exchanging commercial goods with their keen Caribbean counterparts. Ships sailing from Boston, Philadelphia, Charleston, and Savannah carried, along with clothing, manufactured goods, and salted fish, another commodity popular along the wharves of Cap-Français and Port-au-Prince: direct reports regarding the war, diplomacy, and life in America from sea captains and crews.[95] Subsequently, readers in Saint-Domingue began to receive European and American perspectives of the momentous military conflict that would soon arrive at its shores. Only five days after Vergennes received the news about the surprising US triumph at Saratoga, the *Affiches* reported, "We hasten to give the public an excerpt from the *Boston Gazette* that we have just received, which mentions the capitulation agreed upon between [British] General [John] Burgoyne & [US] Major-General [Horatio] Gates."[96] It dedicated the next full page to reprinting the official articles of surrender.

Some historians have centered the US military action as the catalyst for the Franco-American alliance. In the 1870s, historian Thomas Balch described Saratoga as the reason that moved Louis XVI to grant "the entreaties of his ministers and of Franklin."[97] The position is buttressed by contemporary newspaper reports "that after the news of General Burgoyne's defeat, affairs took a new and very favourable turn, especially in France."[98] The victory in New York afforded the US greater esteem among its cynics at Versailles. Other scholars focus more on the diplomatic calculus of Vergennes and the work of the American diplomats.[99] Franklin, early on in the mission, told foreign ministry officials that if France rebuffed the bilateral alliance, the weaker US would be forced to end the war and reconcile its relationship with Britain.[100] He understood that Vergennes feared an Anglo-American rapprochement.[101] An American defeat would embolden the British Empire to attack France's holdings in the Caribbean, including its most valuable sugar colony, Saint-Domingue.[102]

Foreign Minister Vergennes, therefore, assessed a myriad of the fluid economic, military, and diplomatic determinants. He concluded that the American cause in the wake of Saratoga presented the kingdom of France the most opportune moment since 1763 to vigorously pursue its supreme geopolitical goals. Five previous ministers had served as France's chief diplomat since the humiliating treaty ending the Seven Years' War was signed in Paris. Fifteen years later, he possessed the opportunity to direct a strategy to restore French imperial power across the western Atlantic world. During the winter, Vergennes counseled the king to transition French engagement with the Atlantic war from surreptitious aid for the Americans to open conflict with the British.

Historian Larrie D. Ferreiro suggests, "The French-American alliance was agreed to not so much because Saratoga was a great American victory, but rather because Vergennes had already decided that their more numerous defeats, such as those at Long Island and Brandywine, demonstrated that despite their growing abilities, the insurgents were still likely to lose the war without direct intervention, and a reunited Britain was simply too dangerous to contemplate."[103] In that analysis, it seems Franklin's early threats regarding the possibility of the US rejoining the British Empire, despite Vergennes's stoic reception of the Model Treaty, had hit their mark.

The fuller, more expansive reason for the establishment of the Franco-American alliance likely involves varying factors affecting the ultimate outcome. The bilateral relationship provided France a long-awaited, viable opportunity to militarily pursue the nation's fifteen-year vendetta against Britain, which stemmed from the perceived wrongs of the Treaty of 1763. Doubtless, the American military victory indicated to the French foreign minister that Americans could fight capably to defeat the two nations' common foe. It suggested that France's involvement would not be wasted on Americans who might require more and more assistance in a drawn-out war. Saratoga showed that Americans were in it to win, and the American Declaration of Independence had opened the door to diplomatic cooperation in bringing forth a decisive break from Britain. Franklin, for his part, resolutely evinced the nascent US's diplomatic acumen, savvy, and grit to the French crown, the royal court, and an adoring Parisian public. The Franklin-Vergennes negotiations had been ongoing for nearly a year when the news of Saratoga arrived in Europe. In late 1777, prompted by the US military success, after having steadily and acutely taken the measure of the relatively inexpert American commissioners, Vergennes, with nearly three decades of diplomatic experience, seemed to have correctly calculated that he could move them from their government's position of a commerce-only accord.

During the summer of 1776, John Adams had convinced his colleagues in Congress to maintain his model for American foreign policy, which was based solely on economic reciprocity. His long study of international relations and a rather partisan view of US economic forecasts suggested the viability of his plan of treaties. Atlantic world conditions and American prospects for victory appeared differently two years later. Renewed talks in Paris advanced across the winter of 1778, a period that seemed more promising for US interests than when Franklin and his cohort first arrived. It remained evident to Franklin, as it had from the beginning, that the commercial treaty alone did not offer enough incentives to secure French assistance. Therefore, the commissioners offered no resistance to Vergennes's demand that a commercial treaty be accompanied by a military alliance. Franklin accepted that the proposal exceeded their original scope for diplomatic engagement, but he saw in it a necessity and an advantage for his fledgling nation.[104]

On 6 February 1778, Franklin, Deane, and Lee joined Gérard at the Hotel de Lautrec to sign the blueprint for America's first bilateral relationship. They signed two treaties. The treaty of amity and commerce followed almost exactly Adams's original diplomatic principles, known primarily as freedom of the seas, which became fundamental to later US foreign policy.[105] Its more immediate achievement was France's recognition of the United States as an independent country. The second treaty negotiated in-country by Franklin stipulated that the United States and France "[should] make [war with Great Britain] a common cause and aid each other mutually . . . as becomes good & faithful allies."[106] In addition to other provisions, it also pledged US acquiescence if France attacked and captured British colonial territories in the Caribbean.

The Declaration of Independence had succeeded in achieving its objective of securing the diplomatic recognition of a new independent nation. The commissioners in France had succeeded in this mission by believing in their cause and waiting patiently for positive changes and subsequent leverage.[107] Franklin, more than anyone, had won a diplomatic campaign equal in results to Saratoga. In an oft-repeated tribute, biographer Edmund Morgan characterized Franklin's role in the 1778 treaties as "the greatest diplomatic victory the United States has ever achieved."[108]

The Franco-American alliance established in February 1778 went against the diplomatic scope that John Adams had envisioned for the new republic confronting the Atlantic world. Before its conclusion, when bilateral talks had stalled, Congress voted to dispatch Adams to France to assist Benjamin Franklin in negotiating the treaty. He departed Boston on 13 February 1778, a week after Franklin and the others had signed the two treaties with the

French government.[109] Unbeknownst to Adams, who had been an influential revolutionary since the Stamp Act, even before he left home, his diplomatic services in Paris were no longer necessary. He landed at Bordeaux in April. By then, US newspapers had reported "that the Treaty between France & America [was] signed."[110] The earliest reports of the Franco-American alliance came from the French island Martinique, revealing "that Doctor Franklin had been presented to the King of France as Plenipotentiary of the United States; [he] had a very gracious reception, and a long conference with his Majesty."[111] One gazette's front-page story announced the most encouraging news since Saratoga: "Frances acknowledges, the INDEPENDENCE OF AMERICA."[112]

When Adams arrived in Paris, there was nothing more he could do to influence the diplomatic negotiations he had played such a pivotal role in designing. The urgency of the negotiation process had passed. Still, Adams took some solace in the fact that his ideas for US relations with France had yielded diplomatic recognition and garnered the new republic status among Atlantic powers. To his diary, he confided, "I thought the Attentions which had been shewn me . . . since my Arrival at the Capital . . . had been very remarkable and portended much good to our Country. They manifested as I thought, in what estimation the new Alliance with America was held." Vergennes, during their first meeting, told Adams he "hoped the Treaty would be agreable, and the Alliance lasting." Adams responded, "I thought the Treaty liberal and generous—and doubted not of its speedy Ratification."[113]

Scholars suggest Adams, as he had since the summer of 1776, opposed the precepts of the alliance and "blamed Franklin, among other American Francophiles," for a diplomatic strategy that required so little from France.[114] Decades later, when remembering his conversation with Vergennes, in addition to his polite statement, he admitted thinking, "Although the Treaty had gone somewhat farther than the System I had always advocated in Congress and further than my Judgment could yet perfectly approve, it was now too late to make any Objections."[115] Despite any misgivings about the outcome, Adams seemed to accept the Treaty of Alliance as a fait accompli. In a letter to Abigail, he described the alliance as "a great Event indeed in our History, which [could not] fail to have the most important and decisive Effects." He may be forgiven the indulgence of boasting to his wife a major achievement of the Model Treaty by suggesting, "The Trade between the two Countries will vastly increase and the Security of it, will make it more profitable."[116]

After Congress ratified both Franco-American treaties on 4 May, Adams, in a letter to James Warren, husband of the more famous Mercy

Otis Warren, confided, "The longer I live in Europe, and the more I consider our Affairs, the more important our Alliance with France appears to me." The confession appears to be an acknowledgment of the extra efforts Franklin took to secure French cooperation. He further described the Franco-American alliance as "a Rock upon which we may safely build."[117] Some scholars consider the relationship between John Adams and Benjamin Franklin as antagonistic or mysterious.[118] Such characterizations fail to capture the complexity and accomplishments of their diplomatic partnership. Adams prepared and proposed the first intellectual framework for approaching France with diplomatic negotiations, and Franklin built on that foundation as he dealt with real-world conditions. Both men were intellectual giants and played critical roles in the success of the American Revolution. They had worked together effectively on numerous Continental Congress ventures, including the committee that drafted the Declaration of Independence. In Philadelphia, in Franklin's presence, Adams's intellect and oratory had persuaded America's leading men to vote into existence a new nation and to sustain its independence by pursuing the Model Treaty. In Paris, however, Adams and his ideas did not fare so well. By the time of his arrival, Franklin had concluded the Treaty of Alliance. Through no fault of his own, Adams was redundant. Nonetheless, he trusted that Franklin "had generally maintained an honourable Character in the World."[119]

Adams scorned his countryman's methods and procedures. Yet, to defend his colleague's integrity against a rival's attack, he acknowledged Franklin's singular importance to the US diplomatic mission in France. Adams argued as forcefully as he had on the floor of Congress "that Dr. Franklin possessed the Confidence of the French Court and of his own Country, and held her Commission and Authority: and therefore, it was the duty of all of Us, to treat him with respect."[120] As one biographer suggests, "Despite their personal friction, Adams and Franklin were bound together by their shared patriotism and their ardor for America's independence."[121] Franklin and Adams combined mutual brilliance with differences in age and experience to establish America's first effective foreign policy–making duo. Their example would be reproduced, in part, by more famous partners like George Washington and Alexander Hamilton, then Thomas Jefferson and James Madison. The foreign policy that Adams outlined in Philadelphia and the diplomacy Franklin negotiated in Paris resulted in the Franco-American alliance that advanced the American Revolution and became a model for US engagement in transitional affairs across the next century. The consequences of the

Adams–Franklin collaborative diplomacy also played out in the Caribbean. Afro-Caribbean men from Saint-Domingue soon arrived in the United States to contribute to the fight for American independence. Their military service in allied combat with the Continental Army instructed and inspired them, within a decade, to embrace another revolution to challenge France for their colony's sovereignty and the freedom of their people.

Chapter 6

"Armed, Disciplined and Battle-Hardened"

1779–1783

In 1779, Congress appointed Benjamin Franklin as the sole US minister plenipotentiary to France. John Adams, in the meantime, awaited reassignment to another European diplomatic posting but received no word from Congress. He did not even get an official recall order. His time in Paris, however, was over. Assessing his diplomatic sojourn there, he wrote to his wife and best friend, Abigail, "I am much disappointed in not receiving Dispatches from Congress." Seeming to acknowledge professional and personal mistakes during the mission, he expressed to Abigail that "if [he could] get safe to Penns Hill," from where she and John Quincy Adams had watched the Battle of Bunker Hill, "[he should] never repent of [his] Voyage to Europe, because [he had] gained an Insight into several Things that [he] never should have understood without it."[1]

Despite his perceived missteps, Adams's Model Treaty and his presence in Paris made lasting impressions on American foreign policy. He described his contentment with the French nation and, as if to counter contemporary newspaper accounts, stated clearly, "I admire the Parisians prodigiously."[2] He shared with his wife that, in particular, Vice Admiral Charles Henri Hector d'Estaing, commander of the French naval fleet in the western Atlantic world, "[was] allowed by all Europe to be a great and worthy Officer, and by all that [knew] him to be a zealous friend of America."[3]

To reciprocate the professional admiration for one of America's diplomats in Paris, Admiral d'Estaing paid courtesy calls on Abigail Adams five months after Congress ratified the bilateral Treaty of Alliance. Abigail informed John, "I have received great civility and every mark of Respect" from the French officers, and she added, "Count d'Estaing has been exceeding polite to me."[4] With French ships harbored at Boston for repairs, the admiral and Abigail conducted an ad hoc form of social diplomacy aboard the admiral's flagship *Le Languedoc* and at the Adamses' home in Braintree. On one occasion, the ship's crew treated her to "an entertainment fit for a princess."[5] On another evening, she and her guests "were sumptuously entertained with every delicacy that this country produce[d] and the addition of every foreign article that could render [their] feast Splendid."[6] The *Affiches Américaines* newspaper informed readers in Saint-Domingue of d'Estaing's public relations campaign that included a superb banquet aboard his ship for the important ladies of Boston.[7] It was clear to colonial readers in the

Figure 6.1. Abigail Adams. Engraving from portrait by Gilbert Stuart, 1815. Courtesy of the Library of Congress.

French Caribbean that France and the new American nation were becoming fast friends.

Abigail's experiences confirmed the warm diplomatic ties. She offered John a positive review of French comportment and hospitality during their sojourn. Officers from different ships "[had] made [her] several visits" and "dined with [her]" at home, she reported. She considered Admiral d'Estaing "a most agreeable Man, Sedate, polite, affable with a dignity." She also noted "the peaceable quiet disposition both of officers and men . . . which they [had] exhibited." However, French troops did not always receive the same treatment in return. According to Abigail Adams, the required civilities expected to welcome the sailors and soldiers of a desperately needed ally in the US War of Independence "[had] been neglected in the town of Boston."[8]

A French naval officer confided to his journal the level of animosity and the overt signs of suspicion with which Bostonians approached him and his comrades.[9] Abigail's good friend, Mercy Otis Warren, explained that the Americans—Britons until 1776—and the French had been mortal enemies against each other in the Seven Years' War, which ended with the Treaty of Paris in 1763. Despite "the Wish of Mutual Confidence," she surmised, "There has not yet been time to prove the sincerity of Either party."[10] Therefore, feeling "more anxious to have them [their French guests] distinguished," Abigail put in extra efforts toward hospitality and wished "[she] had it in [her] power to entertain every officer in the Fleet."[11]

Back in Paris, John Adams recognized the diplomacy in the encounters between Abigail and d'Estaing. The Adamses as a political duo appreciated the importance of strengthened ties between the American and French peoples in their shared fight against the British.

In his letter, John commended Abigail's efforts and seconded her impressions of their country's allies and best hope for victory: "I am extremely obliged to the Comte D'Estaing and his officers for their Politeness to you, and am very Glad you have had an opportunity, of seeing so much of the French Nation. The accounts from all hands agree that there was an agreeable intercourse, & happy harmony upon the whole between the inhabitants and the Fleet, the more this Nation is known, & the more their Language is understood, the more narrow Prejudices will wear away."[12]

John Adams departed Paris in the spring of 1779. Though unable to speak passable French when he arrived, he had studied and practiced the language diligently during the mission. During his final meeting at Versailles with French Foreign Minister Charles Gravier de Vergennes, the two men had a long conversation, "in French, which [Adams] found [he] could talk as fast as [he] pleased."[13]

In the month before his departure, he reflected on his time in Paris. He recalled, with some sadness, that when he arrived, many people mistook him for Thomas Paine or Samuel Adams, his cousin, "the famous Adams." To them, "he was some Man that nobody had ever heard of before—and therefore a Man of no Consequence."[14] People knew John Adams by the time he left France.

Aboard ship, heading home, he was accompanied by the new French ambassador to the United States, Anne-César de la Luzerne. The two men talked a great deal during the transatlantic voyage. On one occasion, "the Chevalier and [Adams] walking upon deck, he took [Adams] under the arm" and began a lengthy conversation "all in French" about the Franco-American alliance, including details of forthcoming allied military engagement. Adams was very proud that some of the disappointments in France had not changed him. With Ambassador Luzerne, "[he had] conversed with that Frankness that [made] a part of [his] Character." The talk of French military strategy, however, left him with a question: "What becomes of Georgia?"[15] Adams did not yet know that, in just a few months, the bilateral diplomatic plan for which he had laid the intellectual foundation would bring hundreds of Afro-Caribbean soldiers ashore in Georgia to fight for American independence under the French flag.

As John Adams sailed westward, efforts were underway in South Carolina to make Black troops a large part of the Continental Army. US Lieutenant Colonel John Laurens was the son of former Continental Congress president Henry Laurens. The elder Laurens would serve in Paris alongside Adams and Benjamin Franklin at the future Anglo-American peace talks. The Laurens family possessed the largest slave-trading house in the United States, and in a ten-year span, the Charleston firm of Austin and Laurens oversaw the trafficking of over eight thousand African children, women, and men.[16]

The younger Laurens served on General Washington's staff with Alexander Hamilton. His observance of the African-descended soldiers of the First Rhode Island Regiment in combat persuaded him that enslaved Africans could be useful to the American cause. In May 1779, Congress, with some reluctant lobbying from its former president, approved Henry Laurens's proposal to recruit three thousand enslaved men in South Carolina and Georgia.[17] Congress stipulated that the Black soldiers would be mustered into segregated battalions and commanded by white officers. Men of color would not even be allowed to advance to the noncommissioned officer ranks.[18]

Laurens also advocated that, like the Dunmore Proclamation four years earlier, the United States grant enslaved soldiers their freedom in return for their service. However, most Southern white Americans took a different view of soldiers of African descent in the revolution. They considered the arming of Black men to be a threat to their way of life. White Americans in the Southern states lived in fear of the people of the African diaspora whom they daily abused and dehumanized. They worried that training Black soldiers and, potentially, allowing them to live freely in an independent United States would inspire those who remained enslaved to kill their slaveholders and seek their own freedom as well.

Alexander Hamilton encouraged his good friend's efforts to recruit troops, but, as a New Yorker, he held little confidence in Southerners' willingness to challenge their racist, self-interested worldviews. He wrote to Laurens, "I think your black scheme would be the best resource the situation of your country will admit. I wish its success, but my hopes are very feeble. Prejudice and private interest will be antagonists too powerful for public spirit and public good."[19] Laurens communicated with South Carolina Governor John Rutledge, who also temporarily governed Georgia, asserting, "Those very blacks which have hitherto been regarded as our greatest weakness may be converted into our greatest strength." The governor did not support Laurens's plan, and neither did the South Carolina Assembly. The legislators, many of them slaveholders, rejected the recruitment of African-descended troops, despite Congress's endorsement.[20] General Washington, who shared the slaveholding mentality, admitted to Laurens after the proposal's defeat, "I must confess that I am not at all astonished at the failure of your Plans."[21]

Washington understood what Laurens did not: that Southerners were willing to risk losing independence to the British before risking the loss of a racialized system that held tens of thousands of people in the diaspora under their unchallenged authority. Laurens's father explained the political stakes most succinctly as "certainly a great task effectually to persuade Rich Men to part willingly with very source of their wealth"[22] Still, the twenty-five-year-old Laurens believed erroneously that his slaveholding neighbors would change. He wrote to Hamilton, "That I should be inexcusable in the light of a Citizen if I did not continue my utmost efforts for carrying the plan of black levies [recruitment] into execution, while there remains the smallest hope of success."[23] Despite the racialized political disappointment in his home state, in a few months, John Laurens would find himself marching into harm's way on a Georgia battlefield, allied with hundreds of armed Afro-Caribbean soldiers from Saint-Domingue, as they faced together the redoubts and rifle fire of thousands of Black soldiers and workers fighting for their freedom in the service of the British military.

One of France's first major military engagements of the American Revolution occurred in the southern part of North America. The Chasseurs

Volontaires Battalion from Saint-Domingue, composed of over five hundred French-speaking Afro-Caribbean infantrymen, landed at Beaulieu, Georgia, on 12 September 1779. Since Lexington and Concord, Black men had been fighting in US military units during the War of Independence. From the Boston Massacre in 1770, with Crispus Attucks dying along with four others, the blood of men of color had contributed to the attainment of American liberty. The First Rhode Island Regiment, or the "Black Regiment," formed in 1775 and, with the normal strength level of 225 men, fought in about twenty significant battles and campaigns for the duration of the war.

On the British side, the Dunmore Proclamation in 1775 had inspired thousands of African-descended men to escape enslavement by Americans, to serve as successors to the original "Ethiopian Regiment," and to kill American soldiers and militiamen on the battlefield. As John Laurens discovered despondently, white Americans, to safeguard their exploitative notion of white supremacy, refused, in the face of evidence to the contrary, to acknowledge the capacity of fellow African-descended colonists, free and enslaved, to possess the skill or bravery to fight with valor. Despite their prejudice, four years into the war, the presence of Black men serving in the military was not altogether extraordinary.

However, the landing of the Chasseurs Battalion was remarkable and remains historic. It marked the first time in the Atlantic world that hundreds of people of African descent landed together on North American shores as free people, deployed to fight for the independence of others. For 160 years, since the time when twenty people of color arrived in servitude near Jamestown, Virginia, in 1619, fleets of European slave ships had ferried tens of thousands of African men, women, and children toward a lifetime of servitude in British North America. European merchants, ship captains, and enslavers considered these unfortunate African inhabitants to be articles of exchange within the commercial networks of the Atlantic trade system. Extracted violently from their peoples across Africa, millions of innocent spouses, mothers, fathers, sisters, brothers, sons, and daughters crossed the southern Atlantic Ocean—millions of others were buried in it—and eventually were led off the boats to become the perpetual captives of slaveholders. The colony of Georgia, founded in 1733, outlawed slavery in 1735. But, with the advocacy of Reverend George Whitefield and others, colonial leaders repealed the ban on African slavery in 1750.[24] Between 1752 and 1779, the port of Savannah received over 1,400 African people in bondage from Caribbean slave societies.[25]

The Chasseurs Battalion landed about twelve miles south of Savannah's port, aboard European warships, not slave ships. The soldiers of African descent disembarked in formation, not in chains. Instead of wearing filthy rags to affirm and broadcast their degradation, the Afro-Caribbean men came ashore dressed in distinctive uniforms to identify their military rank and unit. They wore the clothing and insignia of a West Indian volunteer corps, in accordance with French military regulations that stipulated an exclusive uniform for each unit. The Chasseurs Battalion was outfitted in a blue coat with a yellow collar, green cuffs, blue lapels, white buttons, and green epaulets; a white waistcoat; pants; and a black tricorn hat with a white-and-yellow plume.[26]

Unlike any other group of African people, the Chasseurs arrived armed in the United States with French imperial-issued rifles and bayonets. They had come to America on behalf of the French king to fight British soldiers alongside American rebels. But they all had individual outlooks on the war and their participation in it. Scholars continue to offer reasons to explain why the Afro-Caribbean men of the Chasseurs Battalion, some free, some enslaved, fought in the American Revolution.[27] Robert Gross's seminal history of the minutemen in New England illustrates that different men across disparate social groups—"farmboys and mechanics," the "governing elite," "young as well as old"—fought together as a unit for a myriad of reasons.[28] Different rationales and motives also existed among the groups of Black and *gens de couleur* men who fought together in Saint-Domingue's Chasseurs Volontaires Battalion. The analysis here focuses on the cohorts of free and enslaved men who sought freedom and equality as they had been doing since the 1769 Revolt. It aims to present US history readers with an expanded view of the service offered to the American cause by the Chasseurs Battalion at the Siege of Savannah, an underappreciated event that illustrates how revolutionary acts were interconnected across the Atlantic world.[29]

In some ways, John Rutledge, the slaveholding South Carolina governor who stymied Laurens's effort to recruit Black Carolinian soldiers, opened a pathway for the Chasseurs to come to America's aid. In December 1778, the British had taken control of Savannah, the southernmost US port city, which had a population of about 7,500 people, most of them enslaved Africans.[30] On 20 July 1779, Rutledge, as the acting military governor of Georgia, wrote to French Admiral d'Estaing, urging him to join the forces of US General Benjamin Lincoln in an allied attempt to wrest Savannah from British control. In a bizarre, woefully inaccurate assessment of British troop strength surrounding the city, Rutledge reportedly assured d'Estaing that "two fifty-gun frigates and a few mulattoes would be sufficient" for the success of the campaign.³¹

After receiving the letter, the French admiral and general broke off his Caribbean campaign, where his expeditionary forces had scored important victories against the British navy, and landed troops in islands like Grenada. With the aid of the Indigenous Afro-Caribbean militia on Saint Vincent, d'Estaing had retaken that island, which the humiliating Treaty of Paris of 1763 had transferred to Britain.³² On 31 August, from the flagship *Le Languedoc*, the French commander responded to Rutledge that the letter had convinced him to change his plans in order "to strike [their] common enemy with the important blow that [Rutledge had] proposed to [him]."³³ Admiral d'Estaing's decisive response and the impending landing of foreign troops in Georgia reassured Americans skeptical of French commitment to the Franco-American alliance. After his failed efforts a year earlier during the Battle of Rhode Island, d'Estaing had caused some Americans to vocally question France's earnestness in assisting the United States.³⁴

D'Estaing had landed in Cap-Français a month earlier—31 July 1779—to a hero's welcome. In a way, his appearance was a triumphant return to Saint-Domingue. He had served as the colony's governor-general for two years during the 1760s. Then, the king's council, reeling from the first Treaty of Paris's concessions of France's North American territories to the British, had tasked him and other French West Indian administrators with strengthening defense fortifications and militarizing the colonial populations. D'Estaing's moves proved widely unpopular and, when taken together with other changes across a turbulent decade, helped to sow the seeds for the 1769 Revolt. An important, additional change that d'Estaing had initiated was to establish the Chasseurs Volontaires d'Amérique, the first battalion of 550 men with African heritage organized in Saint-Domingue as part of the French regular army.

Afro-Caribbean men of different hues had faithfully served the empire within the military ranks, but not in such a distinctive unit that highlighted their Blackness. The service of Captain Etienne Auba of Fort-Dauphin and Cap-Français's Captain Vincent Ollivier dated back to the late seventeenth-century French expeditionary forces at the Raid of Cartagena.³⁵ Both men served as commissioned militia officers of color and were considered living military heroes of the Dominguan community of African heritage. There is no evidence d'Estaing used military policies to counter the increasingly racist societal changes that white administrators and planters championed between the two treaties of Paris. His mission was to enhance Saint-

Figure 6.2. Charles Henry d'Estaing. Print by Henry Bryan Hall. Courtesy of the New York Public Library.

Domingue's military posture to deter or withstand a British invasion. He, unlike many white leaders, including George Washington a decade later, valued the military skills and qualities of Black and white men equally. In addition to the Chasseurs Volontaires d'Amerique, d'Estaing also established the Légion de Saint-Domingue, an integrated unit of Afro-Caribbean and European men. Racially hostile mindsets and regulations dismantled the units after d'Estaing's departure from the island. But he had established a legacy that, throughout the rest of the century, praised and inspired Afro-Caribbean Dominguan military service.

Before his return in 1779, d'Estaing's investment in the participation of soldiers of color in the Dominguan military paid dividends for the colony and the American cause. In the wake of the bilateral Treaty of Alliance ratified the year before, the French government prepared to assist its US allies against Britain. In March 1779, Governor-General Robert d'Argout established two segregated military units. The decision resulted in the Chasseurs' identifiable battlefield achievements, imperial praise, and historical significance. Yet, similar to d'Estaing's in the previous decade, d'Argout's primary concern was not the well-being of African-descended Dominguans. Rather, his actions affirmed the colony's racist *ordre du jour* that Afro-Caribbean inhabitants could not work, serve, or exist as equals alongside their white neighbors.

Only three days before, Superior Council of Port-au-Prince members, following their counterparts at Cap-Français, passed an ordinance to remind Dominguans of mixed parentage that they were not white, a fact "many of them seemed to have forgotten." Using the threat of police detainment and imprisonment, the council prohibited people of African descent from wearing clothes that marked "a reprehensible assimilation with the way white men and women behaved."[36] France needed Afro-Caribbean men to contribute their bodies to war and to die alongside white men. Yet, on the streets of Dominguan cities, they—literally—could not wear the same pants as their white counterparts.

In an article lauding France's entrance into the US War of Independence, the *Affiches* newspaper writer expressed excitement that Saint-Domingue would do its part "to combat the enemies of the State." The newspaper reported the creation of the two units, noting that the Grenadiers "must be composed of Whites" and the Chasseurs "of free Negroes, Mulattoes, and People of color."[37] Oddly, the government stipulated that the twenty-eight drummers in the Chasseurs and the Grenadiers corps detachments be "Negroes or Mulattoes."[38] D'Argout issued the calls for enlistment in both detachments on the same day.

The *Affiches Américaines* reporter lent his prose to the recruitment effort. He asserted that "good Frenchmen, undoubtedly, did not need much prodding to exhibit their natural valor, this innate feeling to the best Nation in the world." Afro-Caribbean and European colonists responded with wildly different degrees of enthusiasm. According to the newspaper, across the colony, every day, "the most brilliant young men" signed up to serve in the expedition. It noted, "Already entire companies are formed, and they are all raring to march."[39] The assessment did not adequately describe the level of white Dominguan apathy toward the war. The Grenadiers mustered just over 150 men, out of a European population of nearly 20,000.

The colony's Afro-Caribbean men demonstrated a far superior level of patriotism and willingness to sacrifice their lives to aid the American effort toward independence. The initial decree called for one battalion of Chasseurs, divided into ten companies of free men, with about six hundred infantrymen.[40] The response from men of color across the colony was overwhelming. Some Chasseurs companies signed up as many as fifteen men a day. In the first month, 950 Black and mixed-parentage men volunteered, prompting the government to raise the cap on enlistments of color, enlarging the unit to accommodate two battalions.[41] According to French Naval Ministry records, the Chasseurs Volontaires de Saint-Domingue, at its height, consisted of 1,030 infantrymen of African descent.[42]

The example of Afro-Caribbean Captains Auba and Olliver assisted the government's recruitment push. Some of the colony's more affluent and well-educated men of any race were among the gens de couleur who volunteered to participate in the American cause for liberty. Free young men of color of Saint-Domingue with the means, like their white counterparts across the Caribbean, traveled to Europe for education and professional advancement. In fact, many of the Chasseurs were as, or more, educated and affluent as many white Americans in the South. According to the battalion commander, "The Chasseurs are nearly all property owners who have abandoned their fortune to serve the King."[43]

Dominguan men of color who enlisted as Chasseurs included Louis Jacques Beauvais, Beauregard, Jean-Baptiste Belley, Martial Besse, Pierre Cangé, Jean-Baptiste Chavannes, Pierre Faubert, Laurent Férou, Lambert, Christophe Mornet, Pierre Pinchinnat, André Rigaud, Césaire Savary, Jérôme Thoby, and Jean-Louis Villatte.[44] Free men of African descent in Saint-Domingue and the United States chose to fight in the US war against Britain, in part to prove to their island and continental neighbors that they deserved equal access to the liberties that European colonial Atlantic inhabitants sought during this revolutionary moment.

The future king of Haiti, Henry Christophe, was an enslaved man in Grenada during the war. In 1779, he had been captured by d'Estaing's squadron during the admiral's victorious battle there against the British. The twelve-year-old boy was likely pressed into service as a drummer for the Chasseurs Battalion.[45] At the mustering stations across Saint-Domingue, it was also a known secret that enslaved Africans numbered among the Chasseurs' ranks. Similar to the colony's free gens de couleur enlistees, bonded Africans sought to prove their mettle and earn their freedom though military service. Despite d'Argout's ordinance that only free men could contribute, an undetermined number of enslaved men, claiming to be free, concealed their servitude to secure a spot in the overseas military expedition.[46]

White officials played along with the ruse to sustain military readiness. The government had foreseen, and likely encouraged, the determination of enslaved men to join the war effort. In the original military regulations, d'Argout made a rather ambiguous offer that bonded Chasseurs would be granted freedom "upon return from the campaign" if given a "certificate of their good services, signed by their Corps commanders and their captain."[47] Governor D'Argout, like Lord Dunmore of the British military, appreciated the capacity and willingness of African-descended people to fight effectively for white liberty, empire, or *patrie* in exchange for freedom.

One officer, in particular, who knew about the freedom-seeking scheme was Colonel Laurent-François Lenoir de Rouvray. The thirty-six-year-old white commander of Saint-Dominguan troops became one of the colony's wealthiest slaveholding planters, and inadvertently, he also became one of most effective recruiters of men who made their way into the Chasseurs Battalion to escape his brutality. The French Naval Ministry even credited Rouvray and his efforts with the extraordinary recruiting of the Chasseurs.[48] The newspaper reported that multiple Africans escaped his captivity in search of freedom. He had literally left his mark on them, branding his name into their chests with hot irons.[49]

In one instance, Rouvray reported that "one of his Negroes, named Stanislaus," had fled his estate in the northeastern commune Terrier-Rouge as a maroon. Against Dominguan law about apparel, he departed wearing a gray frock coat and a green jacket "in the style of M. de Rouvray." Stanislaus was a skilled carpenter and coachman who had previously been enslaved to the service of former Governor-General Louis-Armand-Constantin de Rohan and other Dominguan nobility. Yet the enslaver described him as "a very dangerous scoundrel."[50]

On 16 August 1779, Colonel Rouvray and his Chasseurs Battalion departed the peaceful harbor at Cap-Français as part of the imposing twenty-four-ship armada led by the flagship *Le Languedoc* in the one-thousand-mile journey northward to wage war in British-held Savannah.[51] The Chasseurs Battalion of 545 Afro-Caribbean men made up 15 percent of d'Estaing's expeditionary force of 3,500 men.[52] Admiral d'Estaing's journal listed another 156 men of color serving as part of other French military regiments.[53] French and British accounts show that Britain's military employed some 4,000 men of African descent as soldiers, sailors, and laborers in their successful defense of the city against the allied forces.[54] The total number of Black men from the United States and Saint-Domingue participating at the Siege of Savannah in 1779 was at least 4,700 of the 13,048 men mustered on both sides of the redoubts, making it, at 36 percent, one of the largest assemblies of African-descended combatants in a major battle of the American Revolutionary War.[55]

On 12 September, the French army landed at Beaulieu, twelve miles south of Savannah. The Chasseurs disembarked on American soil and marched toward Savannah as part of the rear guard of a three-column formation.[56]

A few days later, with some 2,400 troops (the bulk of his forces encamped about three miles from Savannah), Admiral d'Estaing performed an extraordinary act of eighteenth-century military leadership.[57] He engaged in drills with the Chasseurs Battalion. To his journal he revealed, "I myself had to carry for several yards cast-iron swivel guns with small field carriages." It was not often that a commander in chief drilled with infantrymen, the lowest-ranking soldiers, and manually hauled portable cannons. Yet he had examined the terrain around the impending Savannah battlefield and surmised, "We were likely to use [the mobile gun carriages] anywhere."[58]

D'Estaing needed the Chasseurs Battalion to perform manual labor as an important part of his fighting forces. He also needed them to know he valued their service. The force commander understood the racial biases under which the Afro-Caribbean infantrymen served. Therefore, he led by example, pulling the guns "in order to convince the commander of the mulattos that yellow and black soldiers, who were being treated like musketeers, could easily perform the same task without dishonoring themselves or tiring themselves too much."[59] It is unknown what prompted d'Estaing to take the unorthodox actions.

The battalion officers may have reported to the admiral their men's concerns about being assigned to excessive work details. They may have reminded him that Article I of Governor-General d'Argout's orders governing the Saint-Dominguan Chasseurs and Grenadiers units guaranteed that both detachments "[would] enjoy the same treatment" as their brothers in arms "of the Colonial Regiments."[60] The Afro-Caribbean men of Saint-Domingue had not come to America to be worked as enslaved people. They were proud, honorable men who volunteered to risk their lives for the liberty of white Americans—and for freedom and equal treatment in Saint-Domingue.

Historical attention has been given to the Chasseurs Battalion for their brave actions securing the French army's rear guard during the eventual retreat at the lifting of the siege.[61] A newspaper also commended the actions of the infantrymen of the diaspora during the troop drawdown, "as it was glorious for them, by the dangers to which they were perpetually exposed, and by the different maneuvers with which they were charged."[62] Moreover, the work of Haitian historian Alfred Nemours draws attention to contributions that indicate "during all the operations of the Siege, the Chasseurs Volontaires, as well as the other troops of Saint Domingue, demonstrated bravery, enthusiasm, endurance, and discipline." D'Estaing wrote in his journal that "the men coming from Saint-Domingue," 85 percent of whom were

Chasseurs Volontaires, "[had] been always on duty for almost a month," both "in the heat of the day and enduring the chill of the night."[63]

The Franco-American army positioned itself a half mile outside the city. The allied order of battle positioned the Chasseurs Battalion at the right of the line extending to the Savannah River.[64] D'Estaing later wrote that Rouvray's detachment had been "charged to occupy a difficult and potentially dangerous post because it formed a fulcrum along the river." He praised Colonel Rouvray's leadership of the Afro-Caribbean battalion throughout the campaign as exhibiting marks of firmness and a great aptitude for military tactics. He added that Rouvray "carried out the orders that [D'Estaing] gave him well," in the manner of "a true soldier."[65]

Historian Franklin Hough dates the beginning of the Siege of Savannah to 23 September.[66] On that day, Rouvray received the command to oversee the construction of a network of trenches that approached the British lines. That evening, three companies of the Chasseurs Battalion and three companies of the Dominguan Grenadiers protected, supported, and assisted work details from the white Grenadiers of Saint-Domingue and at least three hundred white American rebels to construct trenches together.[67] With Black and white men working alongside each other in the trenches, the allied effort yielded great progress overnight, reaching within three hundred yards of the enemy lines. To acknowledge the achievement, "the troops received a rum ration, and M. d'Estaing sent the trench officers a very fine basket of food."[68]

Around daybreak the next morning, the British spotted the trenches, and three companies of light infantrymen attacked the allied detail. The Chasseurs companies took the initial assault of six hundred advancing soldiers. The clash marked the Chasseurs' first firefight of the campaign with white soldiers. The Chasseurs and Grenadiers fought the British troops up close, "at the point of the bayonet," driving them back to their redoubts. Pursuing their aggressors, the Afro-Caribbean troops came within range of British artillery, which opened fire on them.[69]

Admiral d'Estaing praised the Dominguan troops, the vast majority of whom were Black and gens de couleur, for their armed battle against the British. Soon after the Savannah campaign, he wrote in his journal, "The troops demonstrated bravery and discipline during this skirmish."[70] Later, in a report for the French Naval Ministry commending Rouvray's actions as "the commanding officer in charge of the trench the day that the English were forced back," he added that "his Corps served with zeal and precision" during the fight.[71] Defending French and white American troops and their entrenchments, Chasseurs and Grenadiers killed or wounded twenty-one British, including one officer.⁷² Rouvray's command lost twenty-nine Chasseurs and Grenadiers, including four officers, with sixty-six wounded.⁷³ Within twelve hours during the night of 23–24 September, Afro-Caribbean and white soldiers from Saint-Domingue worked together with white Americans, fought together in hand-to-hand combat, and died together in Georgia. Back home in the Caribbean, those same martyrs, connected as comrades in death, had been prohibited by colonial ordinances from wearing the same clothes or eating together as equals.

The French and American troops continued to expand their trenches over the next two weeks as British artillery batteries lobbed shells across the lines to disrupt the construction. On the afternoon of 8 October, orders spread through the allied lines that they would attack British defenses the next day.⁷⁴ On the other side of their entrenchments lay battlements and redoubts constructed by Black workers. Following the example of Lord Dunmore, Georgia's colonial government voted in 1777 to mobilize enslaved men to fight alongside British soldiers in the colony's defense. The law promised freedom to members of the "Ethiopian Regiment" in exchange for military service.⁷⁵

As d'Estaing's expeditionary force sailed from Cap-Français, British governor of Georgia Jacques Marcus Prevost, whose wife, Theodosia, resided in New Jersey, where she was having an illicit affair with US Lieutenant Colonel Aaron Burr, ordered three hundred Black men to repair Savannah's defenses. They erected thirteen redoubts and installed fifteen gun batteries.⁷⁶ According to one newspaper report, while French forces disembarked and marched toward the city, more than two thousand men of African descent under the command of British Lieutenant Colonel John Maitland worked "night and day incessantly engaged in adding to the strength and number of the works."⁷⁷

On 9 October, Admiral d'Estaing tested the battle readiness of the Black Loyalists' fortifications. Their works proved up to the challenge of an allied assault. The battle orders called for the Chasseurs Battalion to join the reserve guard and to go wherever their presence was necessary throughout the day.⁷⁸ Some were deployed to an advanced guard with white Dominguan Grenadiers and white units from the South Carolina and Georgia militias. This interracial allied detachment feigned an assault on the British left flank along the Savannah. The objective of the fake attack was to draw the attention away from the redoubts at the center of the line. The Chasseurs and their fellow soldiers exchanged fire with enemy forces, and fifty men were killed or wounded.⁷⁹ But the false flanking maneuver did not deceive the British. American spies or deserters had warned General Prevost's army of d'Estaing's attack plan.⁸⁰

"Armed, Disciplined and Battle-Hardened" 201

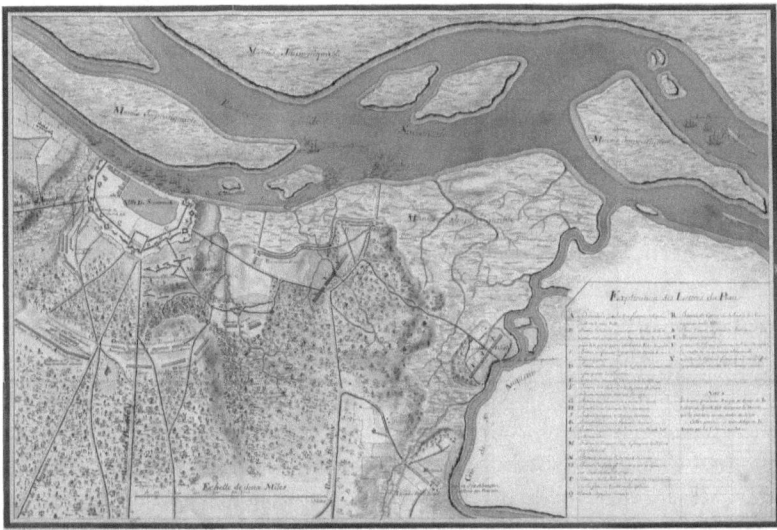

Figure 6.3. Plan of the Siege of Savannah. Map by Antoine François Térence O'Connor, 1779. The map shows the position of American, French, and British military units before the failed Franco-American charge at British battlements on 9 October 1779. The map clearly illustrates the Chasseurs Volontaires Battalion at the extreme-right flank of the French line. Courtesy of the John Carter Brown Library.

Three columns of French troops and two columns of Americans attacked the main body of the fortifications.[81] The violent, failed assault to dislodge the British from Savannah lasted less than one hour before d'Estaing called his forces to withdraw. The allies encountered an impenetrable barrage of cannon, grapeshot, and rifle fire that killed the famed General Casimir Pulaski and severely wounded Admiral d'Estaing. Estimates of allied losses during the doomed attack suggest that around 640 French and 250 Americans were killed and wounded.[82] Hundreds of Black Loyalist soldiers fired on the allied troops who advanced toward the Springhill Redoubt across the British ramparts built by Black labor.[83]

The Siege of Savannah, like no other battle of the American Revolution, extended to a substantial number of Black men from the United States and Saint-Domingue the opportunity to fight for freedom. They fought for similar reasons but joined opposing forces with different political and military objectives. On one side, Black Loyalists chose to join the British imperial forces against white American independence to secure their freedom, and that of their family, from slavery. Chasseurs Battalion soldiers, for their part, fought alongside white American rebels, in some cases, for freedom from slavery and, in others, to persuade their racist Dominguan neighbors to treat them as equal citizens.

The Siege of Savannah proved a failure for the French and American forces brought together by the Treaty of Alliance. Still, US General Lincoln maintained a high regard for his French counterpart. He reported, "Count d'Estaing has undoubtedly the interest of America much at heart. This he has evinced by coming to our assistance, by his constant attention during the Siege."[84] The next day, after the rout, both armies began their retreat from the field of battle. The Americans returned overland to their stronghold in Charleston. The French initiated the weeklong operation to reembark on their naval transports.[85]

Afro-Caribbean and white troops were assigned to guard the retreat. One hundred Chasseurs Battalion members secured the right flank of the column, while other Chasseurs were assigned to different units. The French Consul J. Plombard would return to his post in Charleston with the Americans. Sixty Chasseurs Volontaires were posted to guard the house he occupied in case of British attack.[86] The British, indeed, decided to pursue the withdrawing forces. A unit of Black Loyalists skirmished with a party of white American troops near Lachlan McGillivray's plantation outside Savannah. According to a newspaper account, the Black soldiers drove the rebels "from the buildings on the plantation into the woods. Want of ammunition, however, obliged the Blacks to retreat in the evening." The Loyalists sustained the loss of one man killed and four wounded.[87]

Two days later, Black British soldiers killed two white American rebels in a foraging party and captured two American dragoons.[88] As the French army completed its reembarkation, five companies of Dominguan Chasseurs and Grenadiers evacuated their posts in the trenches and joined the rear guard near the commandeered plantation of white Loyalist Colonel John Mulryne.[89] Members of the Chasseurs Battalion found themselves aboard different ships heading in different directions. After the French fleet's departure from Savannah, the Chasseurs Volontaires de Saint-Domingue were scattered across the Atlantic world.

The dispersal of the Chasseurs Battalion was not planned, and it occurred against the wishes of the Dominguan infantrymen. The decentralized manner of the retreat operations caused Rouvray's command to be broken up without his knowledge or approval. Some of his men boarded ships that returned them to their home port of Cap-Français.[90] Rouvray angrily reported to the French Naval Ministry that Admiral d'Estaing, without consulting him, "deployed 150 or 200 men of [his] Corps to reinforce the garrison in Grenada."⁹¹ About sixty Chasseurs, likely the company ordered to protect French Consul Plombard during the retreat, escorted allied casualties to Charleston and fought with the Americans in the Siege of Charleston the following year.⁹² Another detachment of Chasseurs Volontaires sailed to France aboard *La Provence*. The newspaper writer in Saint-Domingue editorialized that "it must have appeared extraordinary in Europe to see people of color armed, disciplined and battle-hardened." Seeming to refer to race relations, the newspaper suggested that the Chasseurs' presence in France "could indeed be the subject of serious reflection."⁹³

Rouvray had enslaved and brutalized African bodies for profit and social status before, during, and after the Siege of Savannah. Still, to men with whom he served in the Chasseurs Battalion, he proved himself a skilled and dedicated military commander of Afro-Caribbean soldiers, on and off the battlefield. After the battle was over, in ways incongruous with Rouvray as an enslaver, the colonel showed great respect for the personhood and service of the Black and mixed-parentage men under his command. He praised his men, expressing extreme pride in "the Corps of Chasseurs Volontaires that [he] commanded and that served with the greatest Distinction and the greatest valor."⁹⁴

The *Affiches Américaines* reported with assurance that "the Corps served very well" in the United States. In addition, army officers in France who fought at Savannah affirmed Rouvray's approbation for the Chasseurs Battalion.⁹⁵ In his report to the ministry about "the unfortunate affair in Savannah," including d'Estaing's decision to send the Chasseurs to Grenada, Rouvray pleaded for his men, appealing to the navy minister's sense of "justice and [his] humanity that [he] would issue the orders that would return these unfortunate men to their homeland."⁹⁶

On 27 September 1779, three days after the Chasseurs engaged the British in a bloody overnight skirmish in Savannah, the Continental Congress appointed John Adams as the US minister plenipotentiary to negotiate peace and commerce with the British. Adams's allies and opponents in Congress seemed to esteem something positive and encouraging in his diplomatic prowess that scholars and biographers have since undervalued. His unimpressive sojourn to Paris the previous year aside, Adams was the principal architect of America's first significant, successful foreign policy strategy. His championing of commercial connections over military entanglements became a cornerstone of US international affairs.

Revolutionary Americans understood that the new nation, after winning its prized independence, would need the productive trade ties with the Atlantic world's largest economy to sustain its sovereignty. Therefore, they trusted and reassigned Adams to another equally important posting. Adams had arrived home to Braintree, Massachusetts, from Paris, "disgusted and mortified . . . full of disappointment, chagrin, and vexation," around 2 August 1779. His wife, Abigail, bolstered his spirits. The hometown folks also continued to support their favorite son. Within days of his return, they elected him to represent the town at the Massachusetts state constitutional convention that began on 1 September.[97]

The body of 312 delegates selected John Adams, Samuel Adams, and James Bowdoin to serve on the drafting committee. In the time it took d'Estaing to land troops and lose the battle in Georgia, Adams emerged as the "principal Engineer" of the commonwealth's foundational legal document. His two colleagues chose him to draw up the document. He later quipped that he became "a sub-subcommittee of one." As he had done when drafting the Model Treaty three years earlier, he drew on his vast knowledge of history and political philosophy, and he also incorporated many ideas from his own treatise *Thoughts on Government*. Adams completed his draft by 30 October. The convention adopted the constitution the following year.[98]

Adams later wrote of that emotional moment in his life, "Instead of being mortified, it was the proudest of my whole life. I made a Constitution for Massachusetts which finally made the Constitution of the United States."[99] Three years later, the Massachusetts Supreme Judicial Court applied the principle of judicial review and used the constitution's Article 1, drafted by Adams, as the basis to abolish slavery in the state.[100]

In November 1779, around the same time the armed, uniformed members of the Chasseurs Battalion landed in France, presenting an astounding image of Blackness to the French population, John Adams embarked from Boston for a second diplomatic mission. His return trip to the continent retraced with renewed hope the sea path he had taken in disappointment months earlier. No longer acting as Benjamin Franklin's subordinate left to busy himself with meaningless embassy paperwork, Adams was charged and equally empowered as the American plenipotentiary to negotiate an Atlantic treaty in Europe.[101]

Sixty miles north of where John Adams set sail to broker his country's peace with its former imperial ruler, on 12 November, twenty Africans enslaved in New Hampshire petitioned the state's council and House of Representatives for freedom.[102] They used Adams's own language as leverage. Before departing, Adams, only two weeks before, had completed his draft of the Massachusetts Constitution, arguing that "all men are born free and equal, and have certain natural, essential, and unalienable rights; among which may be reckoned the right of enjoying and defending their lives and liberties."[103]

The listed petitioners, identifying proudly as "natives of Africa," similarly asserted "that the God of nature gave them life and freedom, upon the terms of the most perfect equality with other men."[104] Adams and the New Hampshire Africans were practically writing their arguments for transracial human freedom and equality at the same time. Perhaps unwittingly, the Africans picked up Lemuel Haynes's argument in *Liberty Further Extended* that "Liberty, & Freedom, is an innate principle, which is unmovably placed in the human Species . . . and is Coaeval with his Existence."[105] To ensure the clarity of their meaning, they explained, "That freedom is an inherent right of the human species, not to be surrendered, but by consent."[106]

In January 1777, six months after Congress issued the Declaration of Independence, Prince Hall, Peter Bestes, and other African Freemasons had signed their names to a petition to the Massachusetts legislature advocating the abolition of slavery in that state.[107] In their effort, the free men of color argued to the commonwealth's legislative body that their enslaved sisters and brothers "were unjustly dragged, by the cruel hand of Power, from their dearest friends, & some of them even torn from the Embraces of their tender Parents—From a populous, pleasant, & plentiful Country—& in Violation of the Laws of Nature & of Nations & in defiance of all the tender feelings of humanity."[108] The Granite State Africans also highlighted slavery's violation of the laws of nature. With great confidence, they informed white lawmakers that "[they felt] the dignity of human nature" and "[knew] that the God of Nature made [them] free!"[109]

A Portsmouth newspaper covered the Black abolitionist endeavor and reprinted the freedom petition for its readership in full. Despite the elegantly worded appeal and front-page press coverage, however, New Hampshire slaveholders did not follow the example of their Massachusetts neighbors. The petition was read in the House in April 1780, and the legislature granted the petition a hearing the following June.[110] But, in the midst of a fight for greater liberty for white inhabitants, House members decided "that at [that] time the House [was] not ripe for a Determination in this matter: Therefore ordered that the further consideration & determination of the matter be postponed till a more convenient opportunity."[111] Shamefully, it took New Hampshire another four decades to abolish slavery; it did so just six years before the Emancipation Proclamation.

As Africans in Portsmouth published their petition, Phillis Wheatley Peters, in Boston, worked to publish her second book of poetry. Since her first volume, *Poems on Various Subjects*, in 1773 garnered her fame across the Atlantic world, she had gained her freedom and married. The thirty-year-old formerly enslaved female poet continued to write during the US War of Independence. By 1779, she had a collection of thirty-three poems and thirteen letters. She placed six advertisements in the *Boston Evening Post* soliciting subscribers for "300 pages in Octavo." Appreciating the importance of the Franco-American alliance to American independence, Wheatley dedicated her volume "to the Right Hon. Benjamin Franklin, Esq.: One of the Ambassadors of the United States at the Court of France." Yet the book project did not secure enough subscribers and was never printed. Consistent with their distaste for Wheatley's publishing efforts six years earlier, white Bostonians refused to support the hometown Black writer.[112] Still, in 1783, poetry "by the celebrated Phillis Wheatly" headlined a public auction in Salem also featuring "Pliny's *Letters*," "[John] Brown's *Essays*," and "1st vol. [Alexander] Pope's Homer."[113]

In 1779, the minuteman and abolitionist writer of color Lemuel Haynes began training for a ministerial career in northwestern Connecticut. There he learned Latin, theology, and homiletics in exchange for providing labor on the farm where he lodged. The following year, he learned Greek and took up the position of a licensed temporary pastor of a new church in his hometown of Granville, Massachusetts.[114] Five years later, he became, according to Thabiti Anyabwile, "the first African American ordained by any religious body in America."[115] In 1783, Haynes married Elizabeth Babbitt, one of the church's white American parishioners, and the couple established a large family and served together in Christian ministry for over forty years in Vermont.[116]

In 1781, two years after the failed Siege of Savannah, the Franco-American alliance made its most important military impact of the war at the Battle of Yorktown, in Virginia. It was a decisive victory by a coalition force of the Continental Army troops led by General George Washington, with French land force support from army commanders Marie-Joseph Marquis de Lafayette and Jean-Baptiste de Rochambeau and with a French naval force commanded by François Joseph de Grasse. The allied victory led to the surrender of Lieutenant General Charles Cornwallis and marked the final major battle in the North American theater during the US War of Independence. According to Alfred Nemours, Afro-Caribbean soldiers from the Dominguan Chasseurs Battalion served at Yorktown as integrated members of the augmented

Port-au-Prince and Cap-Français regiments mustered under de Grasse.[117] Black soldiers from North America also fought at Yorktown. Some, notably the First Rhode Island Regiment, fought on the American side.[118] In addition, thousands of enslaved Africans from Southern plantations fought with the British, who had promised them freedom.[119]

In the same year, about ten miles west of the famous battlefield, the enslaved Gowan Pamphlet began preaching to a gathering of free and enslaved Black Baptists in Williamsburg, the former capital of Virginia. Pamphlet was the acquaintance of an enslaved preacher named Moses who had assembled the city's first Baptist church in 1776. Moses endured regular beatings from white authorities as he worked to gather and spiritually nurture the founding members of the church.[120] Historical records and accounts suggest that Pamphlet served alongside Moses on wooded land outside of town and assumed the duties of a pastor in 1781 after Moses departed the area.[121] While preaching, he also worked in the King's Arms Tavern, which was owned by his enslaver. Contemporary white Baptist pastor Robert Semple reported that, before coming to the capital, Pamphlet had been preaching in Middlesex County. In Williamsburg, Pamphlet "became popular among the Black congregants, and began to baptize them as well to preach."[122] His pastorate produced a more organized body that practiced more clearly defined Baptist theology and doctrines.[123]

In 1783, white Baptist association leaders, hearing of Williamsburg's Black Baptist church, attempted to muzzle Pamphlet and stifle the congregation's growth. They "advised that no person of colour should be allowed to preach." However, in Semple's estimation, Pamphlet and the Black Baptists "were rebellious, and continued still holding meetings."[124] Pamphlet also became known to Virginians for encouraging Black religious expression and Black liberation.[125] Under his leadership, the church grew to over two hundred members and gained acceptance into the white-governed Dover Baptist Association.[126]

In Savannah, after the Franco-American victory at Yorktown, Black Baptist pastor George Liele prepared to evacuate the city with the departing British military. The thirty-two-year-old formerly enslaved preacher had planted assemblies of the Baptist faith among members of the African diaspora held captive on rice and indigo plantations around coastal Georgia. Historians date Liele's founding of the African Baptist Church in Savannah from 1773 to 1777.[127] In 1779, the congregation that emerged as the state's, and perhaps the country's, first African Baptist church met on a plantation in Brampton, just three miles from the trenches where the Chasseurs Battalion of Saint-

Domingue fought British troops in a deadly skirmish.[128] Liele met, evangelized, and baptized an older enslaved man, Andrew Bryan, at the Brampton church site. Historian Charles Irons describes a mentoring clerical relationship between Liele and Bryan similar to that of Moses and Gowan Pamphlet at the Black Baptist church in Williamsburg.[129]

The end of the Siege of the Savannah signaled the end of Liele's evangelistic endeavors in North America. In July 1782, during the largest exodus of enslaved Africans of the American Revolution, caused by the British evacuation of Savannah, some six thousand women, men, and children of the African diaspora departed US shores in search of freedom in the British Empire.[130] Liele was among them. Though he had become a free man through unclear circumstances during the British occupation of Georgia, he decided to leave the United States along with fellow Black Loyalists and the British military forces.[131] Liele landed in Jamaica and established an African Baptist church on the island.

In 1783, Andrew Bryan assumed the duties of spiritual leadership of the Savannah-area African Baptist population. Under Bryan's leadership, the number of converts grew steadily, and the church members erected a wooden structure for communal worship on a plantation in Yamacraw.[132] Similar to those of his predecessor, Bryan's sermons likely illuminated the transatlantic connections between Black Georgians and the peoples of the African continent. He also explained to abused human beings the biblical teachings describing God's mighty interventions into history on behalf of African-descended people.[133] In a region where the roots of African languages were still in use, Black Baptists introduced a number of traditional African-descended beliefs and practices into their collective Christian worship and individual spiritual experiences.[134]

As their racist counterparts had done to Moses in Virginia, white Georgians persecuted Bryan with physical beatings and accused him of plotting an insurrection because of the success of his pastorate in Black empowerment.[135] In 1790, the year Bryan purchased his freedom, the church moved into Savannah, onto land purchased by Bryan, making it, like the Black church in Williamsburg, the city's first Baptist church, Black or white.[136] The African Baptist Church joined the white-governed Georgia Baptist Association as the largest Baptist church in the state, according to Baptist historian John Asplund's 1790 *Baptist Register*, with 250 members.[137]

The American Revolution afforded thousands of people of the African diaspora the opportunity to attain freedom by departing the independent, proslavery United States with the defeated British armies. George Liele, though he had planted the church in Savannah, decided to leave. Andrew Bryan and Gowan Pamphlet chose to remain in the US, despite remaining in slavery until the 1790s.[138] They preached God's deliverance and Black liberation to enslaved Baptists and built in Georgia and Virginia strong Black congregations with storied histories that still exist today.

Back together in Paris, John Adams and Benjamin Franklin headed the US delegation to the peace talks with Britain. Similar to their first diplomatic mission, the Anglo-American negotiations were slow, complex, and, at times, frustrating. After a year and a half of bargaining, countering, and wordsmithing, on 3 September 1783, Adams affixed his name, on behalf of the United States, to the Treaty of Peace and Friendship (commonly referred to as the Treaty of Paris), officially ending the US War of Independence.

Article I of the Treaty of Paris of 1783 states, "His Britannick Majesty acknowledges the said United States . . . to be Free, Sovereign, and Independent States; that he treats with them as such; and . . . relinquishes all claims to the government, propriety, and territorial rights of the same, and every part thereof."[139]

The declaration by King George III vindicated the collective colonial resistance—including the many petitions, the Stamp Act Congress, newspaper essays, the Boston Massacre, assemblies and meetings, the Boston Tea Party, political treatises, speeches, and protests—by British American subjects beginning with the Stamp Act in 1765. The second Paris treaty affirmed for US citizens the virtues of the Continental Congress, Lexington and Concord, the Declaration of Independence, the Model Treaty, the Articles of Confederation, the Franco-American alliance, the Siege of Savannah, state constitutions, and the victory at Yorktown. After six years of warfare that cost the new nation the lives of some two hundred thousand servicemen, the treaty represented a bilaterial diplomatic effort by the United States and Britain "to forget all past misunderstandings and differences that have unhappily interrupted the good correspondence and friendship which they mutually wish to restore" and to "promote and secure to both perpetual peace & harmony."[140]

The Treaty of Paris also irrevocably changed the Atlantic world in 1783. Twenty years earlier, another treaty in Paris had profound effects on Europe, the Caribbean, and North America. During the Seven Years' War, which precipitated the previous armistice, American colonists had fought with their fellow Britons against the French to move the European imperial balance of power markedly in favor of the British. In 1776, the delegates of thirteen colonies issued a declaration of their separation from the English king and of their new identity as citizens of a western Atlantic republic. Two years

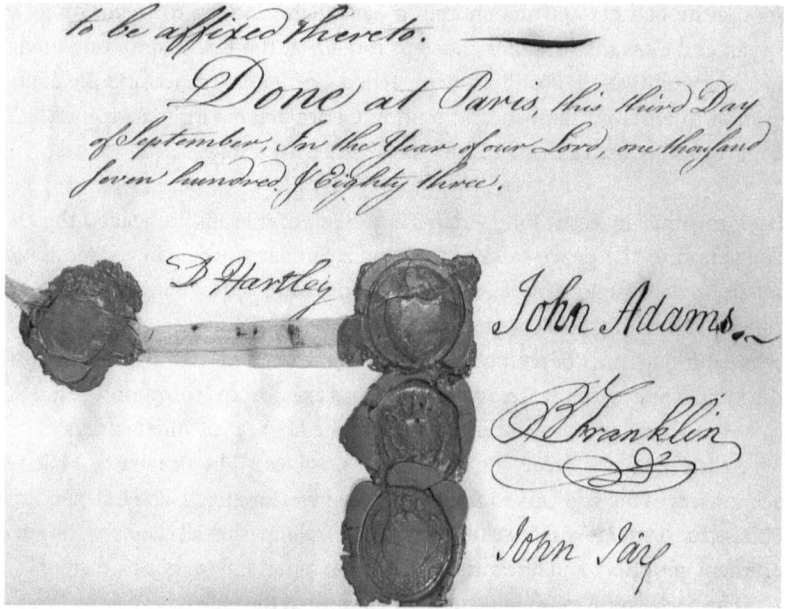

Figure 6.4. Definitive Treaty of Peace between Great Britain and the United States, 1783. Courtesy of the Massachusetts Historical Society.

later, the Americans began fighting alongside former French enemies against former British neighbors, business partners, old friends, and kinsmen. White Americans fought and died for greater liberty to make decisions about taxes, debts, and alliances for themselves, without deferring to the wishes of a monarch and Parliament three thousand miles across the ocean.

From the Stamp Act to Yorktown, Black people in North America, free and enslaved, considered the racialized meanings of Enlightenment ideals like freedom and liberty articulated in American assemblies and newspapers. Before and after the Treaty of Paris of 1763, Africans in diaspora fled plantations, wrote revolutionary poems, joined white American acts of insurrection, established new forms of Black Christian worship, submitted freedom petitions, and fought as minutemen and Continental Army soldiers, all in an appeal for freedom from white American patriots. Still, white Americans clung to slavery after independence. Before British General Cornwallis surrendered at Yorktown, Pennsylvania legislators passed the complicated Gradual Emancipation Act, which for years "freed no one."[141]

John Adams had drafted the Massachusetts Constitution, which, in April 1783, empowered the Supreme Judicial Court to declare slavery "effectively abolished" in the state.[142] In September of that same year, Adams, in Paris, on behalf of the United States, affixed his signature to the treaty to secure peace and harmony. Article VII of the accord sought "perpetual peace" between the two nations by prohibiting Britain from "carrying away any negroes, or other property of the American Inhabitants."[143] By signing the treaty, Adams and his fellow commissioners conceded that the US government considered formerly enslaved Black Loyalists, who had escaped to the British lines, to be property of white American slaveholders. They, however, did not prevent thousands of people of African descent from fleeing American shores during the British evacuation. The 1783 provision required US diplomats in future Anglo-American negotiations—including the Jay Treaty (1794) and the Treaty of Ghent (1814)—to pursue the issue of British refusal to compensate white American enslavers for providing Africans a pathway to freedom during the American Revolution.[144]

The two decades between the two treaties of Paris presented an era of revolution across North America and the Caribbean. In Saint-Domingue, the humiliating military loss represented in the peace of 1763 led white Frenchmen to fear a British invasion and become more race conscious to preserve what they perceived as a weakened regime of white superiority. Versailles-appointed officials implemented policies of militarization, and colonial administrators attempted to restrict economic and social advancement to the white Dominguans. Free Afro-Caribbean colonists used the opportunities that imperial mandates presented to resist racist, local restrictions on their civil and human rights. In 1765, African-descended men joined the segregated Chasseurs Volontaires d'Amérique to defend the colony against a British incursion. Four years later, many used their training to lead and fight against the French army in the 1769 Revolt.

Throughout the 1770s, Saint-Domingue's gens de couleur, similar to their counterparts of color in North America, joined colonial militias in remarkable numbers to prove their fitness for citizenship and social status comparable to that of their white neighbors. They had access to the steady newspaper reports of American revolutionary ideals, republican nation-building efforts, and the results of Adams's and Franklin's transatlantic diplomacy. Affluent Afro-Caribbean men left the island to acquire education and military training abroad. Like the planter class in America, the *grand blancs* remained committed to slavery in the colony. In 1779, hundreds of Black and mixed-parentage men, free and enslaved, served in the Chasseurs Battalion to fight overseas against the British army to honor the Franco-American alliance, to secure US independence, and to bolster their argument for freedom and equality in Saint-Domingue. Advancing liberty was and would continue to be an ongoing collective effort among Atlantic world inhabitants.

Epilogue

"The School of Liberty"

Beyond 1783

In 1783, George III and Louis XVI signed a second *Definitive Treaty of Peace and Friendship, between His Britannick Majesty, and the Most Christian King*, ending a war between their two empires. Twenty years before, the British monarch and the French king's father had signed a Treaty of Paris ending a war between their respective realms. France's military casualties, pivotal naval engagement, and the considerable debt accrued to aid the Americans in the US War of Independence did not alleviate Versailles's losses from the Treaty of Paris of 1763. The allied victory over Britain did not net the French Empire a great deal of territorial gain either. However, Article IX of the 1783 Treaty of Paris returned Gorée Island to the French king. The West African territory had been recaptured by the British in the war. The treaty also ceded to France the Senegal River and control over access to important inland slave-trading posts along the waterway.[1] The British concessions represented an important victory for France's slave trade and the trafficking of Africans to Saint-Domingue and other Caribbean colonies. The Treaty of Paris of 1783 also represented the realization of an important objective for France's involvement in the American Revolution: It tilted the balance of power in the Atlantic world back toward France's direction by depriving the British Empire of a valuable colonial source of economic strength and military power.

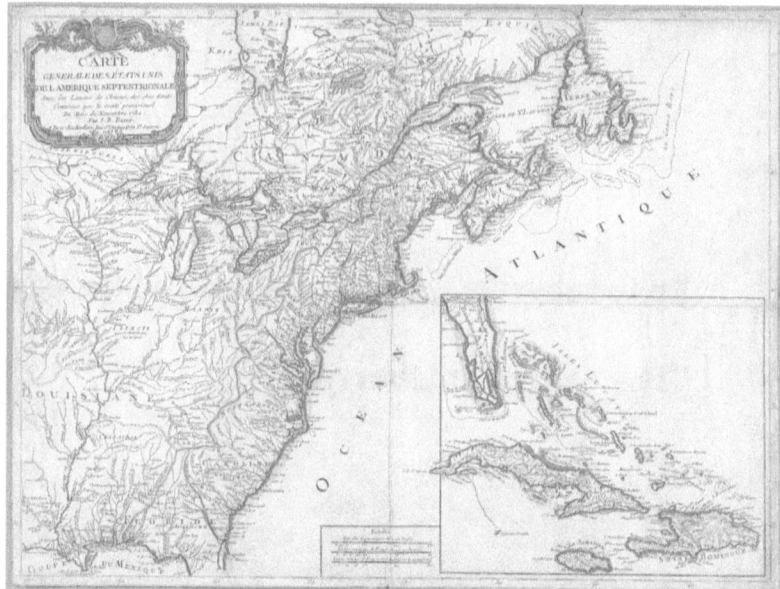

Figure E.1. Map of the United States with the limits of each of the said states, as agreed by the Anglo-American provisional treaty. Map by Jean-Baptiste Eliot, 1783. Courtesy of the John Carter Brown Library.

To mark the importance of the 1783 Treaty of Paris between the two kings, the governor-general of Saint-Domingue, Guillaume de Bellecombe, ordered the revival of the theater production *l'Anglois a Bordeaux* (The Englishman in Bordeaux) and offered the showing free to the public. The play had been written by French playwright Charles-Simon Favart and was first performed in Paris after the Seven Years' War "on the occasion of the Peace of 1763."[2]

The *Comédie du Cap*, located on the *Place de Montarcher* opposite the governor's residence in Cap-Français, had been built in 1765. The 1,500-seat, segregated performance venue was part of the Versailles government's plan to ingratiate itself with Dominguan colonists after the previous military and diplomatic loss to Britain.[3] When the Chasseurs Battalion members returned from duty in the United States, some may have attended the play. Their efforts for freedom and equality, which they had begun before the Savannah campaign, continued after the Treaty of 1783. Though the Naval Ministry formally disbanded the Chasseurs corps in 1781, Afro-Caribbean men who had fought in the American Revolution had also witnessed and experienced

US patriots fighting imperial forces for their liberty. The expeditionary soldiers of color returned to Saint-Domingue as battle-hardened combat veterans who continued to seek, in some cases, freedom from slavery and, in others, enfranchisement as French citizens.[4]

Between the two treaties of Paris, colonial inhabitants of the western Atlantic world, Black and white, became more empowered by the shifting world order in the 1760s. With different motives, they searched for greater freedom and liberty in different places and in daring new ways. Thousands of Caribbean maroons fled island plantations to create free communities hidden within the brush. Crispus Attucks and others of the African diaspora discovered freedom in shipboard life on the seas. Young men of the Caribbean, Black and white, pursued skills and status in academic settings across Europe and North America.

Benjamin Franklin remained in Paris as the US minister after the ratification of the Treaty of 1783. He served his last public office as the president of Pennsylvania, where he served as host for the national convention that produced the US Constitution in 1789. That same year witnessed the invigorated written demands for racial equality and citizenship in Saint-Domingue by Dominguan *gens de couleur* and their allies in Paris during the beginnings of the French Revolution. Some scholars suggest that the participation of Afro-Caribbean men in the Chasseurs Battalion expedition at the Siege of Savannah fueled ideas and actions that led to the Haitian Revolution ten years later.[5] Nineteenth-century Haitian historian Beauvais Lespinasse suggested that, in Savannah, the Chasseurs soldiers persevered, "undoubtedly learning some things at the school of liberty that the young American nation had opened." From their experience in the American Revolution came "the *esprit de corps*" among the Dominguan men of color. And, according to Lespinasse, it was "this powerful spirit which would give birth to the wonders of the revolution in Saint-Domingue."[6] Haitian historian Alfred Nemours likewise argues that the members of the Chasseurs Battalion who fought in Savannah, like Jean-Jacques Chavannes and André Rigaud, learned things from the Americans about fighting imperial forces to secure their liberty. They returned to Saint-Domingue and continued to advocate for freedom and equality.[7]

The impact of the American Revolution on peoples and nations across the Atlantic world within the age of revolutions remains a vibrant area of scholarly exploration.[8] Even before Savannah, dating to the 1760s, the Dominguan population of color, particularly wealthy, educated gens de couleur, would have learned about and followed from newspapers and community conversations the progress of the American Revolution. As this book has illustrated, they would have known about public protests in Boston, the military campaigns of George Washington, the Continental Congress declaration penned by Thomas Jefferson, and the Franco-American alliance secured by Benjamin Franklin.

More research into and continued scholarly historical engagement with the period between revolutions in the US and in Saint-Domingue are needed to advance our knowledge of how combat service in the American Revolution affected the postwar lives and informed the leadership methods of some of the most extraordinary men in the Atlantic world in the late eighteenth and early nineteenth centuries. However, during the Haitian Revolution of the 1790s, Afro-Caribbean veterans of the Chasseurs Battalion who fought in the Savannah campaign undoubtedly made indelible contributions to the abolition of slavery, the achievement of equal citizenship status, and, twenty years after the second treaty in Paris, the founding of an independent Haiti.

Jean-Baptiste Belley, a Black militiaman in Saint-Domingue during the 1769 Revolt, was thirty-three years old when he deployed with d'Estaing's expeditionary force in 1779. There, he had experienced the plausibility of international and interracial collaboration. His career and life afterward exhibited an expanded sense of political and social mobility for Black people.[9] During the Haitian Revolution, Belley was the first Black deputy elected to the National Convention in Paris, where he contributed to the debate that freed enslaved Africans across the French Empire.

Other Dominguan veterans of the American Revolution participated in the Haitian revolutionary march toward freedom, equality, and independence. In the late 1780s, Vincent Ogé, a free, educated, and affluent gens de couleur, returned to Saint-Domingue from Paris to lead, along with Black Chasseurs veteran Jean-Jacques Chavannes, a movement to foment rebellion in northern Saint-Domingue against exclusive white citizenship and enfranchisement. Colonial authorities captured and, in early 1791, executed Chavannes and Ogé cruelly and publicly in Cap-Français, making them the first two martyrs of the Haitian Revolution.

The resistance to white authority by Afro-Caribbeans revived the memory of Makandal, three decades after he had become a martyr for Black freedom in Cap-Français. One author peddled hackneyed, racist tropes about Black Atlantic inhabitants in a fictionalized story to introduce the fabled spiritual leader of African descent to a new generation. Readers of

Figure E.2: Jean-Baptiste Belley. Portrait by Anne-Louis Girodet-Trioson, 1797. Public domain.

the London-based *Universal Magazine of Knowledge and Pleasure* learned that Makandal was born in Africa and enslaved near Cap-Français before joining a Dominguan maroon community in the Limbé Valley mountains. The author, however, portrayed Makandal as a vengeful, skillful poisoner who "threatened the whole colony" before, in 1758, the Superior Council of Cap-Français sentenced him to being publicly burned alive.[10]

Another author took an extremely generous view of trafficking in African bodies to suggest that Makandal, born free, had been "reduced by bad fortune to a state of slavery." The article elaborated on "Makandal's intentions" to destroy the planter class "and lastly, to exterminate the whole race of white men by a general massacre, which would render him the deliver[er] and sovereign of the whole island." The claims in the recitation were so outlandish that the magazine's editor acknowledged in a note that "the author may have embellished this story a little in the narration."[11] Nevertheless, the memory of Makandal and his leadership of members of Saint-Domingue's Black population permeated the white imagination as the Haitian Revolution unfolded.

Six months after Ogé and Chavannes were martyred, hundreds of thousands of enslaved Africans around Cap-Français initiated the revolution's military campaign for freedom. André Rigaud, who had been wounded at Savannah, led the effort to arouse and arm free gens de couleur around Les Cayes in southern Saint-Domingue. Initially, Black insurgents and rebels of color were fighting separately against colonial leaders—as they had been since the American Revolution—for freedom and equality, respectively. Over time, southern insurgents moved to augment the rebellion in the north.

In 1792, the British military invaded Saint-Domingue to wrest the rich colony from France's tenuous control. As commander of the southern revolutionary forces, which included soldiers like fellow Chasseurs veteran Laurent Férou, Rigaud, again, faced British forces, as he had in Savannah. On Dominguan soil, at the head of Afro-Caribbean troops, he forced the invading army to retreat to Jamaica.[12]

As the Haitian Revolution progressed, the myths and fears around the martyred Makandal influenced characterizations of one of the eighteenth century's greatest Atlantic revolutionary leaders, who was Black.[13] Toussaint Louverture had gained freedom from slavery in Saint-Domingue around the age of thirty-three during the American Revolution. Industrious, he became a prosperous landowner and, like many Caribbean fathers, sent his sons Isaac and Placide to study in Europe to achieve a life of education and refinement that had been denied to him during his youth.[14] By the mid-1790s, he had ascended to the helm of the Saint-Domingue revolutionary movement. One of France's counterrevolutionary leaders, General Francois Marie de Kerversau, described Louverture as "respected by the Africans as a sort of Makandal." Historian Pierre Pluchon described him as a "Catholic Makandal" whose strong faith informed his style of leadership and persuaded the formerly enslaved Dominguan population to follow him.[15]

In May 1797, Toussaint Louverture became general-in-chief of Saint-Domingue, two months after John Adams succeeded George Washington as the second president of the United States. After the Treaty of 1783, the Continental Congress had appointed Adams as the first US minister plenipotentiary to Britain. In London today, a historical plaque is located in Grosvenor Square to mark his eighteenth-century ambassadorial residence.[16] But Adams also negotiated agreements with his Caribbean counterparts. Diplomatic relations with the Louverturian regime became a hallmark of his foreign policy as president. Two decades after authoring the Model Treaty, he continued to seek commerce-only partnerships. But in Saint-Domingue, as with France twenty years before, he found that military alliances were required in times of war.

Adams appointed Dr. Edward Stevens, from Saint Croix, to be the US envoy to the Louverturian government. Stevens, during the American Revolution, had left the Caribbean in search of education and professional advancement at King's College and, later, in Scotland. Around the time the second Paris treaty was signed, he returned to his home island as a much-needed physician. In the early 1790s, he joined his childhood friend, and the first US Secretary of the Treasury, Alexander Hamilton, in America's capital city of Philadelphia. There, the two friends resided blocks from each other, as they had as kids in Christiansted. When Stevens departed for his post in Cap-Français as Adams's emissary to Louverture, he took with him written fundamentals for a draft constitution—penned by Hamilton—to be presented to the Dominguan revolutionary government. Hamilton, who had assembled the pro–US Constitution essays in the transformative publication *The Federalist Papers*, engaged his brilliant political mind to aid the western Atlantic world's first government of Black leaders. Hamilton's draft plan of government helped influence the sections on executive leadership and public finance in the Constitution of Saint-Domingue issued by Louverture in 1801.[17]

Louverture and Stevens, two men born and raised on the islands, who had experienced the expansion of freedom and liberty during the 1770s, formed a transracial diplomatic bond that produced mutual advantages for both their governments. One of Louverture's top generals was Henry Christophe, who had reportedly been wounded at Savannah as an enslaved teenage Chasseurs Battalion drummer.[18] During the Haitian Revolution, he rose through the ranks as a Louverturian commander and participated in the campaign's more decisive battles. In a strange turn of events, the twentieth anniversary of the Siege of Savannah found Christophe in southern Saint-Domingue, leading the Siege of Jacmel, which was supported by the US Navy, to defeat Rigaud's attempts to overthrow the revolutionary leadership of Louverture.[19]

During the 1770s, the diplomacy of John Adams and Benjamin Franklin brought Dominguan soldiers to US shores. In the late 1790s, the foreign policy of the Adams administration deployed American forces to the shores of Saint-Domingue. The formerly enslaved Black general Jean-Jacques Dessalines succeeded Louverture as the head of the revolution and, in 1804, declared the independence of Haiti. In the political turmoil following Dessalines's death, Christophe and Rigaud, the two Chasseurs Battalion veterans, contested each other for leadership over the independent Haitian state, which each man had contributed so much to establish.[20]

The Afro-Caribbean men who journeyed to join the white Americans' fight for independence returned from the experience in the revolutionary United States to, within a decade, become leaders in their own revolution against a formidable imperial power. The effects of the Treaty of Paris of 1763 on France led to negative changes in the racial dynamics in Saint-Domingue, prompting Afro-Caribbeans toward actions to secure their freedom. The second Treaty of Paris twenty years later affirmed the political risks that disaffected British colonists, Black and white, had taken during the American Revolution. Following those actions across the decades, Dominguans of color understood that revolutionary writings and military successes were the appropriate means to abolish slavery and achieve equality. The colonial aspirations connecting the United States and Saint-Domingue across the two decades between the treaties of Paris offered mutual encouragement and tangible achievements for both peoples that arguably represent the beginning of the age of revolutions, including movements toward Black freedom in the United States, Haiti, and the subsequent emerging nations across the western Atlantic world.

Acknowledgments

The genesis of this book arose on an evening in the hills along the north coast of the island of Saint Croix, as I looked over the Caribbean Sea toward Saint Thomas. During the COVID-19 pandemic, I benefited from an invaluable opportunity to ruminate on the actions recounted within these pages, in the actual places where some of them occurred nearly three centuries ago. The research trip was funded by the Institute for Advanced Studies in the Humanities at the University of Edinburgh. Though historical monographs generally list one author, they are indeed produced from a combination of financial support and personal encouragement from many people and organizations. The words that follow represent my attempt to express my gratitude. I undertake this task knowing that I will inevitably forget to mention someone or some place. And for the inadvertent omission, I preemptively ask forgiveness.

This book is the product of the space and time needed to write and revise the manuscript, with funding provided by the Ralph and Bessie Mae Lynn Chair of History Endowment at Baylor University. Other generous, crucial sources of research funding include the National Endowment for the Humanities (NEH); the American Philosophical Society; the Kate B. and Hall J. Peterson Fellowship at the American Antiquarian Society; the Mellon

Scholars Program in African American History Fellowship at the Library Company of Philadelphia; the African American Episcopal Historical Collection Research Grant from the Virginia Theological Seminary; the Research Travel Grant from the Center for Latin American Studies and the George A. Smathers Library at the University of Florida; and the Howard H. Peckham Fellowship on Revolutionary America from the William L. Clements Library at the University of Michigan.

The historical analysis in this book is based on evidence gathered from archives and repositories staffed by dedicated professionals who care deeply for the preservation, organization, and accessibility of historical documents and artifacts, including the Archives Nationale d'Outre-Mer, Aix-en-Provence, France; the St. Croix Landmarks Society, Frederiksted; St. John's Episcopal Church, in Christiansted, Saint Croix; the American Antiquarian Society; the Library Company of Philadelphia; the Latin American and Caribbean Collection at the George Smathers Library; the William L. Clements Library; and the Georgia Historical Society.

My research efforts benefited greatly from vital holdings being made accessible through investment in digital humanities by institutions including the John Carter Brown Library Digital Collections; the Bibliothèque Nationale de France Gallica; the Massachusetts Historical Society Digital Collections; the Digital Library of the Caribbean (dLOC); the Association de Généalogie d'Haïti; Internet Archive; Google Books and Timeline; the Digital Library of Georgia; Founders Online of the National Archives; the Library of Congress Digital Collections; and the digital resources of the Albert B. Alkek Library of Texas State University and the Moody Memorial Library at Baylor University.

The book was enriched by the expertise and passion of university research librarians, including Laura Semrau, Ellen Filgo, and Libby Ehlers of the Moody Library at Baylor University and Margaret Vaverek of the Alkek Library at Texas State University. I was writing this book about freedom for oppressed peoples during a period when public libraries came under attack from American citizens for offering readers diverse collections of books about and by people from marginalized groups. Librarians selflessly serve communities across the country. My love of reading was kindled in my hometown public library. The librarians there offered my young mind a passport to places I would later visit and ideas I would embrace as an adult. Despite present book bans and controversaries over libraries across the state of Texas, the dedicated staffs and volunteers of public libraries in the cities of Kyle, Buda, Flatonia, and Waco provided books and accessible spaces to form and refine my words and arguments.

Acknowledgments

The Baylor University family—at the department, college, and university levels—has shown consistent support for this book project, providing necessary funding and research leave. My Baylor colleagues Julie K. deGraffenried, Barry G. Hankins, Robert Elder, Greg Garrett, Coretta M. Pittman, Horace J. Maxile Jr., Stephen Breck Reid, Malcolm Foley, David A. Smith, Thomas S. Kidd, and Lori Baker shared my passion for the book and offered encouragement and empathy throughout the process. Baylor History graduate research assistants Rebeca Joy Blemur, Savannah Flanagan, Allie Lopez, David Nanninga, and Regina Wenger provided expertise and creativity to the project as if it were their own. The skills and professionalism of Baylor History front office colleagues Dianne Schmidt, Tasha Rich, and Emily Leavitt deftly managed the necessary administrative and financial operations for the book.

The Texas State University community supported research for the book with the Verena & Kenneth Wilson Latin American Research Grant from the Center for International Studies, the College of Liberal Arts Research Enhancement Program Grant, and the Research Grant from the Department of History.

The field of academic history is filled with wonderful people who are brilliant, kind, and generous. Some professional colleagues who, in a variety of ways, poured a bit of their expertise, experience, and friendship into me and the project include Leslie M. Alexander, Claire Bourhis-Mariotti, Brandon R Byrd, Marlene L. Daut, John D. Garrigus, Sara Georgini, Robert A. Gross, Leslie M. Harris, Johann N. Neem, Gregory Nobles, Ousmane K. Power-Greene, Alan Taylor, and Karin Wulf.

I have been blessed to participate in wonderful cohorts of fellow writers whose probing questions, thoughtful suggestions, and timely encouragement enriched the book and my writing experience. The Second Book Workshop sponsored by the Society for Historians of the Early American Historians (SHEAR) provided a welcoming atmosphere and sound advice about how to productively begin a new project. The Haitian Studies Association Writing Group, especially Crystal A. Felima and Yveline Alexis, offered collegiality and affirmation. I participated in multiple sessions of the National Center for Faculty Development and Diversity 14-Day Writing Challenge, in which NCFDD facilitators and cohort participants pushed me to write—even—on the difficult days. Colleagues in the Baylor Department of History Works in Progress cohort—Ricardo Álvarez-Pimentel, Emmanuella Amoh, Daniel Barish, Elesha J. Coffman, Marilia Corrêa, Marcelo Boccato Kuyumjian, Andrea L. Turpin, and Daniel J. Watkins —read drafts of chapter 2 and helped me to productively reframe the book's discussion of race and freedom. Facilitators and cohort members of the Baylor University Summer Faculty Institute, including Lenore Wright, Keith Schubert, and Craig Carlson, shared time, space, and innovative methods to steadily advance the writing of the book.

NEH institutes offered archival and digital resources and inspiring collegial cohorts; these institutes included the African American Experience in Georgia's Lowcountry and the Atlantic World Institute at the Georgia Historical Society; the Caribbean Studies Digital History Institute at the University of Florida; and the Teaching the History and Culture of Vast Early America Institute at the Omohundro Institute of Early American History & Culture.

Much of the book was written in safe and inspiring places furnished with friendly encounters provided by amazing people, including Pam and Rick Allen in Waco, Texas; Barbara and Hans Lawaetz in Upper Love, Saint Croix; Michael Gelardi in Belvedere, Saint Croix; Heather Gayle of the Olle Hotel in Flatonia, Texas; and writing havens in Marble Falls and Tehuacana, Texas. Baylor History alum and former regent Ella Wall Prichard offered valuable analytical insight and encouragement. The Starbucks #14349 Barista Team in Kyle, Texas—Nicole's crew, including Ali, Alicia, Beck, Kaitlyn, Stassney, and Tess—in addition to offering coffee and support, exhibited genuine interest with questions about the book and my writing progress.

Vaneesa Cook lent her exceptional skills as a developmental editor—and motivational colleague—to invigorating me as a writer and clarifying the book's narrative and analysis.

The United States in the World series team of Cornell University Press was a phenomenal group with whom to collaborate on the project. Former editor Amy S. Greenberg initially saw the compatibility of my work with the series' mission. Series editors Benjamin A. Coates, Emily Conroy-Krutz, Paul A. Kramer, and Judy Tzu-Chun Wu showed continued confidence in the contributions of the book. Emily, especially, scrutinized each word of the manuscript with care and an experienced eye to make recommendations that more clearly illuminated the arguments and enhanced the framing of the story. The professionalism of CUP editorial director Sarah Grossman moved the book smoothly toward publication. The skill of CUP senior production editor Karen Hwa and the technical expertise of acquisitions assistant Katy Bond helped me greatly in assembling the manuscript. The thoughtful and meticulous copyediting of Angelique Dunn made the book's prose and analysis much more accessible. I am extremely grateful to the anonymous readers who took time from their own work to engage the manuscript closely, ask tough questions, and offer caring suggestions that, together, greatly improved the final volume.

It is hard to explain the immense sense of peace that the furry members of our family, Sable and Neville, gave to me throughout the writing process. I hope they know how much their love means to me.

Our kids, Soleil and RJ (Ronald Jr.), gave me so much strength and inspiration as the book developed. They each read parts of the draft and offered helpful corrections. They endured my many absences from the dinner table with grace, believing in the value of the work I was trying to accomplish. I have tried to write a book that will make them proud and illustrate to them the importance of personal resilience and collective resistance.

And my wife, Colette, was the engine behind this book. She read parts of the manuscript, made incredible suggestions, tangled with me over word choices, and listened thoughtfully to my many frustrations. As I oscillated between doubt and determination, she was my lodestar, steadying me and, gently but firmly, guiding me toward the book's completion. Her unwavering belief and empowering inspiration across the writing journey revealed to me a heretofore unseen truth: Enduring love is a powerful muse. Thank you.

Notes

Prologue

1. *Relation d'une conspiration tramée par les negres dans l'Isle de S. Domingue* (Paris, 1758), 3.
2. *New-Hampshire Gazette* (Portsmouth), 20 January 1758.
3. *New-York Mercury*, 9 January 1758.
4. *New-York Mercury*, 1 May 1758.
5. *New-York Mercury*, 1 May 1758.
6. *Boston Evening Post*, 8 May 1758; *Boston Gazette*, 8 May 1758; *Boston Post-Boy*, 8 May 1758; *Boston News-Letter*, 11 May 1758.
7. *New-York Mercury*, 1 May 1758.
8. John D. Garrigus, *A Secret Among the Blacks: Slave Resistance Before the Haitian Revolution* (Cambridge, MA: Harvard University Press, 2023), 80.
9. Garrigus, *Secret Among the Blacks*, 84; Elizabeth Maddock Dillon and Kate Simpkins, "Makandal and Pandemic Knowledge: Literature, Fetish, and Health in the Plantationocene," *American Literature* 92, no. 4 (2020): 726.
10. Garrigus, *Secret Among the Blacks*, 84.
11. For more on Voltaire's literary, philosophical engagement with Atlantic slavery, see Ingvild Hagen Kjørholt, "Cosmopolitans, Slaves, and the Global Market in Voltaire's *Candide, Ou l'Optimisme*," *Eighteenth-Century Fiction* 25, no. 1 (2012): 61–84; Gianamar Giovannetti-Singh, "Racial Capitalism in Voltaire's Enlightenment," *History Workshop Journal* 94, no. 1 (2022): 22–41; Margaret Watkins, "'Slaves Among Us': The Climate and Character of Eighteenth-Century Philosophical Discussions of Slavery," *Philosophy Compass* 12, no. 1 (2017), https://doi.org/10.1111/phc3.12393.

12. Voltaire, *Candide, ou l'Optimisme* (n.p., 1759), 166.
13. Voltaire, *Candide*, 167.
14. Garrigus, *Secret Among the Blacks*, 86.
15. Garrigus, *Secret Among the Blacks*, 76.
16. Voltaire, *Candide*, 167.
17. Karol K. Weaver, *Medical Revolutionaries: The Enslaved Healers of Eighteenth-Century Saint Domingue* (Urbana: University of Illinois Press, 2006), 90.
18. See Frank Lambert, *"Pedlar in Divinity": George Whitefield and the Transatlantic Revivals, 1737–1770* (Princeton, NJ: Princeton University Press, 1994); Thomas S. Kidd, *George Whitefield: America's Spiritual Founding Father* (New Haven, CT: Yale University Press, 2014); Harry S. Stout, *The Divine Dramatist: George Whitefield and the Rise of Modern Evangelism* (Grand Rapids, MI: W. B. Eerdmans, 1991).
19. Weaver, *Medical Revolutionaries*, 90; Garrigus, *Secret Among the Blacks*, 79.
20. Marlene Daut, *Awakening the Ashes: An Intellectual History of the Haitian Revolution* (Chapel Hill: University of North Carolina Press, 2023), 71.
21. Karen E. Fields and Barbara J. Fields, *Racecraft: The Soul of Inequality in American Life* (London: Verso, 2012), 128–45.
22. Alejandro de la Fuente and Ariela J. Gross, *Becoming Free, Becoming Black: Race, Freedom, and Law in Cuba, Virginia, and Louisiana*, Studies in Legal History (Cambridge: Cambridge University Press, 2020), 4–5, 34–38.
23. *New-York Mercury*, 1 May 1758.
24. Research did not uncover a subsequent follow-up story in the publication—or any other North American newspaper—about the events in Saint-Domingue.
25. *Relation d'une conspiration*, 2, 4.
26. Ronald Angelo Johnson, "Black Literary Engagement with the Haitian Revolution," in *African American Literature in Transition, 1750–1800*, ed. Rhondda Robinson Thomas (Cambridge: Cambridge University Press, 2022), 152–53.
27. *New-York Mercury*, 1 May 1758.
28. *Relation d'une conspiration*, 3–4.
29. Weaver, *Medical Revolutionaries*, 91.
30. Ronald Angelo Johnson, *Diplomacy in Black and White: John Adams, Toussaint Louverture, and Their Atlantic World Alliance* (Athens: University of Georgia Press, 2014), 181.
31. Weaver, *Medical Revolutionaries*, 91.
32. Scholars remain divided over whether the collective acts of resistance to slavery by Black people in Saint-Domingue during the 1750s constituted a rebellion. Monique Allewaert, "Super Fly: François Makandal's Colonial Semiotics," *American Literature* 91, no. 3 (2019): 459–90, https://doi.org/10.1215/00029831-7722092; Dillon and Simpkins, "Makandal and Pandemic Knowledge" 723-35; Garrigus, *Secret Among the Blacks*, 53–74; Weaver, *Medical Revolutionaries*, 76–97; Daut, *Awakening the Ashes*, 351–52n34; "Makandal in Context: French Agronomy in Saint-Domingue," Early Caribbean Digital Archive, accessed 25 May 2024, https://ecda.northeastern.edu/makandal-in-context-french-agronomy-in-saint-domingue/.
33. "Arrêt de Règlement Du Conseil Supérieur du Cap, concernant les empoisonnements, par les esclaves," 11 March 1758, in Emilien Petit, *Traité sur le Gouvernement des Esclaves*, 2 vols. (Paris: Chez Knapen, 1777), 1:204–7.
34. "Arrêt de Règlement Du Conseil Supérieur du Cap, sur la police des esclaves," 7 April 1758, in Petit, *Traité sur le Gouvernement des Esclaves*, 1:307–16.
35. Reports of continued acts of resistance stemming from the "insurrection" piqued the interest of white inhabitants in the Caribbean and Europe. North American newspapers

first reported the Black rebellious activity, along with the vengeful and legal reactions by white officials. New York and Boston editors buried the story among dense reporting of the global war. In September, London newspapers presented the Makandal "insurrection" and its effects as a featured article. They highlighted a letter from Jamaica about Black insurrectionists "who have murder'd a great Number white inhabitants . . . by poisoning the Wells." *London Evening Post*, 23–26 September 1758; *Public Advertiser* (London), 25 September 1758. A pamphlet published in Paris featured a letter from Saint-Domingue dated in November. It suggested that despite burning hundreds of Black people at the stake, officials believed macandalists still planned "to make themselves masters of the colony" by "killing all the whites." *Relation d'une conspiration*, 8.

Introduction

1. Charles-Simon Favart, *L'Anglois a Bordeaux: Comédie en Un Acte et en Vers Libres* (Paris: Chez Duchesne, 1763), 7, 43.

2. Tobias George Smollett, "Art. XI. The Englishman at Bourdeaux, a Comedy," *Critical Review, or, Annals of Literature* 16 (1763): 382–83.

3. Favart, *L'Anglois a Bordeaux*, 38.

4. John Adams, autobiography, June–July 1776, in *Diary & Autobiography of John Adams*, ed. L. H. Butterfield, 4 vols. (Cambridge, MA: Harvard University Press, 1961), 3:338.

5. George Washington, "Farewell Address," 19 September 1796, Founders Online, National Archives, accessed 30 August 2024, http://founders.archives.gov/documents/Washington/05-20-02-0440-0002 (hereafter cited as FONA); Thomas Jefferson, "First Inaugural Address," 4 March 1801, FONA, accessed 30 August 2024, http://founders.archives.gov/documents/Jefferson/01-33-02-0116-0004.

6. Other works that address the complex connections between race and freedom in different parts of the Atlantic world include Yesenia Barragan, *Freedom's Captives: Slavery and Gradual Emancipation on the Colombian Black Pacific* (Cambridge: Cambridge University Press, 2021); Amy Murrell Taylor, *Embattled Freedom: Journeys Through the Civil War's Slave Refugee Camps* (Chapel Hill: University of North Carolina Press, 2018).

7. Abigail Adams to John Adams, 31 March 1776, FONA, accessed 3 August 2024, http://founders.archives.gov/documents/Adams/04-01-02-0241; Abigail Adams to John Adams, 22 September 1774, FONA, accessed 3 August 2024, http://founders.archives.gov/documents/Adams/04-01-02-0107.

8. *Affiches Américaines* (Port-au-Prince), 19 April 1775.

9. For discussions of the contextual approach and the cross-border perspective in scholarly historical literature, see Nathan Perl-Rosenthal, "Atlantic Cultures and the Age of Revolution," *William and Mary Quarterly* 74, no. 4 (2017): 667–96; Bénédicte Zimmermann, "Histoire Croisée: A Relational Process-Based Approach," *Footprint* 14, no. 1 (2020): 7–14, https://doi.org/10.7480/footprint.14.1.4513.

10. A partial list of early US history works includes Serena R. Zabin, *The Boston Massacre: A Family History* (Boston: Houghton Mifflin Harcourt, 2020); Alan Taylor, *American Revolutions: A Continental History, 1750–1804* (New York: W. W. Norton, 2016); Karen Cook Bell, *Running from Bondage: Enslaved Women and Their Remarkable Fight for Freedom in Revolutionary America* (Cambridge: Cambridge University Press, 2021); Joseph J. Ellis, *Revolutionary Summer: The Birth of American Independence* (New York: Vintage Books, 2014); Larrie D. Ferreiro, *Brothers at Arms: American Independence and the Men of France and Spain Who Saved It* (New York: Knopf, 2016);

Gerald Horne, *Negro Comrades of the Crown: African Americans and the British Empire Fight the U.S. before Emancipation* (New York: New York University Press, 2012); Rachel B. Herrmann, *No Useless Mouth: Waging War and Fighting Hunger in the American Revolution* (Ithaca, NY: Cornell University Press, 2019); Douglas R. Egerton, *Death or Liberty: African Americans and Revolutionary America* (Oxford: Oxford University Press, 2009); Robert G. Parkinson, *Thirteen Clocks: How Race United the Colonies and Made the Declaration of Independence* (Chapel Hill: University of North Carolina Press, 2021). A selected list of Haitian historical scholarship includes Wien Weibert Arthus, *Les Grandes Dates de l'Histoire Diplomatique d'Haïti: De la Période Fondatrice à Nos Jours* (Paris: L'Harmattan, 2017); Jean Casimir, *La Nation Haïtienne et l'État* (Paris: Éditions du CIDIHCA, 2022); Jean Coradin, *Histoire Diplomatique d'Haïti, 1804–1843* (Port-au-Prince: Edition des Antilles, 1988); Anthony Georges-Pierre, *L'Exil dans la Politique Haïtienne: De Toussaint Louverture à Aristide* (Pétion-Ville, Haiti: C3 Éditions, 2014); Lewis Ampidu Clorméus and Gaétan Mentor, eds., *Autour de l'Acte de l'Indépendance d'Haïti* (Port-au-Prince: Société Haïtienne d'Histoire, de Géographie et de Géologie, 2014).

11. The narrative framework in this book is informed by "the dialectic between global and local conditions" as presented in Christopher L. Hill, *National History and the World of Nations: Capital, State, and the Rhetoric of History in Japan, France, and the United States* (Durham, NC: Duke University Press, 2008).

12. Jeffrey L. Pasley, *"The Tyranny of Printers": Newspaper Politics in the Early American Republic* (Charlottesville: University Press of Virginia, 2003); Jeffrey Pasley, "Thomas Greenleaf: Printers and the Struggle for Democratic Politics and Freedom of the Press," in *Revolutionary Founders: Rebels, Radicals, and Reformers in the Making of the Nation*, ed. Alfred Young, Gary Nash, and Ray Raphael (New York: Vintage Books, 2011), 355–74; Adolphe Cabon, "Un siècle et demi de journalisme en Haïti," in *Proceedings of the American Antiquarian Society* (Worcester, MA: American Antiquarian Society, 1940), 121–205; Leara Rhodes, "Haitian Contributions to American History: A Journalistic Record," in *Slavery in the Caribbean Francophone World: Distant Voices, Forgotten Acts, Forged Identities*, ed. Doris Y. Kadish (Athens: University of Georgia Press, 2000), 59–67; Robert D. Taber, "Rumor and Repot in Affiches Américaines: Saint-Domingue's American Revolution," Age of Revolutions, 13 September 2017, https://ageofrevolutions.com/2017/09/13/rumor-and-report-in-affiches-americaines-saint-domingues-american-revolution/; Robert D. Taber, "Navigating Haiti's History: Saint-Domingue and the Haitian Revolution," *History Compass* 13, no. 5 (2015): 235–50, https://doi.org/10.1111/hic3.12233.

13. John Adams to Hezekiah Niles, 13 February 1818, FONA, accessed 9 September 2019, http://founders.archives.gov/documents/Adams/99-02-02-6854.

14. Michelle M. Wright, *Physics of Blackness: Beyond the Middle Passage Epistemology* (Minneapolis: University of Minnesota Press, 2015); Karen E. Fields and Barbara Jeanne Fields, *Racecraft: The Soul of Inequality in American Life* (London: Verso, 2012); Alejandro de la Fuente and Ariela J. Gross, *Becoming Free, Becoming Black: Race, Freedom, and Law in Cuba, Virginia, and Louisiana* (Cambridge: Cambridge University Press, 2020); Julius S. Scott, *The Common Wind: Afro-American Currents in the Age of the Haitian Revolution* (New York: Verso, 2018); James Sidbury, *Becoming African in America: Race and Nation in the Early Black Atlantic* (New York: Oxford University Press, 2009); Sharon Block, *Colonial Complexions: Race and Bodies in Eighteenth-Century America* (Philadelphia: University of Pennsylvania Press, 2021); Laurent Dubois and Julius S. Scott, eds., *Origins of the Black Atlantic* (New York: Routledge, 2010); Leslie M. Alexander, *Fear of a Black Republic: Haiti and the Birth of Black Internationalism in the United States* (Champaign: University of Illinois Press, 2023); Gerald Horne, *Confronting Black Jacobins: The United States, the Haitian Revolution, and the Origins of the Dominican Republic* (New York: Monthly Review Press, 2015); Marlene L. Daut, *Tropics of Haiti: Race and the Literary History*

of the Haitian Revolution in the Atlantic World, 1789–1865 (Liverpool: Liverpool University Press, 2015); Doris Y. Kadish and Françoise Massardier-Kenney, eds., *Translating Slavery*, vol. 1, *Gender and Race in French Abolitionist Writing, 1780–1830*, 2nd ed. (Kent, OH: Kent State University Press, 2009); Sue Peabody and Tyler Stovall, eds., *The Color of Liberty: Histories of Race in France* (Durham, NC: Duke University Press, 2003).

15. Leslie M. Harris, "Names, Terms, and Politics," *Journal of the Early Republic* 43, no. 1 (2023): 151.

16. Elise A. Mitchell, "Black and African American," *Journal of the Early Republic* 43, no. 1 (2023): 86.

17. Sidbury, *Becoming African*, 6.

18. Françoise Massardier-Kenney, "Translation Theory and Practice," in *Translating Slavery*, vol. 1, *Gender and Race in French Abolitionist Writing, 1780–1830*, ed. Doris Y. Kadish and Françoise Massardier-Kenney, 2nd ed. (Kent, OH: Kent State University Press, 2009), 11.

19. C. L. R. James, *The Black Jacobins: Toussaint l'Ouverture and the San Domingo Revolution*, 2nd ed. (New York: Vintage Books, 1989), 38.

20. David Geggus, "The Slaves and Free People of Color of Cap Français," in *The Black Urban Atlantic in the Age of the Slave Trade*, ed. Jorge Cañizares-Esguerra, Matt D. Childs, and James Sidbury (Philadelphia: University of Pennsylvania Press, 2013), 107.

21. Daut, *Tropics of Haiti*, 19; Massardier-Kenney, "Translation Theory and Practice," 10–11.

1. "Their Colour Is a Diabolic Die"

1. *The Definitive Treaty of Peace and Friendship, between His Britannick Majesty, the Most Christian King, and the King of Spain* (London: E. Owen and T. Harrison, 1763), 9–22.

2. The value of four million French livres in 1763 equaled roughly 196,000 British pounds in the same year. Rodney Edvinsson, Historical Currency Converter, accessed 5 August 2024, https://www.historicalstatistics.org/Currencyconverter.html.

3. Yvonne Eileen Fabella, "Inventing the Creole Citizen: Race, Sexuality and the Colonial Order in Pre-Revolutionary Saint Domingue" (PhD diss., State University of New York at Stony Brook, 2008), 20.

4. Marlene L. Daut, *Tropics of Haiti: Race and the Literary History of the Haitian Revolution in the Atlantic World, 1789–1865* (Liverpool: Liverpool University Press, 2015), 14.

5. Tom Reiss, *The Black Count: Glory, Revolution, Betrayal, and the Real Count of Monte Cristo* (New York: Crown, 2012).

6. John D. Garrigus, *Before Haiti: Race and Citizenship in French Saint-Domingue* (New York: Palgrave Macmillan, 2011), 115–16.

7. Garrigus, *Before Haiti*, 116–19.

8. *Treaty of Peace and Friendship*, 1763, 14–16; Ignotus, *Thoughts on Trade in General, Our West-Indian in Particular, Our Continental Colonies, Canada, Guadaloupe, and the Preliminary Articles of Peace* (London: printed for John Wilkie, 1763), 76–79; *The Beginning, Progress, and Conclusion of the Late War with Other Interesting Matters Considered* (London: printed for J. Almon, 1770), 25–27.

9. Garrigus, *Before Haiti*, 122.

10. Julia Prest, "Performing the Racial Scale: From Colonial Saint-Domingue to Contemporary Hollywood," *Insights* 10, no. 7 (2017), https://www.iasdurham.org/wp-content/uploads/2021/03/Prest_Performing-the-Racial-Scale-From-Colonial-Saint-Domingue-to-Contemporary-Hollywood.pdf.

11. *Providence (RI) Gazette*, 26 January 1765.

12. *New-York Gazette*, 27 May 1765.

13. Sheila L. Skemp, *The Making of a Patriot: Benjamin Franklin at the Cockpit* (New York: Oxford University Press, 2013), 78.

14. Page Smith, *John Adams*, 2 vols. (Garden City, NY: Doubleday, 1962), 1:74.

15. Robert D. Taber, "Rumor and Repot in Affiches Américaines: Saint-Domingue's American Revolution," *Age of Revolutions*, 13 September 2017, https://ageofrevolutions.com/2017/09/13/rumor-and-report-in-affiches-americaines-saint-domingues-american-revolution/.

16. Edwin S. Gaustad, *Benjamin Franklin* (New York: Oxford University Press, 2006), 66.

17. John Adams, diary entry, 18 December 1765, in *Diary & Autobiography of John Adams*, ed. L. H. Butterfield, 4 vols. (Cambridge, MA: Harvard University Press, 1961), 1:263 (hereafter cited as *DAJA*).

18. John Adams, "A Dissertation on the Canon and the Feudal Law," Founders Online, National Archives, 21 October 1765, http://founders.archives.gov/documents/Adams/06-01-02-0052-0007 (hereafter cited as FONA).

19. John Adams, diary entry, 18 December 1765, *DAJA*, 1:263.

20. John Adams, diary entry, 31 December 1765, *DAJA*, 1:282.

21. *New-York Gazette*, 10 March 1766.

22. John Adams, diary entry, 2 January 1766, *DAJA*, 1:285.

23. *Massachusetts Gazette* (Boston), 28 November 1765.

24. John Adams, diary entry, 2 January 1766, *DAJA*, 1:285.

25. Skemp, *Making of a Patriot*, xiv, 79–80.

26. Skemp, *Making of a Patriot*, 79–81.

27. Skemp, *Making of a Patriot*, 80–84.

28. Gaustad, *Benjamin Franklin*, 66–67.

29. Skemp, *Making of a Patriot*, 86.

30. "Examination Before the Committee of the Whole of the House of Commons, 13 February 1766," FONA, accessed 9 August 2024, http://founders.archives.gov/documents/Franklin/01-13-02-0035.

31. Skemp, *Making of a Patriot*, 87–88.

32. Gaustad, *Benjamin Franklin*, 67, 70–71.

33. Timothy J. Shannon, *Indians and Colonists at the Crossroads of Empire: The Albany Congress of 1754* (Ithaca, NY: Cornell University Press, 1999).

34. *Treaty of Peace and Friendship*, 1763, 9–11.

35. Josephine F. Pacheco, "French Secret Agents in America, 1763–1778" (PhD diss., University of Chicago, 1950), 7.

36. Jonathan R. Dull, *A Diplomatic History of the American Revolution* (New Haven, CT: Yale University Press, 1985), 29.

37. Dull, *Diplomatic History*, 9.

38. François de Pontleroy, quoted in Richard J. Werther, "Scouting the American Revolution: The French Intelligence Community," *Journal of the American Revolution*, 9 April 2020, https://allthingsliberty.com/2020/04/scouting-the-american-revolution-the-french-intelligence-community/.

39. Pacheco, "French Secret Agents," 43–49.

40. Pacheco, "French Secret Agents," 30–35.

41. Rayford W. Logan, *The Diplomatic Relations of the United States with Haiti, 1776–1891* (Chapel Hill: University of North Carolina Press, 1941), 7–8.

42. Pacheco, "French Secret Agents," 59.

43. James H. Hutson, *John Adams and the Diplomacy of the American Revolution* (Lexington: University Press of Kentucky, 2014), 9–10.

44. Étienne François de Choiseul, quoted in Werther, "Scouting the American Revolution."
45. Dull, *Diplomatic History*, 9.
46. Benjamin Franklin to William Franklin, 28 August 1767, FONA, accessed 6 June 2020, https://founders.archives.gov/documents/Franklin/01-14-02-0146.
47. Pacheco, "French Secret Agents," 63–64.
48. Logan, *Diplomatic Relations*, 7.
49. *Boston Gazette*, 16 January 1769.
50. Ryan Hanley, *Beyond Slavery and Abolition: Black British Writing, c.1770–1830* (Cambridge: Cambridge University Press, 2019), 4, 9, 240.
51. Briton Hammon, *Narrative of the Uncommon Sufferings, and Surprizing Deliverance of Briton Hammon* (Boston: Green & Russell, 1760), 3.
52. Frances Smith Foster and Larose Davis, "Early African American Women's Literature," in *The Cambridge Companion to African American Women's Literature*, ed. Angelyn Mitchell and Danille K. Taylor (Cambridge: Cambridge University Press, 2009), 17.
53. Hammon, *Uncommon Sufferings*, 3, 8, 12–13.
54. Italics in the original. Hammon, *Uncommon Sufferings*, 11. See also Robert Desrochers, "'Surprizing Deliverance'? Slavery and Freedom, Language, and Identity in the Narrative of Briton Hammon, 'A Negro Man,'" in *Genius in Bondage: Literature of the Early Black Atlantic*, ed. Vincent Carretta and Philip Gould (Lexington: University Press of Kentucky, 2001), 165.
55. Hammon, *Uncommon Sufferings*, 12.
56. For a discussion of Guinea and Atlantic slavery, see Gwendolyn Midlo Hall, *Slavery and African Ethnicities in the Americas: Restoring the Links* (Chapel Hill: University of North Carolina Press, 2005), 80–126.
57. Karen A. Weyler, *Empowering Words: Outsiders and Authorship in Early America* (Athens: University of Georgia Press, 2013), 96.
58. Hanley, *Beyond Slavery and Abolition*, 7–13.
59. Foster and Davis, "Early African American Women's Literature," 16.
60. Phillis Wheatley, *Poems on Various Subjects, Religious and Moral* (London: A. Bell, 1773), 17.
61. Robert J. Chaffin, "The Townshend Acts Crisis, 1767–1770," in *A Companion to the American Revolution*, ed. Jack P. Greene and J. R. Pole (Hoboken, NJ: Wiley-Blackwell, 2000), 134–50.
62. Wheatley, *Poems on Various Subjects*, 17.
63. Foster and Davis, "Early African American Women's Literature," 16.
64. Hanley, *Beyond Slavery and Abolition*, 240.
65. June Jordan, "The Difficult Miracle of Black Poetry in America or Something Like a Sonnet for Phillis Wheatley," in *Wild Women in the Whirlwind: Afra-American Culture and the Contemporary Literary Renaissance*, ed. Joanne M. Braxton and Andrée Nicola McLaughlin (New Brunswick, NJ: Rutgers University Press, 1990), 22–34; Foster and Davis, "Early African American Women's Literature," 16.
66. Wheatley, *Poems on Various Subjects*, 16, 62.
67. Wheatley, *Poems on Various Subjects*, 18.
68. Vincent Carretta, *Phillis Wheatley: Biography of a Genius in Bondage* (Athens: University of Georgia Press, 2011), 60.
69. Wheatley, *Poems on Various Subjects*, 18; Phillis Wheatley, "On Being Brought from Africa to America," in *The Wiley Anthology of African American Literature*, vol. 1, *1746–1920*, ed. Gene Andrew Jarrett (Hoboken, NJ: Wiley-Blackwell, 2014), 19.
70. Keith Byerman, "Talking Back: Phillis Wheatley, Race, and Religion," *Religions* 10, no. 401 (2019), https://doi.org/10.3390/rel10060401.

71. Wheatley, *Poems on Various Subjects*, 18.
72. Carretta, *Phillis Wheatley*, 105–6, 108.
73. Wheatley, *Poems on Various Subjects*, 9, 11; Carretta, *Phillis Wheatley*, 106.
74. Foster and Davis, "Early African American Women's Literature," 16.
75. David Waldstreicher, "Ancients, Moderns, and Africans: Phillis Wheatley and the Politics of Empire and Slavery in the American Revolution," *Journal of the Early Republic* 37, no. 4 (2017): 727, 732. For fuller treatment of Phillis Wheatley, see David Waldstreicher, *The Odyssey of Phillis Wheatley: A Poet's Journeys Through American Slavery and Independence* (New York: Farrar, Straus and Giroux, 2023); Danielle Legros Georges and Artress Bethany White, eds., *Wheatley at 250: Black Women Poets Re-Imagine the Verse of Phillis Wheatley Peters* (Cambridge, MA: Pangyrus, 2023); Tara Bynum, *Reading Pleasures: Everyday Black Living in Early America* (Urbana: University of Illinois Press, 2023), 23–52; Henry Louis Gates, *The Trials of Phillis Wheatley: America's First Black Poet and Her Encounters with the Founding Fathers* (New York: Basic Civitas Books, 2010).
76. Foster and Davis, "Early African American Women's Literature," 16; Hanley, *Beyond Slavery and Abolition*, 246.
77. Charles Frostin, *Les Révoltes Blanches à Saint-Domingue aux XVIIe et XVIIIe Siècles (Haïti Avant 1789)* (Paris: L'École, 1975), 308.
78. Garrigus, *Before Haiti*, 130.
79. Beauvais Lespinasse, *Histoire des Affranchis de Saint-Domingue. Tome Premier* (Paris: J. Kugelmann, 1882), 151.
80. Garrigus, *Before Haiti*, 130.
81. Lespinasse, *Histoire des Affranchis*, 151.
82. Garrigus, *Before Haiti*, 130.
83. Lespinasse, *Histoire des Affranchis*, 151; Garrigus, *Before Haiti*, 130.
84. Garrigus, *Before Haiti*, 131.
85. Lespinasse, *Histoire des Affranchis*, 152.
86. Garrigus, *Before Haiti*, 131.
87. Lespinasse, *Histoire des Affranchis*, 150, 153–54.
88. Lespinasse, *Histoire des Affranchis*, 150, 154.
89. Lespinasse, *Histoire des Affranchis*, 151, 154.
90. C. L. R. James, *The Black Jacobins: Toussaint l'Ouverture and the San Domingo Revolution*, 2nd ed. (New York: Vintage Books, 1989), 37; David P. Geggus, "The Slaves and Free People of Color of Cap Français," in *The Black Urban Atlantic in the Age of the Slave Trade*, ed. Jorge Cañizares-Esguerra, Matt D. Childs, and James Sidbury (Philadelphia: University of Pennsylvania Press, 2013), 107.
91. Garrigus, *Before Haiti*, 132.
92. Médéric Louis Élie Moreau de Saint-Méry, *Loix et Constitutions des Colonies Françoises de l'Amérique Sous le Vent*, 6 vols. (Paris: l'Auteur, 1785), 5:337 (hereafter cited as *LCCFA*).
93. Frostin, *Les Révoltes Blanches*, 311.
94. Lespinasse, *Histoire des Affranchis*, 154.
95. Frostin, *Les Révoltes Blanches*, 310.
96. *LCCFA*, 5:337.
97. Julien Raimond, *Observations Sur l'Origine et Les Progés du Préjugé des Colons Blancs Contre Les Hommes de Couleur* (Paris: Belin, 1791), 9.
98. Raimond, *Observations Sur l'Origine*, 10.
99. Frostin, *Les Révoltes Blanches*, 311–13, 346.
100. Frostin, *Les Révoltes Blanches*, 312–13; Garrigus, *Before Haiti*, 136–37.
101. *LCCFA*, 5:338.

102. Frostin, *Les Révoltes Blanches*, 312.
103. *Boston Post-Boy*, 8 May 1769.
104. Frostin, *Les Révoltes Blanches*, 347–48.
105. *Georgia Gazette* (Savannah), 21 February 1770.
106. *Boston News-Letter*, 17 November 1769.
107. Frostin, *Les Révoltes Blanches*, 348.
108. *Georgia Gazette* (Savannah), 11 October 1769.
109. *Boston Chronicle*, 14 September 1769.
110. *New-York Gazette*, 23 April 1770.
111. *New-York Gazette*, 8 January 1770 (capitalization and italics in the original).
112. Charles Dickens, *A Tale of Two Cities* (London: Chapman and Hall, 1859), 10.
113. Dickens, *Tale of Two Cities*, 27.
114. Alexander Hamilton to Edward Stevens, 11 November 1769, in *The Papers of Alexander Hamilton, Digital Edition*, ed. Harold C. Syrett (Charlottesville: University of Virginia Press, Rotunda, 2011), https://rotunda.upress.virginia.edu/founders/ARHN.html (hereafter cited as *PAHDE*).
115. Alexander Hamilton to Edward Stevens, 11 November 1769, *PAHDE*.
116. Kethly Millet, "Dessalines, Jean-Jacques," in *Dictionnaire Historique de La Révolution Haïtienne*, ed. Claude Moïse, 2nd ed. (Montreal: CIDIHCA, 2019), 114.
117. Alexander Hamilton to Edward Stevens, 11 November 1769, *PAHDE* (capitalization in the original).

2. "Kill Them! Kill Them!"

1. Alexander Hamilton to Edward Stevens, 11 November 1769, *The Papers of Alexander Hamilton, Digital Edition*, ed. Harold C. Syrett (Charlottesville: University of Virginia Press, Rotunda, 2011), accessed 18 October 2021, https://www.upress.virginia.edu/title/ARHN/ (capitalization in the original).
2. Ron Chernow, *Alexander Hamilton* (New York: Penguin, 2004), 49.
3. *New-York Journal*, 21 June 1770.
4. *New-York Gazette*, 12 February 1770; 19 March 1770; 24 September 1770.
5. *The Beginning, Progress, and Conclusion of the Late War with Other Interesting Matters Considered* (London: printed for J. Almon, 1770), 2, 20, 23, 31.
6. *Beginning, Progress, and Conclusion of the Late War*, 17–18, 32.
7. *New-York Gazette*, 24 September 1770.
8. Joseph S. Tiedemann, *Reluctant Revolutionaries: New York City and the Road to Independence, 1763–1776* (Ithaca, NY: Cornell University Press, 1997), 147–49; Mariam Touba, "The Battle of Golden Hill: New York's Opening Act of Revolutionary Bloodshed," *From the Stacks* (blog), New York Historical Society, 16 January 2020, https://www.nyhistory.org/blogs/the-battle-of-golden-hill-new-yorks-opening-act-of-revolutionary-bloodshed; Arthur Meier Schlesinger, "Political Mobs and the American Revolution, 1765–1776," *Proceedings of the American Philosophical Society* 99, no. 4 (1955): 245; Michael D. Hattem, "'As Serves Our Interest Best': Political Economy and the Logic of Popular Resistance in New York City, 1765–1776," *New York History* 98, no. 1 (2017): 59–60; David C. Humphrey, *From King's College to Columbia, 1746–1800* (New York: Columbia University Press, 1976), 129–44.
9. *New-York Gazette*, 5 March 1770; Serena Zabin, *The Boston Massacre: A Family History* (Boston: Houghton Mifflin Harcourt, 2020), 143.

10. *New-York Gazette*, 5 March 1770.

11. "Crispus Attucks Alias Michael Johnson," Crispus Attucks On-Line Museum, University of Massachusetts, 15 February 2023, accessed 3 March 2023, http://www.crispusattucksmuseum.org/document-crispus-attucks/.

12. Bernard Bailyn, *The Ideological Origins of the American Revolution*, enlarged ed. (Cambridge, MA: Belknap, 1992), v–vi.

13. *Diary of Cotton Mather*, ed. Worthington Chauncey Ford, 2 vols. (Boston: Massachusetts Historical Society, 1911–12), 1:564–65.

14. Cotton Mather, *The Negro Christianized: An Essay to Excite and Assist the Good Work, the Instruction of Negro-Servants in Christianity* (Boston: printed by B. Green, 1706), 22.

15. Mather, *Negro Christianized*, 39, 43.

16. *Diary of Cotton Mather*, 1:176–77.

17. *Boston Gazette*, 2 October 1750.

18. *Boston Gazette*, 2 October 1750.

19. Sharon Block, *Colonial Complexions: Race and Bodies in Eighteenth-Century America* (Philadelphia: University of Pennsylvania Press, 2021), 56, 85, 94, 104, 106.

20. *Boston Gazette*, 20 November 1750.

21. *Diary of Cotton Mather*, 1:177.

22. William Dillon Piersen, *Black Yankees: The Development of an Afro-American Subculture in Eighteenth-Century New England* (Amherst: University of Massachusetts Press, 1988), 55–56.

23. Sylviane A. Diouf, *Slavery's Exiles: The Story of the American Maroons* (New York: New York University Press, 2014), 1–2.

24. Celeste Winston, "Maroon Geographies," *Annals of the American Association of Geographers* 111, no. 7 (2021): 2186.

25. Winston, "Maroon Geographies," 2186–87.

26. Neville A. T. Hall, "Maritime Maroons: Grand Marronage from the Danish West Indies," in *Origins of the Black Atlantic*, ed. Laurent Dubois and Julius Sherrard Scott (New York: Routledge, 2010), 51–52. Julius S. Scott discusses freedom seekers crossing the Caribbean Sea from Jamaica to Cuba in Scott, *The Common Wind: Afro-American Currents in the Age of the Haitian Revolution* (New York: Verso, 2018), 63–68.

27. W. Jeffrey Bolster, *Black Jacks: African American Seamen in the Age of Sail* (Cambridge, MA: Harvard University Press, 1997), 9.

28. Mitchell A. Kachun, *First Martyr of Liberty: Crispus Attucks in American Memory* (New York: Oxford University Press, 2017), 8.

29. Ira Berlin, "From Creole to African: Atlantic Creoles and the Origins of African-American Society in Mainland North America," *William and Mary Quarterly* 53, no. 2 (1996): 251–88; Bolster, *Black Jacks*, 9–10.

30. Peter Linebaugh and Marcus Rediker, *The Many-Headed Hydra: Sailors, Slaves, Commoners, and the Hidden History of the Revolutionary Atlantic* (Boston: Beacon, 2000), 232.

31. "Indeed, Bahamian society, with the existence of subclasses within the white section as well as racial and class crossovers within families at all levels, was already more like a complex social spectrum than the tripartite system claimed by many commentators for Latin America and the Caribbean in general, let alone the simply bifurcated society developing in the American mainland colonies." Michael Craton and Gail Saunders, *Islanders in the Stream: A History of the Bahamian People, Volume One: From Aboriginal Times to the End of Slavery* (Athens: University of Georgia Press, 2011), 147, 151, 156, 172.

32. *The Definitive Treaty of Peace and Friendship, between His Britannick Majesty, the Most Christian King, and the King of Spain* (London: E. Owen and T. Harrison, 1763), 16; Ignotus, *Thoughts*

on Trade in General, Our West-Indian in Particular, Our Continental Colonies, Canada, Guadaloupe, and the Preliminary Articles of Peace (London: printed for John Wilkie, 1763), 72–73. Gorée Island, located off the coast of present-day Dakar, Senegal, served as an important eighteenth-century harbor for European ships carrying human beings to the western Atlantic world. A small doorway through which African women and men reportedly passed to board slave ships is called the Door of No Return. US President Barack Obama and First Lady Michelle Obama toured Gorée Island in 2013 during a diplomatic visit to Senegal. Pictures of America's first presidential couple of African ancestry standing in the passageway popularized the Door of No Return for many Americans. Olga Idriss Davis, "The Door of No Return: Reclaiming the Past Through the Rhetoric of Pilgrimage," *Western Journal of Black Studies* 21, no. 3 (1997): 156–61.

33. Craton and Saunders, *Islanders in the Stream*, 150–52.

34. Craton and Saunders, *Islanders in the Stream*, 152–55, 162.

35. Bolster, *Black Jacks*, 38–39. See also Olaudah Equiano, *The Life of Olaudah Equiano, or, Gustavus Vassa, the African* (Boston: Isaac Knapp, 1837).

36. James Sidbury, *Becoming African in America: Race and Nation in the Early Black Atlantic* (New York: Oxford University Press, 2009), 6–7.

37. Scott, *Common Wind*, 36; Paul Gilroy, *The Black Atlantic: Modernity and Double-Consciousness* (Cambridge, MA: Harvard University Press, 1995).

38. Alison Games, *Migration and the Origins of the English Atlantic World* (Cambridge, MA: Harvard University Press, 2001); Bernard Bailyn, *Atlantic History: Concept and Contours* (Cambridge, MA: Harvard University Press, 2005); Peter A. Coclanis, "Atlantic World or Atlantic/World?," *William and Mary Quarterly* 63, no. 4 (2006): 725–42.

39. Sidbury, *Becoming African*, 6; Françoise Massardier-Kenney, "Translation Theory and Practice," in *Translating Slavery*, vol. 1, *Gender and Race in French Abolitionist Writing, 1780–1830*, ed. Doris Y. Kadish and Françoise Massardier-Kenney, 2nd ed. (Kent, OH: Kent State University Press, 2009), 11.

40. Leslie M. Alexander, *Fear of a Black Republic: Haiti and the Birth of Black Internationalism in the United States* (Champaign: University of Illinois Press, 2023), 7.

41. Block, *Colonial Complexions*, 84–85; Alejandro de la Fuente and Ariela J. Gross, *Becoming Free, Becoming Black: Race, Freedom, and Law in Cuba, Virginia, and Louisiana* (Cambridge: Cambridge University Press, 2020), 34–38.

42. Stephen L. Carter, *Palace Council* (New York: Vintage Books, 2009), 16.

43. Sidbury, *Becoming African*, 6–7.

44. John D. Garrigus, *Before Haiti: Race and Citizenship in French Saint-Domingue* (New York: Palgrave Macmillan, 2011), 118.

45. Scott, *Common Wind*, 29–32.

46. "*Libres de fait* were male and female, black and of mixed race, African and Creole, urban and rural, and specialized and nonspecialized by profession or occupation. Most of them, however, were mixed-race and Creole women of color and their children. Throughout slavery the number of *libres de fait* remained small compared to the total population of free persons with clear titles, which was insignificant compared to the number of slaves in each French colony." Bernard Moitt, "In the Shadow of the Plantation: Women of Color and the Libres de Fait of Martinique and Guadeloupe, 1685–1848," in *Beyond Bondage: Free Women of Color in the Americas*, ed. David Barry Gaspar and Darlene Clark Hine (Champaign: University of Illinois Press, 2004), 37–38.

47. Médéric Louis Élie Moreau de Saint-Méry, *Loix et Constitutions des Colonies Françoises de l'Amérique Sous le Vent*, 6 vols. (Paris: Chez l'Auteur, 1787), 5:291.

48. Moreau, *Loix et Constitutions*, 5:291.

49. Garrigus, *Before Haiti*, 132; John Garrigus, email to author, 28 April 2023.

50. Garrigus, *Before Haiti*, 83, 332n3.

51. Gabriel Debien, *Plantations et Esclaves à Saint-Domingue* (Dakar, Senegal: Université de Dakar Faculté des Lettres et Sciences Humaines, 1962), 45, 50.

52. Pompée Valentin, Baron de Vastey, *The Colonial System Unveiled*, trans. Chris Bongie (Liverpool: Liverpool University Press, 2014), 135n.

53. Vastey, *Colonial System Unveiled*, 135n. Other works that suggest Denis as Paul Carenan's father are Beauvais Lespinasse, *Histoire des Affranchis de Saint-Domingue, Tome Premier* (Paris: J. Kugelmann, 1882), 240; Garrigus, *Before Haiti*, 83.

54. Lespinasse, *Histoire des Affranchis*, 232. Lespinasse wrote further, "This is why Garran Coulon says 'that we included in our islands, under the denomination of colored men, not only all those who came from the mixture of the two colors and their descendants, but also the negroes even originating in Africa or colonies, provided that both had the actual enjoyment of freedom.'"

55. Moreau, *Loix et Constitutions*, 5:290. For information on the Superior Council of Port-au-Prince, see "Histoire de l'ancienne Colonie de Saint-Domingue," infoBretagne.com, accessed 21 April 2023, http://www.infobretagne.com/saint-domingue.htm.

56. The council referred to "Paul, dit [known as, or who called himself] Carenan." Moreau, *Loix et Constitutions*, 5:290.

57. Moreau, *Loix et Constitutions*, 5:290.

58. Moreau, *Loix et Constitutions*, 5:291; Vastey, *Colonial System Unveiled*, 136n.

59. C. L. R. James, *The Black Jacobins: Toussaint l'Ouverture and the San Domingo Revolution*, 2nd ed. (New York: Vintage Books, 1989), 39.

60. Vastey, *Colonial System Unveiled*, 135.

61. Jean-Philippe Garran de Coulon, *An Inquiry into the Causes of the Insurrection of the Negroes in the Island of St. Domingo* (London: J. Johnson, 1792), 10.

62. Garran de Coulon, *Inquiry*, 10.

63. *Affiches Américaines* (Port-au-Prince), 7 February 1770.

64. *Georgia Gazette* (Savannah), 7 February 1770.

65. Moreau, *Loix et Constitutions*, 5:291. Rousseau's wildly popular epistolary novel *La Nouvelle Héloïse* pulled at the heartstrings of readers throughout France. The love Héloïse exhibited was "spiritual," rendering it more meaningful. Yvonne Eileen Fabella, "Inventing the Creole Citizen: Race, Sexuality and the Colonial Order in Pre-Revolutionary Saint Domingue" (PhD diss., State University of New York at Stony Brook, 2008), 181, 200–201; Jean-Jacques Rousseau, *Lettres de Deux Amans, Habitans d'une petite Ville au pied des Alpes* (Amsterdam: Chez Rey, 1761).

66. Moreau, *Loix et Constitutions*, 5:291.

67. Apparently, Nolivos and Bongars freed Paul Carenan and referred their verdict to King Louis XV. To date, no record has been found to verify if the king received, read, or decided on the Carenan appeal. Moreau, *Loix et Constitutions*, 5:291.

68. Lespinasse, *Histoire des Affranchis*, 1:242.

69. Moreau, *Loix et Constitutions*, 5:291. For more on the Code Noir in Paul Carenan's case, see Lespinasse, *Histoire des Affranchis*, 240–41.

70. Moreau, *Loix et Constitutions*, 5:291.

71. Bolster, *Black Jacks*, 11.

72. Scott, *Common Wind*, 76.

73. Scott, *Common Wind*, 3, 19.

74. *Affiches Américaines* (Port-au-Prince), 14 February 1770; 25 July 1770; 5 September 1770. The news reports of the majority of freedom seekers "etampe," or branded, exhibit the exceptional cruelty of white slaveholders in Saint-Domingue. They branded enslaved people "on

their chests with a hot iron" to imprint the name of their enslaver and the parish in which they lived. Jayne Boisvert, "Colonial Hell and Female Slave Resistance in Saint-Domingue," *Journal of Haitian Studies* 7, no. 1 (2001): 62.

75. Scott, *Common Wind*, 55–56, 79; Bolster, *Black Jacks*, 39–41.

76. John Adams, diary entry, 24 September 1775, in *The Works of John Adams, Second President of the United States*, ed. Charles Francis Adams, 10 vols. (Boston: Charles C. Little and James Brown, 1850–56), 2:428.

77. Scott, *Common Wind*, 38–39, 76–77.

78. *New-York Gazette*, 8 January 1770.

79. *Georgia Gazette* (Savannah), 21 February 1770.

80. *Affiches Américaines* (Port-au-Prince), 14 February 1770.

81. *Boston-Gazette*, March 12, 1770.

82. *Boston-Gazette*, 5 March 1770.

83. Zabin, *Boston Massacre*; Kachun, *First Martyr*; Douglas R. Egerton, *Death or Liberty: African Americans and Revolutionary America* (Oxford: Oxford University Press, 2009).

84. Kachun, *First Martyr*, 15; Egerton, *Death or Liberty*, 55.

85. Zabin, *Boston Massacre*, 152.

86. Kachun, *First Martyr*, 16.

87. *Boston Chronicle*, 8 March 1770; *New-York Gazette*, 26 March 1770.

88. For the best treatment of the intimate nature of revolutionary violence in Boston, see Zabin, *Boston Massacre*.

89. Farah Peterson, "Black Lives and the Boston Massacre," *American Scholar*, Winter 2019, accessed 6 July 2021, https://theamericanscholar.org/black-lives-and-the-boston-massacre/.

90. *Beginning, Progress, and Conclusion of the Late War*, 18, 20.

91. Egerton, *Death or Liberty*, 55.

92. Kachun, *First Martyr*, 9–12.

93. Nathan Perl-Rosenthal, *Citizen Sailors: Becoming American in the Age of Revolution* (Cambridge, MA: Belknap, 2015), 52–53; Scott, *Common Wind*, 40–41, 114.

94. Briton Hammon, *Narrative of the Uncommon Sufferings, and Surprizing Deliverance of Briton Hammon* (Boston: Green & Russell, 1760), 1, 6; Bolster, *Black Jacks*, 36.

95. Equiano, *Life of Olaudah Equiano*, 124, 223–24; Scott, *Common Wind*, 71.

96. Bolster, *Black Jacks*, 35–39, 127–28, 161, 167, 230.

97. Scott, *Common Wind*, 79.

98. Bolster, *Black Jacks*, 5.

99. For a discussion of the impact of the presence of British troops in Boston on American revolutionary fervor, in general, and on the Boston Massacre, in particular, see Richard Archer, *As If an Enemy's Country: The British Occupation of Boston and the Origins of Revolution* (New York: Oxford University Press, 2010), 182–206.

100. Paul Revere, "A View of Part of the Town of Boston in New-England and British Ships of War: Landing Their Troops! 1768," News Media and the Making of America, 1730–1865, American Antiquarian Society, accessed 6 April 2023, https://collections.americanantiquarian.org/earlyamericannewsmedia/items/show/27.

101. Benjamin L. Carp, *Rebels Rising: Cities and the American Revolution* (Oxford: Oxford University Press, 2007), 23–29, 45–53; Sidney Kaplan and Emma Nogrady Kaplan, *The Black Presence in the Era of the American Revolution*, rev. ed. (Amherst: University of Massachusetts Press, 1989), 6.

102. *Massachusetts Gazette* (Boston), 15 March 1770; *Boston Chronicle*, 8 March 1770.

103. *Boston Gazette*, 12 March 1770.
104. *Boston Gazette* (Boston), 12 March 1770 (capitalization and alternate spelling in the original).
105. *Boston Gazette*, 12 March 1770; Kachun, *First Martyr*, 17–18; Louise Phelps Kellogg, "The Paul Revere Print of the Boston Massacre," *Wisconsin Magazine of History* 1, no. 4 (1918): 379.
106. *Massachusetts Gazette* (Boston), 15 March 1770.
107. *Boston Gazette*, 12 March 1770.
108. Kellogg, "Paul Revere Print," 380.
109. Kachun, *First Martyr*, 18.
110. *Georgia Gazette* (Savannah), 11 April 1770.
111. Karsten Fitz, "Commemorating Crispus Attucks: Visual Memory and the Representations of the Boston Massacre, 1770–1857," *Amerikastudien / American Studies* 50, no. 3 (2005): 469–70 (italics in the original). See also Kachun, *First Martyr*, 17; Peterson, "Black Lives and the Boston Massacre." Serena Zabin offers one of the best descriptions of Revere's effective changes to Henry Pelham's sketch, without discussing the victims. Zabin, *Boston Massacre*, xi–xvi.
112. Fitz, "Commemorating Crispus Attucks," 470n13.
113. Kellogg, "Paul Revere Print," 380–84.
114. "The Bloody Massacre Perpetrated in King Street, Boston on March 5th 1770 by a Party of the 29th Regiment," Massachusetts Historical Society Collections Online, accessed 6 April 2023, https://www.masshist.org/database/2?ft=Boston%20Massacre&from=/features/massacre/visual&noalt=1&pid=34; "Paul Revere's Engraving of the Boston Massacre, 1770," Gilder Lehrman Institute of American History, accessed 6 April 2023, https://www.gilderlehrman.org/history-resources/spotlight-primary-source/paul-reveres-engraving-boston-massacre-1770; "The Bloody Massacre Perpetrated in King Street Boston on March 5th 1770 by a Party of the 29th Regt.," Library of Congress, accessed 6 April 2023, https://www.loc.gov/item/2008680173/.
115. "Paul Revere's Engraving of the Boston Massacre, 1770."
116. Peterson, "Black Lives and the Boston Massacre."
117. Town of Boston, *A Short Narrative of the horrid Massacre in Boston Perpetrated in the Evening of the Fifth Day of March 1770* (Boston: Edes and Gill, 1770), 5.
118. Boston, *Short Narrative of the horrid Massacre*, 5–8.
119. Boston, *Short Narrative of the horrid Massacre*, 32.
120. Zabin, *Boston Massacre*, 214–15; Kachun, *First Martyr*, 15.
121. Dan Abrams and David Fisher, *John Adams Under Fire: The Founding Father's Fight for Justice in the Boston Massacre Murder Trial* (Toronto: Hanover Square, 2021), 15–16.
122. Peterson, "Black Lives and the Boston Massacre."
123. Peter Shaw, *The Character of John Adams* (Chapel Hill: University of North Carolina Press, 1976), 77–78.
124. Sidbury, *Becoming African*, 38.
125. *Legal Papers of John Adams*, vol. 3, Adams Papers Digital Edition, Massachusetts Historical Society, accessed 11 March 2023, https://www.masshist.org/publications/adams-papers/index.php/view/ADMS-05-03-7-contents (Hereafter cited as *LPJA*, APDE-MHS).
126. "Trowbridge's and Oliver's Charges to the Jury," 5 December 1770, *LPJA*, APDE-MHS.
127. "Adams' Argument for the Defense," 3–4 December 1770, *LPJA*, APDE-MHS.
128. Block, *Colonial Complexions*, 61–67, 84–85, 107–8; de la Fuente and Gross, *Becoming Free, Becoming Black*, 34–38. Adams's oration also included an anti-immigrant bent. In this, however, he invoked the xenophobic term "Irish teagues" only once. "Adams' Argument for the Defense," 3–4 December 1770, *LPJA*, APDE-MHS. The ethnic background of Patrick Carr, Attucks's fellow martyr, was mentioned three times during the trial—twice by Adams. The

lawyers and witnesses referred to Carr as "a native of Ireland." Testimony of John Jeffries, quoted in "Transcript of Remaining Defense Evidence," 30 November–1 December 1770, *LPJA*, APDE-MHS.

129. J. L. Bell, "Newton Prince and the Struggle for Liberty," *Journal of the American Revolution*, 2 December 2014, https://allthingsliberty.com/2014/12/newton-prince-and-the-struggle-for-liberty/.

130. Testimony of Newton Prince, quoted in "Transcript of Remaining Defense Evidence," 30 November–1 December 1770, *LPJA*, APDE-MHS.

131. Testimony of James Bailey, quoted in John Hodgson, *The Trial of William Wemms, James Hartegan, William McCauley, Hugh White, Matthew Kilroy, William Warren, John Carrol, and Hugh Montgomery* (Boston: J. Fleeming, 1770), 24–28.

132. Testimony of Andrew, quoted in "Transcript of Remaining Defense Evidence," 30 November–1 December 1770, *LPJA*, APDE-MHS.

133. Testimony of Andrew, quoted in "Transcript of Remaining Defense Evidence," 30 November–1 December 1770, *LPJA*, APDE-MHS.

134. Testimony of Oliver Wendell, in "Transcript of Remaining Defense Evidence," *LPJA*, APDE-MHS.

135. John Adams, quoted in "Adams' Argument for the Defense," 3–4 December 1770, *LPJA*, APDE-MHS.

136. Robert G. Parkinson, *Thirteen Clocks: How Race United the Colonies and Made the Declaration of Independence* (Chapel Hill: University of North Carolina Press, 2021), 69–70.

137. *Georgia Gazette* (Savannah), 11 April 1770; *Connecticut Journal* (New Haven), 15 March 1770; 12 March 1770; *Pennsylvania Chronicle* (Philadelphia), 26 March 1770; Linebaugh and Rediker, *Many-Headed Hydra*, 232.

138. John Adams, quoted in "Adams' Argument for the Defense," 3–4 December 1770, *LPJA*, APDE-MHS.

139. Peterson, "Black Lives and the Boston Massacre."

140. John Adams, quoted in "Adams' Argument for the Defense," 3–4 December 1770, *LPJA*, APDE-MHS.

141. Archer, *As If an Enemy's Country*, 117; Gerald Horne, *The Counter-Revolution of 1776: Slave Resistance and the Origins of the United States of America* (New York: New York University Press, 2014), 10–11; Zabin, *Boston Massacre*, 63.

142. Nathaniel Philbrick, *Bunker Hill: A City, a Siege, a Revolution* (London: Doubleday, 2013), 24; *Boston Gazette*, 12 March 1770; 28 May 1770.

143. Zabin, *Boston Massacre*, 61–64; Horne, *Counter-Revolution of 1776*, 11; Archer, *As If an Enemy's Country*, 117.

144. John Adams, quoted in "Adams' Argument for the Defense," 3–4 December 1770, *LPJA*, APDE-MHS.

145. Robert Treat Paine, quoted in "Paine's Argument for the Crown," 4–5 December 1770, *LPJA*, APDE-MHS.

146. Peterson, "Black Lives and the Boston Massacre."

147. John Adams, quoted in "Adams' Argument for the Defense," 3–4 December 1770, *LPJA*, APDE-MHS.

148. Benjamin Lynde, quoted in "Lynde's Charge to the Jury," 5 December 1770, *LPJA*, APDE-MHS.

149. John Adams, quoted in "Adams' Argument for the Defense," 3–4 December 1770, *LPJA*, APDE-MHS; Boston, *Short Narrative of the horrid Massacre*, 10.

150. *Boston Evening Post*, 19 November 1770.

242   Notes to Pages 92–96

151. *Boston Evening Post*, 19 November 1770; J. L. Bell, "Whatever Happened to Jesse Saville?," Boston 1775, 24 November 2020, https://boston1775.blogspot.com/2020/11/whatever-happened-to-jesse-saville.html.

152. R. S. Longley, "Mob Activities in Revolutionary Massachusetts," *New England Quarterly* 6, no. 1 (1933): 98–130.

153. *Boston Evening Post*, 19 November 1770.

154. "Verdicts," 5 December 1770, LPJA, APDE-MHS.

155. Bolster, *Black Jacks*, 185.

156. Linebaugh and Rediker, *Many-Headed Hydra*, 237. A recent Attucks biographer, examining Adams's performance, agrees that "the collective evidence of several witnesses does suggest that Attucks was at the forefront of the mob and one of the most aggressive among those accosting the troops." Kachun, *First Martyr*, 17.

157. Moreau, *Loix et Constitutions*, 5:337–40.

158. *New-York Journal*, 6 December 1770.

3. "A Natural Right to Be Free"

1. John Adams to Thomas Hutchinson, 19 July 1773, in *The Works of John Adams, Second President of the United States*, ed. Charles Francis Adams (Boston: Charles C. Little and James Brown, 1850), 2:322.

2. "This address, in the name of the mulatto who was shot by the soldiers in the riot of the 5th of March 1770, seems to have been intended for publication in a newspaper." Editorial note, *Works of John Adams*, 2:322n1.

3. Peter Linebaugh and Marcus Rediker, *The Many-Headed Hydra: Sailors, Slaves, Commoners, and the Hidden History of the Revolutionary Atlantic* (Boston: Beacon, 2000), 237.

4. John Adams to Jedidiah Morse, 5 January 1816, Founders Online, National Archives, accessed 27 March 2023, http://founders.archives.gov/documents/Adams/99-02-02-6564 (hereafter cited as FONA).

5. Douglas R. Egerton, *Death or Liberty: African Americans and Revolutionary America* (New York: Oxford University Press, 2009), 55.

6. *Massachusetts Spy* (Boston), 15 July 1773.

7. J. L. Bell, "Adams Revisits Attucks," *Boston 1775* (blog), 8 March 2014, https://boston1775.blogspot.com/2014/03/adams-revisits-attucks.html.

8. Helen Saltzberg Saltman, "John Adams's Earliest Essays: The Humphrey Ploughjogger Letters," *William and Mary Quarterly* 37, no. 1 (1980): 125–35; John Adams, *Novanglus and Massachusettensis: Political Essays, Published in the Years 1774 and 1775* (Bedford, MA: Applewood Books, 2009).

9. Sandra M. Gustafson, *Eloquence Is Power: Oratory and Performance in Early America* (Chapel Hill: University of North Carolina Press, 2012), 184.

10. *Affiches Américaines* (Port-au-Prince), 13 July 1774.

11. *Connecticut Journal* (New Haven), 24 December 1773.

12. Gustafson, *Eloquence Is Power*, 184n26; Sharon Block, *Colonial Complexions: Race and Bodies in Eighteenth-Century America* (Philadelphia: University of Pennsylvania, 2018), 79. For a fuller explanation of white colonists masquerading as Native Americans, see Benjamin L. Carp, *Defiance of the Patriots: The Boston Tea Party & the Making of America* (New Haven, CT: Yale University Press, 2010), 141–60.

13. *Affiches Américaines* (Port-au-Prince), 25 May 1774.

14. *The Definitive Treaty of Peace and Friendship, between His Britannick Majesty, the Most Christian King, and the King of Spain* (London: E. Owen and T. Harrison, 1763), 16–17; *A Full and Free Inquiry into the Merits of the Peace* (London: printed for T. Payne, 1765), 101–3.

15. Ignotus, *Thoughts on Trade in General, Our West-Indian in Particular, Our Continental Colonies, Canada, Guadaloupe, and the Preliminary Articles of Peace* (London: printed for John Wilkie, 1763), 8–9; Daniel A. Baugh, *The Global Seven Years War, 1754–1763: Britain and France in a Great Power Contest*, 2nd ed. (Abingdon: Routledge, 2021), 555.

16. *Affiches Américaines* (Port-au-Prince), 22 June 1774.

17. For a solid discussion of African groups represented among Saint-Domingue's enslaved population, see "The Slaves of Saint-Domingue," *Colony in Crisis: The Saint-Domingue Grain Shortage of 1789* (blog), 5 May 2016, https://colonyincrisis.lib.umd.edu/2016/05/05/the-slaves-of-saint-domingue/.

18. John Adams, diary entry, 17 December 1773, in *Diary and Autobiography of John Adams*, ed. L. H. Butterfield (Cambridge, MA: Harvard University Press, 1961), 2:86 (hereafter cited as *DAJA*).

19. *Affiches Américaines* (Port-au-Prince), 6 April 1774 ; 22 June 1774.

20. *Affiches Américaines* (Port-au-Prince), 13 July 1774.

21. Lover of Constitutional Liberty, *The Appendix: Or, Some Observations on the Expediency of the Petition of the Africans, Living in Boston* (Boston: printed and sold by E. Russell, 1773), 9.

22. Chernoh M. Sesay, "The Dialectic of Representation: Black Freemasonry, the Black Public, and Black Historiography," *Journal of African American Studies* 17, no. 3 (2013): 380–98; Jared Ross Hardesty, "Disappearing from Abolitionism's Heartland: The Legacy of Slavery and Emancipation in Boston," *International Review of Social History* 65, no. S28 (2020): 145–68; Thomas J. Davis, "Joining the Revolution: African American Writing in the Era of Independence," in *African American Literature in Transition, 1750–1800*, ed. Rhondda Robinson Thomas (New York: Cambridge University Press, 2022), 123–47.

23. Sesay, "Dialectic of Representation," 385.

24. Lover of Constitutional Liberty, *Petition of the Africans*, 10.

25. *Massachusetts Spy* (Boston), 7 January 1773 (capitalization in the original). For more on slavery in Salisbury, Massachusetts, see Kabria Baumgartner and Elizabeth Duclos-Orsello, "African Americans in Essex County, Massachusetts: An Annotated Guide," National Park Service, accessed 13 May 2023, https://www.nps.gov/articles/000/african-americans-in-essex-county.htm.

26. Lover of Constitutional Liberty, *Petition of the Africans*, 10.

27. *Massachusetts Spy* (Boston), 30 July 1772; 6 August 1772; 3 September 1772.

28. Matthew Mason, "North American Calm, West Indian Storm: The Politics of the Somerset Decision in the British Atlantic," *Slavery & Abolition* 41, no. 4 (2020): 723–47; Dana Rabin, "'In a Country of Liberty?': Slavery, Villeinage and the Making of Whiteness in the Somerset Case (1772)," *History Workshop Journal* 72, no. 1 (2011): 5–29. The Somerset case does not seem to have been reported in the Dominguan newspaper *Affiches Américaines*. The scholarly literature does not reveal substantive reactions to the case in the laws regarding slavery in Saint-Domingue. France had addressed the legal question of slavery in the French metropole—the principle at stake for Britain in the Somerset case—in *Jean Boucaux v Verdelin* (1738). Franklin W. Knight, "The Haitian Revolution," *American Historical Review* 105, no. 1 (2000): 103–15; Laurie M. Wood, "Across Oceans and Revolutions: Law and Slavery in French Saint-Domingue and Beyond," *Law & Social Inquiry* 39, no. 3 (2014): 758–82.

29. Graham Russell Hodges, *Slavery and Freedom in the Rural North: African Americans in Monmouth County, New Jersey, 1665–1865* (Madison, WI: Madison House, 1997), 93.

30. Christopher Cameron, *To Plead Our Own Cause: African Americans in Massachusetts and the Making of the Antislavery Movement* (Kent, OH: Kent State University Press, 2014), 50–53.
31. Lover of Constitutional Liberty, *Petition of the Africans*, 9.
32. *Massachusetts Gazette* (Boston), 4 January 1773.
33. *Affiches Américaines* (Port-au-Prince), 10 February 1773.
34. Lover of Constitutional Liberty, *Petition of the Africans*, 10.
35. Davis, "Joining the Revolution," 123–47.
36. *New-York Gazette*, 2 March 1772.
37. *Boston Gazette*, 11 November 1771.
38. *Essex Gazette* (Salem, MA), 22 October 1771; *Providence (RI) Gazette*, 5 October 1771.
39. *New-York Gazette*, 2 March 1772.
40. *Boston Evening Post*, 7 October 1771.
41. Charles Frostin, "Les Colons de Saint-Domingue et La Métropole," *Revue Historique* 237, no. 2 (1967): 410–11.
42. *Affiches Américaines* (Port-au-Prince), 6 January 1773; 10 February 1773; 6 March 1773.
43. Médéric Louis Élie Moreau de Saint-Méry, *Loix et Constitutions des Colonies Françoises de l'Amérique Sous le Vent*, 6 vols. (Paris, 1787), 5:427.
44. Peter Bestes, Sambo Freeman, Felix Holbrook, and Chester Joie, "Boston, April 20th, 1773. Sir. The Efforts Made by the Legislative of This Province in Their Last Session to Free Themselves from Slavery," Library of Congress, accessed 22 May 2023, https://www.loc.gov/resource/rbpe.03701600/?st=text. The petition was published in *Massachusetts Spy* (Boston), 3 June 1773.
45. Felix Holbrook and other Black abolitionists, Petition against Slavery in Massachusetts, "To his Excellency Thomas Hutchinson, Esq; Governor of said Province to the Honourable his Majesty's Council, Representatives in General Court assembled, June, A.D. 1773," quoted in *Massachusetts Spy* (Boston), 29 July 1773; John Trenchard and Thomas Gordon, *Cato's Letters*, no. 60, quoted in *Massachusetts Spy* (Boston), 4 April 1771; Chernoh M. Sesay, "The Revolutionary Black Roots of Slavery's Abolition in Massachusetts," *New England Quarterly* 87, no. 1 (2014): 100.
46. *Massachusetts Spy* (Boston), 29 July 1773.
47. "Instructions Adopted by the Braintree Town Meeting," 24 September 1765, FONA, accessed 18 August 2023, http://founders.archives.gov/documents/Adams/06-01-02-0054-0003; John Adams to Jedidiah Morse, 5 January 1816, FONA, accessed 27 March 2023, http://founders.archives.gov/documents/Adams/99-02-02-6564.
48. *Massachusetts Spy* (Boston), 29 July 1773.
49. Sesay, "Black Roots of Slavery's Abolition," 100.
50. Chernoh M. Sesay, "Emancipation and the Social Origins of Black Freemasonry, 1775–1800," in *All Men Free and Brethren: Essays on the History African American Freemasonry*, ed. Peter P. Hinks and Stephen Kantrowitz (Ithaca, NY: Cornell University Press, 2013), 25.
51. *Boston Evening Post*, 12 March 1770.
52. Vincent Carretta, *Phillis Wheatley: Biography of a Genius in Bondage* (Athens: University of Georgia Press, 2011), 80–99.
53. *New-York Gazette*, 5 November 1770.
54. Cameron, *To Plead Our Own Cause*, 31–33.
55. *American Weekly Mercury* (Philadelphia), 21 August 1740; Andrew M. Pisano, "Reforming the Literary Black Atlantic: Worshipful Resistance in the Transatlantic World," *Studies in Eighteenth-Century Culture* 44, no. 1 (2015): 84–89; John Saillant, "Slavery and Divine Providence in New England Calvinism: The New Divinity and a Black Protest, 1775–1805," *New England Quarterly* 68, no. 4 (1995): 584–86.

56. Frank Lambert, *"Pedlar in Divinity": George Whitefield and the Transatlantic Revivals, 1737–1770* (Princeton, NJ: Princeton University Press, 1994), 204–14; Thomas S. Kidd, *George Whitefield: America's Spiritual Founding Father* (New Haven, CT: Yale University Press, 2014), 58–104, 188–202; Stephen J Stein, "George Whitefield on Slavery: Some New Evidence," *Church History* 42, no. 2 (June 1973): 243–56; Tara Leigh Babb, "'Without a Few Negroes': George Whitefield, James Habersham, and Bethesda Orphan House in the Story of Legalizing Slavery in Colonial Georgia" (MA thesis, University of South Carolina, 2013).

57. George Whitefield, *Three Letters from the Reverend Mr. G. Whitefield* (Philadelphia: printed and sold by B. Franklin, 1740), 14, 16.

58. Katharine Gerbner, *Christian Slavery: Conversion and Race in the Protestant Atlantic World* (Philadelphia: University of Pennsylvania Press, 2018), 4–5, 189–90.

59. Whitefield, *Three Letters*, 15.

60. Thomas Paine, "African Slavery in America," 1775, in *The Writings of Thomas Paine*, ed. Moncure Daniel Conway, 4 vols. (New York: G. P. Putnam's Sons, 1894), 1:8 (hereafter cited as *WTP*).

61. Monica Najar, "Meddling with Emancipation," *Journal of the Early Republic* 25, no. 2 (2005): 162.

62. Albert J. Raboteau, *Slave Religion: The "Invisible Institution" in the Antebellum South* (Oxford: Oxford University Press, 1978), 213–17, 294–95; Andrew Billingsley, *Mighty like a River: The Black Church and Social Reform* (New York: Oxford University Press, 2003), xxi.

63. Edgar Garfield Thomas, *The First African Baptist Church of North America* (Savannah, GA: E. G. Thomas, 1925), 10–12.

64. Charles J. Elmore, *First Bryan, 1778–2001: The Oldest Continuous Black Baptist Church in America* (Savannah, GA: First Bryan Baptist Church, 2002), 10; James M. Simms, *The First Colored Baptist Church in North America. Constituted at Savannah, Georgia, January 20, A.D. 1788* (Philadelphia: J. B. Lippincott, 1888), 256; Whittington Johnson, *Black Savannah, 1788–1864* (Fayetteville: University of Arkansas Press, 1999), 10.

65. John DeVeaux, will, 19 January 1762, Colonial Will Books, Colony of Georgia, RG 49-1-5, Virtual Vault, Georgia Archives, accessed 19 June 2020, https://vault.georgiaarchives.org/digital/collection/cwb.

66. Walter J. Fraser, *Savannah in the New South: From the Civil War to the Twenty-First Century* (Columbia: University of South Carolina Press, 2018), 59; Charles Lwanga Hoskins, *The Trouble They Seen: Profiles in the Life of Col. John H. Deveaux, 1848–1909* (Savannah, GA: C. L. Hoskins, 1989), 66.

67. David T. Shannon, "George Liele: Apostle of Liberation and Faith," in *George Liele's Life and Legacy: An Unsung Hero*, ed. David T. Shannon, Julia Frazier White, and Deborah Van Broeckhoven (Macon, GA: Mercer University Press, 2013), 76; Simms, *First Colored Baptist Church*, 14; Thomas, *First African Baptist Church*, 10–11.

68. Thomas, *First African Baptist Church*, 11.

69. Raboteau, *Slave Religion*, 145.

70. Simms, *First Colored Baptist Church*, 15–16; Shannon, "George Liele," 76.

71. "First African Baptist Church of Savannah," PBS.org, accessed 17 August 2023, https://www.pbs.org/wgbh/aia/part2/2p30.html; "Savannah's History: First African Baptist Church," Savannah.com, 13 February 2023, https://www.savannah.com/savannahs-history-first-african-baptist-church/; "History," First African Baptist Church, accessed 17 August 2023, https://firstafricanbc.com/history.php.

72. Carter G. Woodson, *The History of the Negro Church* (Washington, DC: Associated Publishers, 1921), 43; Raboteau, *Slave Religion*, 139–40; C. Eric Lincoln and Lawrence H.

Mamiya, *The Black Church in the African American Experience* (Durham, NC: Duke University Press, 1990), 23.

73. Charles F. Irons, *The Origins of Proslavery Christianity: White and Black Evangelicals in Colonial and Antebellum Virginia* (Chapel Hill: University of North Carolina Press, 2008), 50; Grant Gordon, *From Slavery to Freedom: The Life of David George, Pioneer Black Baptist Minister* (Hantsport, Nova Scotia: Lancelot, 1992).

74. Woodson, *Negro Church*, 53.

75. I am most grateful for Ella Wall Prichard for her research and work in bringing deserved attention to the archaeological work by the Colonial Williamsburg Foundation to explore more fully the First Baptist Church and the Bray School, which educated free and enslaved Black students during the 1770s. Ella Wall Prichard, "How We're Learning to See and Hear the Black Experience at Colonial Williamsburg," Baptist News Global, 23 September 2021, https://baptistnews.com/article/how-were-learning-to-see-and-hear-the-black-experience-at-colonial-williamsburg/. See also Sarah Kuta, "DNA Evidence Sheds Light on One of America's Oldest Black Churches," *Smithsonian Magazine*, 11 April 2023, https://www.smithsonianmag.com/smart-news/dna-oldest-black-churches-first-baptist-williamsburg-180981962/.

76. Michael E. Ruane, "Beneath a Virginia Parking Lot Rest the Bones of an Old Black Church and, Perhaps, Its Worshipers," *Washington Post*, 17 September 2020.

77. Woodson, *Negro Church*, 53.

78. Linda Rowe, "Gowan Pamphlet: Baptist Preacher in Slavery and Freedom," *Virginia Magazine of History and Biography* 120, no. 1 (2012): 34; Robert B. Semple, *A History of the Rise and Progress of the Baptists in Virginia* (Richmond, VA: R. B. Semple, 1810), 114; Irons, *Origins of Proslavery Christianity*, 48–49.

79. Semple, *History of Baptists in Virginia*, 115.

80. Rowe, "Gowan Pamphlet," 35–37.

81. *Treaty of Peace and Friendship*, 1763, 3, 31, 34.

82. *Treaty of Peace and Friendship*, 1763, 9–11.

83. *Merits of the Peace*, 1765, 10–14.

84. David McCullough, *John Adams* (New York: Simon & Schuster, 2004), 33.

85. John Adams, diary entry, 23 October 1774, *DAJA*, 2:156.

86. John Adams, diary entry, 23 October 1774, *DAJA*, 2:156.

87. Arthur Scherr, "John Adams Confronts Quakers and Baptists During the Revolution: A Paradox of the Quest for Liberty," *Journal of Church and State* 59, no. 2 (2017): 262–63; Nicholas Patrick Miller, *The Religious Roots of the First Amendment: Dissenting Protestants and the Separation of Church and State* (Oxford: Oxford University Press, 2012), 102–6.

88. Biographers commonly repeat that Prince Hall joined or was baptized in the Congregational Church. Given that Boston was a hub of Congregationalist theology and doctrine, the description is not very helpful. That Hall joined the New North Church is plausible, given that Hall and his wife, Flora, baptized their son Prince Africanus at the church in 1784. Chernoh Sesay, "Freemasons of Color: Prince Hall, Revolutionary Black Boston, and the Origins of Black Freemasonry, 1770–1807" (PhD diss., Northwestern University, 2006), 22.

89. John Adams, diary entry, 28 February 1778, *DAJA*, 2:87–88.

90. See Peter P. Hinks and Stephen David Kantrowitz, eds., *All Men Free and Brethren: Essays on the History of African American Freemasonry* (Ithaca, NY: Cornell University Press, 2013); David G. Hackett, *That Religion in Which All Men Agree: Freemasonry in American Culture* (Berkeley: University of California Press, 2014); Danielle Allen, "A Forgotten Black Founding Father: Why I've Made It My Mission to Teach Others About Prince Hall," *The Atlantic*, 10 February 2021, https://www.theatlantic.com/magazine/archive/2021/03/prince-hall-forgotten-founder/617791/; David

A. Taylor, "Black Soldiers Played an Undeniable but Largely Unheralded Role in Founding the United States," *Smithsonian Magazine*, 24 February 2021, https://www.smithsonianmag.com/history/black-soldiers-played-undeniable-largely-unheralded-role-founding-united-states-180977083/.

91. Sesay, "Freemasons of Color," 21.
92. McCullough, *John Adams*, 63.
93. Sesay, "Freemasons of Color," 21.
94. James E. McClellan, *Colonialism and Science: Saint Domingue in the Old Regime* (Chicago: University of Chicago Press, 2010), 105.
95. Sesay, "Freemasons of Color," 58–59, 60, 64.
96. Allen, "Forgotten Black Founding Father"; Sesay, "Black Roots of Slavery's Abolition," 126.
97. Sesay, "Freemasons of Color," 57.
98. Hinks and Kantrowitz, *All Men Free and Brethren*, 2–3; Theda Skocpol, Ariane Liazos, and Marshall Ganz, *What a Mighty Power We Can Be: African American Fraternal Groups and the Struggle for Racial Equality* (Princeton, NJ: Princeton University Press, 2006), 2, 34.
99. Maurice Wallace, "'Are We Men?': Prince Hall, Martin Delany, and the Masculine Ideal in Black Freemasonry, 1775–1865," *American Literary History* 9, no. 3 (1997): 397; "Muster Books and Pay Lists (WO 12/5171–5172): 38th (1st Staffordshire) Regiment of Foot: 1775–1789," Loyalist Collection, accessed 8 June 2021, https://loyalist.lib.unb.ca/node/4721.
100. Hinks and Kantrowitz, *All Men Free and Brethren*, 1.
101. Wallace, "'Are We Men?,'" 397; Sesay, "Emancipation and the Social Origins of Black Freemasonry," 27; Sesay, "Freemasons of Color," 60–61.
102. Jan C. Jansen, "In Search of Atlantic Sociability: Freemasons, Empires, and Atlantic History," *Bulletin of the German Historical Institute* 57 (2015): 75–76, 88–89, 96; John D. Garrigus, "A Secret Brotherhood?: The Question of Black Freemasonry Before and After the Haitian Revolution," *Atlantic Studies* 16, no. 3 (2019): 323; Peter P. Hinks, "'To Commence a New Era in the Moral World': John Telemachus Hilton, Abolitionism, and the Expansion of Black Freemasonry, 1784–1860," in Hinks and Kantrowitz, *All Men Free and Brethren*, 52–53.
103. Jansen, "In Search of Atlantic Sociability," 76.
104. Jansen, "In Search of Atlantic Sociability," 78–80; Garrigus, "A Secret Brotherhood," 324; Stefan-Ludwig Hoffmann, *Civil Society, 1750–1914* (New York: Red Globe, 2006), 22.
105. Jansen, "In Search of Atlantic Sociability," 93–98.
106. Alain Le Bihan, "La Franc-Maçonnerie dans les Colonies Françaises aux XVIII siècle," *Annales Historiques de la Révolution Française* 46, no. 215 (1974): 39.
107. Garrigus, "Secret Brotherhood," 329; Jan C. Jansen, "Brothers in Exile: Masonic Lodges and the Refugees of the Haitian Revolution, 1790s–1820," *Atlantic Studies* 16, no. 3 (2019): 354.
108. Michel R. Doret, *André Rigaud: La Vraie Silhouette* (Bloomington, IN: Xlibris, 2011), 49; George Jean-Charles, "Rigaud, André," in *Dictionnaire Historique de la Révolution Haïtienne*, ed. Claude Moïse, 2nd ed. (Montreal: CIDIHCA, 2019), 219; François Roc, *Dictionnaire de la Révolution Haïtienne, 1789–1804* (Montreal: Éditions Guildives, 2006), 347.
109. Michel-Rolph Trouillot, "The Inconvenience of Freedom: Free People of Color and the Political Aftermath of Slavery in Dominica and Saint-Domingue/Haiti," in *The Meaning of Freedom: Economics, Politics, and Culture After Slavery*, ed. Frank McGlynn and Seymour Drescher (Pittsburgh: University of Pittsburgh Press, 1992), 175n16; Georges Jean-Charles, "Rigaud, Andre," in Moïse, *Dictionnaire Historique de la Révolution Haïtienne*, 219.
110. Éliane Seuran, *Vincent Ogé: un héros des Antilles assassiné le sombre destin d'un homme de couleur à l'Aube de la Révolution Française* (Versailles: Via romana, 2017), 13–15. Alexandre Pétion,

a future Haitian revolutionary and president of the Republic of Haiti, was born in 1770 in Port-au-Prince to Ursule, a free woman of color, and Pascal Sabès, a wealthy white inhabitant. His parents later sent him to study goldsmithing in France. Trouillot, "Inconvenience of Freedom," 176n21.

111. Trouillot, "Inconvenience of Freedom," 176n16.
112. Roc, *Dictionnaire de la Révolution Haïtienne*, 348.
113. Doret, *André Rigaud*, 59, 142, 144.
114. Christine Levecq, *Black Cosmopolitans: Race, Religion, and Republicanism in an Age of Revolution* (Charlottesville: University of Virginia Press, 2019), 81, 84, 87.
115. "Chavannes, Jean Baptiste," in *Appletons' Cyclopædia of American Biography*, ed. James Grant Wilson and John Fiske, 7 vols. (New York: D. Appleton, 1900), 1:595; Tessie P. Liu, *A Frail Liberty: Probationary Citizens in the French and Haitian Revolutions* (Lincoln: University of Nebraska Press, 2022), 111.
116. Georges Jean-Charles, "Bauvais, Louis Jacques ou Beauvais," in Moïse, *Dictionnaire Historique de la Révolution Haïtienne*, 45; Roc, *Dictionnaire de la Révolution Haïtienne*, 36; Bernard Beaupère, *Histoire Du Prytanée National Militaire* (Paris: Charles-Lavauzelle, 1985).
117. John D. Garrigus, *A Secret Among the Blacks: Slave Resistance Before the Haitian Revolution* (Cambridge, MA: Harvard University Press, 2023), 3, 10–11.
118. Beauvais Lespinasse, *Histoire des Affranchis de Saint-Domingue*, Premier Tome (Paris: J. Kugelmann, 1882), 273.
119. Thomas Paine, "African Slavery in America," 1775, *WTP*, 1:4.
120. Thomas Paine, "African Slavery in America," 1775, *WTP*, 1:7.
121. Ron Chernow, *Alexander Hamilton* (New York: Penguin, 2004), 51.
122. Chernow, *Alexander Hamilton*, 51, 53; Thomas Vinciguerra, "Alexander Hamilton, King's College, and the Roots of Philolexian," Philolexian Society, Columbia University, 15 May 2017, http://www.columbia.edu/cu/philo/legacy_content/content/archives/history/.
123. Chernow, *Alexander Hamilton*, 52.
124. Chernow, *Alexander Hamilton*, 55.
125. Chernow, *Alexander Hamilton*, 56.
126. Signe Haubroe Flygare, "The Free Negro Company of Christiansted: Struggles for Equality, 1773–1799," *Scandinavian Journal of History* 41, no. 4/5 (2016): 586–87, 590, 599.
127. *Royal Danish American Gazette* (Christiansted, Saint Croix), 15 May 1773; 26 May 1773; 3 July 1773. For more on efforts to recapture freedom seekers from slavery in Saint Croix, see Enrique Corneiro, *Runaway Virgins: Danish West Indian Slave Ads, 1770–1848*, 2nd ed. (Richmond, TX: Triple E Enterprise, 2018).
128. *Royal Danish American Gazette* (Christiansted, Saint Croix), 4 January 1775.
129. Alexander Hamilton, "The Farmer Refuted, &c.," [23 February] 1775, FONA, accessed 20 August 2023, http://founders.archives.gov/documents/Hamilton/01-01-02-0057.
130. Hamilton, "Farmer Refuted."
131. *Massachusetts Spy* (Boston), 29 July 1773.
132. Hamilton, "Farmer Refuted."

4. "No More Talk of Reconciliation"

1. Chernoh Sesay, "Freemasons of Color: Prince Hall, Revolutionary Black Boston, and the Origins of Black Freemasonry, 1770–1807" (PhD diss., Northwestern University, 2006), 20.

2. John Adams, *Novanglus, and Massachusettensis: Or, Political Essays, Published in the Years 1774 and 1775* (Boston: Hews & Goss, 1819), 138–39.

3. Abraham Hews and Sylvester Goss, "To the Public," in Adams, *Novanglus, and Massachusettensis*, ii (capitalization and italics in the original).

4. John Adams to Hezekiah Niles, 13 February 1818, Founders Online, National Archives, accessed 9 September 2019, http://founders.archives.gov/documents/Adams/99-02-02-6854 (hereafter FONA) (capitalization and spelling in the original).

5. Alan Taylor, *The Internal Enemy: Slavery and War in Virginia, 1772–1832* (New York: W. W. Norton, 2013), 9, 421.

6. Robert A. Gross, *The Minutemen and Their World*, 25th anniversary ed. (New York: Hill and Wang, 2001), 59–61.

7. Robert A. Gross, *The Minutemen and Their World*, rev. ed. (New York: Picador, 2022), 120.

8. Gross, *Minutemen*, rev. ed., 90, 119–20; John F. Hannigan, "King's Men and Continentals: War and Slavery in Eighteenth-Century Massachusetts" (PhD diss., Brandeis University, 2021), 151–63, 171–87.

9. Pete Seymour, "Prince Estabrook of Lexington," National Park Service, May 2020, https://www.nps.gov/people/prince-estabrook-of-lexington.htm; George Quintal, *Patriots of Color: "A Peculiar Beauty and Merit," African Americans and Native Americans at Battle Road and Bunker Hill*, classic reprint (n.p.: Forgotten Books, 2022), 97; John Hannigan, "Patriots of Color Service on April 19, 1775," National Park Service, 12 October 2021, https://www.nps.gov/articles/000/john-hannigan-patriots-of-color-paper-4.htm; Alice M. Hinkle, *Prince Estabrook: Slave and Soldier* (Lexington, MA: Pleasant Mountain, 2001).

10. Secretary of the Commonwealth, *Massachusetts Soldiers and Sailors of the Revolutionary War* (Boston: Wright and Potter, 1900), 227; Albion Benjamin Wilson, *History of Granville, Massachusetts* (Hartford: Connecticut Printers, 1954), 63–64.

11. Hannigan, "Patriots of Color Service on April 19, 1775."

12. Wilson, *History of Granville*, 192.

13. John Saillant, *Black Puritan, Black Republican: The Life and Thought of Lemuel Haynes, 1753–1833* (Oxford: Oxford University Press, 2003), 51; Ruth Bogin, "'Liberty Further Extended': A 1776 Antislavery Manuscript by Lemuel Haynes," *William and Mary Quarterly* 40, no. 1 (1983): 85–86.

14. Ruth Bogin, "'The Battle of Lexington': A Patriotic Ballad by Lemuel Haynes," *William and Mary Quarterly* 42, no. 4 (October 1985): 499; Secretary of the Commonwealth, *Massachusetts Soldiers and Sailors*, 227.

15. Saillant, *Black Puritan, Black Republican*, 51.

16. Lemuel Haynes, quoted in Bogin, "'Battle of Lexington,'" 501.

17. Lemuel Haynes, quoted in Bogin, "'Battle of Lexington,'" 501 (strikethrough in the original).

18. Lemuel Haynes, quoted in Bogin, "'Battle of Lexington,'" 503–4.

19. Stacey B. Day, ed., *Edward Stevens: Gastric Physiologist, Physician and American Statesman* (Montreal: Cultural and Educational Productions, 1969).

20. Ron Chernow, *Alexander Hamilton* (New York: Penguin, 2004), 63, 67.

21. David Waldstreicher, "Ancients, Moderns, and Africans: Phillis Wheatley and the Politics of Empire and Slavery in the American Revolution," *Journal of the Early Republic* 37, no. 4 (2017): 724.

22. Vincent Carretta, *Phillis Wheatley: Biography of a Genius in Bondage* (Athens: University of Georgia Press, 2011), 153–54; Sidney Kaplan and Emma Nogrady Kaplan, *The Black Presence in the Era of the American Revolution*, rev. ed. (Amherst: University of Massachusetts Press, 1989), 184.

23. Phillis Wheatley to George Washington, 26 October 1775, FONA, accessed 22 August 2023, http://founders.archives.gov/documents/Washington/03-02-02-0222-0001.

24. David Waldstreicher, *The Odyssey of Phillis Wheatley: A Poet's Journeys Through American Slavery and Independence* (New York: Farrar, Straus and Giroux, 2023), 291–99; Kaplan and Kaplan, *Black Presence in the American Revolution*, 186; *The Virginia Gazette*, published in the colony's capital, Williamsburg, printed Wheatley's poem and letter on 20 March 1776. Carretta, *Phillis Wheatley*, 157.

25. Carretta, *Phillis Wheatley*, 154.

26. Phillis Wheatley, "To His Excellency, George Washington," 1775, Phillis Wheatley Historical Society, accessed 22 August 2023, http://www.phillis-wheatley.org/to-his-excellency-george-washington/.

27. Chernow, *Alexander Hamilton*, 66.

28. George Washington to Phillis Wheatley, 28 February 1776, FONA, accessed 22 August 2023, http://founders.archives.gov/documents/Washington/03-03-02-0281.

29. Francine Uenuma, "Enslaved by George Washington, This Man Escaped to Freedom—and Joined the British Army," *Smithsonian Magazine*, 14 June 2023, https://www.smithsonianmag.com/history/enslaved-by-george-washington-this-man-escaped-to-freedomand-joined-the-british-army-180982362/.

30. Carretta, *Phillis Wheatley*, 157.

31. Alexander Hamilton to Edward Stevens, 11 November 1769, in *The Papers of Alexander Hamilton, Digital Edition*, ed. Harold C. Syrett (Charlottesville: University of Virginia Press, Rotunda, 2011), https://rotunda.upress.virginia.edu/founders/ARHN.html.

32. Chernow, *Alexander Hamilton*, 72, 81.

33. *Affiches Américaines* (Port-au-Prince), 13 December 1775.

34. Robert D. Taber, "'Le Sens Commun': Atlantic Pathways and Imagination in Saint-Domingue's *Affiches Américaines*," *Latin Americanist* 61, no. 4 (2017): 569–70, 573; Jeremy D. Popkin, "A Colonial Media Revolution: The Press in Saint-Domingue, 1789–1793," *Americas* 75, no. 1 (2018): 5, 6.

35. Taber, "'Le Sens Commun,'" 571.

36. Robert D. Taber, "Rumor and Report in *Affiches Américaines*: Saint-Domingue's American Revolution," *Age of Revolutions*, 13 September 2017, https://ageofrevolutions.com/2017/09/13/rumor-and-report-in-affiches-americaines-saint-domingues-american-revolution/.

37. Taber, "Rumor and Report."

38. Taber, "'Le Sens Commun,'" 578.

39. Taber, "'Le Sens Commun,'" 569, 574–75.

40. *Affiches Américaines* (Port-au-Prince), 6 September 1775.

41. *Affiches Américaines* (Port-au-Prince), 20 September 1775.

42. *Affiches Américaines* (Port-au-Prince), 27 September 1775. An example of Lieutenant Edward Thoroton Gould's report in US newspapers can be found in *The Virginia Gazette* (Williamsburg), 3 June 1775.

43. Taber, "Rumor and Report."

44. Sesay, "Freemasons of Color," 140.

45. *Affiches Américaines* (Port-au-Prince), 4 October 1775.

46. American artist John Trumbull immortalized Joseph Warren in the painting *The Death of General Warren at the Battle of Bunker's Hill, 17 June 1775*, Museum of Fine Arts Boston, accessed 19 June 2023, https://collections.mfa.org/objects/34260/the-death-of-general-warren-at-the-battle-of-bunkers-hill;jsessionid=A59CEF39096386B40022A62675136 10B.

47. "Lord Dunmore's Proclamation, 1775," Gilder Lehrman Institute of American History, accessed 20 June 2023, https://www.gilderlehrman.org/history-resources/spotlight-primary-source/lord-dunmores-proclamation-1775.

48. Italics as original. "Lord Dunmore's Proclamation, 1775."

49. *Pennsylvania Evening Post* (Philadelphia), 12 December 1775; Woody Holton, "'Rebel Against Rebel': Enslaved Virginians and the Coming of the American Revolution," *Virginia Magazine of History and Biography* 105, no. 2 (1997): 182; Benjamin Quarles, *The Negro in the American Revolution*, 35th anniversary ed. (Chapel Hill: University of North Carolina Press, 1996), 28; *New-York Gazette*, 18 December 1775; *Connecticut Journal* (New Haven), 20 December 1775. For more on the Ethiopian Regiment, see Justin Iverson, *Rebels in Arms: Black Resistance and the Fight for Freedom in the Anglo-Atlantic* (Athens: University of Georgia Press, 2022), 64–90.

50. Quarles, *Negro in the American Revolution*, 23–27; Holton, "'Rebel Against Rebel,'" 182.

51. Despite reporting on the military actions of British units commanded by Lord Dunmore, including the participation of Black troops, the *Affiches Américaines* featured no stories about the Dunmore Proclamation promising freedom to enslaved men in Virginia who would serve in the British military. Further treatment of the Dunmore Proclamation can be found in Gerald Horne, *The Counter-Revolution of 1776: Slave Resistance and the Origins of the United States of America* (New York: New York University Press, 2014), 219–36; Robert G. Parkinson, *Thirteen Clocks: How Race United the Colonies and Made the Declaration of Independence* (Chapel Hill: University of North Carolina Press, 2021), 111–16; Douglas R. Egerton, *Death or Liberty: African Americans and Revolutionary America* (Oxford: Oxford University Press, 2009), 70–71.

52. *Pennsylvania Ledger* (Philadelphia), 30 December 1775; Quarles, *Negro in the American Revolution*, 28–29.

53. *Norwich (CT) Packet*, 25 December 1775.

54. Horne, *Counter-Revolution of 1776*, 223.

55. John Adams, diary entry, 24 September 1775, in *The Works of John Adams, Second President of the United States*, ed. Charles Francis Adams, 10 vols. (Boston: Charles C. Little and James Brown, 1850), 2:428 (hereafter cited as *WJA*).

56. *Pennsylvania Ledger* (Philadelphia), 4 November 1775.

57. Robert L. Watts, "Rethinking Our Outlines/Redrawing Our Maps: Representing African Agency in the Antebellum South, 1783–1829" (PhD diss., Temple University, 2011), xxiii–xxiv, 35–36, 127n318, 134.

58. *Constitutional Gazette* (New York), 3 January 1776.

59. *New-York Gazette*, 18 December 1775; *Connecticut Journal* (New Haven), 20 December 1775.

60. Minutes of the Conference Between a Committee of Congress, Washington, and Representatives of the New England Colonies, 18[–24] October 1775, FONA, accessed 26 June 2023, http://founders.archives.gov/documents/Franklin/01-22-02-0142.

61. General Orders, 12 November 1775, FONA, accessed 26 June 2023, http://founders.archives.gov/documents/Washington/03-02-02-0326 (spelling in the original).

62. Parkinson, *Thirteen Clocks*, 122–23.

63. George Washington to John Hancock, 31 December 1775, FONA, accessed 27 June 2023, http://founders.archives.gov/documents/Washington/03-02-02-0579. See also Joseph J. Ellis, "Washington Takes Charge: Confronting the British in Boston in 1775," *Smithsonian Magazine*, January 2005, https://www.smithsonianmag.com/history/washington-takes-charge-107060488/.

64. General Orders, 30 December 1775, FONA, accessed 26 June 2023, http://founders.archives.gov/documents/Washington/03-02-02-0575 (spelling in the original).

65. George Washington, Commission to Robert Breck, 24 January 1776, FONA, accessed 27 June 2023, http://founders.archives.gov/documents/Washington/03-03-02-0126.

66. Sudhir Hazareesingh, *Black Spartacus: The Epic Life of Toussaint Louverture* (New York: Farrar, Straus, and Giroux, 2020), 30.

67. In this book, in reference to the leader of the Haitian Revolution, Toussaint, a name given to him, is used during the period of his enslavement. Louverture, the name he chose for himself and used as his signature on his official letterhead, is used during the period after he secured his freedom.

68. Ronald Angelo Johnson, *Diplomacy in Black and White: John Adams, Toussaint Louverture, and Their Atlantic World Alliance* (Athens: University of Georgia Press, 2014).

69. John Adams to William Tudor, 12 April 1776, FONA, accessed 28 June 2023, http://founders.archives.gov/documents/Adams/06-04-02-0041.

70. Marie Antoinette Ménier, Jean Fouchard, and Gabriel Debien, "Toussaint Louverture Avant 1789: Légendes et Réalités," *Conjonction: Bulletin de l'Institut Francais d'Haïti* 134, no. 1 (1977): 69; Philippe R. Girard, *Toussaint Louverture: A Revolutionary Life* (New York: Basic Books, 2016), 53–54; Jacques de Cauna, ed., *Toussaint Louverture et l'Indépendance d'Haïti: Témoignages Pour Un Bicentenaire* (Paris: Karthala, 2004), 7, 57, 63.

71. Hazareesingh, *Black Spartacus*, 31.

72. Jean Fouchard, *Les Marrons de la Liberté* (Paris: Editions de l'École, 1972), 103–29; Girard, *Toussaint Louverture*, 28–29; Christine Levecq, *Black Cosmopolitans: Race, Religion, and Republicanism in an Age of Revolution* (Charlottesville: University of Virginia Press, 2019), 77–78.

73. Louverture, after becoming leader of Saint-Domingue two decades later, found his beloved sister Geneviéve in the southern city Les Cayes. Hazareesingh, *Black Spartacus*, 28.

74. Girard, *Toussaint Louverture*, 54.

75. In this instance, *Creole* indicates that one was born in the western Atlantic world. *Affiches Américaines* (Port-au-Prince), 5 September 1772. On the case of James Somerset, see Dana Rabin, "'In a Country of Liberty?': Slavery, Villeinage and the Making of Whiteness in the Somerset Case (1772)," *History Workshop Journal* 72, no. 1 (2011): 5–29.

76. The fate and future of the Africans after they regained their freedom aboard ship has escaped the notice of historians. *Affiches Américaines* (Port-au-Prince), 9 September 1772.

77. *Essex Gazette* (Salem, MA), 7 July 1772.

78. *Royal Danish American Gazette* (Christiansted, Saint Croix), 12 September 1772.

79. Alexander Hamilton to *The Royal Danish American Gazette*, 6 September 1772, FONA, accessed 29 June 2023, http://founders.archives.gov/documents/Hamilton/01-01-02-0042. For more on the famous hurricane in Saint Croix that influenced events in the life of Alexander Hamilton, see Bob Henson, "Inside the 1772 St. Croix Hurricane That Drove Hamilton to America," *Washington Post*, 26 September 2020, https://www.washingtonpost.com/weather/2020/09/26/alexander-hamilton-hurricane/; Marvin McAllister, "Toward a More Perfect Hamilton," *Journal of the Early Republic* 37, no. 2 (2017): 279–88; Gertrude Franklin Horn Atherton, ed., *A Few of Hamilton's Letters, Including His Description of the Great West Indian Hurricane of 1772* (New York: Macmillan, 1903).

80. *Royal Danish American Gazette* (Christiansted, Saint Croix), 3 October 1772.

81. Hazareesingh, *Black Spartacus*, 24–28; Girard, *Toussaint Louverture*, 54–55.

82. "Chavannes, Jean Baptiste," in *Appletons' Cyclopædia of American Biography*, ed. James Grant Wilson and John Fiske, 7 vols. (New York: D. Appleton, 1900), 1:595; Levecq, *Black Cosmopolitans*, 81.

83. Girard, *Toussaint Louverture*, 56; Hazareesingh, *Black Spartacus*, 30–31; Ménier, Fouchard, and Debien, "Toussaint Louverture Avant 1789," 68.

84. David McCullough, *John Adams* (New York: Simon & Schuster, 2004), 76, 163.

85. Joseph J. Ellis, *Revolutionary Summer: The Birth of American Independence* (New York: Vintage Books, 2014).

86. John Adams to Abigail Adams, 3 July 1776, Adams Family Papers: An Electronic Archive, Massachusetts Historical Society, accessed 25 May 2016, https://www.masshist.org/adams/adams-family-papers (hereafter cited as AFP-MHS).

87. Worthington Chauncey Ford, Gaillard Hunt, and John Clement Fitzpatrick, eds., *Journals of the Continental Congress, 1774–1789*, 34 vols. (Washington, DC: Library of Congress, 1904–37), 5:507.

88. John Adams to Abigail Adams, 3 July 1776, AFP-MHS.

89. L. Carroll Judson, *A Biography of the Signers of the Declaration of Independence* (Philadelphia: J. Dobson, and Thomas, Cowperthwait, 1839), 283.

90. John Adams, autobiography, in *Diary and Autobiography of John Adams*, ed. L. H. Butterfield (Cambridge, MA: Harvard University Press, 1961), 3:383, 386 (hereafter cited as *DAJA*).

91. John Adams, diary entry, 1 July 1776, *DAJA*, 3:395–98.

92. John Adams, autobiography, *WJA*, 3:58.

93. John Adams to Samuel Chase, 1 July 1776, *WJA*, 9:415

94. For a detailed description of the impression of Adams and others regarding his performance in Philadelphia, see Peter Shaw, *The Character of John Adams* (Chapel Hill: University of North Carolina Press, 1976), 98–105.

95. John Adams, autobiography, *WJA*, 3:56; Richard Stockton to John Adams, 12 September 1821, FONA, accessed 14 September 2024, https://founders.archives.gov/documents/Adams/99-02-02-7545.

96. Thomas Jefferson, quoted in Daniel Webster, *A Discourse in Commemoration of the Lives and Services of John Adams and Thomas Jefferson* (Boston: Cummings, Hilliard, 1826), 32–22.

97. McCullough, *John Adams*, 129.

98. John Adams to Mercy Otis Warren, 17 August 1807, FONA, accessed 24 July 2023, http://founders.archives.gov/?q=John%20Adams%20to%20Mercy%20Otis%20Warren%2017%20August%201807&s=1111311111&sa=&r=3&sr=.

99. *Affiches Américaines* (Port-au-Prince), 3 July 1776.

100. *Affiches Américaines* (Cap-Français), 17 July 1776.

101. John Adams to Abigail Adams, 19 March 1776, FONA, accessed 24 July 2023, http://founders.archives.gov/documents/Adams/04-01-02-0235; William Tudor to John Adams, 29 February 1776, FONA, accessed 24 July 2023, http://founders.archives.gov/documents/Adams/06-04-02-0013; John Adams to William Tudor, 12 April 1776, FONA.

102. John Adams to Abigail Adams, 19 March 1776, FONA.

103. *Affiches Américaines* (Port-au-Prince), 20 November 1776.

104. *Affiches Américaines* (Port-au-Prince), 11 December 1776.

105. *Affiches Américaines* (Port-au-Prince), 8 January 1777.

106. *Affiches Américaines* (Port-au-Prince), 8 January 1777.

107. John Adams, diary entry, 2 January 1766, *DAJA*, 1:285.

108. *Affiches Américaines* (Port-au-Prince), 8 January 1777.

109. *Affiches Américaines* (Port-au-Prince), 8 January 1777.

110. Edward Stevens to Alexander Hamilton, 23 December 1777, in Day, *Edward Stevens*, 25.

111. The Harveian Society awarded Edward Stevens the gold medal in 1778 at the annual Harveian Oration. The previous year's recipient was Charles Darwin, great-uncle of the famous Charles Darwin, author of *The Origin of Species*. Stevens's "Dissertatio De Alimentorum Concoctione" on digestion, completed in 1777, influenced the research of noted Italian biologist and physiologist Lazzaro Spallanzani. Edward Stevens to Alexander Hamilton, 23 December 1777, in Day, *Edward Stevens*, 19–20.

Notes to Pages 153–160

112. Edward Stevens to Alexander Hamilton, 23 December 1777, in Day, *Edward Stevens*, 26.

113. Thomas Paine, *Common Sense: Addressed to the Inhabitants of America* (Philadelphia: printed by R. Bell, 1776), Project Gutenberg, accessed 9 September 2019, https://www.gutenberg.org/files/147/147-h/147-h.htm.

114. John Adams to Abigail Adams, 3 July 1776, AFP-MHS.

5. "Articles of Entangling Alliance"

1. John Adams, "Memorial to the States General," 19 April 1781, Founders Online, National Archives, accessed 5 August 2023, http://founders.archives.gov/documents/Adams/06-11-02-0204 (hereafter cited as FONA).

2. Thomas Paine, *Common Sense: Addressed to the Inhabitants of America* (Philadelphia: printed by R. Bell, 1776), Project Gutenberg, accessed 9 September 2019, https://www.gutenberg.org/files/147/147-h/147-h.htm.

3. John Adams to James Warren, 7 October 1775, FONA, accessed 5 August 2023, http://founders.archives.gov/documents/Adams/06-03-02-0096.

4. James Grant, *John Adams: Party of One* (New York: Farrar, Straus and Giroux, 2005), 171.

5. Samuel Flagg Bemis, *The Diplomacy of the American Revolution*, 7th ed. (Bloomington: Indiana University Press, 1967), 46.

6. George Bancroft, *History of The United States from the Discovery of the American Continent*, 10 vols., 9th ed. (Boston: Little, Brown, 1874), 8:142.

7. Worthington Chauncey Ford, Gaillard Hunt, and John Clement Fitzpatrick, eds., *Journals of the Continental Congress, 1774–1789*, 34 vols. (Washington, DC: Library of Congress, 1904–37), 3:392 (hereafter cited as *JCC*).

8. Jonathan R. Dull, *A Diplomatic History of the American Revolution* (New Haven, CT: Yale University Press, 1985), 49.

9. Thomas Balch, *The French in America during the War of Independence of the United States, 1777–1783* (Philadelphia: Porter & Coates, 1891), 54n65.

10. Dull, *Diplomatic History*, 49–50; Walter Isaacson, *Benjamin Franklin: An American Life* (New York: Simon & Schuster, 2003), 321.

11. Pierre Penet and Emmanuel de Pliarne to George Washington, 18 December 1775, FONA, accessed 6 August 2023, http://founders.archives.gov/documents/Washington/03-02-02-0530; George Washington to John Hancock, 14 December 1775, FONA, accessed 6 August 2023, http://founders.archives.gov/documents/Washington/03-02-02-0503; Balch, *French in America*, 79.

12. James H. Hutson, *John Adams and the Diplomacy of the American Revolution* (Lexington: University Press of Kentucky, 1980), 20–22.

13. Nearly two decades later, Britain invaded and attempted to wrest Saint-Domingue from France during the instability and upheavals of the Haitian Revolution.

14. John Adams, diary entry, 1 March 1776, in *Diary & Autobiography of John Adams*, ed. L. H. Butterfield, 4 vols. (Cambridge, MA: Harvard University Press, 1961), 2:235 (hereafter cited as *DAJA*).

15. Médéric Louis Élie Moreau de Saint-Méry, *Loix et Constitutions des Colonies Françoises de l'Amérique Sous le Vent*, 6 vols. (Paris: l'Auteur, 1784–90), 5:721 (hereafter cited as *LCCFA*).

16. *LCCFA*, 5:337. There were at least three Mallet brothers from Les Côteaux parish in southern Saint-Domingue: Jean-Pierre, Charles, and François. "Index Moreau de Saint-Mery," Association Généalogie et Histoire de la Caraïbe, accessed 24 August 2023, https://www.ghcaraibe.org/livres/ouvdiv/stmery/stmery-M.html. Historian John Garrigus identified Jean-

Pierre and Charles Mallet as participants in the 1769 Revolt. John D. Garrigus, *Before Haiti: Race and Citizenship in French Saint-Domingue* (New York: Palgrave Macmillan, 2011), 134–36.

17. Charles Frostin, *Les Révoltes Blanches à Saint-Domingue aux XVIIe et XVIIIe Siècles* (Paris: l'École, 1975), 314.

18. LCCFA, 5:722.

19. Frostin, *Les Révoltes Blanches*, 312; LCCFA, 5:721.

20. LCCFA, 5:721.

21. John Adams, diary entry, 1 March 1776, *DAJA*, 2:235.

22. The no-military-connection stipulation, in 1776, seemed impractical, given the weary state of the Continental Army. John Adams, diary entry, March–April 1776, *DAJA*, 2:236.

23. *JCC*, 5:428–29. The *Journals of the Continental Congress* can be accessed through the Library of Congress Digital Collections, https://www.loc.gov/item/05000059/.

24. J. H. Powell, "Speech of John Dickinson Opposing the Declaration of Independence, 1 July 1776," *Pennsylvania Magazine of History and Biography* 65, no. 4 (1941): 458–81; Bernhard Knollenberg, "John Dickinson vs. John Adams: 1774–1776," *Proceedings of the American Philosophical Society* 107, no. 2 (1963): 143.

25. *JCC*, 5:501–2.

26. Robert Kagan, *Dangerous Nation* (New York: Knopf, 2006), 41.

27. Powell, "Speech of John Dickinson," 470; Hutson, *John Adams and the Diplomacy of the American Revolution*, 2–8.

28. John Adams, autobiography, April 1778, *DAJA*, 4:38.

29. David Armitage, "The Declaration of Independence in World Context," *OAH Magazine of History* 18, no. 3 (2004): 62. See also David Armitage, *The Declaration of Independence: A Global History* (Cambridge, MA: Harvard University Press, 2007).

30. *Connecticut Gazette* (New London), 19 July 1776.

31. *New-England Chronicle* (Boston), 22 August 1776.

32. *Norwich (CT) Packet*, 2 September 1776.

33. Richard Henry Lee and James Wilson were later added to the committee. *JCC*, 5:431, 709–10.

34. Hutson, *John Adams and the Diplomacy of the American Revolution*, 27–28.

35. John Adams, autobiography, *DAJA*, 3:338.

36. John Adams, "A Plan of Treaties," 18 July 1776, Adams Papers Digital Edition, Massachusetts Historical Society, https://www.masshist.org/publications/adams-papers/index.php/view/ADMS-06-04-02-0116-0002 (hereafter cited as APDE-MHS); *JCC*, 5:575–76.

37. John Adams, autobiography, *DAJA*, 3:338.

38. Thomas Jefferson, quoted in Daniel Webster, *A Discourse in Commemoration of the Lives and Services of John Adams and Thomas Jefferson* (Boston: Cummings, Hilliard, 1826), 32–33.

39. John Adams, autobiography, *DAJA*, 3:338.

40. Hutson, *John Adams and the Diplomacy of the American Revolution*, 2–8.

41. John Adams, autobiography, *DAJA*, 3:338; *JCC*, 5:768–78.

42. *JCC*, 5:813.

43. *JCC*, 5:770.

44. *JCC*, 5:814.

45. Continental Congress, "Plan of Treaties as Adopted (with Instructions)," 17 September 1776, APDE-MHS, accessed 31 July 2023, https://www.masshist.org/publications/adams-papers/index.php/view/ADMS-06-04-02-0116-0004. For additional information on and insight into the evolution of the diplomatic instructions, see Continental Congress, "Instructions to Benjamin Franklin, Silas Deane, and Arthur Lee as Commissioners to France," 24 September–22

October 1776, FONA, accessed 9 August 2023, http://founders.archives.gov/documents/Franklin/01-22-02-0371.

46. A fuller treatment of Médéric Louis Élie Moreau de Saint-Méry can be found in Sara E. Johnson, *Encyclopédie Noire: The Making of Moreau de Saint-Méry's Intellectual World* (Chapel Hill: University of North Carolina Press, 2023).

47. *LCCFA*, 5:707–8; Abigail Adams to John Adams, 21 July 1776, FONA, accessed 31 August 2023, http://founders.archives.gov/documents/Adams/04-02-02-0033.

48. Lemuel Haynes, quoted in Ruth Bogin, "'Liberty Further Extended': A 1776 Antislavery Manuscript by Lemuel Haynes," *William and Mary Quarterly* 40, no. 1 (1983): 94 (spelling in the original).

49. Lemuel Haynes, quoted in Bogin, "'Liberty Further Extended,'" 95–96 (spelling and italics in the original).

50. Lemuel Haynes, quoted in Bogin, "'Liberty Further Extended,'" 96 (spelling in the original).

51. Lemuel Haynes, quoted in Bogin, "'Liberty Further Extended,'" 95, 99 (spelling and italics in the original).

52. Some biographers, including Richard Newman, do not explain why Haynes did not publish "Liberty Further Extended." John Saillant suggests the essay was not intended to be private. Rita Roberts hypothesized that Haynes considered that abolitionist activism could negatively affect his personal and career goals. Ruth Bogin uncovered the work in the Wendell Family Papers at the Houghton Library of Harvard University and published it in the *William and Mary Quarterly* in 1983. She describes the extant manuscript as "a second or later draft of a statement clearly intended for publication." Lemuel Haynes, quoted in Bogin, "'Liberty Further Extended,'" 89; Richard Newman, *Lemuel Haynes: A Bio-Bibliography* (New York: Lambeth, 1984), 67–68; John Saillant, *Black Puritan, Black Republican: The Life and Thought of Lemuel Haynes, 1753–1833* (Oxford: Oxford University Press, 2003), 15; Rita Roberts, "Patriotism and Political Criticism: The Evolution of Political Consciousness in the Mind of a Black Revolutionary Soldier," *Eighteenth-Century Studies* 27, no. 4 (1994): 586.

53. Secretary of the Commonwealth, *Massachusetts Soldiers and Sailors of the Revolutionary War* (Boston: Wright and Potter, 1900), 7:39.

54. Roberts, "Patriotism and Political Criticism," 570.

55. Margaret Humphreys, "A Stranger to Our Camps: Typhus in American History," *Bulletin of the History of Medicine* 80, no. 2 (2006): 276.

56. *LCCFA*, 5:744. See also *LCCFA*, 5:741.

57. *Affiches Américaines* (Port-au-Prince), 9 March 1776; 13 April 1776.

58. *LCCFA*, 5:744.

59. *LCCFA*, 5:744.

60. *LCCFA*, 5:338.

61. For an unknown reason, Haynes drafted the latter sentence twice and struck through the sentence twice. Bogin, "'Liberty Further Extended,'" 97–98 (capitalization and spelling in the original).

62. Bemis, *Diplomacy of the American Revolution*, 48.

63. Congress elected Thomas Jefferson as a commissioner. He declined, and Congress appointed Arthur Lee to accompany Franklin and Deane. Congress, "Instructions to Benjamin Franklin, Silas Deane, and Arthur Lee as Commissioners to France," 24 September–22 October 1776, FONA, accessed 9 August 2023, http://founders.archives.gov/documents/Franklin/01-22-02-0371.

64. *JCC*, 5:827, 833–34.

65. Isaacson, *Benjamin Franklin*, 337–38.

66. Isaacson, *Benjamin Franklin*, 338; Jonathan R. Dull, *Franklin the Diplomat: The French Mission* (Philadelphia: American Philosophical Society, 1982), 14.
67. Dull, *Franklin the Diplomat*, 14.
68. Edwin S. Gaustad, *Benjamin Franklin* (New York: Oxford University Press, 2006), 98.
69. Dull, *Franklin the Diplomat*, 14.
70. *Essex Journal* (Newburyport, MA), 6 February 1777.
71. *New-York Gazette*, 17 March 1777.
72. *Pennsylvania Evening Post* (Philadelphia), 5 April 1777.
73. *Freeman's Journal* (Portsmouth, NH), 22 March 1777.
74. *Pennsylvania Evening Post* (Philadelphia), 5 April 1777; 19 April 1777.
75. *Providence (RI) Gazette*, 22 February 1777.
76. *Affiches Américaines* (Port-au-Prince), 25 June 1777; 18 November 1777; 7 July 1778; 14 July 1778.
77. *Affiches Américaines* (Port-au-Prince), 25 November 1777.
78. *Affiches Américaines* (Cap-Français), 17 November 1778.
79. *Pennsylvania Evening Post* (Philadelphia), 19 April 1777.
80. *New-York Gazette*, 17 March 1777.
81. *New-York Gazette*, 14 April 1777.
82. *New-York Gazette*, 17 March 1777.
83. *New-York Gazette*, 14 April 1777.
84. *Independent Chronicle* (Boston), 8 May 1777.
85. *Essex Journal* (Newburyport, MA), 6 February 1777.
86. *Pennsylvania Evening Post* (Philadelphia), 19 April 1777.
87. *Essex Journal* (Newburyport, MA), 6 February 1777.
88. Dull, *Franklin the Diplomat*, 16, 21; Gaustad, *Benjamin Franklin*, 251–52.
89. Bemis, *Diplomacy of the American Revolution*, 49; Edmund S. Morgan, *Benjamin Franklin* (New Haven, CT: Yale University Press, 2002), 260–61.
90. Dull, *Franklin the Diplomat*, 26–27.
91. Richard Henry Lee, *Life of Arthur Lee, Joint Commissioner of the United States to the Court of France*, 2 vols. (Boston: Wells and Lilly, 1829), 1:334.
92. Lee, *Life of Arthur Lee*, 1:335.
93. Dull, *Franklin the Diplomat*, 29.
94. Robert D. Taber, "'Le Sens Commun': Atlantic Pathways and Imagination in Saint-Domingue's *Affiches Américaines*," *Latin Americanist* 61, no. 4 (2017): 571.
95. Taber, "'Le Sens Commun,'" 575.
96. *Affiches Américaines* (Port-au-Prince), 9 December 1777.
97. Balch, *French in America*, 85.
98. *Providence (RI) Gazette*, 25 April 1778.
99. For a fuller discussion of Saratoga's role in the Franco-American alliance, see Seth Jacobs, *Rogue Diplomats: The Proud Tradition of Disobedience in American Foreign Policy*. (Cambridge: Cambridge University Press, 2020), 35–36.
100. Isaacson, *Benjamin Franklin*, 338.
101. Edmund S. Morgan, *The Birth of the Republic, 1763–89*, 4th ed. (Chicago: University of Chicago Press, 2012), 83.
102. Larry D. Ferreiro, "The French-American Treaty of Alliance, 1778," Patrimoines Partagés—France Amériques, Bibliothèque Nationale de France, accessed 6 September 2023, https://heritage.bnf.fr/france-ameriques/en/treaty-1778-article.

103. Larrie D. Ferreiro, *Brothers at Arms: American Independence and the Men of France and Spain Who Saved It* (New York: Knopf, 2016), 99.
104. Dull, *Franklin the Diplomat*, 30.
105. Jacobs, *Rogue Diplomats*, 35–36.
106. "The Franco-American Treaty of Alliance, 6 February 1778," FONA, accessed 13 September 2024, https://founders.archives.gov/documents/Franklin/01-25-02-0476.
107. Dull, *Franklin the Diplomat*, 32.
108. Edmund Morgan, quoted in Isaacson, *Benjamin Franklin*, 349.
109. Hutson, *John Adams and the Diplomacy of the American Revolution*, 34.
110. *Exeter (NH) Journal*, 28 April 1778.
111. *Connecticut Courant* (Hartford), 21 April 1778.
112. *Freeman's Journal* (Portsmouth, NH), 21 April 1778 (capitalization in the original).
113. John Adams, diary entry, 11 April 1778, *DAJA*, 2:298–99.
114. Grant, *John Adams*, 4.
115. John Adams, autobiography, *DAJA*, 4:48.
116. John Adams to Abigail Adams, 19 April 1778, APDE-MHS, accessed 31 May 2016, https://www.masshist.org/digitaladams/archive/doc?id=L17780419ja&rec=sheet&archive=&hi=&numRecs=&query=&queryid=&start=&tag=&num=10&bc=/digitaladams/archive/browse/letters_1778_1779.php.
117. John Adams to James Warren, 4 August 1778, FONA, accessed 4 August 2023, http://founders.archives.gov/documents/Adams/06-06-02-0267.
118. Isaacson, *Benjamin Franklin*, 350–51; Morgan, *Benjamin Franklin*, 279.
119. John Adams, autobiography, *DAJA*, 4:87.
120. John Adams, autobiography, *DAJA*, 4:88.
121. Isaacson, *Benjamin Franklin*, 351.

6. "Armed, Disciplined and Battle-Hardened"

1. John Adams to Abigail Adams, 2 December 1778, Adams Papers Digital Edition, Massachusetts Historical Society, accessed 31 May 2016, https://www.masshist.org/digitaladams/archive/doc?id=L17781202ja&rec=sheet&archive=&hi=&numRecs=&query=&queryid=&start=&tag=&num=10&bc=/digitaladams/archive/browse/letters_1778_1779.php (hereafter cited as APDE-MHS) (spelling has been corrected).
2. John Adams to Abigail Adams, 13 February 1779, APDE-MHS, accessed 31 May 2016, https://www.masshist.org/digitaladams/archive/doc?id=L17790213ja&rec=sheet&archive=&hi=&numRecs=&query=&queryid=&start=&tag=&num=10&bc=/digitaladams/archive/browse/letters_1778_1779.php.
3. John Adams to Abigail Adams, 6 November 1778, APDE-MHS, accessed 23 September 2023, https://www.masshist.org/publications/adams-papers/index.php/view/AFC03d097.
4. Abigail Adams to John Adams, 21 October 1778, Founders Online, National Archives (hereafter FONA), accessed 31 May 2016, http://founders.archives.gov/documents/Adams/04-03-02-0090 (spelling has been corrected).
5. Abigail Adams to John Adams, 21 October 1778, FONA (spelling has been corrected).
6. Abigail Adams to John Adams, 25 October 1778, FONA, accessed 31 May 2016, http://founders.archives.gov/documents/Adams/04-03-02-0091.

7. *Affiches Américaines* (Cap-Français), 24 November 1778.

8. Abigail Adams to John Adams, 21 October 1778, 25 October 1778, FONA (spelling has been corrected).

9. *Extrait Du Journal d'un Officier de La Marine de l'Escadre de M. Le Comte d'Estaing* (n.p., 1782), 48–50.

10. Mercy Otis Warren to John Adams, 15 October 1778, APDE-MHS, accessed 23 September 2023, https://www.masshist.org/publications/adams-papers/index.php/volume/PJA07/pageid/PJA07p141.

11. Abigail Adams to John Adams, 25 October 1778, FONA.

12. John Adams to Abigail Adams, 18 December 1778, FONA, accessed 31 May 2016, http://founders.archives.gov/documents/Adams/04-03-02-0111 (spelling has been corrected).

13. John Adams, diary entry, 3 March 1779, FONA, accessed 4 October 2023, http://founders.archives.gov/documents/Adams/01-02-02-0009-0002.

14. John Adams, diary entry, 11 February 1779, in *Diary & Autobiography of John Adams*, ed. L. H. Butterfield, 4 vols. (Cambridge, MA: Harvard University Press, 1961), 2:351 (hereafter cited as *DAJA*).

15. John Adams, diary entry, 21 June 1779, *DAJA*, 2:386–89.

16. "Slavery & Justice Report," 2006, Brown University Steering Committee on Slavery and Justice, accessed 4 October 2023, https://slaveryandjustice.brown.edu/report/2006-report.

17. Alan Taylor, *American Revolutions: A Continental History, 1750–1804* (New York: W. W. Norton, 2016), 231–32.

18. Antoinette Dorothy Bettasso, "'In Justice and the Public Good': John Laurens and the Fight for the Continental Black Battalion" (MA thesis, Kansas State University, 2019), 80.

19. Alexander Hamilton to John Laurens, 11 September 1779, FONA, accessed 19 September 2023, http://founders.archives.gov/documents/Hamilton/01-02-02-0446.

20. Bettasso, "'In Justice and the Public Good,'" 33, 83.

21. George Washington to John Laurens, 10 July 1782, FONA, accessed 4 October 2023, http://founders.archives.gov/documents/Washington/99-01-02-08890.

22. Taylor, *American Revolutions*, 233.

23. John Laurens to Alexander Hamilton, 14 July 1779, FONA, accessed 19 September 2023, http://founders.archives.gov/documents/Hamilton/01-02-02-0321.

24. Karen Cook Bell, "Atlantic Slave Trade to Savannah," 19 September 2002, *New Georgia Encyclopedia*, accessed 20 September 2023, https://www.georgiaencyclopedia.org/articles/history-archaeology/atlantic-slave-trade-to-savannah/.

25. Numbers of enslaved people from the Caribbean courtesy of "Intra-American Slave Trade—Database," SlaveVoyages, accessed 20 September 2023, https://www.slavevoyages.org/american/database. See also Jefferson Hall, "The Savannah Port and Its 18th Century Slave Trade," *Fact-Checking Savannah's History* (blog), 22 August 2019, https://savannahhistory.home.blog/2019/08/22/the-18th-century-slave-trade-and-the-savannah-port/.

26. Médéric Louis Élie Moreau de Saint-Méry, *Loix et Constitutions des Colonies Françoises de l'Amérique Sous le Vent*, 6 vols. (Paris: l'Auteur, 1785), 5:862 (hereafter cited as *LCCFA*); René Chartrand, *The French Army in the American War of Independence* (London: Osprey, 1995), 26, 34.

27. A solid summary of the historiographical discussions among scholars of Saint-Domingue and early Haiti history is presented in Nicole Willson, "Vestiges of Black Internationalism: The Chasseurs Volontaires de Saint-Domingue in History and Memory," *Kalfou* 7, no. 1 (2020): 119–27. Scholars note that a hope to improve civic and social status and a degree of aggressive persuasion and compulsion by Dominguan officials served as different inducements for Afro-Caribbean service in the Chasseurs Battalion. John D. Garrigus, *Before Haiti: Race and Citizenship*

in *French Saint-Domingue* (New York: Palgrave Macmillan, 2011), 205–7; Stewart R. King, *Blue Coat or Powdered Wig: Free People of Color in Pre-Revolutionary Saint Domingue* (Athens: University of Georgia Press, 2001), 75–77.

28. Robert A. Gross, *The Minutemen and Their World*, 25th anniversary ed. (New York: Hill and Wang, 2001), 59–67.

29. In recent years, inspiring traditions around the Chasseurs Battalion's actions have encouraged local, civic, and public history portrayals of the historic unit of Black and mixed-parentage infantrymen from Saint-Domingue. In 2009, the Miami-based Haitian-American Historical Society completed its construction of the Haitian Monument in Franklin Square in Savannah, Georgia. "Chasseurs Volontaires de Saint-Domingue," Historic Savannah, accessed 8 September 2024, https://savannahgavisitors.com/attractions/historic-district/momuments/1599-chasseurs-volontaires-de-saint-domingue; "Savannah, Georgia's, Haitian Monument on Franklin Square," Library of Congress, 25 May 2017, https://www.loc.gov/item/2017880481/; "Haitian Monument (Savannah, Georgia)," Contemporary Monuments to the Slave Past, 8 October 2007, https://www.slaverymonuments.org/items/show/1169; Léa Maguire, "Haitian Soldiers at the Battle of Savannah (1779)," *BlackPast* (blog), 28 January 2018, https://www.blackpast.org/global-african-history/haitian-soldiers-battle-savannah-1779/; Robert Scott Davis, "Black Haitian Soldiers at the Siege of Savannah," *Journal of the American Revolution*, 22 February 2021, http://allthingsliberty.com/2021/02/black-haitian-soldiers-at-the-siege-of-savannah/. The analysis presented here offers to US history readers a fresh approach to situating French archival sources, an exploration of newspaper coverage of the servicemen, and French-language scholarship by scholars of the history of Saint-Domingue and early Haiti. Little French-language scholarship about the Chasseurs Volontaires de Saint-Domingue is found in North American–based historical literature on the American Revolution. Alfred Nemours, *Haïti et la Guerre de l'Indépendance Américaine* (Port-au-Prince: Henri Deschamps, 1952); Pierre Force, "Race et Citoyenneté Dans La Carrière et Les Écrits de Charles Henri d'Estaing (1729–1794)," *L'Esprit Créateur* 56, no. 1 (2016): 68–81; Boris Lesueur, "Les Troupes Coloniales Aux Antilles Sous l'Ancien Régime," *Histoire, Économie et Société* 28, no. 4 (2009): 3–19; German Arciniegas, "L'Amérique Noire Dans la Lutte Pour la Liberté," *La Nouvelle Revue Des Deux Mondes*, 1974, 622–29; Warrington Dawson, "Les 2112 Français Morts Aux États-Unis De 1777 à 1783 en Combattant Pour L'indépendance Américaine," *Journal de La Société des Américanistes* 28, no. 1 (1936): 1–154; René de Kerallain, "Bougainville à l'Escadre du Cte d'Estaing: Guerre d'Amérique, 1778–1779," *Journal de La Société des Américanistes* 19 (1927): 155–206.

30. Charles Lwanga Hoskins, *Yet with a Steady Beat: Biographies of Early Black Savannah* (Savannah, GA: Gullah, 2001), 9.

31. Benjamin Kennedy, ed., *Muskets, Cannon Balls, and Bombs: Nine Narratives of the Siege of Savannah in 1779* (Savannah, GA: Beehive, 1974), 43, 128n3.

32. Nemours, *Haïti et l'Indépendance Américaine*, 9. See also Julie Chun Kim, "The Caribs of St. Vincent and Indigenous Resistance During the Age of Revolutions," *Early American Studies* 11, no. 1 (2013): 117–32.

33. Nemours, *Haïti et l'Indépendance Américaine*, 15.

34. Kennedy, *Muskets, Cannon Balls, and Bombs*, ix.

35. *LCCFA*, 5:720, 902–3; Christine Levecq, *Black Cosmopolitans: Race, Religion, and Republicanism in an Age of Revolution* (Charlottesville: University of Virginia Press, 2019), 86; John D. Garrigus, *Before Haiti: Race and Citizenship in French Saint-Domingue* (New York: Palgrave Macmillan, 2011), 205; Christina Proenza-Coles, "Freedom Seekers: On Black Colonialists in Seventeenth-Century America," *Lapham's Quarterly*, 19 March 2019, https://www.laphamsquarterly.org/roundtable/freedom-seekers.

36. *LCCFA*, 5:855–56. In 1779, Governor-General Robert d'Argout, in a show of white supremacist solidarity, opposed the commissioning of Pierre Chapuizet, whose mother descended from Africa, in a white militia unit. David Allen Harvey, "The Chapuizet Affair: Race, Honor, and Politics in Prerevolutionary Saint-Domingue," *French Historical Studies* 44, no. 4 (2021): 583–612.

37. *Affiches Américaines* (Cap-Français), 6 April 1779.

38. *LCCFA*, 5:860.

39. *Affiches Américaines* (Cap-Français), 6 April 1779.

40. *LCCFA*, 5:862.

41. John D. Garrigus, "Catalyst of Catastrophe?: Saint-Domingue's Free Men of Color and the Battle of Savannah, 1779–1782," *Revista/Review Interamericana* 22, no. 1–2 (1992): 118; *LCCFA*, 5:876.

42. "Lenoir de Rouvray, Laurent François, Colonel Commandant le Corps des Chasseurs Volontaires de Saint-Domingue, Habitant de la Partie du Sud," Archives Nationales d'Outre-Mer, AN COL E 278, 101, accessed 16 November 2016, https://recherche-anom.culture.gouv.fr/ark:/61561/up424wqruqwm/daogrp/0 (hereafter cited as ANOM).

43. Laurent-François de Rouvray to Minister of the Navy, 12 November 1779, ANOM, AN COL E 278, 84.

44. Nemours, *Haïti et l'Indépendance Américaine*, 72; Claude Moïse, ed., *Dictionnaire Historique de La Révolution Haïtienne*, 2nd ed. (Montreal: CIDIHCA, 2019), 45–46, 49, 65, 157, 196, 219, 245.

45. Paul Clammer, *Black Crown: Henry Christophe, the Haitian Revolution and the Caribbean's Forgotten Kingdom* (London: Hurst, 2023), 19–21.

46. After the Savannah campaign, the Dominguan newspaper reported on captured Black freedom seekers who explained to officials they were free and had served as Chasseurs Volontaires in the 1779 expedition of Admiral d'Estaing. *Affiches Américaines* (Cap-Français), 16 January 1781; 31 July 1781.

47. *LCCFA*, 5:868.

48. Charles Henri d'Estaing to Minister of the Navy, 29 February 1780, ANOM, AN COL E 278, 89.

49. *Affiches Américaines* (Cap-Français), 26 October 1779; 4 July 1780.

50. *Affiches Américaines* (Port-au-Prince), 12 January 1779.

51. For the date of embarkment from Cap-Français, see *Journal d'un Officier de M. Le Comte d'Estaing*, 1782, 127; Kennedy, *Muskets, Cannon Balls, and Bombs*, 5.

52. This study uses Admiral d'Estaing's journal estimate of 545 Chasseurs Volontaires who fought at Savannah. It also acknowledges that the counting of Black people in the eighteenth-century Atlantic world was generally imprecise. Charles Henri d'Estaing and Antoine François Térence O'Connor, *Journal du Siege de Savannah Septembre, et Octobre 1779* (n.p., 1779), 72. Estimates of the Chasseurs Battalion's strength during the Siege of Savannah vary from five hundred to one thousand infantrymen. See *Journal d'un Officier de M. Le Comte d'Estaing*, 1782, 131; Nemours, *Haïti et l'Indépendance Américaine*, 50; Kennedy, *Muskets, Cannon Balls, and Bombs*, 32; Charles C. Jones, ed., *The Siege of Savannah in 1779: As Described in Two Contemporaneous Journals of French Officers in the Fleet of Count Destaing* (Albany, NY: Joel Munsell, 1874), 20, 39, 50; Franklin Benjamin Hough, *The Siege of Savannah, by the Combined American and French Forces, under the Command of Gen. Lincoln, and the Count d'Estaing, in the Autumn of 1779* (Albany, NY: J. Munsell, 1866), 95, 173.

53. D'Estaing and O'Connor, *Journal du Siege de Savannah*, 72.

54. Similar to the numbers for the Chasseurs Battalion, estimates of Black troop and labor strength in the British army during the Siege of Savannah vary widely. See d'Estaing and O'Connor, *Journal du Siege de Savannah*, 72; Hough, *Siege of Savannah*, 100, 173; Jones, *Siege of*

Savannah, 29, 40; Rita Folse Elliott and Daniel T. Elliott, *Savannah Under Fire, 1779: Expanding the Boundaries* (Savannah, GA: Coastal Heritage Society, 2011), 53; Nemours, *Haïti et l'Indépendance Américaine*, 51.

55. D'Estaing and O'Connor, *Journal du Siege de Savannah*, 71–72.

56. Nemours, *Haïti et l'Indépendance Américaine*, 50.

57. Alexander A. Lawrence, *Storm over Savannah: The Story of Count d'Estaing and the Siege of the Town in 1779*, rev. ed. (Athens: University of Georgia Press, 2021), 35, https://ugapress.manifoldapp.org/projects/storm-over-savannah-the-story-of-count-d-estaing-and-the-siege-of-the-town-in-1779.

58. D'Estaing and O'Connor, *Journal du Siege de Savannah*, 15; Kennedy, *Muskets, Cannon Balls, and Bombs*, 49.

59. D'Estaing and O'Connor, *Journal du Siege de Savannah*, 15; Kennedy, *Muskets, Cannon Balls, and Bombs*, 49.

60. LCCFA, 5:863.

61. George P. Clark, "The Role of the Haitian Volunteers at Savannah in 1779: An Attempt at an Objective View," *Phylon* 41, no. 4 (1980): 356–66.

62. *New-Jersey Gazette* (Trenton), 7 June 1780.

63. Charles Henri d'Estaing, quoted in Nemours, *Haïti et l'Indépendance Américaine*, 53.

64. Jones, *Siege of Savannah*, 20–21.

65. Charles Henri d'Estaing to Minister of the Navy, 29 February 1780, ANOM, AN COL E 278, 90.

66. Hough, *Siege of Savannah*, 21, 162.

67. D'Estaing and O'Connor, *Journal du Siege de Savannah*, 25; Nemours, *Haïti et l'Indépendance Américaine*, 53; Kennedy, *Muskets, Cannon Balls, and Bombs*, 15–16; Jones, *Siege of Savannah*, 22; Leara Rhodes, "Haitian Contributions to American History: A Journalistic Record," in *Slavery in the Caribbean Francophone World: Distant Voices, Forgotten Acts, Forged Identities*, ed. Doris Y. Kadish (Athens: University of Georgia Press, 2000), 62.

68. Notes in d'Estaing's journal regarding the allied forces' muster roll indicated that white Grenadiers, the Chasseurs Battalion, and 60 percent of the white American troops could be used to dig trenches. D'Estaing and O'Connor, *Journal du Siege de Savannah*, 71–72; Kennedy, *Muskets, Cannon Balls, and Bombs*, 16–17, 54.

69. Kennedy, *Muskets, Cannon Balls, and Bombs*, 16–17; Jones, *Siege of Savannah*, 22; *Independent Ledger* (Boston), 10 January 1780; *New-Jersey Gazette* (Trenton), 7 June 1780.

70. Kennedy, *Muskets, Cannon Balls, and Bombs*, 56.

71. Charles Henri d'Estaing to Minister of the Navy, 29 February 1780, ANOM, AN COL E 278, 90.

72. Jones, *Siege of Savannah*, 22n1.

73. Kennedy, *Muskets, Cannon Balls, and Bombs*, 55; Nemours, *Haïti et l'Indépendance Américaine*, 54. There are no casualty listings for American troops from the bloody skirmish, likely meaning the white Americans digging the trenches were unarmed and detailed as workers.

74. Kennedy, *Muskets, Cannon Balls, and Bombs*, 20.

75. When the British army evacuated Savannah in July 1782, some five thousand Black Loyalists left with them. Hoskins, *Yet with a Steady Beat*, 9–10.

76. *Independent Ledger* (Boston), 10 January 1780.

77. *New-Jersey Gazette* (Trenton), 8 December 1779.

78. Jean-Rémy de Tarragon and Benjamin Franklin Stevens, *Pechot—Journal of the Siege of Savannah by the French Troops under Count Estaing from 1 September to 18 October 1779*, (n.p., 1895), 18–20; Nemours, *Haïti et l'Indépendance Américaine*, 50, 57.

79. Nemours, *Haïti et l'Indépendance Américaine*, 57–58, 60, 63; Hough, *Siege of Savannah*, 165; Jones, *Siege of Savannah*, 30; Rhodes, "Haitian Contributions to American History," 62; *Independent Ledger* (Boston), 10 January 1780.

80. Kennedy, *Muskets, Cannon Balls, and Bombs*, 36, 68; Jones, *Siege of Savannah*, 27.

81. Hough, *Siege of Savannah*, 164.

82. Kennedy, *Muskets, Cannon Balls, and Bombs*, 68; Jones, *Siege of Savannah*, 37–38.

83. Sylvia R. Frey, *Water from the Rock: Black Resistance in a Revolutionary Age* (Princeton, NJ: Princeton University Press, 1991), 97; Hoskins, *Yet with a Steady Beat*, 10; Kennedy, *Muskets, Cannon Balls, and Bombs*, 68.

84. General Benjamin Lincoln, 22 October 1779, quoted in Hough, *Siege of Savannah*, 155.

85. Nemours, *Haïti et l'Indépendance Américaine*, 65.

86. Tarragon and Stevens, *Pechot*, 24–27; Nemours, *Haïti et l'Indépendance Américaine*, 68.

87. *Independent Ledger* (Boston), 10 January 1780.

88. Hough, *Siege of Savannah*, 78.

89. *Independent Ledger* (Boston), 10 January 1780; Jones, *Siege of Savannah*, 48.

90. Nemours, *Haïti et l'Indépendance Américaine*, 89.

91. Laurent-François de Rouvray to Minister of the Navy, 12 November 1779, ANOM, AN COL E 278, 83 (underline in the original).

92. Garrigus, *Before Haiti*, 210; Nemours, *Haïti et l'Indépendance Américaine*, 74, 81; Levecq, *Black Cosmopolitans*, 90. See also Clément Lanier, "Les Nègres d'Haïti Dans la Guerre d'Indépendance Américaine," 25 April 1933, *Genése: Journal Généalogique et Historique*, Association de Généalogie d'Haïti, accessed 16 January 2016, https://www.agh.qc.ca/articles/?id=31; Robert Scott Davis, "Black Haitian Soldiers at the Siege of Savannah," *Journal of the American Revolution*, 22 February 2021, http://allthingsliberty.com/2021/02/black-haitian-soldiers-at-the-siege-of-savannah/.

93. A description of Afro-Caribbean soldiers in the battalion of Chasseurs Volontaires of Saint-Domingue after the Siege of Savannah in 1779. *Affiches Américaines* (Cap-Français), 2 May 1780.

94. Laurent-François de Rouvray to Minister of the Navy, 12 November 1779, ANOM, AN COL E 278, 82–83 (underline in the original).

95. *Affiches Américaines* (Cap-Français), 2 May 1780.

96. Laurent-François de Rouvray to Minister of the Navy, 12 November 1779, ANOM, AN COL E 278, 82, 84.

97. James H. Hutson, *John Adams and the Diplomacy of the American Revolution* (Lexington: University Press of Kentucky, 1980), 51–52.

98. "John Adams & the Massachusetts Constitution," Mass.gov, accessed 19 September 2023, https://www.mass.gov/guides/john-adams-the-massachusetts-constitution.

99. Hutson, *John Adams and the Diplomacy of the American Revolution*, 51.

100. Ronald Angelo Johnson, *Diplomacy in Black and White: John Adams, Toussaint Louverture, and Their Atlantic World Alliance* (Athens: University of Georgia Press, 2014), 55–56; "Massachusetts Constitution and the Abolition of Slavery," Mass.gov, accessed 16 April 2023, https://www.mass.gov/guides/massachusetts-constitution-and-the-abolition-of-slavery.

101. Hutson, *John Adams and the Diplomacy of the American Revolution*, 55.

102. The petition was written in the name of twenty Black men: Nero Brewster, Pharoah Rogers, Prince Whipple, Seneca Hall, Peter Warner, Cato Warner, Pharaoh Shores, Winsor Moffatt, Garrett Colton, Kittindge Tuckerman, Peter Frost, Romeo Rindge, Cato Newmarch, Cesar Gerrish, Zebulon Gardner, Quam Sherburne, Samuel Wentworth, Will Clarkson, Jack Odiorne, and Cipio Hubbard. See Ben Leubsdorf, "234 Years Later, N.H. Legislature Might

Answer Slaves' Plea for Freedom," 28 February 2013, *Concord Monitor*, accessed 17 September 2023, https://www.concordmonitor.com/Archive/2012/12/SlaveryPetition1779-CM-010613.

103. "Massachusetts Constitution," 193rd General Court of the Commonwealth of Massachusetts, accessed 19 September 2023, https://malegislature.gov/Laws/Constitution.

104. *New-Hampshire Gazette* (Portsmouth), 15 July 1780.

105. Lemuel Haynes, quoted in Ruth Bogin, "'Liberty Further Extended': A 1776 Antislavery Manuscript by Lemuel Haynes," *William and Mary Quarterly* 40, no. 1 (1983): 94 (spelling in the original).

106. *New-Hampshire Gazette* (Portsmouth), 15 July 1780.

107. Chernoh M. Sesay, "The Revolutionary Black Roots of Slavery's Abolition in Massachusetts," *New England Quarterly* 87, no. 1 (2014): 126.

108. "Petition to the Massachusetts Legislature," 13 January 1777, National Constitution Center, accessed 20 September 2023, https://constitutioncenter.org/the-constitution/historic-document-library/detail/prince-hall-petition-to-the-massachusetts-legislature.

109. *New-Hampshire Gazette* (Portsmouth), 15 July 1780.

110. *New-Hampshire Gazette* (Portsmouth), 6 May 1780; 15 July 1780.

111. Leubsdorf, "234 Years Later." See also Mark J. Sammons and Valerie Cunningham, *Black Portsmouth: Three Centuries of African-American Heritage* (Durham: University of New Hampshire Press, 2004); Arnie Alpert, "1779 Petition for Liberation from Slavery," New Hampshire Radical History, 28 April 2021, https://www.nhradicalhistory.org/story/1779-petition-for-liberation-from-slavery/; "N.H. Posthumously Frees 14 Revolutionary War Slaves," *USA Today*, 7 June 2013, https://www.usatoday.com/story/news/nation/2013/06/07/nh-emancipates-war-slaves/2401273/.

112. "Phillis Wheatley, 1753–1784," Poetry Foundation, accessed 23 June 2021, https://www.poetryfoundation.org/poets/phillis-wheatley; Vincent Carretta, "Phillis Wheatley: Researching a Life," *Historical Journal of Massachusetts* 43, no. 2 (2015): 79.

113. *Salem (MA) Gazette*, 13 November 1783.

114. Bogin, "Liberty Further Extended," 86; Richard D. Brown, "'Not Only Extreme Poverty, but the Worst Kind of Orphanage': Lemuel Haynes and the Boundaries of Racial Tolerance on the Yankee Frontier, 1770–1820," *New England Quarterly* 61, no. 4 (1988): 510; Thabiti M. Anyabwile, *The Faithful Preacher: Recapturing the Vision of Three Pioneering African-American Pastors* (Wheaton, IL: Crossway Books, 2007), 19.

115. Thabiti M. Anyabwile, *The Faithful Preacher: Recapturing the Vision of Three Pioneering African-American Pastors* (Wheaton, IL: Crossway, 2007), 18–19.

116. Richard Newman, *Lemuel Haynes: A Bio-Bibliography* (New York: Lambeth Press, 1984), 13.

117. Nemours, *Haïti et l'Indépendance Américaine*, i; Charles E. Hatch, *Yorktown and the Siege of 1781*, rev. ed. (Washington, DC: National Park Service, 1957), 11.

118. Elizabeth M. Collins, "Black Soldiers in the Revolutionary War," US Army, 4 March 2013, https://www.army.mil/article/97705/black_soldiers_in_the_revolutionary_war.

119. "African Americans at Yorktown," National Museum of American History, 26 June 2018, https://americanhistory.si.edu/american-revolution/yorktown-triumph-alliance/african-americans-yorktown.

120. Charles F. Irons, *The Origins of Proslavery Christianity: White and Black Evangelicals in Colonial and Antebellum Virginia* (Chapel Hill: University of North Carolina Press, 2008), 49.

121. Antonio T. Bly, "Breaking with Tradition: Slave Literacy in Early Virginia, 1680–1780" (PhD diss., College of William & Mary, 2006), 188; Ella Wall Prichard, "How We're Learning to See and Hear the Black Experience at Colonial Williamsburg," *Baptist News Global*, 23 September

2021, https://baptistnews.com/article/how-were-learning-to-see-and-hear-the-black-experience-at-colonial-williamsburg/; Linda Rowe, "Gowan Pamphlet: Baptist Preacher in Slavery and Freedom," *Virginia Magazine of History and Biography* 120, no. 1 (2012): 3–31; "Asplund's First Register 1794," Project Gowan Pamphlet, 22 October 2014, https://gowanpamphlet.wordpress.com/gowan-pamphlet/document-archive/asplunds-first-register-1794/.

122. Robert B. Semple, *A History of the Rise and Progress of the Baptists in Virginia* (Richmond, VA: R. B. Semple, 1810), 114–15.

123. Rowe, "Gowan Pamphlet."

124. Semple, *Baptists in Virginia*, 115; Frey, *Water from the Rock*, 37.

125. Irons, *White and Black Evangelicals*, 51.

126. "Asplund's First Register"; Semple, *Baptists in Virginia*, 115.

127. Milton C. Sernett, *African American Religious History: A Documentary Witness* (Durham, NC: Duke University Press, 2000), 44.

128. James M. Simms, *The First Colored Baptist Church in North America* (Philadelphia: J. B. Lippincott, 1888), 15; Carter G. Woodson, *The History of the Negro Church* (Washington, DC: Associated Publishers, 1921), 44.

129. Irons, *White and Black Evangelicals*, 51.

130. Frey, *Water from the Rock*, 106.

131. Edgar Garfield Thomas, *The First African Baptist Church of North America* (Savannah, GA: E. G. Thomas, 1925), 16; Frey, *Water from the Rock*, 38; Irons, *White and Black Evangelicals*, 50; Woodson, *Negro Church*, 44.

132. Simms, *First Colored Baptist Church*, 16.

133. James Sidbury, *Becoming African in America: Race and Nation in the Early Black Atlantic* (New York: Oxford University Press, 2009), 71.

134. Frey, *Water from the Rock*, 39.

135. Thomas, *First African Baptist Church*, 33–35; Irons, *White and Black Evangelicals*, 51; Simms, *First Colored Baptist Church*, 21.

136. Andrew Billingsley, *Mighty like a River: The Black Church and Social Reform* (New York: Oxford University Press, 2003), 18.

137. John Asplund, *The Annual Register of the Baptist Denomination, in North-America; to the First of November, 1790* (Richmond, VA: Dixon, Nicolson, and Davis, 1792), 40–41. The register lists the white Baptist church of Andrew Marshall in Kioka as also having 250 members. In 1788, Abraham Marshall ordained Andrew Bryan as the pastor of the African Baptist church. Simms, *First Colored Baptist Church*, 20.

138. Billingsley, *Mighty like a River*, 18; Rowe, "Gowan Pamphlet."

139. Charles Jenkinson, *A Collection of All the Treaties of Peace, Alliance, and Commerce, between Great-Britain and Other Powers*, 3 vols. (London: J. Debrett, 1785), 3:412.

140. Jenkinson, *Collection of Treaties*, 3:411. Casualty data for the US War of Independence provided by the US Department of Veterans Affairs. "America's Wars," Department of Veterans Affairs, November 2023, https://www.va.gov/opa/publications/factsheets/fs_americas_wars.pdf.

141. "Black Founders: The Free Black Community in the Early Republic," Library Company of Philadelphia, accessed 8 September 2024, https://www.librarycompany.org/blackfounders/section4.htm.

142. "Massachusetts Constitution and the Abolition of Slavery," Mass.gov, accessed 16 April 2023, https://www.mass.gov/guides/massachusetts-constitution-and-the-abolition-of-slavery.

143. Jenkinson, *Collection of Treaties*, 3:415.

144. Steven Brady, *Chained to History: Slavery and US Foreign Relations to 1865* (Ithaca, NY: Cornell University Press, 2022), 10–18.

Epilogue

1. Charles Jenkinson, *A Collection of All the Treaties of Peace, Alliance, and Commerce, between Great-Britain and Other Powers*, 3 vols. (London: J. Debrett, 1785), 3:354, 359.
2. *Affiches Américaines* (Cap-Français), 18 February 1784.
3. Lauren R. Clay, *Stagestruck: The Business of Theater in Eighteenth-Century France and Its Colonies* (Ithaca, NY: Cornell University Press, 2013).
4. Ministry of the Navy, 4 July 1781, Archives Nationales d'Outre-Mer, AN COL E 278, 101, accessed 16 November 2016, https://recherche-anom.culture.gouv.fr/ark:/61561/up424wqruqwm/daogrp/0 (hereafter cited as ANOM); Alfred Nemours, *Haiti et l'Indépendance Américaine* (Port-au-Prince: Henri Deschamps, 1952), 107.
5. Nicole Willson, "Vestiges of Black Internationalism: The Chasseurs Volontaires de Saint-Domingue in History and Memory," *Kalfou* 7, no. 1 (2020): 119–27; Leara Rhodes, "Haitian Contributions to American History: A Journalistic Record," in *Slavery in the Caribbean Francophone World: Distant Voices, Forgotten Acts, Forged Identities*, ed. Doris Y. Kadish (Athens: University of Georgia Press, 2000), 64–65; Nemours, *Haïti et La Guerre de l'Indépendance Américaine*, 107; Beauvais Lespinasse, *Histoire des Affranchis de Saint-Domingue. Tome Premier* (Paris: J. Kugelmann, 1882), 191–95.
6. Lespinasse, *Histoire des Affranchis*, 264.
7. Nemours, *Haïti et l'Indépendance Américaine*, 107.
8. Nathan Perl-Rosenthal, *The Age of Revolutions: And the Generations Who Made It* (New York: Basic Books, 2024); Elizabeth Maddock Dillon and Michael J. Drexler, eds., *The Haitian Revolution and the Early United States: Histories, Textualities, Geographies* (Philadelphia: University of Pennsylvania Press, 2016); Jonathan E. Bosscher, "The United States and Haiti, 1791–1863: A Racialized Foreign Policy and Its Domestic Correlates" (MA thesis, Bowling Green State University, 2008); Patrice L. R. Higonnet, *Sister Republics: The Origins of French and American Republicanism* (Cambridge, MA: Harvard University Press, 1988).
9. Christine Levecq, *Black Cosmopolitans: Race, Religion, and Republicanism in an Age of Revolution* (Charlottesville: University of Virginia Press, 2019), 87–91.
10. "The Negro Makandal, an Authentic History," *Universal Magazine of Knowledge and Pleasure* 82, no. 570 (1788): 90–95.
11. "Account of a Remarkable Conspiracy Formed by a Negro in the Island of St. Domingo," *Literary Magazine and British Review* 2 (1789): 22–27.
12. Georges Jean-Charles, "Rigaud, André," in *Dictionnaire Historique de la Révolution Haïtienne*, ed. Claude Moïse, 2nd ed. (Montreal: CIDIHCA, 2019), 130, 219–20.
13. Karol K. Weaver, *Medical Revolutionaries: The Enslaved Healers of Eighteenth-Century Saint Domingue* (Urbana: University of Illinois Press, 2006), 95.
14. Sudhir Hazareesingh, *Black Spartacus: The Epic Life of Toussaint Louverture* (New York: Farrar, Straus and Giroux, 2020), 28–29.
15. Francois Marie de Kerversau and Pierre Pluchon, quoted in Weaver, *Medical Revolutionaries*, 96.
16. "John Adams," London Remembers, accessed 9 September 2024, https://www.londonremembers.com/memorials/john-adams/; "John Adams' Lease for the American Legation at No. 8 Grosvenor Square," 9 June 1785, Founders Online, National Archives, accessed 9 September 2024, http://founders.archives.gov/documents/Adams/06-17-02-0095.
17. Ronald Angelo Johnson, *Diplomacy in Black and White: John Adams, Toussaint Louverture, and Their Atlantic World Alliance* (Athens: University of Georgia Press, 2014), 176–77.

18. Paul Clammer, *Black Crown: Henry Christophe; The Haitian Revolution and the Caribbean's Forgotten Kingdom* (London: Hurst, 2023), 33–41.

19. Kethly Millet, "Christophe, Henry," in Moïse, *Dictionnaire Historique*, 67.

20. Michel R. Doret, *André Rigaud: La Vraie Silhouette* (Bloomington, IN: Xlibris, 2011), 57; Clammer, *Black Crown*, 174.

Index

1769 Revolt, 53–59, 71, 77–83, 93, 102, 135, 156, 160–61, 172, 193, 216

abolition, 77, 100–104, 118, 120–21, 138–42, 154, 204–6, 220. *See also* freedom: emancipation
Adam (Saint Croix), 120
Adams, Abigail, 14, 147–48, 183, 186, *187*, 188, 204
Adams, John, 13–17, 34–37, 43–45, 78–80, 86–97, 100–105, 111–12, *127*, 144; and Boston Massacre trial, 16, 86–95, 112; as diplomat, 13–14, 143, 155, 158, 164–67, 182–90, 203–4, 209–12, 218–19; and foreign policy, 13–14, 155–56, 158–68, 171–74, 178–88, 218–19; and nation-building, 155–56, 204, 211; as president, 218; and religion, 110–11; and revolution, 17, 34–35, 125–28, 147–54; and slavery issue, 14, 35, 100–104, 139–40, 154, 204, 211
Adams, John Quincy, 186
Adams, Samuel, 63, 83, 96, 189, 204

Affiches Américaines, 32–33, 97–98, 134–37, 145, 150–52, 171, 175–80, 187, 195, 203. *See also* print culture
African (as term). *See* racial terminology
Ahyssa (Saint-Domingue), 167–68
Alexander, Leslie, 69
Andrew (Boston Massacre witness), 88–91
Anglican Church, 109–10
Anyabwile, Thabiti, 206
Archer, Richard, 91
Armitage, David, 163–64
Articles of Confederation, 163–64, 209
Asplund, John, 208
Attucks, Crispus, 20, 63–72, 76–96, 101, 104, 107, 111, 125–26, 140, 145, 215
Auba, Etienne, 193, 196

Babbitt, Elizabeth, 206
Backus, Isaac, 111
Bahamas, 20, 67–68, 82, 90, 161, 236n31
Bailey, James, 89
Bailyn, Bernard, 63

Index

balance of power, 13, 25, 29, 38–41, 155, 161–63, 209–10, 213–14
Balch, Thomas, 180
Ball, Lebbeus, 129
Baptist Church, 101, 106–11, 207–9
Barbados, 2, 34–35, 152
Batt, John, 114
Beauvais, Louis Jacques, 116–20, 196
Bellamy, Joseph, 130
Bellecombe, Guillaume de, 214
Belley, Jean-Baptiste, 116–17, 120, 146, 196, 216, *217*
Belot, Mr. (Saint-Domingue), 75
Bemis, Samuel Flagg, 158
Benezet, Anthony, 118
Berlin, Ira, 67
Besse, Martial, 196
Bestes, Peter, 112, 205
Betty (Savannah), 75
Black (as term), 5–6, 17–19. *See also* racial terminology
Black literature. *See* literature: Black literature
Black soldiers, 28, 120, 138–47, 152, 170–71, 185, 189–207, 210–20. *See also* French colonies: colonial military
Bliss, Daniel, 129
Boisrond, Francois, 160
Bolster, Jeffrey, 81–82
Bongars, Alexandre-Jacques de, 75–76
Bonvouloir, Julien-Alexandre Achard de, 159
Boston Massacre, 16, 63–64, 72, 76–95, 104, 209; depictions of, 84–95; and trial, 87–93
Boston Tea Party, 11, 46, 96–97, 116, 119, 168, 209
Boury, Jacques, 52
Boussole (Saint-Domingue), 171
Bowdoin, James, 85–86, 204
Brandywine, Battle of, 181
Breck, Robert, 142
Brewster, Nero, 263n102
British colonies: and class, 14, 47, 95, 112–15, 121; and colonial governance, 10–13, 25–26, 36, 62, 93, 209; and colonial military, 25–26, 34, 36, 128–35, 137; and colonial rebellions, 10–14, 32–36, 42–43, 62, 80, 86, 93, 135–38, 147–48, 155–56, 209, 216; and colonial taxation, 12, 32–42, 46–47, 80, 86, 96–98; and debts, 10–12, 25–26, 32, 97. *See also* Bahamas; Barbados; Jamaica
Brown, William, 64–67, 80
Bryan, Andrew, 107, *108*, 207–9
Bunker Hill, Battle of, 137, 186
Burgoyne, John, 153, 179–80
Burr, Aaron, 200
Burr, Theodosia Bartow, 200

Cabon, Adolphe, 15
Caldwell, James, 81–83
Cangé, Pierre, 196
Carenan, Denis, 71–76
Carenan, Marie-Jeanne, 14, 71–76
Carenan, Paul, 16, 70–76
Carr, Patrick, 83
Carretta, Vincent, 48, 132
Carter, Stephen L., 69
Charpentier, Victor-Thérèse, 168
Chapuizet, Pierre, 261n36
Chase, Samuel, 158
Chasseurs Volontaires d'Amerique, 28–29, 193–94, 211
Chasseurs Volontaires de Saint-Domingue, 190–204, 206–7, 212–19. *See also* Black soldiers; French colonies: military
Châtelet, duc de. *See* D'Haraucourt, Louis-Marie-Florent
Chaumont, Jacques-Donatien Le Ray de, 179
Chavannes, Jean-Baptiste, 116, 144, 146, 172, 196, 216, 218
Chernow, Ron, 119
Choiseul, Étienne François de, 28–32, 37–43, 49
Christophe, Henry, 146–47, 196, 219
Church of England. *See* Anglican Church
Clarke, Jonas, 129
Clarkson, Will, 263n102
class. *See* British colonies: class; French colonies: class
colonial solidarity, 14, 33–40, 55–57, 69, 112, 135–37, 147, 150–54, 164, 200–210, 215, 220. *See also* interracial resistance
Colton, Garrett, 263n102

Constitution. *See* US Constitution
Continental Army, 141, 151–53, 170, 178–79, 185, 189–90, 209–10
Continental Congress, 14, 110, 121, 125–36, 141–65, 172, 175–78, 183–84, 189–90, 209, 218
Cooper, Myles, 60–61, 119
Cornwallis, Charles, 206, 210
Cornwell, Joseph, 63
Craft, Thomas, 168
Creoles, 19–20, 27, 67, 145, 237n46
Cruger, Nicholas, 120

Danish West Indies, 66, 120. *See also* Saint Croix
D'Argout, Robert, 194–95, 197–200
D'Estaing, Charles Henri Hector (Jean Baptiste), 29–32, 49–50, 160, 186–87, 192–93, *194*, 195–204, 216
D'Haraucourt, Louis-Marie-Florent, 40, 42
Dangeville, Anne Catherine, 9
Daut, Marlene, 19, 28
Deane, Silas, 172–75, 179, 182
De Grasse, Francois Joseph, 206–7
Declaration of Independence, 13, 138, 148, *149*, 150–52, 155–56, *157*, 159, 163–68, 172, 180–84, 205, 209
Delaunay, Jacques, 52–55, 64, 71, 77, 79, 82, 93, 160
Delaunay, Julien, 71
Delaunay, Marie-Jeanne. *See* Carenan, Marie
Depa, Rose Bossy, 115–16
Désir, Philippe-Jasmin, 147
Dessalines, Jean-Jacques, 58–59, 219–20
Deveaux, John Benjamin, 107
diaspora (African): and British communities, 1–8, 108–9, 112–14, 121–22, 208–9; and French Caribbean communities, 1–8, 28–29, 63, 66–69, 76–82, 103, 114–22, 215. *See also* maroon communities
Dickens, Charles, 56
Dickinson, John, 46, 148–49, 158, 163–64
Diouf, Sylviane A., 66
Diver, Jinny, 120
Doret, Michel R., 116

Duane, James, 148
Duclos, Jean-Jacques. *See* Dessalines, Jean-Jacques
Dull, Jonathan, 41
Dumas, Alexandre, 28
Dumas, Thomas-Alexandre, 28
Dunmore Proclamation, 138–41, 189–91, 251n49. *See also* Murray, John (Earl of Dunmore)
Dunmore, Earl of. *See* Murray, John
Durand de Distroff, Francois-Marie, 39–42

Edes, Benjamin, 83
education, 57–60, 116–19, 130, 132, 153, 196, 218
Edwards, Jonathan, 105, 130
Egerton, Douglas, 81
Ellis, Joseph, 147
Enlightenment thought, 3–4, 14, 57, 101, 112, 121, 210
Equiano, Olaudah, 68, 82
Estabrook, Prince, 129
Ethiopian Regiment, 138–39, 145, 191, 200
Etienne (Saint-Domingue), 171
Exeter, 145

Faubert, Pierre, 196
Faucette, Rachel, 58
Favart, Charles-Simon, 9–10, 214
Febula (Saint Croix), 120
Férou, Laurent, 196, 218
Ferreiro, Larrie D., 181
First Continental Congress. *See* Continental Congresses
Fitz, Karsten, 85
Franco-American alliance, 13–14, 37–43, 153, 157–67, 173–88, 193–209, 212, 216
Franco-British rivalry, 10–14, 25–26, 29, 37–40, 153, 157–66, 173–75, 180–81, 188, 209, 213, 218. *See also* Seven Years' War; Treaty of Paris (1763)
François (Saint-Domingue), 145
Franklin, Benjamin, 13, 32, 41–45, 141, 156–59, 162, 164–65, 204, 206; as diplomat, 32, 35–37, 42, 172–75, *176*, 177–86, 189, 209–12, 215, 219–20
Franklin, William, 42
Fraser, Walter, 107

freedom: Black notions of, 3–4, 13–17, 20, 45, 48, 53, 57, 63, 98–104, 113, 117–21, 131, 138, 168–69, 201–5, 210–11, 215; and emancipation, 20, 100–102, 121, 138–41, 154, 190–92, 200–211, 216; white notions of, 10, 13–17, 20, 35, 43, 63, 98, 113, 118, 121, 210, 215. *See also* abolition; liberty; slavery: escapees
Freemasonry, 112–17, 125–26, 137, 205
Free Negro Company, 120
free people of color, 20, 27, 30, 50–53, 57, 72–75, 82, 101, 111–12, 116–20, 144, 211–18
French colonies: and class, 7, 14, 18–19, 27–30, 49–51, 70, 77, 102, 114–20, 211–12; and colonial defense, 25–29, 38–40, 49, 54, 160, 164, 180, 211, 218; and colonial governance, 5–6, 8, 11–12, 25–30, 36, 49–52, 63, 93, 156, 160–61, 213–14; and colonial military, 2–3, 13–14, 27–31, 49–54, 116–20, 160–61, 164, 190–212, 215, 218–19; and colonial rebellions, 10–11, 52–58, 93, 156, 211–12, 216–19; and debts, 12; and emigration, 63, 70; and taxation, 30. *See also* 1769 Revolt; Haitian Revolution
French Revolution, 215
Fristoe, William, 110
Frost, Peter, 263n102

Gage, Thomas, 137
Gano, John, 111
Gardner, Zebulon, 263n102
Garran-Coulon, Jean, 74–75
Garrigus, John, 70, 117
Gascoigne, Edward, 44
Gates, Horatio, 179–80
gender, 14, 16, 48, 187
Geneviéve (Toussaint Louverture's sister), 145
gens de couleur, 18–19, 27–28, 50–53, 63, 147, 192, 199, 211, 215–18. *See also* Black soldiers; free people of color; French colonies: colonial military
George III, King, 14, 25–26, 32–40, 45–47, 55, 97, 152, 177, 209, 213
George, David, 108–9
Gérard, Conrad Alexandre, 174, 179, 182

Gerbner, Katharine, 106
Gerrish, Cesar, 263n102
Gill, John, 83
Gilroy, Paul, 69
Goddard, Robert, 80
Goss, Sylvester, 126
Gould Thoroton, Edward, 136
Gray, Samuel, 83
Great Awakening, 105
Great Britain. *See* British colonies
Grenada, 167, 193, 196, 203
Grenadiers, 195–202. *See also* French colonies: colonial military
Grenville, George, 35–36
Gross, Robert, 129, 192
Gustafson, Sandra, 95

Haitian Revolution, 3, 6–7, 16–17, 30–31, 48, 54–56, 98, 115–17, 126–28, 143–47, 151, 172, 215–20
Hale, Nathan, 58
Hall, Neville A. T., 67
Hall, Flora, 246n88
Hall, Prince, 111–16, 125–26, 137, 205
Hall, Prince Africanus, 246n88
Hall, Seneca, 263n102
Hamilton, Alexander, 57–61, 118, *119*, 120–21, 131–35, 146, 152–53, 189–90, 219
Hammon, Briton, 43–45, 47–48, 81–82, 130
Hancock, John, 81, 83–84, 91, 112–14
Hannibal (New York), 2
Harris, Leslie, 18
Harrison, Benjamin, 158, 164
Harry (Mount Vernon), 133
Hastings, Selina, 105
Hayden, Josiah, 129
Haynes, Lemuel, 129–30, *131*, 132, 142, 168–73, 205–6
Hews, Abraham Jr., 126
Hickling, John, 80
Hodges, Graham, 100
Holbrook, Felix, 98–104, 116, 121
Hopkins, Samuel, 130
Hoskins, Charles, 107
Hough, Franklin, 199
Hubbard, Cipio, 263n102
human rights, 3, 211
Hutchinson, Thomas, 83, 94–95, 98

Hyppolite (Toussaint Louverture's father), 146

interracial resistance, 11, 13–17, 20–22, 29, 53–58, 63, 98–102, 113–39, 147, 160, 194–220. *See also* colonial solidarity
Irishmen, 113–14, 125, 240n128
Irons, Charles, 208

Jack, John, 129
Jamaica, 34–35, 55–57, 114, 160–61, 208, 218
James, C. L. R., 19, 74
Jay Treaty (1794), 211
Jay, John, 133, 158
Jean-Baptiste (Saint-Domingue), 145
Jeannette (Saint-Domingue), 171
Jefferson, Thomas, 14, 48, 149–50, 158, 162, 164, 168, 184
Johnson, Michael. *See* Attucks, Crispus
Johnson, Thomas, 158
Jordan, June, 47
Jotham, Luther, 129

Kachun, Mitchell, 81
Kagen, Robert, 163
Kalb, Baron Johann, 39–41
Kerversau, Francois Marie de, 218
Kilroy, Matthew, 92
King, Richard, 88
King's College (Columbia University), 57–58, 60–62, 118–19, 132–33
Knox, Henry, 147

Labadie, Guillaume, 52
Lafayette, Marquis de, 153, 176, 206
La Provence, 203
Laurens, Henry, 189
Laurens, John, 153, 189–92
Lazare, François, 144
Lazare, Marie-Josèph, 144
Lazare, Marie-Rose, 144
Le Bihan, Alain, 115
Leclerc, Mr. (Saint-Domingue), 145
Le Languedoc, 187, 197
Lee, Arthur, 172–75, 179, 182
Lee, Richard Henry, 151, 162, 166–67, 178–79

Legge, William (Earl of Dartmouth), 136
Legion of Saint-Domingue, 29–30, 49, 194. *See also* Black soldiers; French colonies: military
Léonore (Saint-Domingue), 14
les affranchis. *See* free people of color
Lespinasse, Beauvais, 53, 72, 76, 215
Levecq, Christine, 116
Lexington and Concord, Battle of, 3, 14, 17, 42–43, 118–30, 136, 155, 168, 170, 191
liberty, 8, 16–20, 22, 35, 45, 78, 118, 121, 127–28, 147, 168, 205, 212. *See also* freedom
Liele, George, 107–9, 207–9
Lincoln, Benjamin, 147, 192, 202
Lincoln, C. Eric, 108
literature, 56, 98, 101; Black literature, 43–49, 57, 105–6, 129–33, 168–73, 205–6. *See also* print culture
Logan, Rayford, 42
Long Island, Battle of, 178, 181
Louis XV, King, 9, 25–27, 38, 49–55, 160
Louis XVI, King, 160–61, 175, 180, 213
Louverture, Isaac, 218
Louverture, Placide, 218
Louverture, Toussaint, 7–8, 56–57, *143*, 144–47, 218–19
Loyalists, 61–63, 88, 92, 119, 129; and Black Loyalists, 107–8, 140, 152, 200–203, 208–11
Luzerne, Anne-Cesar de la, 189
Lynde, Benjamin, 91–92

macandalists, 5–8. *See also* Makandal
Magdeleine (Saint-Domingue), 145
Madison, James, 184
Maitland, John, 200
Makandal, 1–8, 14, 28, 55–57, 117, 172, 216–18, 228n35
Mallet, François, 160
Mallet, Jean-Pierre, 53–55, 160
Mansfield, William, 99–100
maroon communities, 4–6, 28, 63, 66–67, 78, 103, 197, 215–18
martyrdom, 1–2, 6–7, 55, 70, 79, 82–85, 92, 102, 116, 200, 216–18
Mather, Cotton, 64–67
Maverick, Samuel, 83–84

McClellan, James, 112
McCullough, David, 150
McGillivray, Lachlan, 202
military. *See* British colonies: colonial military; Chasseurs Volontaires; Continental Army; French colonies: colonial military; ships: war
Mitchell, Elise, 18
Mocco Sam (Saint Croix), 146
Model Treaty, 22, 163–68, 172–73, 178–86, 203–4, 209, 218
Moffatt, Winsor, 263n102
Moitt, Bernard, 71
Montgomery, Edward, 87–89, 92
Moreau, Médéric Louis Élie, 30–31, 58, 167–68
Morgan, Edmund, 182
Mornet, Christophe, 196
Morris, Robert, 164
Moses (Black preacher), 109, 207–9
Mulryne, John, 202
Murray, John (Earl of Dunmore), 101, 128, 137–41, 145, 152, 189, 197, 200

Najar, Monica, 106
Napoleon I, 56
Napoleonic Wars, 126
natural rights/law, 3–4, 14, 103, 121–22, 205
Nemours, Alfred, 198, 215
Newmarch, Cato, 263n102
Newmock, Moses, 82
newspapers. *See* print culture
Niles, Hezekiah, 126–27
Nolivos, Pierre Gédéon de, 75–76, 101–2
Norton, Fletcher, 136

Odiorne, Jack, 263n102
Ogé, Jacques, 116
Ogé, Vincent, 6–7, 55, 58, 116, 172, 216–18
Ollivier, Vincent, 193, 196
Ossé, Angélique, 116
Otis, James Sr., 100

Pacheco, Josephine, 40
Paine, Robert Treat, 91
Paine, Thomas, 106, 118, 144, 153–56, 189
Pamphlet, Gowan, 108–9, 207–9
Parker, John, 129

Pasley, Jeffrey, 15
Paul (Saint-Domingue), 171
Pauline (Toussaint Louverture's mother), 146
Pelham, Henry, 85
Pemberton, Samuel, 85–86
Pendleton Declaration, 140–41, 151
Pendleton, Edmund, 140
Penet, Pierre, 159
Perl-Rosenthal, Nathan, 81
Peterson, Farah, 85, 87, 90–91
Phillis (Savannah), 75
Pinchinnat, Pierre, 196
plantations, 1–4, 12, 31–32, 78, 117; Black ownership of, 14–16, 29–30, 52, 71–76, 102, 116
Pliarne, Emmanuel de, 159
Plombard, J., 202–3
Pluchon, Pierre, 218
Poncet (Saint-Domingue), 171
Pontleroy, Francois, 39–40
Preston, Thomas, 87
Prevost, Jacques Marcus, 200–201
Prichard, Ella Wall, 108
Prince (Lexington), 129
Prince, Newton, 88–89
print culture: and Black resistance, 2–3, 6, 15, 45–49, 55–56, 78–79, 98–104, 128, 145–47, 150–51, 251n49; and dissent, 14–16, 31, 43–47, 55–56, 60–62, 79, 96–102, 126, 134–37, 150–52, 216, 228n35; and war/diplomacy, 1, 61, 125–27, 134–35, 146–52, 156–57, 164, 175–80, 183, 187, 195–96, 203, 216. *See also* literature
Pulaski, Casimir, 201

Quamina (Saint Croix), 146

Raboteau, Albert, 107–8
racial identity, 48, 69, 82; and dehumanization, 6, 17, 28, 47–48, 144–45, 170–73; and legal categories, 5–6, 19–20, 28–31, 50–52, 58, 64, 68–76, 168–71, 211; and social categories, 5–6, 11, 17–20, 27–31, 47–51, 58, 69–74, 82, 88, 112, 211, 236n31
racial terminology, 5–6, 17–20, 65, 69–71, 88–90. *See also* Creoles

Raimond, Julien, 54, 144
Ralph (New York), 2
religion: and Black religion, 4–8, 98, 105–12, 169–70, 206–9; and Christianity, 47–48, 64–66, 98, 100, 105–12, 130, 169–70, 206–9; and itinerant preachers, 4–5, 105–6, 207
republics/republicanism, 12, 17, 35, 48, 103–4, 126–27, 144, 163, 209, 211
Revere, Paul, 83–87, 90, 112–14, 125
Rhodes, Leara, 15
Richardson, Ebenezer, 62–63
Rigaud, André, 58, 115–20, 146–47, 196, 218–19
Rigaud, André Sr., 116
Ringe, Romeo, 263n102
Rochambeau, Jean-Baptiste, 206
Roche, Matthew, 75
Rogers, Pharaoh, 263n102
Rohan, Louis-Armand-Constantin de, 49–55, 75, 197
Rose, David, 130
Rousseau, Jean-Jacques, 75
Rouvray, Laurent-Francois Lenoir de, 197, 199, 202–3
Rowe, Linda Hunter, 109
Russell, Ezekiel, 104
Russell, John, 25
Rutledge, John, 190, 192–93

Saillant, John, 130
Saint Croix, 57–60, 67, 82, 118–121, 133, 145–46, 153, 219, 221
Saint-Méry, Médéric Louis Élie Moreau de. *See* Moreau, Médéric Louis Élie
Saintonge (Saint-Domingue), 171
Salem, Peter, 141
Sam (Savannah), 75
Sannitte (Saint-Domingue), 171
Sara (Saint Croix), 146
Sarah (Savannah), 75
Saratoga, Battle of, 153, 179–83
Savary, Césaire, 196
Savill, Jesse, 92
Scott, Julius, 69, 77, 81
Second Continental Congress. *See* Continental Congresses
Seider, Christopher, 62–63, 79

Semple, Robert Baylor, 109, 207
Sesay, Chernoh, 104, 112
Seven Years' War, 1, 34, 44; causes of, 12, 111; conclusion of, 8–10, 25–28, 36, 38–39; and debts, 10–12. *See also* Treaty of Paris (1763)
Sewell, Elias, 129
Sherburne, Quam, 263n102
ships: and communication, 31–32, 63, 77–78, 187; and freedom, 67–68, 77, 81–82, 93, 101; and merchant, 2–3, 42, 63, 68, 77, 180; and slave ships, 35, 145, 191–92, 237n32; and war, 2, 187, 197, 203
Shores, Pharaoh, 263n102
Siege of Boston, 137, 141
Siege of Charleston, 203
Siege of Jacmel, 219
Siege of Savannah, 147, 189, 192–93, 197–200, *201*, 202–9, 215–16, 219
Skemp, Sheila, 36
slavery: and advertisements, 2, 65, 75, 120, 145–46; criticisms of, 4, 14, 35, 48, 98–101, 104, 118–21, 131, 169–73, 204–5, 211–12; debates on, 14, 100–106, 118–21, 212, 216; and escapees, 2, 4, 35, 63–67, 78, 97–103, 120–22, 144–46, 167, 197, 211; expansion of, 10, 12, 73, 191–92; as political term, 19–20, 28, 35, 47, 50, 76, 103–4, 129, 137; and religion, 64–67, 103–9, 118, 206–9; resistance to, 2–8, 66, 77, 97–99, 117, 120–22, 143–46, 156, 167–72, 204–6; and self-liberation, 4, 8, 14, 28–29, 53–67, 76–78, 97–103, 117–22, 138, 144–46, 167, 172, 196, 205; and slave treatment, 1–6, 15, 28, 48, 99, 104, 144–45, 167–72; and trafficking, 2–4, 12, 20, 30, 35, 68–69, 75, 100, 115, 120, 145, 170, 191–92, 213, 237n32
Smith, Hezekiah, 111
Somerset v. Stewart case, 99–100
Somerset, James, 99, 145
Sons of Liberty, 62–63, 79, 85, 91–92, 119
Stamp Act, 32–45, 63, 77, 86, 104, 130, 134, 137, 147–48, 152, 183, 209
Stanislaus (Saint-Domingue), 197
Stevens, Edward, 57–62, 66, 79, 116, 118–19, 131–34, 152–53, 219
Stockton, Richard, 149

Stono Rebellion, 57
Sugar Act, 32, 35
Superbus (Saint Croix), 146
Symmond, Thomas, 82

Taber, Robert, 15
Tacky's Revolt, 57
Talleyrand-Perigord, Charles-Maurice de, 38
Taylor, Alan, 127
Tea Act, 95–96. *See also* Boston Tea Party
Thibou, Daniel, 146
Thoby, Jérôme, 196
Thomas, Edgar, 107
Thomas, Isaiah, 99–100, 104, 112
Toussaint, Francois Dominique. *See* Louverture, Toussaint
Townshend Acts, 45, 62, 86
Townshend, Charles, 45
trade, 42, 136, 152, 156, 161–62, 165, 179–84, 204, 218. *See also* Model Treaty; ships: merchant; slavery: trafficking
trans-colonial solidarity. *See* colonial solidarity
Treaty of Ghent (1814), 211
Treaty of Paris (1763), 8–17, 20, 25–39, 61, 69, 96–97, 109–10, 151–53, 157–61, 166, 181, 193, 209, 213, 220
Treaty of Paris (1778), 13
Treaty of Paris (1783), 10–14, 17, 22, 209, *210*, 211–14, 218, 220
Treaty of Ryswick (1697), 25
Trimmer (Savannah), 75
Trouillot, Michel-Rolph, 116
Trowbridge, Edmund, 88
Tuckerman, Kittindge, 263n102
Tudor, William, 150

US Constitution, 204, 215, 219

Valentin (Saint-Domingue), 171
Vastey, Baron de, 72
Vattel, Emmerich de, 172–73
Vergennes, Charles Gravier, 38, 40, 159, 173, *174*, 175, 179–81, 188–89
Villatte, Jean-Louis, 196
violence: and executions, 2–3, 6–7, 54–55, 85, 92, 102, 160, 172, 216–18; fears of Black violence, 86–92, 95, 109, 138–40, 190, 208, 217, 229n35; and torture, 6–7, 90–92, 144–45, 156–57, 171–72, 208. *See also* 1769 Revolt; Boston Massacre; Haitian Revolution
Voltaire, 4–5, 178

Waldstreicher, David, 48, 132
Walton, George, 149
Warner, Cato, 263n102
Warner, Peter, 263n102
Warren, James, 14, 183–84
Warren, Joseph, 85–86, 112, 137
Warren, Mercy Otis, 183–84, 188
Washington, George, 14, 112, 128–41, *142*, *143*, 147, 153, 158–62, 179, 184, 189, 206, 218; and race, 190, 194. *See also* Continental Army
Waverage (New York), 63
Wentworth, Samuel, 263n102
Wheatley Peters, Phillis, 14, 45, 46, 47–48, 76–77, 104–5, 111, 113, 129–33, 169, 206
Whipple, Prince, 263n102
white (as term), 6
Whitefield, George, 5, 105–6, 130, 139, 191
Wilson, John, 91
Winston, Celeste, 66
women's rights, 14
Woodson, Carter G., 108

Yale College, 58
Yorktown, Battle of, 206–7, 209–10

www.ingramcontent.com/pod-product-compliance
Lightning Source LLC
Chambersburg PA
CBHW031346230426
43670CB00006B/449